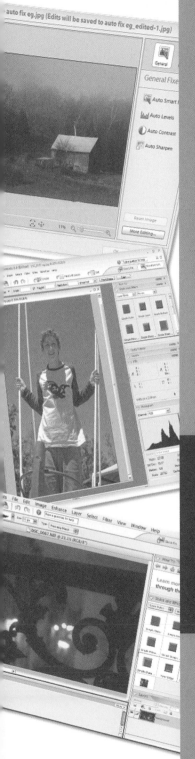

Adobe Photoshop Elements 7

A visual introduction to digital photography

Philip Andrews

AMSTERDAM • BOSTON • HEIDELBERG • LONDON • NEW YORK • OXFORD
PARIS • SAN DIEGO • SAN FRANCISCO • SINGAPORE • SYDNEY • TOKYO
Focal Press is an imprint of Elsevier

Focal Press is an imprint of Elsevier
Linacre House, Jordan Hill, Oxford OX2 8DP, UK
30 Corporate Drive, Suite 400, Burlington, MA 01803, USA

First edition 2009

British Library Cataloguing in Publication Data
A catalogue record for this book is available from the British Library

Library of Congress Cataloging-in-Publication Data
A catalog record for this book is available from the Library of Congress

ISBN: 978-0-240-52157-2

For information on all Focal Press publications
visit our website at www.focalpress.com

Printed and bound in Canada

Layout and design by Karen and Philip Andrews in Adobe InDesign CS3

Picture credits
With thanks to the great guys at www.ablestock.com for their generous support in supplying the cover picture and the tutorial images for this text. Copyright © 2008 Hamera and its licensors. All rights reserved. All other images and illustrations by Karen and Philip Andrews © 2008. All rights reserved.

08 09 10 11   11 10 9 8 7 6 5 4 3 2 1

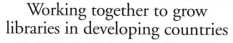

Working together to grow
libraries in developing countries

www.elsevier.com | www.bookaid.org | www.sabre.org

ELSEVIER   BOOK AID International   Sabre Foundation

Contents

Book resources and support movies can be found at **www.photoshopelements.net**

Book resources and support movies can be found at **www.photoshopelements.net**

Book resources and support movies can be found at **www.photoshopelements.net**

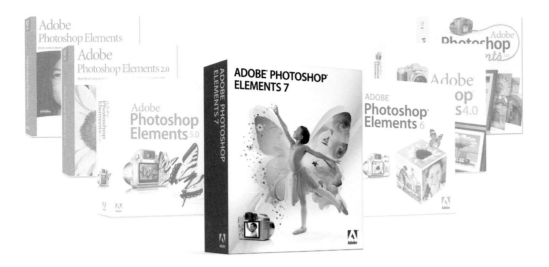

Foreword

In the mid-1980s a group of professional photographers, including myself, were invited to attend an early demonstration of the Quantel Graphics Paintbox system in action at a digital retouching house in Covent Garden, London. We all sat spellbound as we saw our scanned images instantly transformed by the magic of this new computer system. This was my first glimpse of the future of photography in a digital age. From that day forward I always wanted to have my own computer retouching system and take control of the magic pen myself. However, I was soon brought back down to earth when I was told how much one of these systems would cost. Back in those days digital retouching services were the preserve of an elite number of businesses such as advertising agency clients, as these were the only people who could afford to pay the equivalent of a good week's salary for an hour of electronic retouching time.

A few years later, Photoshop made its first appearance – an image-editing program that was designed to run on a desktop computer. From these humble beginnings Adobe Photoshop has grown to become the leading image-editing computer program used by graphic designers, artists, web designers and photographers from all around the world. Millions of people are now able to scan, capture and retouch their own photographs on desktop computers both at home and at work – in fact, I have heard all sorts of people from the bank manager to my hairdresser describe the amazing things they have been able to do to their pictures using a computer.

Whenever I present seminars on Photoshop techniques, I am always pleased to note the mixed age range and makeup of the audiences who attend these events. Digital image editing has been truly democratized now that everyone can afford to play. I use the word play deliberately, because even after all the years I have been using Photoshop, I still get a buzz whenever I am sitting at the computer transforming my pictures.

FOREWORD

Photoshop Elements is essentially a cut-down version of Photoshop, yet it contains nearly all the image manipulation power of the parent program, but in an easy-to-use interface. Although Adobe have limited the range of some of the more advanced Photoshop features and functions, they have included a host of cool features such as the File Browser in the Organizer workspace and the Photomerge feature. Adobe Photoshop Elements is therefore an exciting program in its own right, and is fun to use as well, but it is also a powerful tool, capable of handling a number of professional tasks.

Philip Andrews is a skilled and enthusiastic teacher and here he has produced a very well-written book that will help you, the reader, to quickly get to grips with all aspects of the program. The book is clearly illustrated throughout and you will find that Philip has thoughtfully included a number of practical tips on how to capture better photographs. On top of this, he shows you more than how to operate the program – he also demonstrates how to use Photoshop Elements with examples of practical assignments. In my experience I have found that readers always find it much easier to understand a program when they are provided with project examples that have a logical purpose to them. Philip's book is in every respect refreshingly direct and easy to understand.

Whatever your interest, I am sure that you are going to get a lot of interesting use out of Photoshop Elements. Whether you are into manipulating photographs, wishing to build better websites or producing better looking prints, this book will help you to master all the necessary tools contained in the program.

The learning curve has just got shallower!

Martin Evening
www.martinevening.com, www.photoshopforphotographers.com

Introduction

Here at Adobe, we believe that we make great software but, just as a car manufacturer would never consider publishing a street index, we rely on gifted authors to provide our users with directions and guidelines on how to make the most of our products.

This task is not a simple one. It requires a good understanding of the product, the digital imaging environment and, most of all, the user. Philip Andrews is unique in that he is an author who possesses all these qualities. He has an ongoing professional photographic practice, lectures at universities and colleges, holds a position as an Adobe Ambassador in Australia and has authored over 400 articles and 34 books worldwide.

With these credentials you would imagine that his texts are informative but a little stuffy and academic – not true! In this, the seventh edition of his best selling Photoshop® Elements book, he again uses a very comfortable and easy-to-understand style that leads the reader carefully through the basics and then onto the more advanced techniques needed to edit and enhance their digital images. He not only provides 'must have' information about Photoshop Elements and how to use it, but also introduces the reader to important general digital concepts that puts the package firmly in the context of current imaging technology.

The book is dotted with great illustrations and pictures and, via the video tutorial and resources download section of the associated website, readers have the opportunity to follow the step-by-step techniques using many of these same images that are featured in the text. In addition, the chapter dealing with putting 'Theory into Practice' shows how you can use Photoshop Elements to enhance your digital photography projects in the context of a real life application.

I believe that with Philip providing you with such a good 'street index' to our Photoshop Elements 7 software, you will be creating fantastic digital images in next to no time at all.

Good luck and have fun with your image making.

Jane Brady
Senior Product Marketing Manager, Design Suites,
Adobe Systems Incorporated

Acknowledgements

Always for Kassy-Lee, but with special thanks to Adrian and Ellena for putting up with a 'would-be author' for a father for the last few months. Yes it is over...until next time at least!

Thanks also to the enthusiastic and very supportive staff at Focal Press whose belief in quality book production has given life to my humble ideas – yet again! Special thanks to Ben Denne and Melissa Read for as everyone knows, but doesn't acknowledge nearly enough, 'good book production is definitely a team effort'.

My appreciation goes to Jane Brady for her support and kind introduction, and cheers also to Martin Evening, the 'Guru of GUI', and Don Day and Richard Coencas for their technical and 'pixel-based' guidance.

And thanks once more to Adobe for bringing image enhancement and editing to us all through their innovative and industry-leading products, and the other hardware and software manufacturers whose help is an essential part of writing any book of this nature. In particular I wish to thank technical and marketing staff at Adobe, Microsoft, Sony, Canon, Nikon and Epson.

And finally my thanks to all the readers who continue to inspire and encourage me with their generous praise and great images. Keep e-mailing me to let me know how your imaging is going.

Philip Andrews

1

The Buzz of Digital Photography

Apart from the initial years of the invention of photography, I can't think of a more exciting time to be involved in making pictures. In fact, I believe that Fox Talbot, as one of the fathers of the medium, would have little difficulty in agreeing that over the last few years the world of imaging has changed forever. Digital photography has become the two buzz-words on everyone's lips. Increasing levels of technology coupled with comparatively affordable equipment have meant that sophisticated imaging jobs that were once the closely guarded domain of industry professionals are now being handled daily by home and business users.

This book introduces you to the techniques of the professionals and, more importantly, shows you how to use these skills to produce high quality images for yourself and your business. With the text centered on Adobe's Photoshop Elements package and completely revised to cover the new features in version 7 as well as the tools common to the previous versions of the program, you will learn the basics of good digital production from the point of capturing the picture, through simple manipulation techniques, to outputting your images for print and web. To help reinforce your understanding, you can practise with many of the same images that I have used in the step-by-step demonstrations by downloading them from the supporting website (***www. photoshopelements.net***). A good selection of video tutorials can also be found on the site, giving me the chance to guide you personally through your skills building tasks. There are also links to other relevant websites and information about the other Elements book I write. You will find a web icon (like this one 🌐) placed through out the book to identify when such web content is available. See Figure 1.1.

Also, you will find a real life project in Chapter 15 showing you how to use your new-found skills to enhance your own images and create a professional-looking photo book. Source files and comprehensive video tutorials for this project can also be found on the website, giving you the opportunity to practise your skills on a real world task. See Figure 1.2.

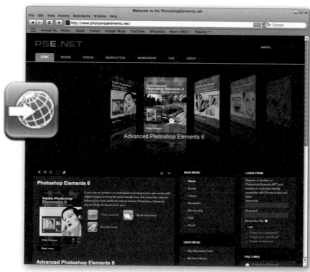

Figure 1.1 *The book's associated website contains practice images as well as video tutorials that are designed to build your skills and knowledge. Look for the 'on the web' icon throughout the text. This indicates that there are either associated practise images, or a video tutorial available on **www. photoshopelements.net**, for the technique.*

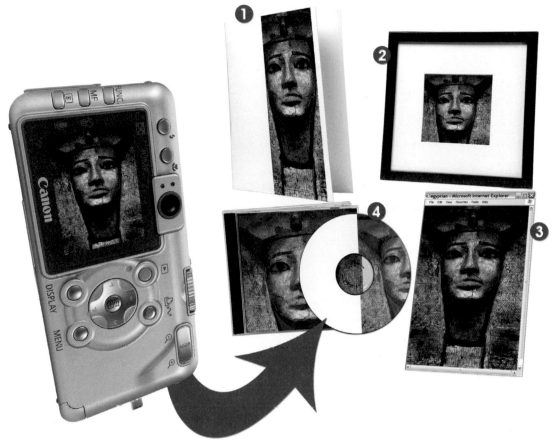

Figure 1.2 Digital imaging skills can be used to manipulate and enhance images so that they can be used in a variety of personal and business publications and products. (1) Presentation folder. (2) Framed print. (3) Web page. (4) CD artwork.

The beginning – the digital photograph

Computers are amazing machines. Their strength is in being able to perform millions of mathematical calculations per second. To apply this ability to working with images, we must start with a description of pictures that the computer can understand. This means that the images must be in a digital form. This is quite different from the way our eye, or any film-based camera, sees the world. With film, for example, we record pictures as a series of 'continuous tones' that blend seamlessly with each other. To make a version of the image that the computer can use, these tones need to be converted to a digital form. The process involves sampling the image at regular intervals and assigning a specific color and brightness to each sample. In this way, a grid of colors and tones is created which, when viewed from a distance, will appear like the original image or scene. Each individual grid section is called a picture element, or pixel. See Figures 1.3 and 1.4.

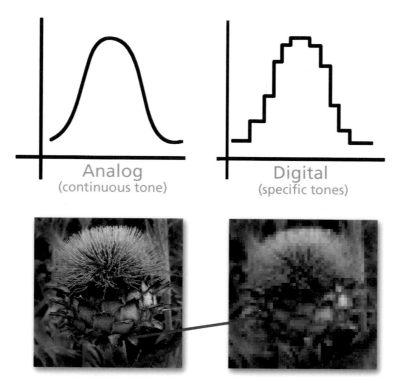

Analog
(continuous tone)

Digital
(specific tones)

Figure 1.3 *Continuous tone images have to be converted to digital form before they can be manipulated by computers.*

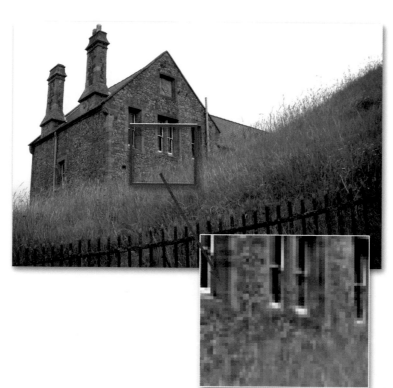

Figure 1.4 *A digital picture is made up of a grid of picture elements or pixels.*

Making the digital image

Digital files can be created by taking pictures with a digital camera or by using a scanner to convert existing prints or negatives into pixel form. Most digital cameras have a grid of sensors, called charge-coupled devices (CCDs), in the place where traditional cameras would have film. Each sensor measures the brightness and color of the light that hits it. When the values from all sensors are collected and collated, a digital picture results. See Figure 1.5.

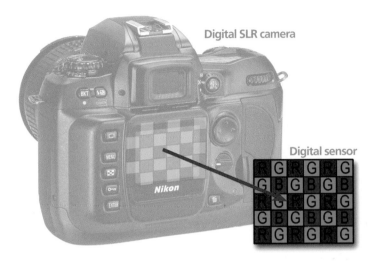

Digital SLR camera

Figure 1.5 *The CCD or CMOS sensor takes the place of film in digital cameras.*

Digital sensor

Scanners work in a similar way, except that these devices use rows of CCD sensors that move slowly over the original, sampling the picture as they go. Generally, different scanners are needed for converting film and print originals; however, some companies are now making products that can be used for both. See Figure 1.6.

Quality factors in a digital image

The quality of the digital file is largely determined by two factors – the number of pixels and the number and accuracy of the colors that make up the image. The number of pixels in a picture is represented in two ways – the dimensions, i.e. 'the image is 900 × 1200 pixels', or the total pixels contained in the image, i.e. 'it is a 3.4 megapixel picture'.

Generally, a file with a large number of pixels will produce a better quality image overall and provide the basis for making larger prints than a picture that contains few pixels. See Figure 1.7. The second quality consideration is the total number of colors that can be recorded in the file. This value is usually referred to as the 'color or bit depth' of the image. The current standard is known as 24-bit color or 8 bits per Red, Green and Blue channel. A picture with this depth is made up of a selection of a possible 16.7 million colors. In practice this is the minimum number of colors needed for an image to appear photographic. In the early years of digital imaging, 256 colors (8 bits of color per channel) were considered the standard. Though good for the time, the color quality of this type of image is generally unacceptable nowadays. In fact, new camera and scanner models are now capable of 12 bits per channel (36-bit color altogether) or even 16 bits per channel (48-bit color altogether). This larger bit depth helps to ensure greater color and tonal accuracy. See Figure 1.8.

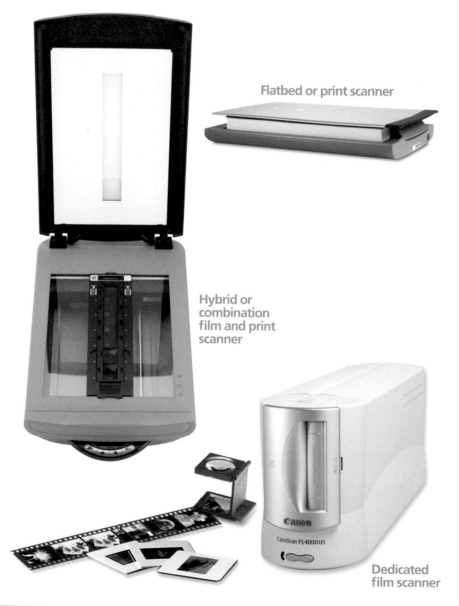

Flatbed or print scanner

Hybrid or combination film and print scanner

Dedicated film scanner

Figure 1.6 *Photographs and negatives, or slides, are converted to digital pictures using either film or flatbed scanners.*

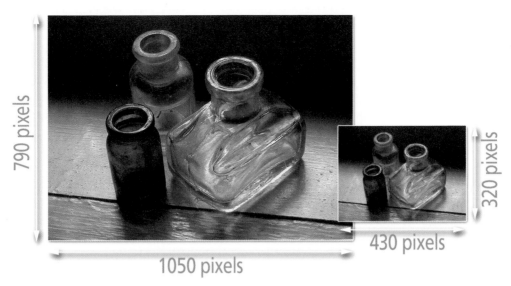

Figure 1.7 *The size of a digital image is measured in pixels. Images with large pixel dimensions are capable of producing big prints and are generally better quality.*

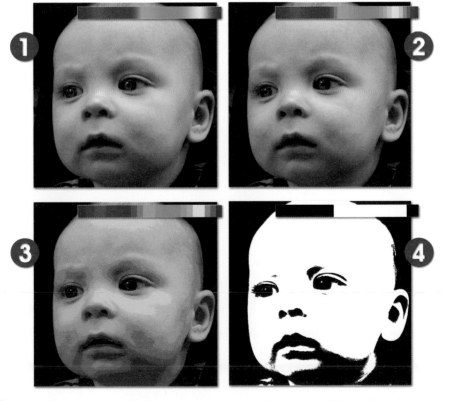

Figure 1.8 *Color or bit depth determines the number of colors possible in a digital file. Confusingly the number of colors is often referred to as 'bits per color channel' with most files being made up of three channels – Red, Green and Blue. This gives a total of three times the bits per channel. (1) 8 bits per color channel or 24-bit total color (16.7 million colors). (2) 8-bit total color (256 colors). (3) 4-bit total color (16 colors). (4) 1-bit total color (two colors).*

The steps in the digital process

The digital imaging process contains three separate steps – capture, manipulate and output. See Figure 1.9. Capturing the image in a digital form is the first step. It is at this point that the color, quality and detail of your image will be determined. Careful manipulation of either the camera or scanner settings will help ensure that your images contain as much of the original's information as possible. In particular, you should ensure that delicate highlight and shadow details are evident in the final image.

If you notice that some 'clipping', or loss of detail, is occurring in your scans, try reducing the contrast settings. If your camera pictures are too dark, or light, adjust the exposure manually to compensate. It is easier to capture the information accurately at this point in the process than try to recreate it later.

Manipulation is where the true power of the digital process becomes evident. It is here that you can enhance and change your images in ways that are far easier than ever before. Altering the color, contrast or brightness of an image is as simple as a couple of button clicks. Changing the size or shape of a picture can be achieved in a few seconds and complex manipulations like combining two or more images together can be completed in minutes rather than the hours, or even days, needed with traditional techniques. See Figure 1.10. Manipulation gives digital illustrators the power to take a base image and alter it many times so that it can be used in a variety of situations and settings. Once changed, it is possible to output this same image in many ways. It can be printed, used as an illustration in a business report, become part of a website, be sent to friends on the other side of the world as an email attachment, or projected onto a large screen as a segment in a professional presentation.

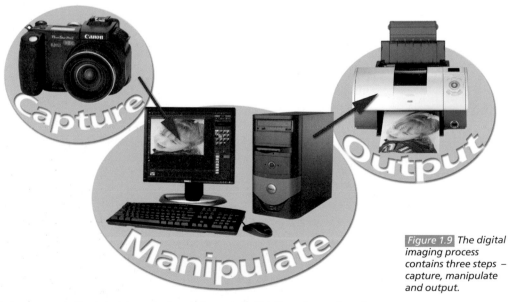

Figure 1.9 *The digital imaging process contains three steps – capture, manipulate and output.*

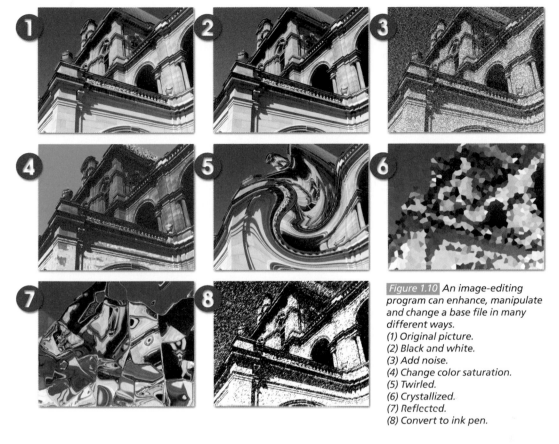

Figure 1.10 An image-editing program can enhance, manipulate and change a base file in many different ways.
(1) Original picture.
(2) Black and white.
(3) Add noise.
(4) Change color saturation.
(5) Twirled.
(6) Crystallized.
(7) Reflected.
(8) Convert to ink pen.

Where does Photoshop Elements fit into the process?

Photoshop Elements is a program that can be used for enhancing, manipulating, printing, presenting and organizing your digital photographs. Put simply, this means that it is the pivot point for the whole digital imaging process. See Figure 1.11. Its main job is to provide the tools, filters and functions that you need to manage, change and alter your pictures. Elements is well suited for this role as it is built upon the same core structure as Adobe's famous professional-level program Photoshop. Many of the functions found in this industry-leading package are also present in Elements but, unlike Photoshop, Adobe has made Elements easier to learn and, more importantly, easier to use than its professional cousin. In this way, Adobe has thankfully taken into account that although a lot of users need to produce professional images as part of their daily jobs, not all of these users are, or want to be, imaging professionals. See Figure 1.12. In addition, Elements contains features designed to download digital pictures from your camera, or scanner, directly into the program, as well as functions that allow you to output easily your finished images to web or print. When used in conjunction with other programs, like desktop publishing packages, it is also possible to include Elements' enhanced images in professionally prepared brochures, advertisements and reports.

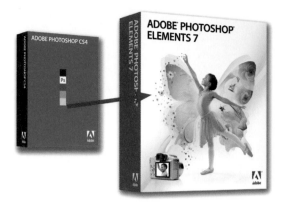

Figure 1.11 Photoshop Elements is built on the same editing engine as its professional cousin Photoshop.

Photoshop Elements 7

Rather than sitting back and basking in the reflected glory of the success of the first few releases of Elements (versions 1.0, 2.0, 3.0, 4.0, 5.0 and 6.0), Adobe has been hard at work improving what was already a great product. Version 7, just like the releases before it, is a state-of-the-art image-editing program full of the features and functions that digital photographers and desktop image makers desire the most. Far from being overshadowed by the power and dominance of its bigger brother Photoshop CS4, Elements has quickly become the editing and enhancement 'weapon of choice' by many who count picture making as their passion. Completely revised to cover all versions of the program, this book will help you learn about the core technology and functions that are shared by Photoshop and Elements, and will also introduce you to the great range of features that are unique to Elements.

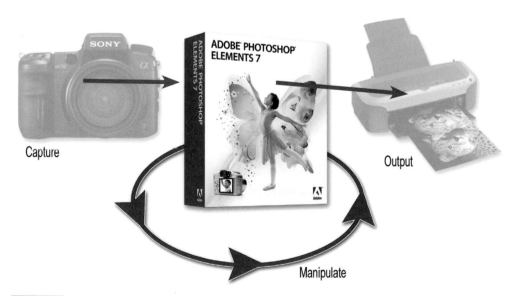

Figure 1.12 Elements is the center of the imaging process, providing the ability to import, manipulate and output digital pictures.

Book resources and video tutorials can be found at **www.photoshopelements.net**

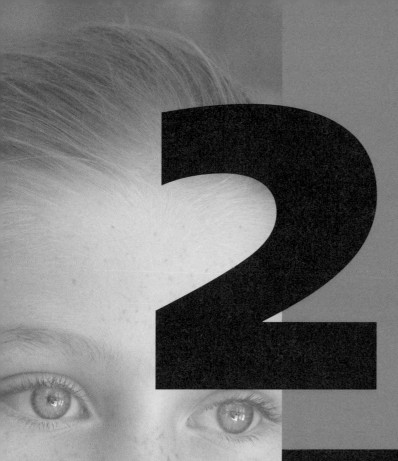

2

Introducing Photoshop Elements 7

Adobe Photoshop Elements 7 – new tools and features

The Photoshop Elements 7 workflow

The interface

Photoshop Elements is the type of software tool that photographers, designers and illustrators use daily to enhance and change their photos. There are many companies who make programs designed for this purpose and in this field Adobe has a substantial advantage over most of its competitors because it also produces the flagship for the industry – Photoshop. Now in its eleventh version, this product, more than any other, has forged the direction for image-editing and enhancement software worldwide. In fact, the tools, functions and interface that are now standard to graphics packages everywhere owe a lot to earlier versions of Photoshop.

With the release of Elements, Adobe recognized that not all digital imaging consumers are the same. Professionals do require a vast array of tools and functions to facilitate almost any type of image manipulation, but there is a significant and growing number of users that want the robustness of Photoshop but don't require all the 'bells and whistles'. This makes Elements sound like a cut-down version of Photoshop, and to some extent it is, but there is a lot more to this package than a mere subset of Photoshop's features. Adobe has taken the time to listen to its customers, and has designed and included in Elements a host of extra tools and features that are not available in Photoshop. It's this combination of proven strength and new functions that makes Elements the perfect imaging tool for digital camera and scanner owners who need to produce professional-level graphics economically.

Adobe Photoshop Elements 7 – new tools and features

The release of version 7 of the program builds upon the firm foundation and user following that the previous editions secured. The revision contains a variety of new tools and features that I predict will fast become regularly used favorites. At the time of going to press this release is a Windows-only version and builds extensively on the extra organization and management features that were added in 3.0 and were originally part of the Photoshop Album package. One of the biggest changes is the extending of this management function to now include the features found at **www.photoshop. com**. This expansion to include a dedicated webspace designed to work seamlessly with Photoshop Elements is a change that shouldn't be overlooked as many believe that it flags the future of the program. The web is such an all-pervading presence in most people's lives now that it seems natural that Elements should spread its imaging wings online.

Table 2.1 details some of the changes that are 'New for 7' and compares them with features found in previous versions of Photoshop and Elements. The new or revised features are also highlighted throughout the book with the 'New for 7' symbol ![symbol]. Video tutorials detailing how to use these new features are also located on this book's website, **www.photoshopelements.net**, and indicated in the text with an on the web symbol ![symbol]. Unlike some of the previous versions of the program, version 7 is a Windows-only release and so this text contains no Macintosh equivalents.

Apart from the inclusion of a host of new and revamped features like the Smart Brush tool, quick fixes for common problems (such as whitening teeth, creating bluer skies and improving skin color) and the new Scene Cleaner feature the program now includes a variety of web linked options available directly in the Organizer workspace. The big push with this release is certainly centred around the building of a thriving Photoshop Elements community. This is plain to see right from the start with membership options available on the Welcome Screen and the ability to share via, publish to, and backup your pictures to www.photoshop.com distributed throughout the program. With membership to this new Elements' community comes rewards. Adobe promises regular delivery of new and inspiration content, great tutorials from leading Elements' experts (yes even yours truly) and masses of online storage space for your photos. In addition Elements members can share their images and movies with their friends and relatives privately or choose the public option and show the world the images they have created. This level of connectivity is powered by the links to www,photoshop.com and the features that are available in Photoshop Express. See Figure 2.1. The one downside to the community concept is that in initial release these options will only be made available to Elements' users based in the United States.

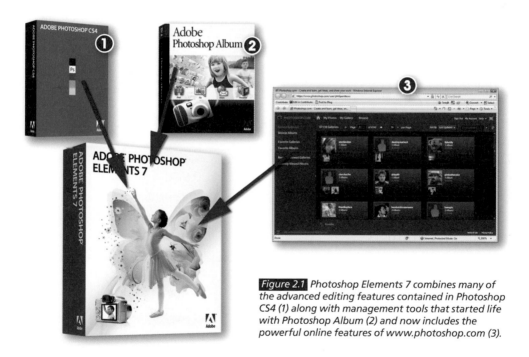

Figure 2.1 *Photoshop Elements 7 combines many of the advanced editing features contained in Photoshop CS4 (1) along with management tools that started life with Photoshop Album (2) and now includes the powerful online features of www.photoshop.com (3).*

The Photoshop Elements 7 workflow

Elements 7 provides a workflow solution from the moment you download your files from camera, scanner or the Net, through organization and manipulation phases and then onto printing (photos, books) or sharing the pictures electronically (online gallery, slide shows, e-mail attachments). Understanding how the various components in the system fit together will help you make the most of the software and its powerful new features. See Figure 2.2.

Feature	v7.0	v6.0	v5.0	v4.0	v3.0	v2.0	v1.0	CS4	CS3
Table 2.1 Summary of features of different versions of Adobe Photoshop Elements and Adobe Photoshop.			PHOTOSHOP ELEMENTS					PHOTOSHOP	
• Content delivered to Elements	✓	✗	✗	✗	✗	✗	✗	✗	✗
• Auto synchronized backup	✓	✗	✗	✗	✗	✗	✗	✗	✗
• View photos from anywhere	✓	✗	✗	✗	✗	✗	✗	✗	✗
• Public or private online galleries	✓	✗	✗	✗	✗	✗	✗	✗	✗
• Smart Brush tool	✓	✗	✗	✗	✗	✗	✗	✗	✗
• Fast fixes for common problems	✓	✗	✗	✗	✗	✗	✗	✗	✗
• New text search box	✓	✗	✗	✗	✗	✗	✗	✗	✗
• Tag photos as you download	✓	✗	✗	✗	✗	✗	✗	✗	✗
• Artwork panel	✓	✓	✓	✗	✗	✗	✗	✗	✗
• Quick Selection tool	✓	✓	✗	✗	✗	✗	✗	✗	✓
• Photomerge Group Shot	✓	✓	✗	✗	✗	✗	✗	✗	✗
• Photomerge Faces	✓	✓	✗	✗	✗	✗	✗	✗	✗
• Photomerge Scene Cleaner	✓	✗	✗	✗	✗	✗	✗	✗	✓
• Photo Collage project	✓	✓	✓	✗	✗	✗	✗	✗	✗
• Photo Books (revamped)	✓	✓	✗	✗	✗	✗	✗	✗	✗
• Direct copy to CD/DVD	✓	✓	✗	✗	✗	✗	✗	✗	✗
• Organize, Edit, Create, Share workflow modules	✓	✓	✗	✗	✗	✗	✗	✗	✗
• Full, Quick and Guided	✓	✓	✗	✗	✗	✗	✗	✗	✗
• Photoshop Showcase	✓	✓	✗	✗	✗	✗	✗	✗	✗
• Guided Edit tutorials	✓	✓	✗	✗	✗	✗	✗	✗	✗
• Organizer auto enhance options	✓	✓	✗	✗	✗	✗	✗	✗	✗
• Smart Albums	✓	✓	✗	✗	✗	✗	✗	✗	✗
• Flipbooks	✓	✓	✓	✗	✗	✗	✗	✗	✗
• Correct Camera Distortion	✓	✓	✓	✗	✗	✗	✗	✗	✓
• Convert to Black and White	✓	✓	✓	✗	✗	✗	✗	✗	✓
• Multi-session DVD/CD ROM	✓	✓	✓	✗	✗	✗	✗	✗	✗
• Expanded Version Sets	✓	✓	✓	✗	✗	✗	✗	✗	✓
• Arrange and Distribute objects	✓	✓	✓	✗	✗	✗	✗	✗	✓
• Photo Creations – Auto Fill	✓	✓	✓	✗	✗	✗	✗	✗	✗
• Multi-page documents	✓	✓	✓	✗	✗	✗	✗	✗	✓
• Video format support in Organizer	✓	✓	✓	✗	✗	✗	✗	✗	✓
• Yahoo Photo Map	✓	✓	✓	✗	✗	✗	✗	✗	✗
• Auto Stacking	✓	✓	✓	✗	✗	✗	✗	✗	✗
• Multi-disk backup	✓	✓	✓	✗	✗	✗	✗	✗	✗
• Online backups	✓	✓	✓	✗	✗	✗	✗	✗	✗
• Flash galleries	✓	✓	✓	✗	✗	✗	✗	✗	✗
• Adjust Sharpening control	✓	✓	✓	✗	✗	✗	✗	CS4	CS3
• Advanced Adobe Photo Downloader Utility	✓	✓	✓	✗	✗	✗	✗	✗	✓
• Shared media collections with Viiv technology	✓	✓	✓	✗	✗	✗	✗	✗	✓
• Color Curves	✓	✓	✓	✗	✗	✗	✗	✗	✓
• Automatic Red Eye Fix	✓	✓	✓	✓	✗	✗	✗	✗	✗
• Magic Selection Brush	✗	✗	✓	✓	✗	✗	✗	✗	✗
• Automatic Face Tagging	✓	✓	✓	✗	✗	✗	✗	✗	✗
• Magic Extractor	✓	✓	✓	✓	✗	✗	✗	✗	✓

Feature	v7.0	v6.0	v5.0	v4.0	v3.0	v2.0	v1.0	CS4	CS3
• Straighten tool	✓	✓	✓	✓	✗	✗	✗	✗	✓
• Order Prints pane	✓	✓	✓	✓	✗	✗	✗	✗	✗
• Desktop wallpaper from photos	✓	✓	✓	✓	✗	✗	✗	✗	✗
• Convert or remove ICC profiles	✓	✓	✓	✓	✗	✗	✗	✗	✓
• View slide shows via Windows Media Center	✓	✓	✓	✓	✗	✗	✗	✗	✗
• Add captions to multiple files	✓	✓	✓	✓	✗	✗	✗	✗	✓
• Adjust Skin Tone feature	✓	✓	✓	✓	✗	✗	✗	✗	✗
• Remove JPEG artifacts	✓	✓	✓	✓	✗	✗	✗	✗	✓
• Create paragraph text	✓	✓	✓	✓	✗	✗	✗	✗	✓
• Multi-select layers	✓	✓	✓	✓	✗	✗	✗	✗	✓
• Defringe command	✓	✓	✓	✓	✗	✗	✗	✗	✓
• WYSIWYG font previews	✓	✓	✓	✓	✗	✗	✗	✗	✓
• Revised File Info dialog	✓	✓	✓	✓	✗	✗	✗	✗	✓
• Revamped Slide Show editor	✓	✓	✓	✓	✗	✗	✗	✗	✗
• Find by metadata or Version Set	✓	✓	✓	✓	✗	✗	✗	✗	✗
• Preview pictures in Full Screen	✓	✓	✓	✓	✗	✗	✗	✗	✗
• Macintosh and Windows version	✓	✓	✗	✓	✓	✓	✓	✗	✓
• Import Outlook or vCard contacts	✓	✓	✓	✓	✗	✗	✗	✗	✗
• Camera Raw file support	✓	✓	✓	✓	✓	✗	✗	✗	✓
• 16 bit per channel file support	✓	✓	✓	✓	✓	✗	✗	✗	✓
• Shadow/Highlights control	✓	✓	✓	✓	✓	✗	✗	✗	✓
• Cookie Cutter cropping tool	✓	✓	✓	✓	✓	✗	✗	✗	✗
• Quick Fix editor	✓	✓	✓	✓	✓	✗	✗	✗	✗
• Auto Smart fix enhance feature	✓	✓	✓	✓	✓	✗	✗	✗	✗
• Spot Healing Brush	✓	✓	✓	✓	✓	✗	✗	✗	✗
• Photo Browser with Date View	✓	✓	✓	✓ WIN	✓ WIN	✗	✗	✗	✗
• Project/Photo/Organize Bin	✓	✓	✓	✓	✓	✗	✗	✗	✗
• Color Variations	✓	✓	✓	✓	✓	✓	✓	✗	✗
• Hints palette	✓	✓	✓	✓	✓	✓	✓	✗	✓
• PDF slide show	✓	✓	✓	✓	✓	✓	✗	✗	✓
• Save for Web option	✓	✓	✓	✓	✓	✓	✓	✗	✓
• Recipes (How to) palette	✓	✗	✗	✓	✓	✓	✓	✗	✗
• Photomerge panoramic stitching	✓	✓	✓	✓	✓	✓	✓	✗	✓
• Get Photos from mobile phone	✓	✓	✓	✓	✓ WIN	✗	✗	✗	✗
• Adjustment layers	✓	✓	✓	✓	✓	✓	✓	✗	✓
• Filter browser	✓	✓	✓	✓	✓	✓	✓	✗	✓
• Picture Package for multiple prints	✓	✓	✓	✓	✓	✓	✓	✗	✓
• Web Photo Gallery wizard	✓	✓	✓	✓	✓	✓	✓	✗	✓
• Tag and Album creation	✓	✓	✓	✓	✓	✗	✗	✗	✗
• Effects browser	✓	✓	✓	✓	✓	✓	✓	✗	✗
• Red Eye Brush	✓	✓	✓	✓	✓	✓	✓	✗	✗
• Painting tools	✓	✓	✓	✓	✓	✓	✓	✗	✗
• Web-based photo printing	✓	✓	✓	✓	✓	✓	✓	✗	✓
• Save as JPEG 2000	✓	✓	✓	✓	✓	✓	✗	✗	✗
• Attach to E-mail feature	✓	✓	✓	✓	✓	✓	✗	✗	✗

1. START-UP

The **Welcome screen** is the first dialog box that the user sees when opening Elements 7. From this screen you can choose to organize, edit, create or share your pictures. These four options correlate to different parts of the photographer's workflow and so with new images you will start with organization and work your way through the editing and creating phases before sharing your masterpieces with family and friends. On the left of the screen are some new community options that include member's sign in, Your Account, Backup Settings, Web Gallery and Tutorial entries.

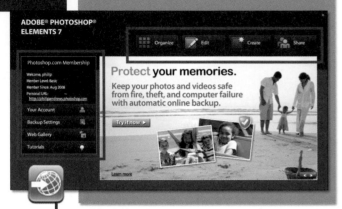

2. GET PHOTOS

Selecting the **Get Photos and Videos** option in the Organizer opens the Adobe Photo Downloader feature (APD) where you can preview, select and transfer files. APD is a sophisticated photo transfer utility for use with card readers and connected cameras as well as files and folders.

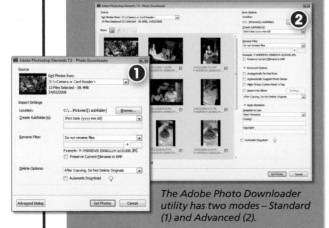

The Adobe Photo Downloader utility has two modes – Standard (1) and Advanced (2).

Figure 2.2 The Photoshop Elements workflow moves from download through editing and enhancing to output.

3. ORGANIZE

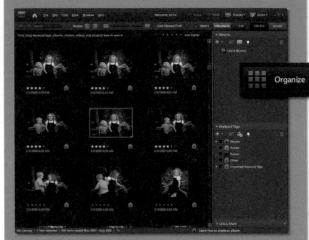

Organize

The **Organizer** workspace of Elements 7 works like a 'super' file browser, allowing you to manage, search, tag and back up all the photos in your picture catalog. You can view the photographs via the Photo Browser window or using the Date View. Pictures can be grouped into Albums (collections) and you can find specific images via the unique 'keyword tags' that you attach to the files.

In **Date View** images are grouped and displayed based on the date they were taken.

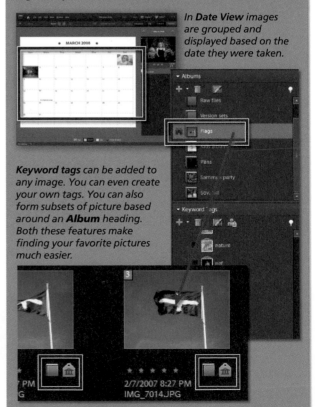

Keyword tags can be added to any image. You can even create your own tags. You can also form subsets of picture based around an **Album** heading. Both these features make finding your favorite pictures much easier.

4. EDIT

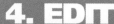

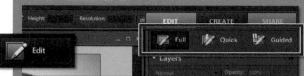

Version 7 contains three editing workspaces – Full (1), Quick (2) and Guided (3). Switching between the edit modes is as simple as clicking the tab in the top right of the Edit workspace.

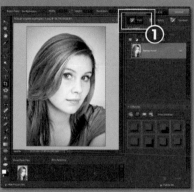

*The **Full (1)** editor contains all the familiar editing and enhancement tools that Elements users have come to expect. It is here that you can take full control over the manipulation and fine-tuning of your pictures. You can also add text, play with layers, create multi-picture composites and combine all manner of special effects with your original photo.*

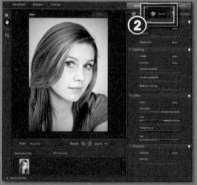

*The **Quick (2)** editor (previously Quick Fix) provides a series of one-click, single slider or semi-automatic fixes for common problems with lighting, contrast, color and sharpness. All the controls are contained in the one screen for speed or application.*

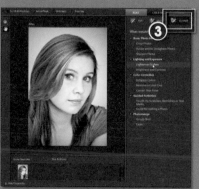

*The **Guided (3)** editor was first introduced in Elements 7 and combines a step-by-step instructional approach with the single click or simplifies controls of the Quick editor workspace.*

5. CREATE

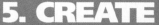

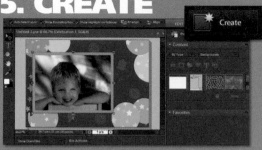

*Building on the success of the Photo Creation projects in version 5.0, the newly named **Create** options, have been revised and streamlined for versions 6 and 7. Via these features Elements provides users with a multitude of ways to use your favorite images to produce items such as Photo Books, online galleries and slide shows. Rather than being a completely separate workspace, as was the case in the previous versions, users can make a variety of creations directly inside the Editor workspaces. Here you can quickly browse and use selections from hundreds of frames, themes, backgrounds, clip-art and effects.*

6. SHARE

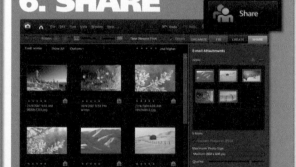

In Photoshop Elements 7 the creation and sharing components of the program have been broken into two sections. Though some areas, like producing your own web galleries, fall neatly into both camps, there are other options such as sending images by e-mail or ordering prints online that are only available in the new Share task pane.

As well as being able to output to a desktop printer, you can print online, place an order for your Photo Book to be published, or even create greeting cards all from inside Elements.

The interface

The program interface is the link between the user and the software. Most graphics packages work with a system that includes a series of menus, tools, palettes and dialog boxes. These devices give the user access to the features of the program. The images themselves are contained in windows that can be sized and zoomed. In this regard Elements is no different. Version 7 carries on the same look and feel that we saw in version 6 with a dark gray surround to most windows and a special Task pane that sits on the right of both Organizer and Editor workspaces. Clicking any of these 'task' headings will set up the workspace for the desired action (creating, sharing, editing, etc.) and listing a range of options in the pane itself. See Figure 2.3.

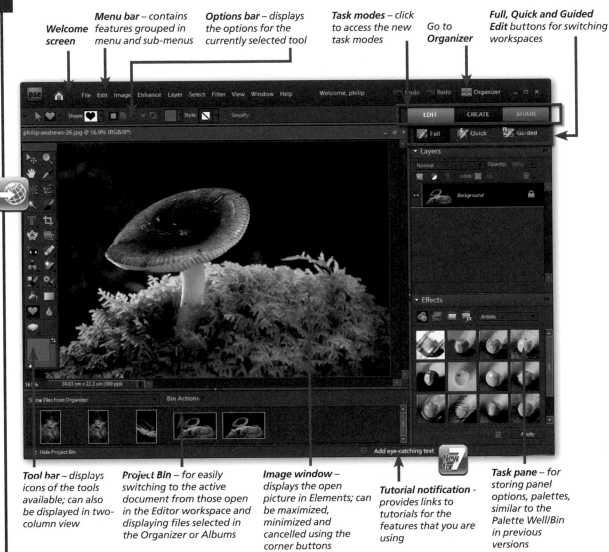

Welcome screen

Menu bar – contains features grouped in menu and sub-menus

Options bar – displays the options for the currently selected tool

Task modes – click to access the new task modes

Go to Organizer

Full, Quick and Guided Edit buttons for switching workspaces

Tool bar – displays icons of the tools available; can also be displayed in two-column view

Project Bin – for easily switching to the active document from those open in the Editor workspace and displaying files selected in the Organizer or Albums

Image window – displays the open picture in Elements; can be maximized, minimized and cancelled using the corner buttons

Tutorial notification - provides links to tutorials for the features that you are using

Task pane – for storing panel options, palettes, similar to the Palette Well/Bin in previous versions

Figure 2.3 The interface for the Windows-only release of Elements 7 Full edit workspace.

Book resources and video tutorials can be found at **www.photoshopelements.net**

Photoshop Elements 7 contains three different editing workspaces – Full, Quick, and Guided. For many editing and enhancement tasks you will be using the Full editor, so over the next few pages we will look at the various parts of this screen and how they are used to allow you to interact with and change your pictures. Later on in the chapter we will also examine the interface of other parts of the Elements system such as the Organizer, Quick, Guided editor and Create, Share options. At the time of publication Photoshop Elements 7 is supplied as a Windows-only package, whereas previous editions of the program have been released in two forms to suit both the Macintosh and Windows platforms.

You control the look of Photoshop Elements 7

One of the most striking and immediately obvious changes for Elements 6 was the look of the interface. Not all users liked the change and in version 7 the Adobe engineers have provided a Interface Brightness control that lets the user decide how dark or light the interface is. Located along with other system settings in the Preferences (Editor: Edit > Preferences > General) a simple slider controls the look of the interface. The Reset Brightness button returns the control to the default setting. See Figure 2.4.

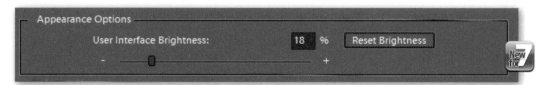

Figure 2.4 *In response to user requests the brightness of the interface for the Elements Editor workspace can be lightened or darkened using the new Appearance Options located in the General section of the editor preferences (Edit > Preferences > General).*

New tools and features

As with every new version of Photoshop Elements Adobe has added new features and updated existing tools for this release. These changes include great new productivity tools such as:

• The new **Smart Brush Tool** allows users to paint on changes to their photos. By combining the selection abilities of the Quick Selection tool and the enhancement powers of Adjustment layers, the new tool automatically seeks out picture parts as you paint and then applies the changes non-destructively to the photo. The new feature is available in two different variations: the Smart Brush Tool, for changes to larger parts of the photo, and the Detail Smart Brush Tool, for making changes to smaller, specific image parts such as teeth and eyes in a portrait. The user selects the type of enhancements to apply from a range of over 65 that ship with Elements before proceeding to paint on the changes to the picture. See Figure 2.5.

• Carrying on the Elements' tradition of pushing the abilities of the stitching power of the Photomerge feature, Elements 7 sees the introduction of a new option – the **Photomerge Scene Cleaner**. Using the feature you can build a composite image from selected parts of several photos. The typical application of this is the removal of tourists from front of landmark buildings. Simply shoot a variety of source photos of the landmark and then pick the best bits from each.

• New tools have been added to the **Quick Fix** editing space. Now sitting alongside the Red Eye Removal tool, there is the Toothbrush (whiten teeth) and Bluer Skies brushes as well as the very cool Black and White Paintbrush. The inclusion of these tools in the Quick Fix workspace borrows some of the power editing ease of the new Smart Brush Tool from the Full Edit workspace.

• The **Guided Edit** workspace gets new step by step enhancement options that include Effects such as Pencil Sketch and Old Fashioned and Adjustments like using Levels and fixing distortion, but the big news is the addition of the new **Action Player**. This new feature has been created to allow Elements users to play Photoshop Actions. Actions are a series of saved editing steps that can be applied to an image by replaying via the Action Player. The program ships with a set of pre-made actions but it is also possible to create your own actions in Photoshop and then install them into Elements. Expect to see Elements users the world over creating and swapping their favorite enhancement actions. See Figure 2.6.

• The **Surface Blur** filter has been added to the list of Blur filters available in Photoshop Elements. When used carefully, this filter is particularly good for softening surface texture in areas such as mottled skin. See Figure 2.7.

• Elements now integrates more tightly with Adobe's online presence, **Photoshop.com.** It is true that in previous versions of the package it has been possible to upload completed Web Galleries to free webspace provided by Adobe but in this release the web integration goes way beyond simple site hosting. Now registered Elements users get extra features such as being able to synchronize their favorite Organizer Albums with a version online providing automatic backup of their best pictures. Just as before, your Elements-created web galleries can be published online, but now these images can not only be viewed from almost any computer but

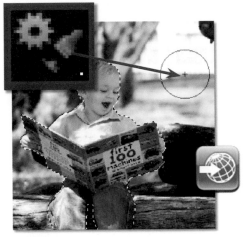

Figure 2.5 The Smart Brush Tool selects and changes image parts in the one action. Using one of a range of preset enhancement options you can paint on the changes with the new tool.

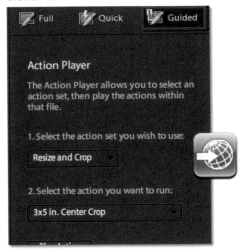

Figure 2.6 The Action PLayer in the Guided Edit workspace is designed for playing recorded Photoshop actions and can be used for applying sophisticated changes to a photo.

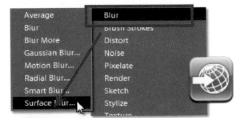

Figure 2.7 Adding a single new blur filter may seem like a strange inclusion except that the Surface Blur filter is good for softening textured areas.

also with specific mobile phones via **Photoshop. com Mobile**. See Figure 2.8.

• There are two levels of membership available for Elements users, a free option that provides the new features above and a paid '**Plus**' level which provides extra benefits for the Elements enthusiast. These include regular deliveries of extra templates for the creative projects you undertake in Elements or online, access to special inspirational tutorials and videos designed to build your skills, and more backup space for safely archiving your images.

• Finding the images you want quickly and easily is a constant challenge for any photographer. Photoshop Elements 7 adds to its already impressive array of 'Find'; options with a new **Text Search** which can locate pictures using keywords, dates and file information. See Figure 2.9.

Revamped favorites

In addition to these new features version 7 also showcases improved versions of many of the program's existing tools and functions that have proven to be firm favorites with image makers worldwide. Revamped features include:

• In the previous version of Elements the Artwork palette became a pivot point for a lot of users when looking to create a different look for their projects. In this release even more background, themes, clip art and effects have been included.

• Users were introduced to some stunning animated web gallery templates in the last release. In version 7 you have more choice of online album styles .

• The Adobe Photo Downloader (APD) now includes a new Import into Album option that creates a new Elements' Album entry and then adds the photos that you are downloading to it; all in one action. See Figure 2.10.

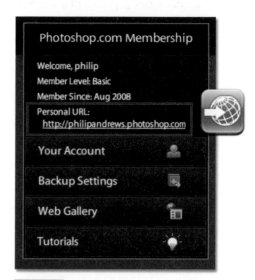

Figure 2.8 Becoming a member to the new Photoshop Elements community has many benefits including your own web address at Photoshop.com.

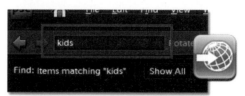

Figure 2.9 Emulating the search features found in both Mac and Windows, Elements now has its own Text Search feature located at the top of the Organizer workspace. With this feature you can quickly locate pictures based on keywords, file information and dates.

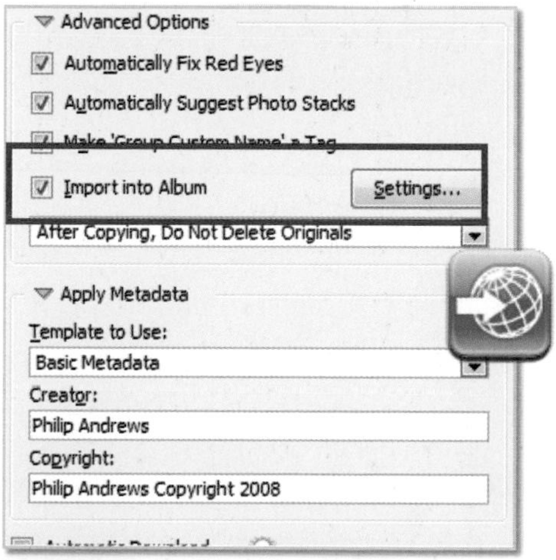

Figure 2.10 Adobe Photo Downloader now includes a special setting that adds transferred images to a new Elements Album.

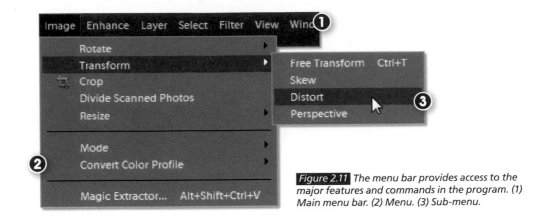

Figure 2.11 The menu bar provides access to the major features and commands in the program. (1) Main menu bar. (2) Menu. (3) Sub-menu.

Menus

Most image-editing programs contain a menu bar with a range of choices for program activities. In addition to the standard File, Edit, View, Window and Help menus, Elements contains five other specialist headings designed specifically for working with digital pictures. See Figure 2.11.

The **Image** menu contains features that change the shape, size, mode and orientation of the picture. Grouped under the **Enhance** heading is a range of options for altering the color, contrast and brightness of images, as well as the new Auto Sharpen, Adjust Sharpness and Convert to Black and White features. All functions concerning image layers and selections are contained under the **Layer** and **Select** menus. The special effects that can be applied to images and layers are listed under the **Filter** menu and in this latest release the Unsharp Mask filter has been moved to the Enhance menu.

Selecting a menu item is as simple as moving your mouse over the menu, clicking to show the list of items, and then moving the mouse pointer over the heading you wish to use. With some selections a second menu (sub-menu) appears, from which you can make further selections. See Figure 2.11.

Some menu items can also be selected using a combination of keyboard strokes called shortcuts. The key combinations for these features are also listed next to the item in the menu list. For example, the Free Transform can be selected using the menu selections Image > Transform > Free Transform or with the key combination of Ctrl + T (the Control key and the letter 'T').

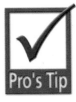

Because Photoshop Elements 7 has several different workspaces or modes that you can work within, I will indicate the workspace first before the menu sequence required to select a feature. For instance, to select the Free Transform feature (as pictured in Figure 2.11) from inside the Standard Editor space the notation would be **Editor: Image > Transform > Free Transform**.

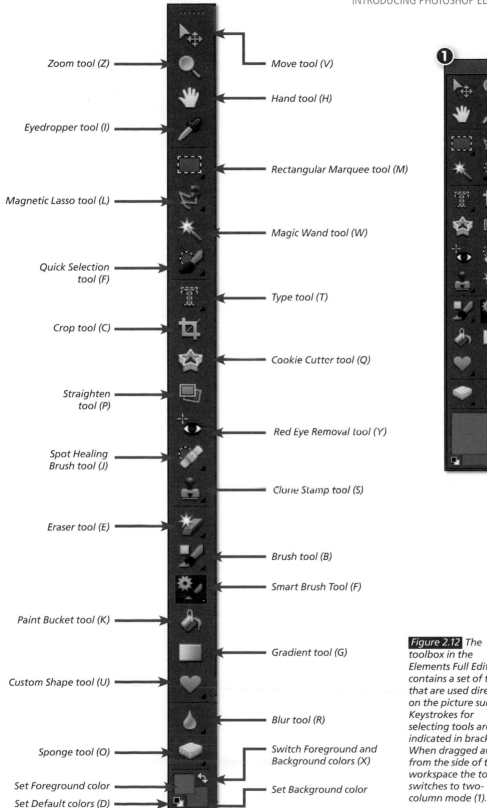

Zoom tool (Z)

Move tool (V)

Hand tool (H)

Eyedropper tool (I)

Rectangular Marquee tool (M)

Magnetic Lasso tool (L)

Magic Wand tool (W)

Quick Selection tool (F)

Type tool (T)

Crop tool (C)

Cookie Cutter tool (Q)

Straighten tool (P)

Red Eye Removal tool (Y)

Spot Healing Brush tool (J)

Clone Stamp tool (S)

Eraser tool (E)

Brush tool (B)

Smart Brush Tool (F)

Paint Bucket tool (K)

Gradient tool (G)

Custom Shape tool (U)

Blur tool (R)

Sponge tool (O)

Switch Foreground and Background colors (X)

Set Foreground color

Set Background color

Set Default colors (D)

Figure 2.12 The toolbox in the Elements Full Editor contains a set of tools that are used directly on the picture surface. Keystrokes for selecting tools are indicated in brackets. When dragged away from the side of the workspace the tool bar switches to two-column mode (1).

Tools

Unlike menu items, tools interact directly with the image and require the user to manipulate the mouse to define the area or extent of the tool's effect. Over the years the number and types of tools found in digital photography packages have been distilled to a common few that find their way into the toolbox of most programs. Amongst these familiar items are the Magnifying Glass or Zoom tool, the Brush, the Magic Wand, the Lasso and the Cropping tool. See Figure 2.12 on page 23. In addition to these few, each company produces a specialized set of customized tools that are designed to make particular jobs easier. Of these, Elements users will find the Red Eye Removal tool, Custom Shape, the Selection Brush, Cookie Cutter, Straighten, Healing Brush and the Quick Selection tool particularly useful.

Some tools contain extra or hidden options which can be viewed by clicking and holding the mouse key over the small triangle in the bottom right-hand corner of the Tool button. Alternatively the sub-menu may list a variety of tools related to the one currently selected. Selecting a new option from those listed will replace the current icon in the toolbox with your new choice. To switch back simply reselect the original tool or repeatedly press the tool's hotkey. See Figure 2.13.

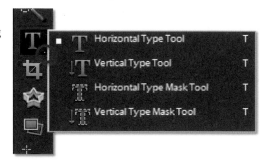

Figure 2.13 Click and hold the triangle in the bottom right of the tool icon to reveal the tool's other options or related tool choices.

Tool types

The many tools available in Photoshop Elements can be broken into several different groups based on their function or the task that they perform.

Selection tools

Selection tools are designed to highlight or isolate parts of an image for editing. This can be achieved by drawing around a section of the picture using either the Marquee or Lasso tools or by using the Magic Wand tool to define an area by its color. The Selection Brush tool allows the user to select an area by painting the selection with a special brush tool. Careful selection is one of the key skills of the digital imaging worker. Often, the difference between good quality

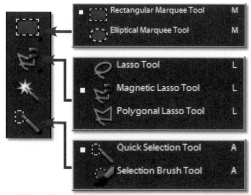

Figure 2.14 Selection tools are used to isolate a specific area in a picture. This can be achieved by drawing around the picture part or you can create the selection based on color.

enhancement and a job that is coarse and obvious is based on the skill taken at the selection stage. Also included in this group is the new Quick Selection tool that selects picture parts interactively as you drag the brush over the image surface. See Figure 2.14.

Painting/drawing tools

Although many photographers and designers will employ Elements to enhance images captured using a digital camera or scanner, some users make pictures from scratch using the program's drawing tools. Illustrators, in particular, generate their images with the aid of tools such as the Paint Bucket, Airbrush and Pencil. However. it is possible to use drawing or painting tools on digital photographs. In fact, the judicious use of tools like the Brush can enhance detail and provide a sense of drama in your images. Also included in this grouping are the Eraser tool, which comes in handy for cleaning up drawn illustrations and photographs alike, the Gradient tool used for filling areas with a blend from one color to another, and the Custom Shape tool. Unlike the other tools in this group the Custom Shape tool creates vector-based or sharp-edged graphics. This tool is especially good for producing regularly shaped areas of color that can be used as backgrounds for text. It is interesting to see that Adobe has included the new Smart Brush Tool in this grouping. Certainly its 'paint on' workflow is similar to other options found here, but the fact that most users will apply the tool to photographic images is different to the strengths of the other tools. See Figure 2.15.

Enhancement tools

These tools are designed specifically for use on existing pictures. Areas of the image can be sharpened or blurred, darkened or lightened and smudged using features like the Burn or Dodge tool. The Red Eye Brush is great for removing the 'devil'-like eyes from flash photographs and the Clone Stamp tool is essential for removing dust marks, as well as any other unwanted picture details. The Spot Healing tool works like an advanced version of the Clone Stamp. See Figure 2.16.

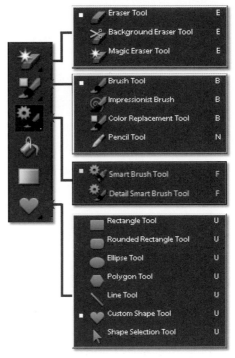

Figure 2.15 *Painting and drawing tools are used to add details to existing images or even create whole pictures from scratch. Also included in this section of the toolbar is the new Smart Brush Tool.*

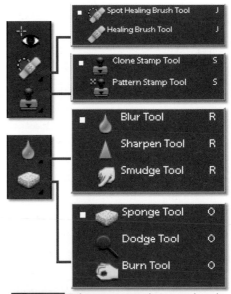

Figure 2.16 *Enhancement tools are used to alter existing images to improve their overall appearance.*

Move and view tools

The Hand tool helps users navigate their way around images. This is especially helpful when the image has been 'zoomed' beyond the confines of the screen. When a picture is enlarged to this extent it is not possible to view the whole image at one time; using the Hand tool the user can drag the photograph around within the window frame. The Zoom tool allows you to get closer to, or further away from, the picture you are working on and the Move tool is used to select, and move, individual picture parts within the picture itself. See Figure 2.17.

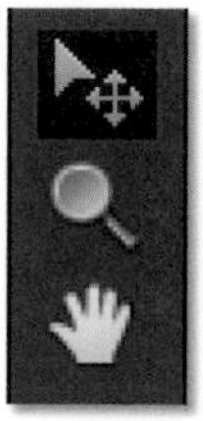

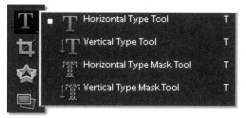

Figure 2.17 *The Hand tool is used to navigate around enlarged pictures, whereas the Zoom tool alters the magnification of the image on screen.*

Text tools

Combining text with images is an activity that is used a lot in business applications. Elements provides the option to apply text horizontally across the page, or vertically down the page. It is also possible to drag the cursor on the image to create Paragraph text. In addition, since version 2.0, two special text masking options have been included that can be used in conjunction with images to produce spectacular effects. See Figure 2.18.

Figure 2.18 *The Text tool is used to add type and type masks to images.*

Cropping and straightening tools

The final group of tools is designed for removing unwanted sections of the image and straightening crooked pictures. Using the standard and familiar Crop tool we can drag a marquee around the part of the picture that we wish to keep and then double-click inside the frame to remove the image areas outside the selection. The Cookie Cutter tool, first introduced in version 3.0, takes the idea further by providing the ability to crop your picture to a specific shape on the rectangular canvas. See Figure 2.19.

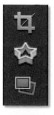

Figure 2.19 *The Crop and Cookie Cutter tools are used for changing the shape of your pictures and removing unwanted edge sections.*

The Straighten tool is used to correct pictures that are slightly crooked by click-dragging a line along the edge of objects that are meant to be horizontal. After letting the mouse go, Elements rotates the photo so that the marked line becomes horizontal. Using the Control (Ctrl) key while drawing also allows you to straighten vertically.

Options bar

Each tool and its use can be customized by changing the values in the options bar. See Figure 2.20. It is located below the shortcuts bar at the top of the screen. The default settings are displayed automatically when you select the tool. Changing these values will alter the way that the tool interacts with your image. For complex tools, like the Brush, more settings can be found by selecting the More button located to the extreme right of the bar.

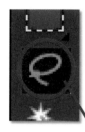

Figure 2.20 The options bar contains all the settings for the currently selected tool. The way that a tool behaves is based on the values found here.

Palettes, panels and panes

Palettes are small windows that help users enhance their pictures by providing extra information about images or by listing a variety of modification options. See Figure 2.21. Palettes can be docked in the Palette Bin (Palette Well for versions 1.0 and 2.0) or dragged and dropped onto the main editing area. Commonly used functions can be grouped by dragging

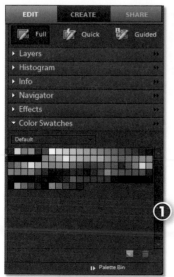

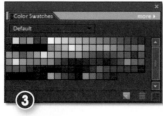

Figure 2.21 Palettes (1) and Panel (2) listings provide a visual summary of image enhancement tools and features. Panel contents remain fixed in the pane area of the workspace whereas palettes are able to be dragged from here to the main workspace where they become stand-alone entities (3).

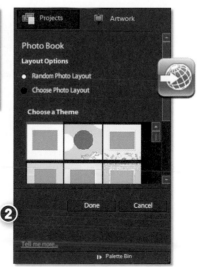

each palette by their tab onto a single palette window. To save space only have open those palettes that you need for the editing or enhancing job at hand. Close the remaining palettes by clicking the Close button in the top of the palette window or drag them to the retractable Palette Bin so that they are out of the way.

In addition to palettes Photoshop Elements 6 and 7 also contain panels. These are essentially the same as palettes in that they list settings or controls, but they differ because they can't be dragged onto the main workspace. Most panels are associated with the new Task Modes (Create, Share, etc.), whereas palettes are used in the Full edit workspace and owe their heritage to Photoshop.

Guided edits

The Guided edit workspace was introduced in Elements 6. It combines the step-by-step instructions that used to be found in the How To feature with the direct enhancement control of the Quick edit space. Selecting the Guided tab from the Edit task pane displays a list of the tutorials that ship with Elements. See Figure 2.22. Clicking a tutorial heading will reveal subheadings for specific topics. Selecting a heading topic will display a set of instructions together with associated buttons and controls. For instance, in the example here, two Rotate buttons (rotate left and rotate right) are displayed in the panel. Clicking either of these buttons will perform the same action as selecting the same options from the Image > Rotate menu.

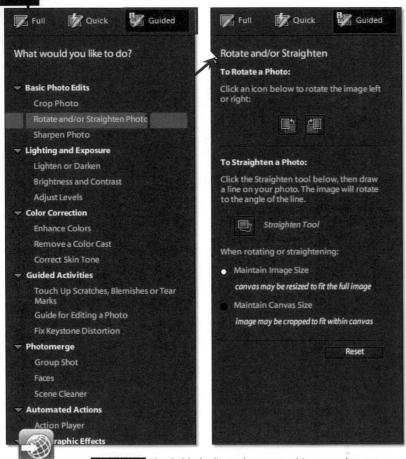

Figure 2.22 *The Guided edit workspace combines step-by-step instruction with embedded enhancement or edit controls.*

Guided edit is best used for learning how to use new tools and techniques or, as is the case with the Photomerge Faces, Photomerge Scene Cleaner and Group Shot options, as a way to step through complex techniques. The Guided Activities > Guide for Editing a Photo entry contains a collection of guided edits that are useful when correcting images. These include crop, lighten, darken, touch up and sharpen.

The Quick editor (previously Quick Fix editor)

The Quick editor (Enhance > Quick Fix), which was introduced in version 2.0 of Elements, cleverly combined a variety of commonly used enhancement and correction tools into a single image control center. With this feature the user no longer needed to access each individual tool or menu item in turn – rather all the options are available in one place. The feature proved so popular that in Elements 3.0 a completely new editing option, called the Quick editor, was introduced. The component is accessed via the Quick Fix entry in the Edit menu at the top right of the Organizer workspace or via the Quick button under the Edit task mode in the Editor workspace. The Quick edit workspace has the same before and after layout as the original Elements 2.0 dialog and contains a reduced tool and feature set designed to facilitate the fast application of the most frequent of all enhancement activities undertaken by the digital photographer. New for version 7 is the inclusion of extra touch up tools at the bottom of the pane on the right. See Figure 2.23.

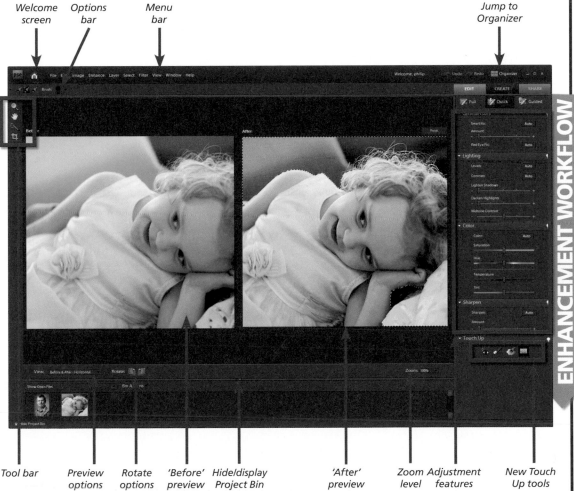

Welcome screen · Options bar · Menu bar · Jump to Organizer

ENHANCEMENT WORKFLOW

Tool bar · Preview options · Rotate options · 'Before' preview · Hide/display Project Bin · 'After' preview · Zoom level · Adjustment features · New Touch Up tools

Figure 2.23 The Quick editor brings together all your most commonly used tools and adjustment features into one easy- and quick-to-use workspace.

Book resources and video tutorials can be found at **www.photoshopelements.net**

The Zoom, Hand, Crop, and Quick Selection tool (and the nested Selection Brush), located in a small tool bar to the left of the screen, are available for standard image-editing changes and the fixed Palette Bin, to the right, contains the necessary features to alter and correct the lighting, color, orientation (Rotate), red eye (automatically) and the sharpness of your pictures. At the base of these controls is a new Touch Up section containing the Red Eye Removal tool and three new options - Toothbrush (for whitening teeth), Bluer Skies (for changing dull skies to blue) and the Black and White Brush (for altering parts of the photo to monochrome).

One of the best aspects of the Quick editing option is the fact that the user can choose to apply each image change automatically, via the Auto button, or manually using the supplied sliders. This approach provides both convenience and speed when needed, with the option of a manual override for those difficult editing tasks. The adjustment features are arranged in a fashion that provides a model enhancement workflow to follow – simply move from the top to the bottom of the tools starting with picture rotation, working through lighting and color alterations and, lastly, applying sharpening.

The Organizer workspace (Photo Browser or Date View)

Along with the Quick editor, Elements 3.0 also introduced a new sophisticated file browsing and management workspace called the Organizer. Previous to this Elements incorporated an older style File Browser feature which provided a quick way to visually locate your images but didn't contain the range of search, tag and display options that the Organizer workspace boasts. See Figures 2.24 and 2.25.

Once the picture files have been imported (Organizer: File > Get Photos and Videos) into Elements they can be viewed by date taken, their associated tags and even their folder location. Pairs of pictures can be viewed side by side with the Organizer: Display > Compare Photos Side by Side

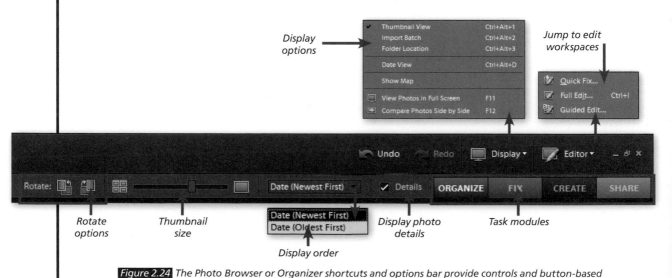

Figure 2.24 *The Photo Browser or Organizer shortcuts and options bar provide controls and button-based access to a range of organizing, editing and sharing options for selected thumbnail images.*

Book resources and video tutorials can be found at **www.photoshopelements.net**

Welcome screen · Menu bar · Thumbnail size · Sort order · Display options · Tags pane · Albums pane

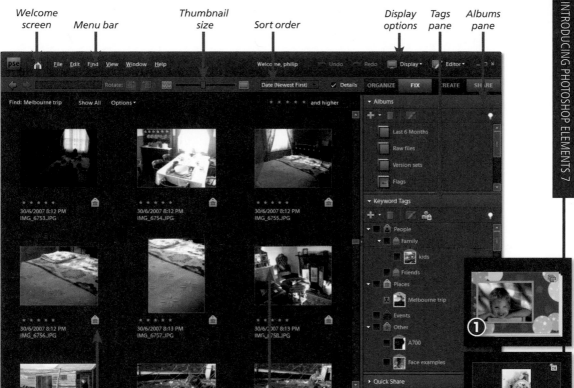

Album icon · Image thumbnails · Quick Share pane

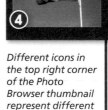

Figure 2.25 *The Organizer or Photo Browser workspace adds extra search, management and viewing options to your collections of images. Simple auto enhancement options can be applied directly from the thumbnail display using the entries in the new Fix task pane without having to enter the main editing application window.*

feature to help choose the best shot from a series of images taken of the same subject. Instant slide shows of whole albums, or just those pictures selected from the browser, can be created and displayed using the Organizer: Display > View Photos in Full Screen feature.

Simple editing tasks, such as the automatic adjustment of levels, contrast and/ or sharpness along with simple orientation and crop changes can be performed directly from inside the browser with the auto enhance features in the Fix pane. Finding your favorite pictures has never been easier as you can search by date, caption, filename, history, media type, tag and color similarity (to already selected photos).

Different icons in the top right corner of the Photo Browser thumbnail represent different file types.
(1) Multi-page .PSE.
(2) Online gallery.
(3) Slide Show.
(4) Video.

Photo Creations become Create and Share options

In version 3.0 Adobe added a separate Photo Creations workspace to Elements. The feature used a wizard approach to create great projects with your pictures. It is these sets of guided projects that have helped set Elements apart from other image-editing programs. Much of the program's popularity is based on the ease with which users can convert a group of their photos into a finished project.

Carrying on the tradition, version 7 sees these photo projects broken into two separate groups and listed in the Create and Share Task panes. The step-by-step wizard approach remains but the separate workspace of earlier days is gone. Now you can commence the creation process from either the Organizer or Edit workspaces by selecting the desired project from the appropriate Task pane. See Figure 2.26.

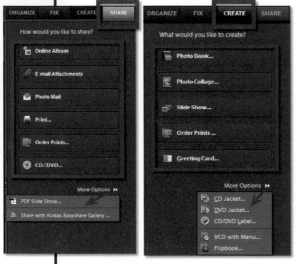

Figure 2.26 *The Create and Share task panes in the Organizer and Editor workspaces provide button-based access to a range of organizing, editing and sharing options for selected thumbnail images.*

The Create and Share panes are the starting point for the production of slide shows, greeting and postcards, online galleries, photo books and collages and Video CD (VCD) presentations. Whole albums, several individually selected files from the Organizer or images open in the Editor, can be used as a basis for the projects. The steps involved in creating the project are clear and precise, with sophisticated and professional results being available in minutes rather than hours, which would be the case if manually produced.

Project Bin (previously the Photo Bin)

In versions 6 and 7 of Elements, substantial changes have been made to what used to be called the Photo bin, now titled the Project Bin. Now when working with Projects (photo books, photo collages, etc.) selecting auto-fill will use the contents of the bin to populate the frames. Also photos can be dragged from the bin into frames, or onto other framed photos. If you have several files open in the editor workspace, you can quickly create an album with them by choosing Save Bin as an Album from the Bin Actions menu. If you use Save Bin as an Album with an existing album's name, the bin's files will be added to that album.

Project Bin behaviors:

- To show a photo in the bin, double-click its thumbnail.

- Ctrl-click or Shift-click on thumbs to select multiple thumbs, then use context menu to Open, Close, Rotate, Duplicate, etc.

- Photos in albums or in Show Files from Organizer are not open in the Editor until you double-click them.

Book resources and video tutorials can be found at **www.photoshopelements.net**

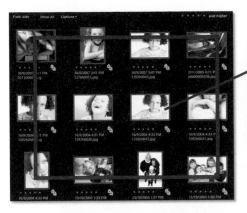
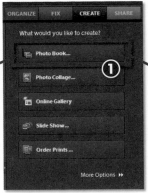
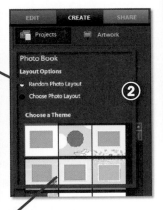
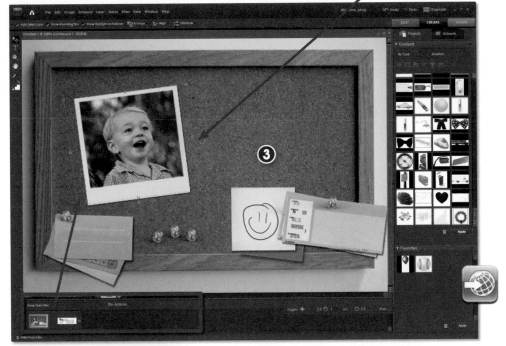
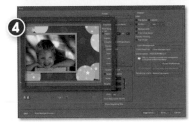
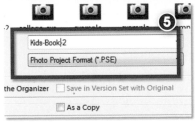

Figure 2.27 The Create options provide step-by-step guides to producing projects such as photo books, collages, slideshows, album pages, greeting cards, and online galleries. (1) You can access the project options via the entries in the new Create task pane. (2) Most Create options now use a common wizard to select the size, layout and style for the project. (3) After clicking OK the projects are created as a multi-page document in the Editor workspace. The pages are stored in a special stack in the Project Bin. Extra frames, photos, shapes, text and graphics can be added at this point. (4) The finished creation can then be printed on a desktop printer or via the online options. The multi-page document is saved in the new .PSE or Photoshop Project format (5).

Book resources and video tutorials can be found at **www.photoshopelements.net**

- Bin Actions works on all photos in the bin, whether they are selected or not.

- You don't have to open the photos in an album to use them in a project or in Group Shot/Faces.

- For Group Shot/Faces, you should select at least two thumbs in the bin that you want to use, otherwise all thumbs will be used.

Options in the Bin Actions menu:

- Show Open Files: Shows files currently open in the Editor.

- Show Files from Organizer: Shows any files currently selected in the Organizer. If the selection changes (e.g. files are added to or removed from selection), the bin updates dynamically.

- Albums: Shows the files in a given album.

- Album Group: Shows all the files of all albums in the group.

- Create/Share: Opens the Create or Share workspace.

- Print Bin Photos: If a single photo or PSE document in the bin, opens the Editor's Print dialog. If several photos in the bin, opens the Organizer's Print dialog.

Version 7 Creations

As well as changing the way that you access creations, versions 6 and 7 contain a modified mix of creation offerings. The major change is the revision of the Photo Layout project so that now we have a Photo Book option, for the production of multi-page documents to be printed and bound online, and the Photo Collage option, which provides the same theme-based layout but for printing at the desktop. Like Photo Layout in version 5.0, these are based around free form, multi-page projects that are produced using a simple step-by-step wizard.

This way of working flows through to other project options (CD/DVD Jacket, Greeting Card, CD/DVD Label). The wizard contains three basic steps – choose project page size, select the theme (matched frame design and background) and then nominate the layout, or number of images per page. Next you click OK and Photoshop Elements creates multiple pages and automatically inserts the photos in the layouts on these pages. At this stage, the project becomes a standard multi-page document– a format which was introduced in version 5.0 and really finds its legs here. See Figure 2.27. Whilst the project is in the Edit space you can adjust the style settings (drop shadows, etc.), add extra pictures, surround them with frames, add text and other graphics or shapes, or even change each page's theme. When complete, you save projects in the .PSE, or new Photo Project format.

Multi-page documents can be printed directly on your desktop printer or, if the Photo Book option was selected, sent to an online print or book service, such as the one offered by Kodak's EasyShare gallery, for professional printing and binding. The completed book is then returned in the mail.

For more details on creating photo projects using the PSE format and the Create/Share options found in Photoshop Elements 7, go to Chapters 10 and 14.

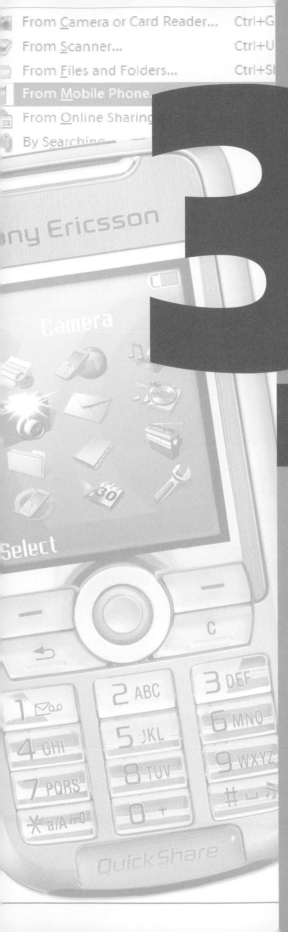

From Camera or Card Reader...   Ctrl+G

From Scanner...   Ctrl+U

From Files and Folders...   Ctrl+Sl

From Mobile Phone.

From Online Sharing

By Searching

3

First Steps

As a simple introduction to the program, this chapter will take you through the first basic steps involved in digital photography from downloading your pictures from your camera to the computer to holding an enhanced print in your hand.

We won't get involved in any manual or complex editing or enhancement techniques – there will be plenty of time for these in the next couple of chapters – instead, we will look at the various ways that you can get your images from your camera or scanner into the program, and see how you can manage the pictures once they are there. Then we will select an individual photograph, rotate and crop the image, save the changed file and finally print the picture. So let's get started.

Import and manage your photos | **START HERE**

Edit and enhance photos within the Full, Quick or Guided edit workspaces

Use your photos in Photo Books, calendars, collages, slide shows or web galleries

Share photos via e-mail, in web galleries, with prints and on CD or DVD

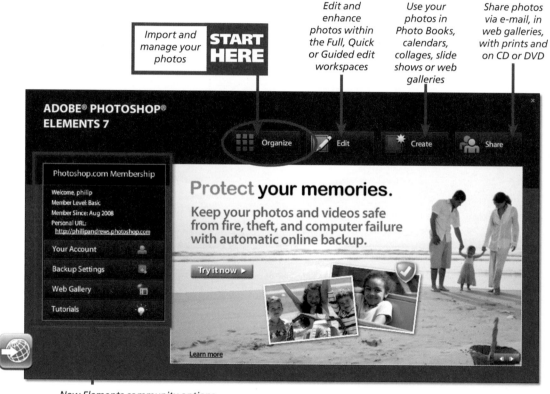

New Elements community options (initially available only in the USA)

Figure 3.1 *The Elements Welcome screen appears as the user opens the program. The screen can also be displayed by selecting the house icon (1) at the left end of either the Organizer or Edit workspaces.*

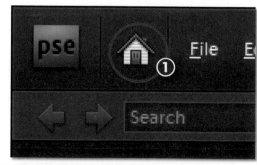

The Welcome screen

When Elements is first opened, the user is presented with a Welcome screen containing several options. See Figure 3.1. The selections are broken into different types of imaging activities and, depending on where you are in the workflow, will determine your entry point into the program.

So to start let's overview the options in the Welcome screen.

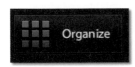

Organize – Designed as the first port of call for downloading your pictures from cameras, scanners and mobile phones, this selection takes you to the Organizer component of the Elements system. Start here when first introducing your pictures into Elements and when managing your photos.

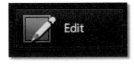

Edit – This selection takes you directly to the Edit workspace where you can choose between three different editing modes - Full, Quick and Guided. *Full* provides you with the most powerful enhancement and editing tools and features available in Elements. *Quick* provides more manual control than is available with the Auto Fix features in the Organizer space, but less than that found in the more sophisticated Full edit area. The *Guided Edit* workspace provides the user with step-by-step instructions on how to enhance their images.

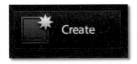

Create – This button takes you to the Create options in the both the Organizer and Editor workspaces. Here you can use your photos in the production of items such as photo books, calendars, collages, slide shows, greetings cards, web galleries and CD or DVD jackets. Slightly different Create options are available in the different workspaces.

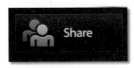

Share – Selecting this option from the Welcome screen displays the options in the Share tab of the Organizer workspace. Here you can choose from a variety of ways to present or distribute your photos. Options include creating an online gallery, attaching photos to your e-mails, producing Photo Mail, placing an order for printing by a web photo laboratory, saving copies of the pictures to CD or DVD or sending to an online gallery or even your mobile phone.

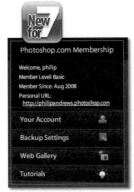

Photoshop Elements Community options: New for Photoshop Elements 7 is the inclusion of a range of community options available right inside the program. We first glimpse these new inclusions at the Welcome screen. Here you can create or modify your own Photoshop. com account settings, access a web gallery of your photos, get advice and inspiration from a series of special Elements tutorials (including some great ones from yours truly) and adjust your online backup settings. Two levels of membership are available – Basic (free) and Plus which, for a small payment, upgrades your online storage space and gets you extra regular Photoshop Elements tips, tricks and tutorials.

Book resources and video tutorials can be found at **www.photoshopelements.net**

Step 1: Getting your pictures into Elements

Over the history of the development of Photoshop Elements one of the most significant additions to the program has been the Organizer or Photo Browser/Date View workspace. This feature provides a visual index of your pictures and can be customized to display the images in Browser mode, Date mode or sorted by keyword tags or collection. Unlike the standard file browsers of previous editions, which created the thumbnails of your pictures the first time that the folder was browsed, the Organizer or Photo Browser as it is also called, creates the thumbnail during the process of adding your photographs to a collection.

To start your first collection simply select the Organize option from the Welcome screen and then proceed to the Organizer: File > Get Photos and Videos menu option. Select one of the listed sources of pictures provided and follow the steps and prompts in the dialogs that follow.

Organizer: File > Get Photos and Videos > From Camera or Card Reader

To start we will download photographs from a memory card or camera. This will probably be the most frequently used route for your images to enter the Elements program. Select the From Camera or Card Reader option from the File > Get Photos and Videos menu. Next you will see the Adobe Photo Downloader (APD) dialog. This feature is designed to quickly and easily transfer images from camera to computer. APD contains the option of using either a Standard or Advanced dialog. See Figure 3.2. The Advanced option not only provides thumbnail previews of the images stored on the camera or card but the dialog also contains several features for sorting and managing files as they are downloaded. But let's start simply, with the options in the Standard dialog.

Standard Dialog Workflow

After finding and selecting the source of the pictures (the card reader or camera) you will then see a thumbnail of the first file stored on the camera or memory card. By default all pictures on the card will be selected ready for downloading and cataloging.

Next set the Import Settings. Browse for the folder where you want the photographs to be stored and if you want to use a subfolder select the way that this folder will be named from the Create Subfolder drop-down menu. To help with finding your pictures later it may be helpful to add a meaningful name, not the labels that are attached by the camera, to the beginning of each of the images. You can do this by selecting an option from the Rename File drop-down menu and adding any custom text if needed. It is at this point that you can choose what action Elements will take after downloading the files via the Delete Options menu.

It is a good idea to choose the Verify and Delete option as this makes sure that your valuable pictures have been downloaded successfully before they are removed from the card. Clicking

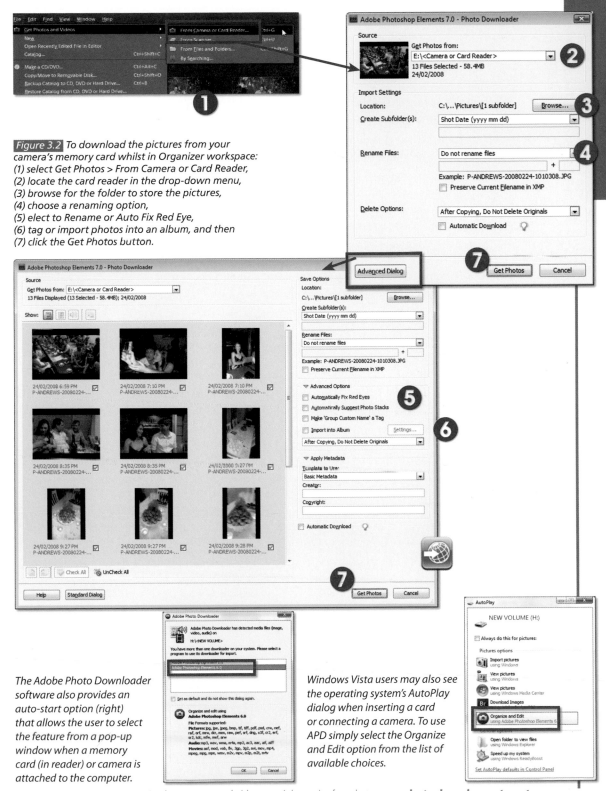

Figure 3.2 *To download the pictures from your camera's memory card whilst in Organizer workspace:*
(1) select Get Photos > From Camera or Card Reader,
(2) locate the card reader in the drop-down menu,
(3) browse for the folder to store the pictures,
(4) choose a renaming option,
(5) elect to Rename or Auto Fix Red Eye,
(6) tag or import photos into an album, and then
(7) click the Get Photos button.

The Adobe Photo Downloader software also provides an auto-start option (right) that allows the user to select the feature from a pop-up window when a memory card (in reader) or camera is attached to the computer.

Windows Vista users may also see the operating system's AutoPlay dialog when inserting a card or connecting a camera. To use APD simply select the Organize and Edit option from the list of available choices.

Book resources and video tutorials can be found at **www.photoshopelements.net**

the Get Photos button will transfer your pictures to your hard drive – you can then catalog the pictures in the Organizer workspace. For more choices during the download process you will need to switch to the Advanced mode. See Figure 3.2.

Advanced Mode Workflow

Selecting the Advanced Dialog button at the bottom left of the Standard mode window will display a larger Photo Downloader dialog with more options and a preview area showing a complete set of preview thumbnails of the photos stored on the camera or memory card. If for some reason you do not want to download all the images, then you will need to deselect the files to remain by unchecking the tick box at the bottom right-hand of the thumbnail.

Note: Only files that are selected in Adobe Photo Downloader can be deleted from the camera. This means they have to be downloaded and added to the catalog (even if they're already there from a previous download) before they are deleted.

This version of the Photo Downloader contains the same 'Location for saving transferred files', Rename and 'Delete after importing' options that are in the Standard dialog. In addition, this mode contains the following options (see Figures 3.3 and 3.4):

Automatically Fix Red Eyes – This feature searches for and corrects any red eye effects in photos taken with flash.

Automatically Suggest Photo Stacks – Select this option to get the downloader utility to display groups of photos that are similar in either content or time taken. The user can then opt to convert these groups into image stacks or keep them as individual thumbnails in the Organizer.

Make 'Group Custom Name' as a Tag – To aid with finding your pictures once they become part of the larger collection of images in your Elements catalog, you can group tag the photos as

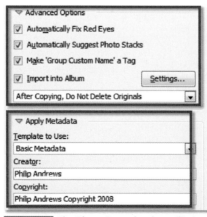

Figure 3.3 The Photo Downloader utility's Advanced mode contains several new options including auto stacking, auto tagging and adding metadata on the fly. This is in addition to the great Auto Red Eye Fix feature that was introduced in version 4.0.

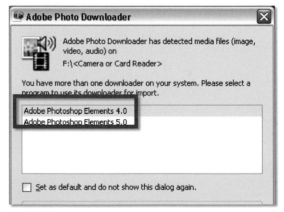

Figure 3.4 If you are upgrading from a previous version of Elements and have retained that version of the program alongside the new version, then selecting the Get Photos and Videos > From Camera or Card Reader option will display the warning seen here. Use this dialog to select the downloader version that you wish to use.

you download them. Adding tags is the Elements equivalent of including searchable keywords with your pictures. This task is normally handled once the photos are in the Organizer work-space but from version 5.0 a new automated way to add the same tag to all the photos downloaded in a single session was introduced. The tag name used is the same as the title added in the Rename section of the Photo Downloader utility.

Import into Album – New for Photoshop Elements 7 is the ability to create albums for the photos you are transferring inside the Adobe Photo Downloader. After selecting the Import to Album option you can click the Settings button. This will display a new pop-up window where you can either select an existing album or create a new one. Being able to download directly into albums will greatly speed up the time taken to locate image to be used in Elements projects. See Figure 3.5.

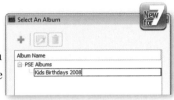

Figure 3.5 *Using the new Import to Album option allows you to create a new album for the images you are downloading.*

Apply Metadata (Author and Copyright) – With this option you can add both author name and copyright details to the metadata that is stored with the photo. Metadata, or EXIF data as it is sometimes called, is saved as part of the file and can be displayed at any time with the File Info (Editor) or Properties (Organizer) options in Elements or with a similar feature in other imaging programs.

Automatic Downloads

Both the Standard and Advanced dialogs contain the option to use automatic downloading the next time a camera or card reader is attached to the computer. The settings used for the auto download, as well as default values for features in the Advanced mode of the Photo Downloader, can be adjusted in the Organizer: Edit > Preferences > Camera or Card Reader dialog.

Organizer: File > Get Photos and Videos > From Scanner

The Organizer: Get Photos and Videos > From Scanner option enables users to obtain images directly from the scanners they have connected to their computers. A dialog asking the user to 'Select an input source' and choose a download folder and image quality may appear if your scanner is not automatically detected. To continue, select the device from the list and click OK. Next, the scanner driver window will be displayed. In this dialog you can preview the picture and adjust the settings that will govern the scanning process. See Figure 3.6. The default settings for importing files from an attached scanner can be adjusted in the Scanner area in the Edit > Preferences dialog.

Start by performing a Preview scan (some scanners handle this step automatically). This will produce a quick low-resolution picture of the print or negative. Using this image as a guide, select the area to be scanned with the Marquee or Cropping tool. Next, adjust the brightness, contrast and color of the image to ensure that you are capturing the greatest amount of detail

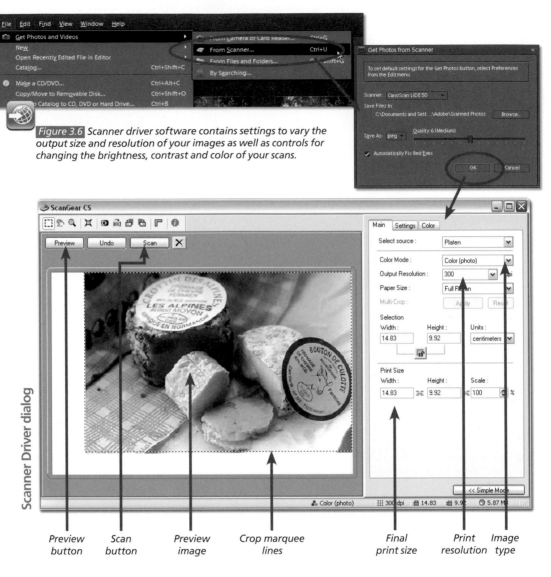

Figure 3.6 *Scanner driver software contains settings to vary the output size and resolution of your images as well as controls for changing the brightness, contrast and color of your scans.*

Scanner Driver dialog

Preview button   Scan button   Preview image   Crop marquee lines   Final print size   Print resolution   Image type

possible. Now input your scan sizes, concentrating on ensuring that the final dimensions and resolution are equal to your needs. As a rough guide, remember that if your original print or film frame is small you will need to scan at a high resolution in order to produce a reasonable file size. Large print originals, on the other hand, can be scanned at lower resolutions to achieve the same file size. Sound a little confusing? It can be, but most scanner software is designed to help you through the maze.

The Scanner Driver dialog is designed and supplied by the same company that manufactures the scanner itself. When the Organizer: File > Get Photos and Videos > From Scanner option is selected the Elements program goes in search of this driver software and displays it in a separate window on screen. When you alter settings you are controlling the scanning process only. All of this process happens outside of Elements and, once completed, the scanned file is then passed to the Elements program. This is the reason why after scanning you sometimes need to close the Control dialog to see the finished image waiting in the Elements workspace behind.

The Driver dialog detailed left is supplied with Canon scanners. Your own scanner control may appear different from this one but all but the most basic machines will have options for changing size, resolution, contrast, brightness and color. Look to your manual or the online Help option for your model to locate the controls.

Ensuring enough pixels for the job

When you capture an image using a print or film scanner, you are creating a digital file. Unlike the situation with most digital cameras, where the largest pixel dimensions of the file are fixed by the size of the sensor, images made via a scanner can vary in size depending on the settings used to create them. To make sure that you have enough pixels for your requirements, it is important to remember that the quality of the image, and the size that it can be printed, are determined, in part, by its pixel dimensions. It is therefore good practice to choose the pixel dimensions for your image based on what that picture will be used for. An image that is destined to become a poster will need to have substantially more pixels than one needed for a postage stamp. 'Just how many more pixels are needed?' is a good question. The answer can be found in the numbers you input in the scanner dialog.

The final dimensions of your digital picture should be input directly into the Width and Height boxes of the control. Next, the output resolution that you will use when printing your picture is placed in the Resolution box. The scanner driver will usually handle the rest, working out the exact file size needed to suit your requirements.

If you are unsure what resolution to input, use the settings in the following table as a starting point. See Table 3.1. If your picture is to be printed at a variety of sizes, scan your image for the largest size first and then use the tools in Elements (Editor: Image > Resize > Image Size) to downsize the digital file when necessary. Making large images smaller preserves much of the quality of the original but the reverse is not true. Enlarging small files to create the correct resolution needed for a big print job will always produce a poor quality file, especially when it is compared to one that was scanned at the right size in the first place. See Figure 3.7.

How the image will be used	The final print resolution to select
Screen or web use only	72 dots per inch (dpi)
Draft quality inkjet prints	150 dpi
Large posters (that will be viewed from a distance)	180-220 dpi
Photographic quality inkjet printing	240–360 dpi
Magazine printing	300 dpi

Table 3.1 Different image outcomes require different levels of output resolution. Use the values in this table as a guide when sizing your photo.

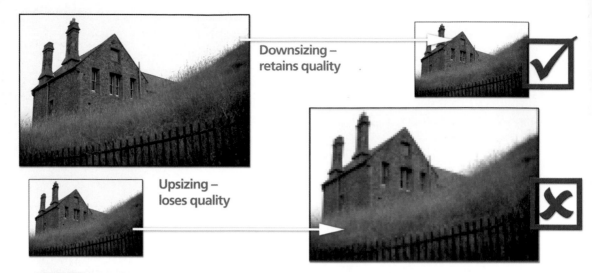

Downsizing – retains quality

Upsizing – loses quality

Figure 3.7 Downsizing images is acceptable but enlarging always produces a final picture that is poor in quality. It is better to rescan the original if you need to print it bigger. Only enlarge a small picture as a last resort.

Editor: Image > Divide Scanned Photos

For those readers with many pictures to scan, the Divide Scanned Photos feature will prove a godsend. With this feature you can scan several prints at once on a flatbed scanner and then allow Elements to separate each of the individual pictures and place them in a new document.

To ensure accurate division of photos, place a colored backing sheet on top of the prints to be scanned. This helps the program distinguish where one picture starts and the other ends. See Figure 3.8.

Figure 3.8 The Divide Scanned Photos options provides a quick way to separate pictures that have been scanned together.

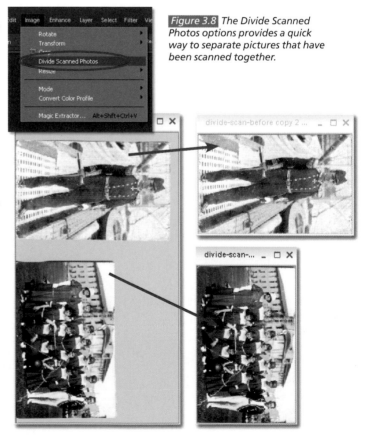

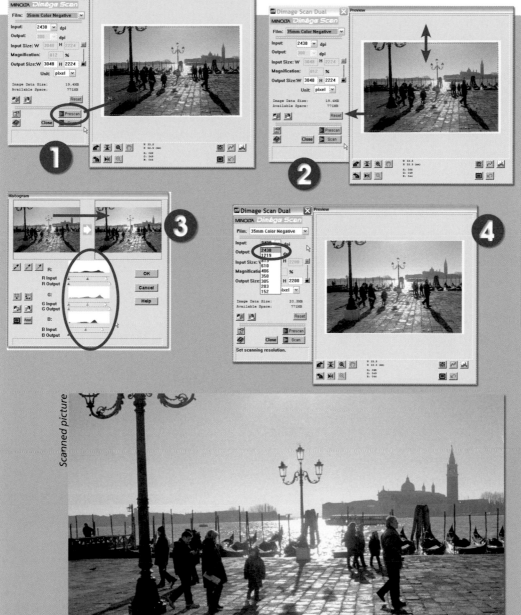

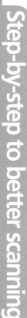

Step-by-step to better scanning

Scanned picture

Scanning summary
Making a scan is a four-step process that starts with previewing the image (1). Next, the area to be scanned is selected (2), the brightness, contrast and color changed (if needed) (3), and finally the output dimensions and resolution set (4).

Organizer: File > Get Photos and Videos > From Files and Folders

Acting much like the File > Open option common to most programs, this selection provides you with the familiar window that allows you to browse for and open pictures that you have already saved to your computer. Though slightly different on Windows and Macintosh machines, you generally have the option to view your files in a variety of ways. Windows users can choose between Thumbnails, Tiles, Icons, List and Detail Views using the drop-down menu from the top of the window. See Figure 3.9. The Thumbnail option provides a simplified File Browser View of the pictures on your disk and it is this way of working that will prove to be most useful for digital photographers. After selecting the image, or images, you wish to import into the Photo Browser or Organizer, select the Get Photos button.

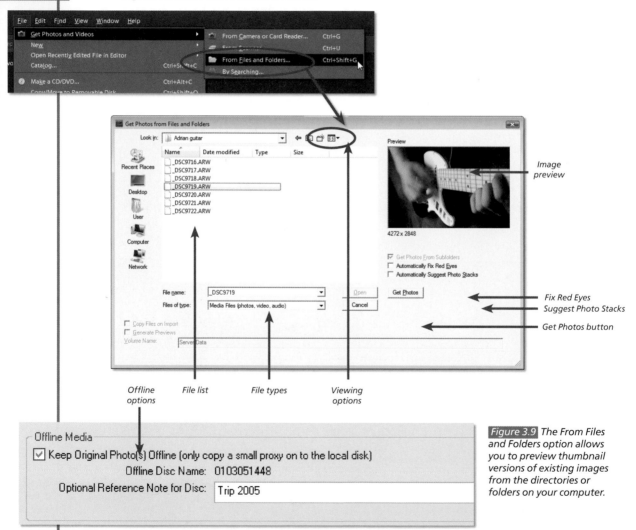

Offline options   File list   File types   Viewing options

Figure 3.9 The From Files and Folders option allows you to preview thumbnail versions of existing images from the directories or folders on your computer.

When working with images from CDs or DVDs the Offline Media options allow you to import small thumbnail versions of the pictures that you have stored on CD-ROMs, DVDs or other media that can be disconnected from your computer. Elements catalogs these pictures and allows you to search and organize the thumbnails just like any other picture.

How to multi-select the files to import

Pro's Tip

To select several images or files at once hold down the Ctrl key whilst clicking onto the pictures of your choice. To select a complete list of files without having to pick each file in turn click on the first picture and then, whilst holding down the Shift key, click on the last file in the group.

Organizer: File > Watch Folders

You can set up an alternative way to automatically add photos to your Organizer workspace with the Watched Folders option found in the File Menu. This is a particularly useful option when you have devices such as mobile phones that download images to specific directories on your computer when they are connected. Using the Watch Folder system you can point Photoshop Elements at the same folder that the phone uses and the program is smart enough to know when new pictures are saved to the folder and Elements will automatically add them to your Organizer library. The option does not link your computer directly to your mobile phone (you will need the software that came with the unit for that), but rather watches the default folder where your phone pictures are downloaded. When new pictures are added to the folder, Elements either adds them to your catalog automatically or notifies you of the new files and asks permission to add them. See Figure 3.10.

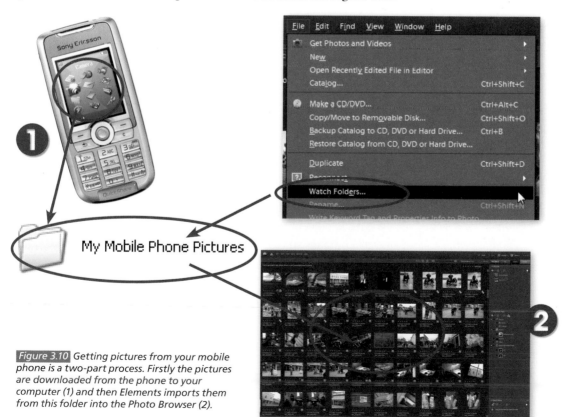

Figure 3.10 *Getting pictures from your mobile phone is a two-part process. Firstly the pictures are downloaded from the phone to your computer (1) and then Elements imports them from this folder into the Photo Browser (2).*

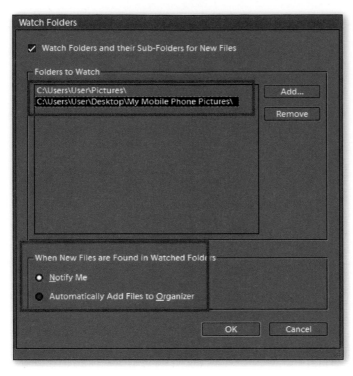

Figure 3.11 *When selecting the Watched Folders option Elements displays a dialog where you can Add or Remove folders that the program will watch.*

To make sure that you can import your mobile phone pictures directly into Elements select the default download folder using the options in the Watch Folders dialog. This window will be displayed when selecting the File > Watch Folders menu option. In the dialog displayed browse for the folder that you use to store your mobile phone pictures. Click OK to set the folder as the default and choose whether to be notified when new photos are found or have them automatically added to the Organizer. See Figure 3.11.

This feature can also be used by photographers who like to remotely control their cameras from an attached laptop. Called tethered shooting, the images are downloaded directly from the camera to the laptop hard drive and then automatically imported into Photoshop Elements.

Organizer: File > Get Photos and Videos > By Searching

The Get Photos and Videos > By Searching option provides a speedy way to locate all the folders connected to your computer that contain pictures that you may want to add to your Organizer catalogs. After you set the search options and click the Search button, Elements will weave its way through your computer hunting down folders that contain candidate picture files. By default the program will not locate files in the GIF or PNG formats (both of which are almost exclusively used for web pages). If you are looking for these file types then you will need to use the Get Photos > From Files and Folders option. You can also choose to exclude small pictures and those images contained in system or program folders. Both these options should be selected to speed up the search process. Once the folder list has been compiled, which usually only takes a few seconds, you can select (or multi-select) the folders whose images you wish to import. Clicking the Import Folders button will then add the pictures contained into the catalog of the Photo Browser. See Figure 3.12.

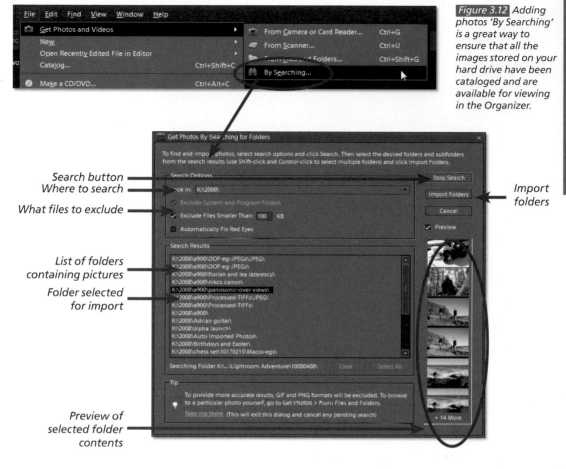

Figure 3.12 Adding photos 'By Searching' is a great way to ensure that all the images stored on your hard drive have been cataloged and are available for viewing in the Organizer.

Search button
Where to search

What files to exclude

List of folders
containing pictures
Folder selected
for import

Import
folders

Preview of
selected folder
contents

Other options for getting your photos into Elements

Although my recommendation is that you always import and organize your pictures via the Organizer and Get Photos features, there will be times when you need to access existing files, or even newly photographed images, whilst in one of the Elements editor modes – Quick Fix or Full Edit. The follow options give you just this type of access.

Editor: File > Open

Working in much the same way as the Get Photos > From Files and Folders option, selecting File > Open presents you with the standard Windows file browser. From here you can navigate from drive to drive on your machine before locating and opening the folder that contains your pictures. You can refine the display options by selecting the specific file type (file ending) to be displayed and as we have already noted you can also choose the way to view the files. In Figure 3.13 the thumbnail view was selected so that it is possible to quickly flick through a folder full of pictures to locate the specific image you are after.

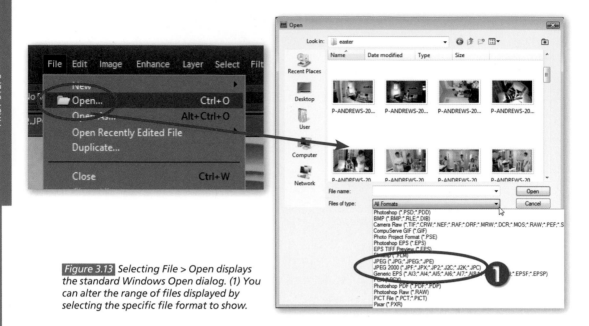

Figure 3.13 *Selecting File > Open displays the standard Windows Open dialog. (1) You can alter the range of files displayed by selecting the specific file format to show.*

Editor: File > Open As

On the odd occasion that a specific file won't open using the File > Open command you can try to open the file in a different format. Do this by selecting the File > Open As option and then choosing the file you want to open. After making this selection pick the desired format from the Open As pop-up menu, and click the Open button. This action forces the program to ignore the file format it has assumed the picture is saved in and treat the image as if it is saved as the file type you have selected. If the picture still refuses to open, then you may have selected a format that does not match the file's true format, or the file itself may have been damaged when being saved. See Figure 3.14.

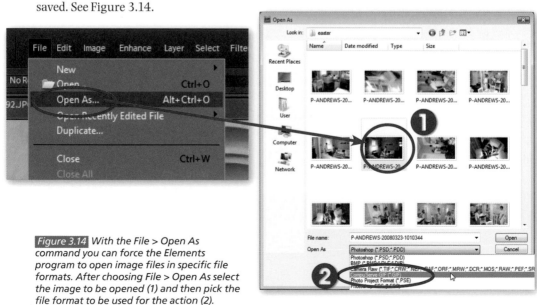

Figure 3.14 *With the File > Open As command you can force the Elements program to open image files in specific file formats. After choosing File > Open As select the image to be opened (1) and then pick the file format to be used for the action (2).*

This feature is also used for open files where the extension is unknown. This is particularly useful if a picture is saved on a Macintosh machine without a file extension and then transferred to a computer running the Windows operating system which requires a file extension to open it.

Opening raw files

Raw files are a special capture file format and are unlike other imaging files that you deal with in Photoshop Elements. Rather than being able to be opened directly into the Editor workspace, they must first be converted from the capture format (.CR2 for Canon, .NEF for Nikon, .ARW for Sony, etc.) to a standard imaging format (TIFF, JPEG, PSD). This is not to say that raw files can't be managed in the Organizer, on the contrary, raw files downloaded with the Adobe Photo Downloader and added to the Elements' library behave like other file formats for the majority of the time. With a couple of exceptions:

1. When applying any of the auto features (plus cropping) listed in the Fix panel, the enhancement is applied to a converted copy of the file and then this new picture is stacked with the raw original.

2. When opening raw files into any mode of the editing space, the picture is first opened in Adobe's conversion utility, Adobe Camera Raw (ACR), where special raw based enhancements are applied and then a converted version of the file is opened into the editing space. Any changes made in ACR are remembered with the file and reflected in the Organizer's preview. See Figure 3.15.

What does this mean in reality? Yes it means that there is an extra step in the editing process, but the increased level of control offered by raw shooting and careful conversion is worth it. For a more comprehensive look at raw formats and how to use them with Photoshop Elements go to Chapter 6.

Figure 3.15 *Raw files need to be converted before they are can be edited or enhanced in Photoshop Elements.*

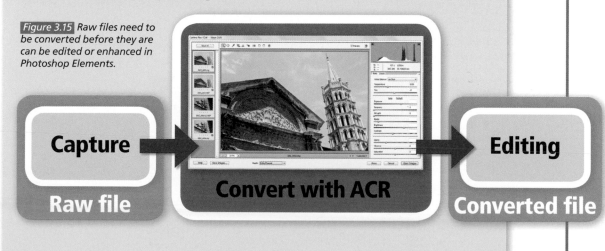

Capture
Raw file
Convert with ACR
Editing
Converted file

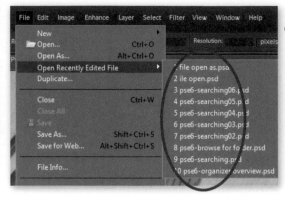

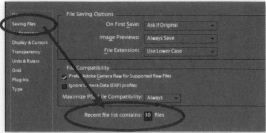

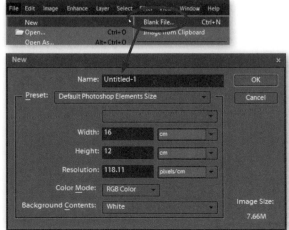

Figure 3.16 *The Open Recently Edited File list displays the last few pictures that you have opened in the Editor workspace. The number of files that are included on this list is determined by the 'Recent file list contains' option in the Saving Files preferences.*

Editor: File > Open Recently Edited File

As you browse, open and edit various pictures from your folders, Elements keeps track of the last few files and lists them under the File > Open Recently Edited Files menu item. This is a very handy feature as it means that you can return quickly to pictures that you are working on without having to navigate back to the specific folder where they are stored. By default Photoshop Elements lists the last 10 files edited. You can change the number of files kept on this menu via the Recent File List setting in the Editor: Edit > Preferences > Saving Files window. Don't be tempted to list too many files as each additional listing uses more memory. See Figure 3.16.

Editor: File > Place

Though not strictly an opening action, the File > Place command is very important as it provides the Elements user with the ability to insert pictures with transparent backgrounds into Photo Book or Photo Collage projects. Normally photos are added to these projects by dragging the images from the Project Bin but this action doesn't suit photos where the backgrounds have been removed. Instead open the project file and then use File > Place to insert your image.

Figure 3.17 *The File > New > Blank File dialog box is used for setting the dimensions, resolution and mode of new image documents. There are a variety of preset sizes available in the File > New dialog. To choose a new preset select the Preset group first from the upper menu (1) and then choose a specific document template from the second menu immediately below it (2).*

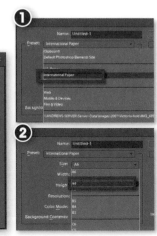

Editor: File > Organize Open Files

This option adds files that are currently open in the Editor workspace to the Organizer catalog, if they're not already there and they don't need resaving. It is important to note that some formats that you can open in the Full edit workspace are not supported in the Organizer. These include: PICT, EPS, Photoshop Raw and SCT.

Creating new documents

Editor: File > New > Blank File

The File > New > Blank File option creates an Elements picture from the settings selected in the New dialog box. The box has sections for the image's name, width, height, resolution and mode. The background content of the image can be chosen from the list at the bottom of the box and you can also choose an existing template from a range of document types from the drop-down Preset menu. See Figure 3.17.

At this stage it is important to remember that the quality of the image, and the size that it can be printed, are determined, in part, by its pixel dimensions. As we saw in the scanner section earlier in the chapter, you should choose your image's pixel dimensions based on what you intend to use the picture for. Small prints need fewer total pixels than those images intended for large posters. To ensure that your document will suit your end purpose, input the final dimensions of your product directly into the Width and Height boxes. Next, add the resolution that you will use when outputting your image in the Resolution box. Be sure to check that the resolution unit is set to 'pixels/inch' not 'pixels/cm'; inadvertently picking the wrong option here will have you creating huge images needlessly. If you are unsure what print resolution to input, use the guide in Table 3.1 (see p. 43).

Editor: File > New > Image from Clipboard

Many programs contain the options to copy (Edit > Copy) and paste (Edit > Paste) information. For the most part, these functions occur within a single piece of software, but occasionally the process can also be used to copy an image, or some text, from one program and place it in another. Previous versions of Elements provided different pathways for making a new file

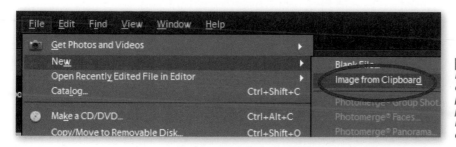

Figure 3.18 *The New > Image from Clipboard dialog box is used for pasting already copied pictures as a layer in a new Elements document.*

from pictures stored in the computer's memory, but since version 3.0 a specialist Image from Clipboard item can be found under the File > New menu. See Figure 3.18.

Once a picture has been copied to memory, selecting the New > Image from Clipboard option automatically creates a new document of the correct size to accommodate the copied content and pastes the picture in as a new layer. There is no need to guess the size of the copied picture as Elements automatically determines this when it creates the new document.

It is worth noting that if there is no image stored in memory then this option will be 'grayed out' (unavailable) in the menu list.

Photomerge options

One of the most popular features of all those included in Elements is the special stitching tool called Photomerge. In version 6 the feature was completely revamped to provide substantially better results, with less effort on the behalf of the photographer, than in previous versions. Also, two new Photomerge options were added – Photomerge Group Shot and Photomerge Faces. In version 7.0 a new, more powerful blending option has been added in the form of the Scene Cleaner. All of these options make use of the alignment and blending technologies that are core to Photomerge to produce composite images from the contents of several photos. See Figure 3.19.

All of the Photomerge options in the File > New menu in the Organizer workspace are grayed out (can't be selected) until two or more thumbnails are selected from the Photo Browser. Once the photos are multi-selected, choosing a Photomerge option will transfer the images to the Edit workspace and proceed with the stitching task.

Editor/Organizer: File > New > Photomerge Group Shot

The Photomerge Group Shot combines the best bits of several photos into a single final image. One of its best uses is to solve the age-old problem of trying to get all the members of a group photograph looking good in the same picture. Using Photomerge Group Photo, the photographer takes several photos of the same grouping and then, back at the desktop, he or she combines the best 'looks' of the group members into a single picture using just a few pencil strokes. The best way to get to know your way around this feature is to select the Photomerge > Group Shop option from the Guided edit panel and follow the steps listed. For more details go to Chapter 11.

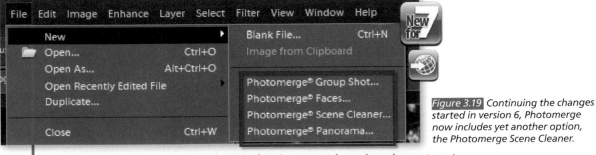

Figure 3.19 Continuing the changes started in version 6, Photomerge now includes yet another option, the Photomerge Scene Cleaner.

Editor/Organizer: File > New > Photomerge Faces

Photomerge Faces is designed to combine facial parts from several different images into a single picture, this option has the capabilities of producing some really bizarre and fun results. For more details on how to use this new feature go to Chapter 11.

Editor/Organizer: File > New > Photomerge Scene Cleaner

Designed as an aid for the travel photographer who regularly manages to capture tourists in the middle of their shots of great monuments, the new Photomerge Scene Cleaner option has the abiltity to stitch together different parts of a multiple photos to produce a single photo. Using this feature the travel photographer can capture several images of the monument with the tourists in different positions and then piece together different sections of the scene to produce a photo sans-tourist.

In another application (see Figure 3.20), the Scene Cleaner can be used to integrate the 'best bits' of several candid photos of the kids to form a composite that features the best expressions for each child in a single photo. For step by step instructions go to Chapter 11.

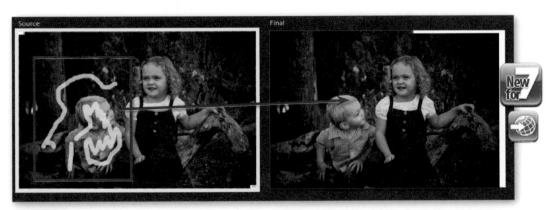

Figure 3.20 *The Photomerge Scene Cleaner is used for combining different parts of multiple photos into a single seamless composition.*

Editor/Organizer: File > New > Photomerge Panorama

The Photomerge Panorama option is used for stitching several overlapping photos to form a wide vista photo. After choosing the source photos in the Organizer, selecting the File > New > Photomerge Panorama option will present you with the Photomerge dialog. As well as providing space to add the files to use for the stitching, there are five Layout options on the left of the window. The Interactive Layout entry moves the files into the familiar Photomerge workspace that featured prominently in previous versions of the program. The other four options align and blend the images automatically into a single wide-angle panorama. See Figure 3.21. For more details on how to use the Photomerge feature see Chapter 11.

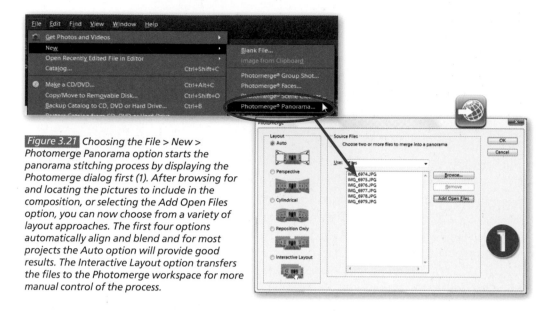

Figure 3.21 Choosing the File > New > Photomerge Panorama option starts the panorama stitching process by displaying the Photomerge dialog first (1). After browsing for and locating the pictures to include in the composition, or selecting the Add Open Files option, you can now choose from a variety of layout approaches. The first four options automatically align and blend and for most projects the Auto option will provide good results. The Interactive Layout option transfers the files to the Photomerge workspace for more manual control of the process.

Editor: File > Import > Frame From Video

Almost hidden from view in a new position on the File > Import menu is the Frame From Video option. With the increase in popularity of digital video, it was a great move on Adobe's part to include this feature in version 2.0 of the program. The option gives the users the opportunity to capture still frames from a variety of stored video formats. The Frame From Video dialog employs familiar video player buttons to play, rewind and fast forward the selected footage. The Grab button snatches still frames from the playing video and places them into Elements ready for editing. Though images captured in this fashion are rarely of equal quality to those sourced from a dedicated stills camera or scanner, there are occasions when a feature such as this fits the bill.

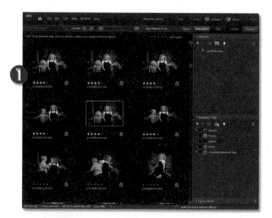
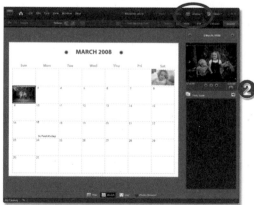

Figure 3.22 You can view cataloged pictures in the Organizer workspace in two fundamentally different ways. Switch views using the options in Display menu located at the top right of the window.
(1) Photo Browser View – based on a thumbnail view with an associated timeline at the top.
(2) Date View – photos organized according to the date they were shot.

Step 2: Viewing your pictures

After importing your pictures into the Organizer, users can then choose to display them in Photo Browser or Date mode. Files can be tagged with appropriate keywords, to help when searching for specific pictures later, or grouped into album collections of images with similar subjects. Although this is not the place to undertake major editing tasks you can apply simple enhancements (mostly automatic) using the features in the new Fix panel such as Auto Smart Fix, Auto Color, Auto Levels and Auto Red Eye Fix. We will look at these options more fully in step 5 of this First Steps introduction.

To apply more complex changes to your photographs you can jump from the Organizer directly to the Edit workspace which contains Full, Quick and Guided Edit modes. In the same way you can also use selected pictures or albums as the basis for producing one of the many photo projects available via the Create panel. But don't think that the Organizer's prowess ends there – the images you select can also be printed, e-mailed to your friends, shared online and even sent to a mobile phone all from this one window using the options in the Share panel. See Figure 3.22.

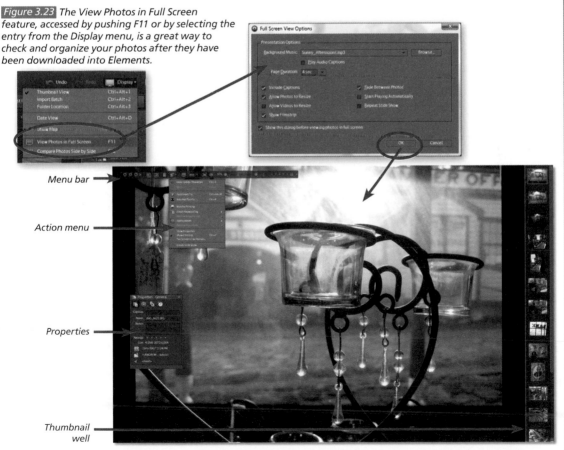

Figure 3.23 *The View Photos in Full Screen feature, accessed by pushing F11 or by selecting the entry from the Display menu, is a great way to check and organize your photos after they have been downloaded into Elements.*

Menu bar

Action menu

Properties

Thumbnail well

View Photos in Full Screen display

Organizer: Display > View Photos in Full Screen (F11)

The View Photos in Full Screen option provides an instant slide show of the files that you have currently displayed in the Photo Browser. Seeing the photos full size on your machine is a good way to edit the shots you want to keep from those that should be placed in the 'I will remember not to do that next time' bin. With the provided menu you can play, pause or advance to next or last photos using the VCR-like controls. You can enlarge or reduce the size that the picture appears on screen with the Magnification slider (Zoom Level control). For quick magnification changes there are also Fit to Window and Actual Pixels buttons. But the real bonus of the feature is the list of actions that you can perform to pictures you review. You can automatically enhance, add and remove tags, mark the file for printing and add the file to a chosen collection using the choices listed under the Action menu. Specific picture properties such as tag, history and metadata are available by hitting the Alt + Enter keys to display the Properties window. See Figure 3.23 on the previous page.

As well as showing all the photos currently in the browser you can also multi-select the images to include in the review session before starting the feature, or even limit those pictures displayed to a particular album. The Full Screen View options can be set when the feature is first opened or accessed via the last item on the Action menu.

First stop – View Photos in Full Screen

The options available in the Full Screen view feature make this a great place to check the results of a day's shooting. You can flick through the images that you have recorded, sorting the good ones into a newly created album, adding ratings, and deleting the not so good examples of your photographic prowess. If you prefer to keep all the images together and just add keyword tags to selected files then this is easily achieved here as well.

Organizer: Display > Compare Photos Side by Side (F12)

Closely linked to the View Photos in Full Screen feature detailed above is the Compare Photos Side by Side option, which allows users to display two similar pictures side by side. This is a great way to choose between several images taken at the same time to ensure that the best one is used for printing or passed on to the editor for enhancement. See Figure 3.24.

To select the images to display click onto one of the Compare workspaces (left or right in the example) and then click on a thumbnail. Now select the other workspace and click the comparison image thumbnail. All the same Full Screen adjustment and organizational controls are available in the Compare Photos feature, including the Zoom control, which provides the ability to examine candidate files more closely.

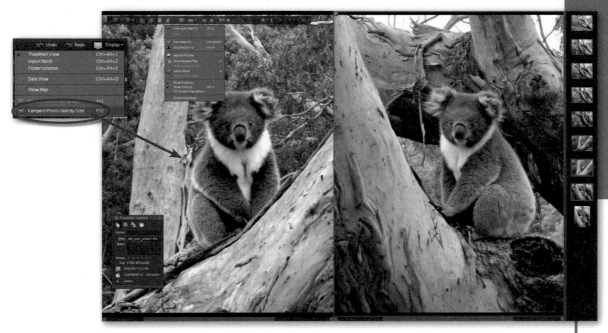

Figure 3.24 *The Compare Photos Side by Side feature provides the opportunity for you to review the quality of similar photos in Full Screen mode.*

By pressing the 'X' key you can switch the pictures from left to right. This technique can be very useful when sorting similar shots. For example, when editing bracketed photos you can keep moving the better shot to the left (whilst flicking through the alternative options on the right) until you find the perfect exposure and then flag that one for printing.

Comparing apples with apples

Clicking the Sync Pan and Zoom button (chain icon) will magnify both pictures to the same zoom level when either picture is changed. The feature also scrolls both pictures in unison, allowing the same specific areas of a photograph to be examined without the need to independently move each image.

Editor: View > Zoom In and Zoom Out

Images displayed in the Editor workspace can be viewed at a variety of different magnifications. To alter the size of the picture on screen, use either the menu option View > Zoom In or Zoom Out, or the Zoom tool. Clicking on a photo with the tool selected will enlarge the picture and clicking with the Alt key held down will reduce the size. Clicking and dragging will draw a marquee, which will then enlarge the selected part to fill your window. Double-clicking the Zoom tool automatically displays the image at 100%. Double-clicking the Hand tool fits to screen. Holding down the Shift key while zooming (with the Zoom tool) or panning (with the Hand tool) applies the changes to all open photos in the Edit workspace. See Figure 3.25.

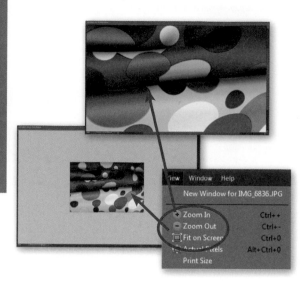
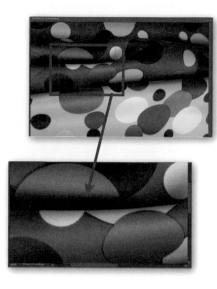

Figure 3.25 *Images can be enlarged or reduced on screen by using either the Zoom In or Out feature (View > Zoom In or Out) or the Zoom tool.*

Editor: Window > Navigator

When the picture is enlarged beyond the boundaries of the window, you will only be able to see a small section of the image at one time. To navigate around the picture, use the Hand tool to click and drag the picture within the box. Alternatively, Elements contains a special Navigator window, where you can interactively enlarge and reduce image size, as well as move anywhere around the image boundaries. See Figure 3.26.

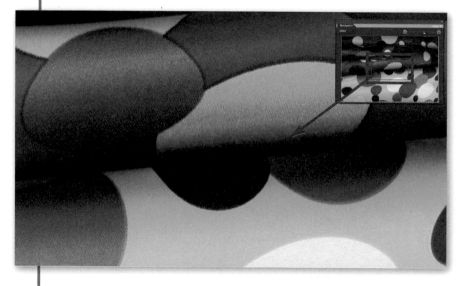

Figure 3.26 *The Navigator palette provides both zoom and movement control in one feature. If you have a large screen, this is a good palette to have visible all the time.*

Book resources and video tutorials can be found at **www.photoshopelements.net**

Step 3: Image rotating

One of the first tasks to undertake on pictures that you have downloaded from your camera or scanner is to correct their orientation. This, of course, is only true for those images that were taken with the camera on the side, or prints that were inadvertently scanned the wrong way up. You can rotate your pictures back to their rightful orientation in the Photo Browser or View Photos in Full Screen features or in any of the Elements Editor workspaces. Use the steps below to reorientate your photos depending on the workspace you have open.

Photo Browser: Select the thumbnail of the picture that needs rotating and then select Rotate 90° Left or Right from either the Edit menu or the right-click menu. See Figure 3.27.

View Photos in Full Screen: Either wait until the image you need to rotate is displayed on the main screen, or select it from the Thumbnail well on the left of the window, and then click one of the Rotate buttons located in the tool bar.

Full Editor: To rotate the whole picture using the Image > Rotate > 90° Left or Right options. Rotating the photo 180° will turn the picture upside down. Flipping the canvas provides a mirror image of the original. The other options in the Rotate menu are for rotating separate layers in an image. For more information on layers see Chapter 6.

Quick editor: As well as using the same menu commands detailed for the Full Edit above, you can also click on the Rotate buttons displayed at the bottom of the preview area.

Guided editor: Select the Rotate and/or Straighten options from the Basic Photo Edits section of the main Guided menu. Select either the Rotate Left or Rotate Right buttons to pivot the picture.

Adobe Photo Downloader: You can also rotate photos in the Advanced section of the Photo Downloader utility. Just click on the thumbnail and then select the appropriate Rotate button.

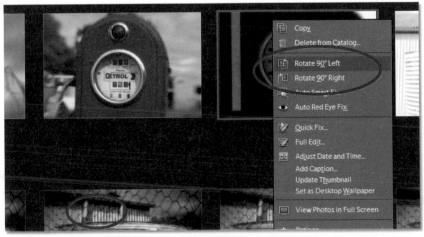

Figure 3.27 To rotate images in the Organizer workspace either select the Rotate 90° Left or Right option from the Edit menu or choose from the same options in the right-click pop-up menu. As an alternative you could also click one of the Rotate buttons at the top of the Photo Browser window. Single or multi-selected photos can be rotated in this way.

Step 4: Cropping and straightening

Cropping

Cropping a picture can help add drama to an image by eliminating unneeded or unwanted detail. It can also be a good method for altering the orientation of a crooked scan. Again there are several different ways of cropping your pictures depending on which Elements workspace you are using, but all are dependent on selecting the portion of the image you wish to retain, using either the Marquee or Crop tools.

Quick and Full editors: With the first approach you need to select the Marquee tool and then click and drag the tool over the image to define a selection (of the area you wish to keep). Then, to apply the crop, choose Image > Crop from the menu bar. See Figure 3.28.

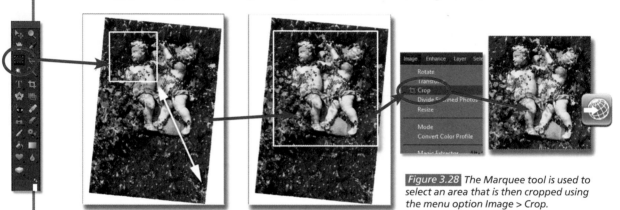

Figure 3.28 The Marquee tool is used to select an area that is then cropped using the menu option Image > Crop.

Guided editor: After selecting the Crop Photo option from the Basic Photo Edits menu, you will notice that a cropping marquee is automatically added to the photo. Use the corner or side handles to adjust the shape and size of the crop before clicking Done to apply the settings. Alternatively you can select a specific crop size from the Crop Box Size menu. See Figure 3.29.

Figure 3.29 The Crop Photo section of the Guided editor panel automatically applies a crop marquee to the image. The user then adjusts the size and shape via the side and corner handles or with the options in the Crop Box Size menu.

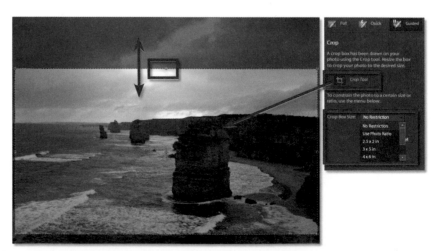

Cropping in the Organizer: First introduced in Photoshop Elements 6 was the ability to crop photos from inside the Organizer workspace. After selecting the thumbnail choose the Crop option from the Fix panel. The Crop Photo Dialog is displayed. Here you can use the Crop tool to reshape or resize the marquee that is previewed on the photograph. It is also possible to select from a variety of preset sizes or add in your own custom ratio for the crop using the Aspect Ratio menu. Clicking the Apply button performs the crop and displays the results on screen. The Undo button can be used to reverse cropping changes and the OK button crops a duplicate of the original photo before saving them both in a Version Set in the Organizer. When cropping a raw file the feature creates a copy of the picture in a different format and applies the crop to this photo. See Figure 3.30.

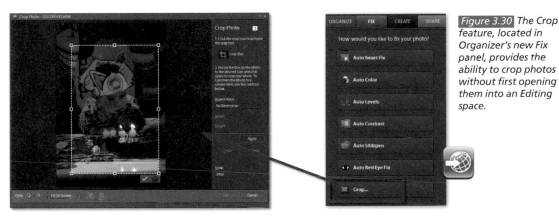

Figure 3.30 The Crop feature, located in Organizer's new Fix panel, provides the ability to crop photos without first opening them into an Editing space.

If you want a little more control then try using the specialist Crop tool. Looking like a set of darkroom easel arms, it is present in both editors' tool bars. Once the tool is selected click and drag on the image surface. You will see a marquee-like box appear. The box can be resized at any time by dragging the handles positioned at the corners or sides. When you are satisfied with the changes, crop the image by either clicking the green tick button at the bottom of the crop marquee or by double-clicking inside the crop marquee. See Figure 3.31.

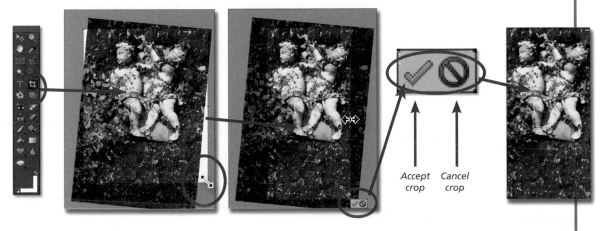

Accept   Cancel
crop   crop

Figure 3.31 The Crop tool allows adjustment of the selection via the handles positioned at the corners and sides of the Bounding box.

Book resources and video tutorials can be found at **www.photoshopelements.net**

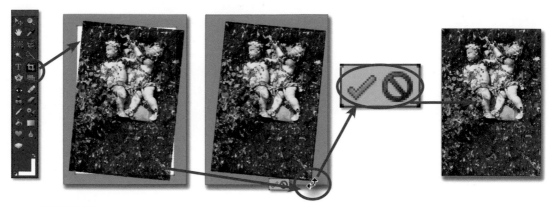

Figure 3.32 *Rotating the Crop tool's selection provides the option for straightening crooked images.*

Auto Straightening

The crop marquee, in the Editor workspaces, can also be rotated to suit an image that is slightly askew. You can rotate the selection box by clicking and dragging the mouse pointer outside the edges. Now when you click the OK button the image will be cropped and straightened. See Figure 3.32. If this all seems a little too complex, Elements also supplies automatic Straighten Image and Straighten and Crop Image functions. Designed especially for people like me, who always seem to get their print scans slightly crooked, these features can be found at the bottom of the Image > Rotate menu.

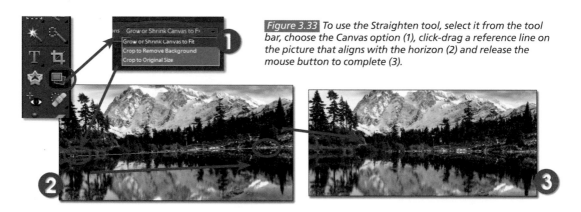

Figure 3.33 *To use the Straighten tool, select it from the tool bar, choose the Canvas option (1), click-drag a reference line on the picture that aligns with the horizon (2) and release the mouse button to complete (3).*

The Straighten tool

A new tool was added in Elements 4.0 to help you straighten the horizon lines in your photos. Called the Straighten tool, you can automatically rotate your pictures so that any line is aligned horizontally. Start by selecting the tool from the tool bar and then click-drag the cursor to draw a line parallel to the picture part that should be horizontal. Once you release the mouse button Elements automatically rotates the photo to ensure that the drawn line (and the associated picture part) is horizontal in the photo. See Figure 3.33.

But don't stop there. The tool also has the ability to straighten vertically which can be very usefully for making the edges of buildings vertical. Hold down the Ctrl key while you drag the Straighten tool along a vertical line and then release the mouse button.

When rotating the image, Elements can handle the resulting crooked edges of the photo in three different ways. The three approaches are listed in the drop-down menu in the options bar. They are:
Grow Canvas to Fit – The canvas size is increased to accommodate the rotated picture. With this option you will need to manually remove the crooked edges of the photo with the Crop tool.
Crop to Remove Background – After rotating Elements automatically removes the picture's crooked edges. This results in a photo with smaller dimensions than the original.
Crop to Original Size – The photo is rotated within a canvas that is the size of the original picture. This option creates a photo which contains some edges that are cropped and others that are filled with the canvas color.

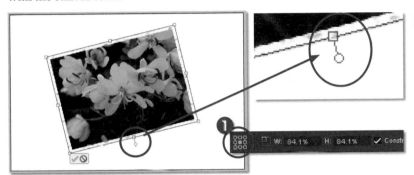

Figure 3.34 *In addition to the resizing handles that are normally found on the edges of layer content, there is also a rotate handle in the middle of the bottom edge. Click and drag to pivot the image around a central reference point. To pivot around an edge or corner click on a new reference in the feature's options bar to establish a new pivot point (1).*

Other rotation controls

When Adobe first introduced Frame layers (in version 5.0) they also created a new way to rotate layer content in Elements. Like the corner handles that appear on the edges of the layers when using the Free Transform feature, the new rotate handle provides a click and drag pivoting option. In addition to their use with frame, the rotate handles are also available with the Image > Transform > Free Transform and Image > Rotate > Free Rotate Layer commands. By default the layer content pivots around the center but you can also pivot from the corner or edges of the layer. Just select another Reference Point location in the feature's options bar. See Figure 3.34.

Step 5: Automatic corrections

First some background

One of the real strengths of the Elements program is that the editing and enhancement capabilities of the software are built upon the industry standard Photoshop platform. But as most people who have had a play with Photoshop will tell you, this 'killer' application is not an easy beast to tame, let alone master. This is where Elements steps in. It combines the majority of the editing abilities of Photoshop with an easier interface and therefore a much simpler learning curve. Version 7 continues this tradition by providing a variety of levels of enhancement and editing tools for the

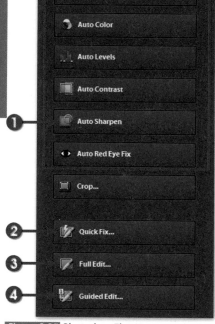

Figure 3.35 *Photoshop Elements contains a range of editing and enhancement features grouped according to complexity and degree of user control. These editing options are available in the Fix panel in the Organizer.*
(1) These auto options provide automatic corrections from within the Organizer workspace.
(2) The image is sent to Elements' Quick Fix editor workspace.
(3) The image is sent to Elements' Full editor workspace to be edited.
(4) The image is sent to the Edit workspace and the Guided edit panel is displayed.

digital photographer. They are skillfully arranged from the automatic 'press this button now' type tools that provide quick and accurate results for the majority of pictures, through to the more sophisticated and user-controlled features required for completion of more complex, professional-level, correction tasks. Organizer's Fix panel, first introduced in version 6.0, collates all these editing choices and is a great place to start. See Figure 3.35.

In the later part of this chapter we will concentrate on the quick and automatic correction tools that are part of the Organizer workspace only. These tools will provide a good starting point for the majority of changes that you will want to make to your digital photographs and, somewhat more importantly, they will give you good results quickly without having to understand too much about the underlying theory of how the tool works and how best to use it.

As your skills develop, however, you will probably want to take a little more control over the editing and enhancement process and for this reason Chapters 5 and 6 will introduce you to the range of more sophisticated tools and features that are part of the Guided, Quick and Full edit workspaces.

The editing and enhancement options presented in the later chapters are capable of results that rival the professionals. But that's coming up; for the moment let's look at the quick and efficient changes we can make using the tools available in the Organizer.

Organizer: Fix panel > Auto options

There are six auto enhancement features listed in the Fix panel in the Organizer. This is an increase of four over the last version of Elements. As well as Auto Smart Fix and Auto Red Eye Fix features, now there is Auto Color, Auto Levels, Auto Contrast, and Auto Sharpen. All of these features can be applied to individually selected, or multi-selected, pictures in the Organizer workspace.

The **Auto Smart Fix** option analyses the colors and tones in the picture before automatically adjusting the brightness, contrast and color cast in the photo. For general images this auto-only solution produces good results but if you are unhappy with the changes simply select the Edit > Undo option to return the picture to its original state. See Figure 3.36.

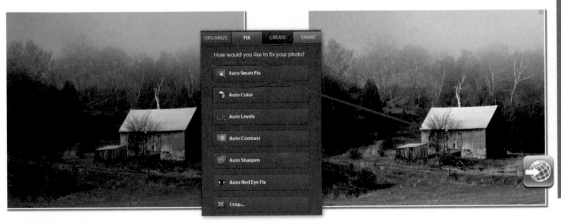

Figure 3.36 Auto Smart Fix adjusts the color, brightness and contrast of the picture in a single step.

The **Auto Color** option concentrates its enhancement on the colors in a photo. This feature works well with neutralizing color casts resulting from taking pictures under mixed or colored lighting. See Figure 3.37.

Auto Levels provides similar color balancing abilities to Auto Color but with the added benefit of also tweaking the contrast of the photo.

The **Auto Contrast** feature ignores the color in a photo and just works with balancing the spread of the tones. This option works particularly well when trying to brighten and add some zap to photos taken under cloudy conditions. See Figure 3.38 on the next page.

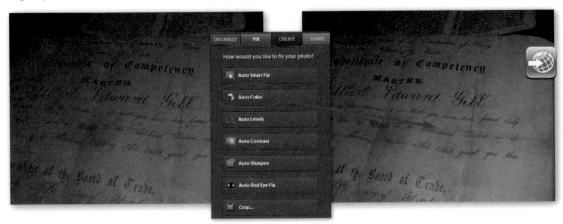

Figure 3.37 The Auto Color feature neutralizes the wayward colors that sometimes appears when a photo has been taken under mixed lighting.

The **Auto Sharpen** control applies a set amount of sharpening to the photo to make the edges in the photo appear more crisp.

Note: The four auto enhancement options grouped in the Fix panel can also be accessed inside both the Full and Quick modes of Elements' editing workspace. See Chapter 5 for more details on each of these features.

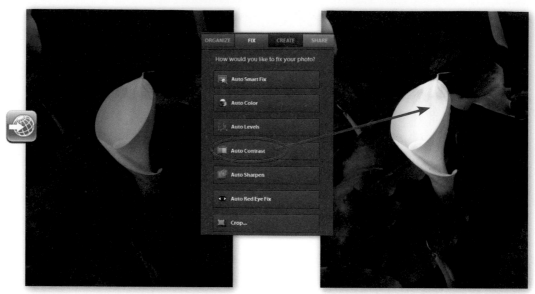

Figure 3.38 *The Auto Contrast feature neutralizes the wayward colors that sometimes appears when a photo has been taken under mixed lighting.*

The **Auto Red Eye Fix** feature is part of the new red eye correction technology that has been added into all levels of the Elements program. You can now automatically remove the dreaded red eye effect at the time of downloading your pictures from a memory card or camera, when importing files from a folder or from inside the Photo Browser. For the last option simply right-click the offending photo and select the Auto Red Eye Fix option from the displayed menu. If the automatic function doesn't eliminate the problem you can manually remove red eye in the Full Edit or Quick Fix editor workspace using the Red Eye Removal tool. Adobe offers two options for red eye correction as some times the auto algorithm produces unexpected results. See Chapter 4 for more details.

Version Sets

The changed file that results from these auto adjustments is not saved over the top of the original; instead a new version of the image is saved with a file name that is appended with the suffix '_edited' attached to the original name. This way you will always be able to identify the original and edited files. The two files are 'stacked' together in the Photo Browser with the latest file displayed on top. The stack of photos representing different editing stages in the picture's history is called a Version Set and is identified with an icon in the top right of the picture showing a pile of photos. To see the other images in the version stack simply click the Expand button to see the images in the Version Set. Alternatively you can right-click the thumbnail image and select Version Set > Reveal Photos in Version Set. See Figure 3.39.

Using the other options available in this pop-up menu the sets can be expanded or collapsed, the current version reverted to its original form or all versions flattened into one picture. Version Set options are also available via the Photo Browser Edit menu.

Figure 3.39 *The Organizer keeps separate versions of your edited files and groups them in Version Sets. Options for the display (expand/collapse) of Versions Sets can be accessed either from the right-click menu or via the Edit > Version Set menu in the Organizer workspace.*

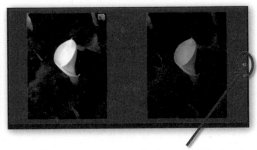

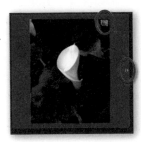

Click the button here to expand/collapse the Version Set

Undo, Revert and Undo History

With so many options available for changing images, it's almost inevitable that occasionally you will want to reverse a change that you have made. One way to step back through your changes is to select an earlier permutation of your picture via the Version Sets feature as detailed above, but Elements also provides several other methods to achieve this.

The Undo control, Edit > Undo, will successfully take your image back to the way it was before the last change. The Undo command is available in all Elements' workspaces. If you are unhappy with all the alterations you have made since opening the file, you can use the Revert feature, Edit > Revert (previously File > Revert), to exchange the last saved version of your file with the one currently on screen. Revert options are available in the editing workspaces in Elements. See Figure 3.40.

The Undo History palette (Window > Undo History) provides complete control over the alterations made to your image. Each action is recorded as a separate step in the palette. Reversing any change is a simple matter of selecting the previous step in the list. See Figure 3.41.

Figure 3.40 *Image changes can be reversed by using either the Undo (Edit > Undo) feature or Revert options (File > Revert).*

Figure 3.41 *The Undo History palette provides the facility to step backwards through the most recent image changes.*

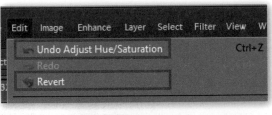

History steps

Current step displayed

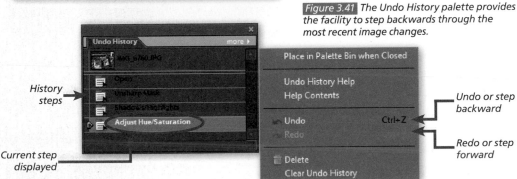

Undo or step backward

Redo or step forward

FIRST STEPS

Step 6: Printing

The falling price of quality inkjet printers means that more and more people are now able to output photographic quality prints right at their desktop. To get you started quickly we will look at the print options available from the Photo Browser but keep in mind that these features are also available from the editing workspaces as well. For more details on printing see Chapter 12.

The Print Selected Photos feature (see Figure 3.42) provides users with a common place to start the print process. This feature largely replaces the Print Preview option found in earlier versions of the program. To display the feature you can select the Print item from the File menu or select the same option from the pop-up menu displayed when you click the Print shortcut button. See Figure 3.43.

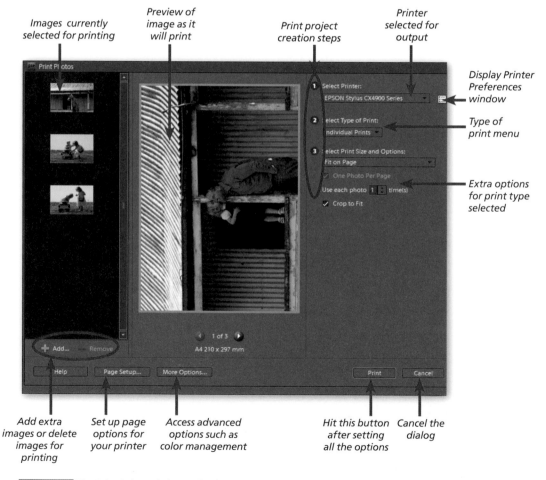

Images currently selected for printing • *Preview of image as it will print* • *Print project creation steps* • *Printer selected for output* • *Display Printer Preferences window* • *Type of print menu* • *Extra options for print type selected* • *Add extra images or delete images for printing* • *Set up page options for your printer* • *Access advanced options such as color management* • *Hit this button after setting all the options* • *Cancel the dialog*

Figure 3.42 *The Print Selected Photos dialog is the pivot point for all your printing activities. From this one spot you can output individual photos, contact sheets, picture packages and label sets. See Chapter 11 for more details on advanced printing tasks.*

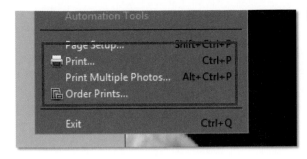

Figure 3.43 After selecting files in the Organizer workspace, or opening images into the Editor, the Elements Print options can be accessed via the File menu. The options include:
Print: *Print using a desktop printer.*
Print Multiple Photos: *Prints the current files that are open in the Editor workspace.*
Order Prints: *Print using an online service.*

Before accessing the feature select the image or images that you want to print. Don't worry if you need to add more pictures when you are in the dialog as the great guys at Adobe have kindly added an Add Photos button at the bottom left of the screen. The process for creating a print project is as easy as setting the options in sections 1, 2 and 3 of the dialog.

Section 1: Start by selecting the printer that will output the image from those listed for your computer. At this stage you should also check that the actual settings for the printer match the type of image you are printing and the media (paper) you are using. Do this by adjusting the settings in the Printer Preferences window which can be displayed by clicking the button next to the printer drop-down menu.

Section 2: Next, choose the type of print you wish to create. See Figure 3.44. There are four options to select from:

• Individual Prints – designed for printing a single photograph per page,
• Contact Sheets – used for creating a sheet of small thumbnails of a group of selected pictures,
• Picture Packages – ideal for putting several larger photos on a single page using templates, and
• Labels – creates a page of label-sized pictures that match commercially available label sheets.

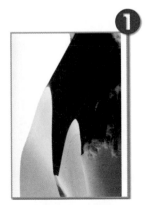
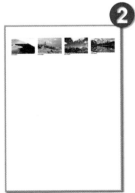
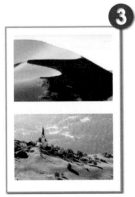
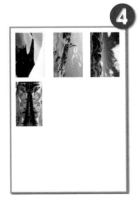

Figure 3.44 You can select a range of different print types from the Print Selected Photos dialog. The options include (1) Individual Prints, (2) Contact Sheets, (3) Picture Packages with a variety of images per page templates and (4) Labels to suit standard sheet label sizes and shapes.

Section 3: The options available in this section change according to the print type that you selected in the previous step. For instance, when you select Individual Prints you can then choose the size that you want the image to be on the page, the number of times the same picture will be repeated, the number of photos to print on each page and whether to allow the program to crop the picture in order to fill the full page. See Figure 3.45.

After adjusting the settings in each of the sections of the Print Selected Photos dialog click the Print button to output your photograph. Now sit back and enjoy your first digital photograph.

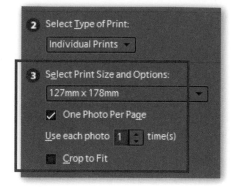

Figure 3.45 The options available in section 3 are determined by the print type in section 2.

More printing options

See Chapter 12 for further details on the array of print options available to Photoshop Elements users.

Step 7: Saving

Whilst you are making changes to your photos, the picture is stored in the memory (RAM) of the computer. With the alterations complete, the file should then be saved to a hard drive or disk. In previous versions of Elements the user needed to perform this saving step habitually after completing editing, and this still remains the case for images edited in the Standard and Quick Fix editor workspaces. But as we have already seen, for the changes made directly from the Photo Browser, Elements automatically saves the edited file and the original together in a Version Set. These auto save actions are terrific for the new user as they reduce the chance of overwriting the original file or losing changes that have taken valuable time to complete.

Editor: File > Save

Saving images edited in either the Quick Fix or Full Edit workspace is a three-step process that starts by choosing File > Save from the menu bar. With the Save dialog open, navigate through your hard drive to find the directory or folder you wish to save your images in. Next, type in the name for the file and select the file format you wish to use. To include the edited file in a Version Set with the original, click-check the Save in Version Set with Original box at the bottom of the dialog. See Figure 3.46.

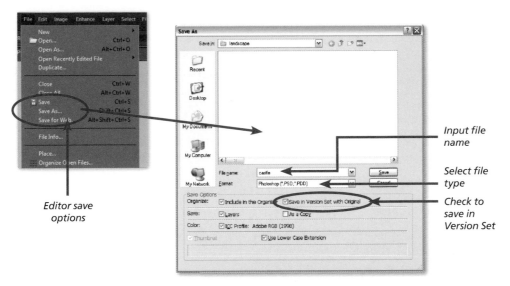

Editor save
options

Input file
name

Select file
type

Check to
save in
Version Set

Figure 3.46 *Saving images is an important part of the imaging process, as it is this step that commits all changes permanently to memory. For most users the Photoshop or PSD format should be used. Other file types have characteristics, like compression, that make them a better choice when sharing files, especially across the Internet. Use the File > Save As option to save your picture in other formats.*

Editor: File > Save As

For most images you should use the Photoshop or PSD format. This option gives you a file that maintains all of the specialized features available in Elements. This means that when you next open your image you will be able to continue to use items like layers and editable text. If, on the other hand, you want to share your images with others, either via the web or over a network, then you can choose to save your files in other formats, like JPEG or TIFF. Each of these options can provide more compact files than PSD, but doesn't support all of Elements' advanced features.

To save a file in a format other than the PSD file type select the File > Save As option, selecting a different option from the drop-down format menu.

To coincide with the introduction of the new multi-page creations in Photoshop Elements 5.0, Adobe released a new file format that was capable of storing the individual pages, their content and settings. Called the Photoshop Elements format, or .PSE, it contains all of the characteristics of the PSD file type but with the added ability of being able to save multiple pages (documents) in the one file.

'The formats I use'

Elements, like its industry-leading brother Photoshop, can open and save files in a multitude of different file formats. It's great to have such a choice, but the big question that most new digital photographers ask is 'What format should I use?'

And like most of the big questions in life there is no single answer to this query. The best way to decide is to be clear about what you intend to use the image for. Knowing the 'end use' will help determine what file format is best for your purposes. Until we look more closely at format characteristics like compression, use the way I work as a starting point. My approach is outlined below.

At the *scanning* or *image capture* stage, I tend to favor keeping my files in a TIFF or raw format. The save options in most scanning software will usually give you the option to save as a TIFF straight after capture and many digital cameras offer the option to store pictures as either raw or TIFF files. If I need to use JPEG with my camera to increase the number of shots I can fit on my compact flash cards, I change the format to TIFF or PSD after downloading. This way, I don't have to be concerned about any further loss of image quality derived from opening and saving JPEG files, but I still get the advantages of good compression. As an added bonus, I can also use the files on both Mac and IBM platforms.

When *manipulating* or *adjusting*, I always use the PSD or the Photoshop and Photoshop Elements format, as this allows me the most flexibility. I can use, and maintain, a number of different layers which can be edited and saved separately. Even when I share my work, I regularly supply the original PSD file so that last minute editing or fine-tuning can continue right up to going to press. If, on the other hand, I don't want my work to be easily edited, I supply the final image in a TIFF format that can be opened by both Mac and Windows machines.

With the introduction of *multi-page* documents from version 5.0, any projects produced with the new creations options are saved in the new Photoshop Elements file format or PSE.

Table 3.2 *This table lists the characteristics of different file types and their suitability for use with different tasks. * Photoshop Elements doesn't support the CMYK color mode.*

File Type	Compression	Color Modes	Layers	Metadata	Uses
Photoshop (.PSD)	✘	RGB, CMYK*, Indexed color, Grayscale	✔	✔	Desktop publishing (DTP), Internet, publishing, photographic work
Photoshop Elements (.PSE)	✘	RGB, Indexed color, Grayscale	✔	✔	The new Elements multi-page document format used for saving creation projects and their contents
GIF (.GIF)	✔	Indexed color	✘	✘	Internet
JPEG (.JPG)	✔	RGB, CMYK*, Grayscale	✘	✔	DTP, Internet, publishing, photographic work
TIFF (.TIF)	✔	RGB, CMYK*, Indexed color, Grayscale	✔	✔	DTP, Internet, publishing, photographic work
PNG (.PNG)	✔	RGB, Indexed color, Grayscale	✘	✘	Internet
Digital Negative (.DNG)	✔	Raw color data	✘	✔	A format used for saving the raw file data from your digital camera

If the final image is to be used for *web*, then I use GIF, PNG or JPEG depending on the number of colors in the original and whether any parts of the image contain transparency. There is no firm rule here. A balance between size and image quality is what is important, so I will try each format and see which provides the best mix. Only GIF and PNG have transparency options. See Table 3.2.

Step 8: Organizing your pictures

Over the last couple of releases Adobe has packed Photoshop Elements with a range of management and organizational features that help bring order to the vast number of picture files that we are all accumulating on our hard drives.

Many of these features are contained in the Organizer workspace. Here images are not just pre-viewed as thumbnails but can be split into different catalogs, located as members of different groups or searched for based on the keywords associated with each photo. Unlike a traditional browser system, which is folder based (that is, it displays thumbnails of the images that are physically stored in the folder), the Elements Photo Browser creates a catalog version of the pictures and uses these as the basis for searches and organization. This makes the process fast and efficient. With this approach it is possible for one picture to be a member of many different groups and to contain a variety of different keywords. So with this in mind let's look at how to use **Tags** (Elements' title for keywords) and **Albums** (aka Collections in earlier versions) to help manage our photos.

Keyword Tags

Tags are special keywords that can be attached to photographs and are used to help sort, organize and display sets of pictures in the Organizer workspace. The tagging feature is located in the new Organize panel on the right of the Photo Browser workspace. See Figure 3.47. The features here allow you to create, manage and add and remove tags from pictures. Multiple tags can be applied to the one picture and then all the photographs in the browser can be searched for the individual images that feature a specific tag.

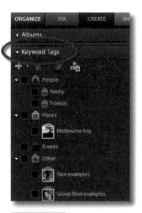

Figure 3.47 *The Keyword Tags panel in the Organize area at the right of the Photo Browser workspace houses current keyword tags and allows you to create new tags, categories and sub-categories.*

By default several different categories of tags are included in the Elements Tags pane – People, Places, Events, Favorites, Hidden and Other. New categories and sub-categories can be created via the New button in the top left of the pane.

Tags are applied to a picture by selecting and dragging them from the pane onto the thumbnail or alternatively the thumbnail can be dragged directly onto the Tags pane. Multiple tags can be attached to a single picture by multi-selecting the tags first and then dragging them to the appropriate thumbnail.

Albums

A Photoshop Elements' Album (previously called a Collection) is another way that you can order and sort your photos. After creating an album you drag selected images from the Photo Browser to the Album panel, or vice versa, where they can be used to make a new photo project or displayed using the Full Screen slide show feature. See Figure 3.48. Unlike when working with tags, pictures grouped in an album are numbered and can be sequenced. To quickly add photos to an album, drag the collection onto the multiple selected photos.

The same photo can be a part of several different albums. When adding your photos to an album you are not duplicating these photos but rather adding the pictures to a visual list of the group's contents. In this way, only one copy of the original photo is stored on the computer but it can be viewed and used in many ways. To display all photos in your library after showing the contents of an album, select the Show All button at the top left of the workspace.

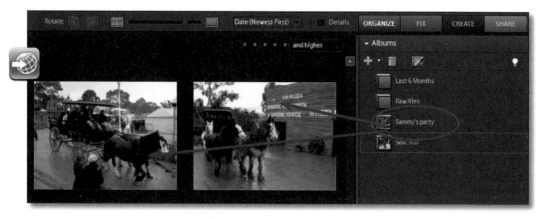

Figure 3.48 *Albums are the Photoshop Elements way to group your photos into different subject or project groups. Use the options in the Albums panel in the Task pane to create new albums. Click and drag the Album icon to any photo in the workspace to add it to the group.*

Smart Albums

Smart Albums were introduced to the organizational line up in Elements in version 6.0. This special album type is made up of the results of searches performed on your Photoshop Elements library. There are two ways to create a Smart Album.

You can perform a search using any of the options listed under the Find menu and then select the New Smart Album option from the '+' drop-down menu at the top left of the Album panel. Add in a title and click OK. Automatically the photos displayed in the workspace are added to the Smart Album.

Alternatively, you can select the option to 'Save this Search Criteria as a Smart Album', at the bottom of any of the Find dialogs. After the search is performed the results are automatically added to the newly created Smart Album.

Why call this type of album 'Smart'? Well, the contents of the album are not static. Every time you select the Smart Album entry, the search is performed again (based on the criteria you initially used), and any new candidate photos are added to the group. This way the album is always up to date. See Figure 3.49.

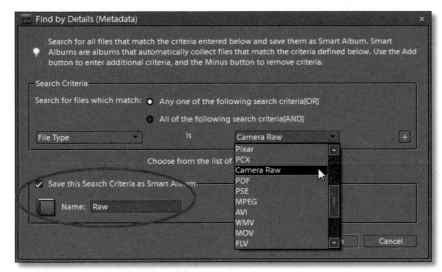

Figure 3.49 One of the easiest ways to create a Smart Album is to select the Save this Search Criteria as Smart Album option at the bottom of the Find dialog.

Stacks and Auto Stacks

The idea of grouping together like photos in a single stack was first introduced in version 3.0 of the program. The ability to auto stack images as they are downloaded from camera, imported into Elements from folders or even when displayed in the Organizer workspace became a reality in the last edition. See Figure 3.50.

To auto stack pictures already in your catalog select a group of thumbnails and then choose Automatically Suggest Photo Stacks from either the Edit > Stack or the right-click pop-up menus. To stack when importing choose the Automatically Suggest Photo Stacks option in the Get Photos and Videos dialog. Either of these two options will then display a new window with alike pictures pre-grouped. Choosing the Stack All Groups button converts the groups to stacks. The Remove Group button prevents the group of pictures being made into a stack.

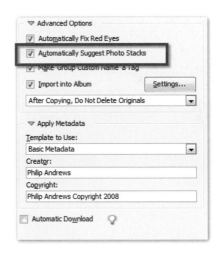

Figure 3.50 The Automatically Suggest Photo Stacks option is available when you import photos from folder, camera or memory card. The feature groups like photos ready for conversion to stacks.

Step 9: Backing up your files

There is no doubt that for most of us the many digital photographs that are saved on our computers are irreplaceable both in terms of their content and also the countless hours spent in capturing and enhancing. Given this scenario it is always puzzling to me that most people do not make duplicates or backups of such a valuable asset. Thankfully Adobe includes an easy-to-use Backup feature in Elements. The last step in your photographic workflow should be to regularly back up your photos,

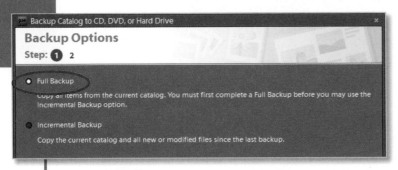

Organizer: File > Backup Catalog to CD, DVD or Hard Drive

The feature is designed for copying your pictures (and catalog files) onto a hard drive, DVD or CD for archiving purposes. Follow the steps in the wizard to make a copy or backup of all the photos you have currently listed in your Photo Browser. Simply activate the feature and follow the wizard's step-by-

Figure 3.51 *Elements contains its own backup options making protecting your precious photos a simple task of using the feature regularly.*

step prompts to create your own backup. See Figure 3.51. For big catalogs the feature estimates the space required for creating the backup copy of the catalog and, after selecting the drive that will be used for archiving, the feature also determines the number of disks required to complete the action. To restore a catalog from a set of backup disks use the File > Restore Catalog option in the Organizer workspace.

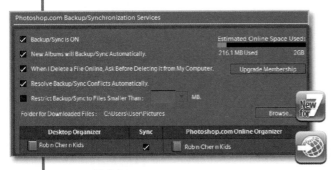

Organizer: Edit > Preferences > Backup/Synchronization

New for Photoshop Elements 7 is the ability to backup selected files from your catalog online. Users with a Photoshop.com account can use the space allocated with their account to store no just their web galleries but also their albums as well. When creating a new Album you are given the choice if you want the album to be backed up online. Choosing the option will then instruct Elements to synchronize the contents of the album

Figure 3.52 *Version 7.0 introduces automated Backup and Synchronization of selected albums.*

with a copy stored at Photoshop.com. The key settings for this process can be found in the Backup/ Synchronization section of the Elements preferences (located in the Edit menu).

More details about managing your photographs with Elements can be found in the next chapter.

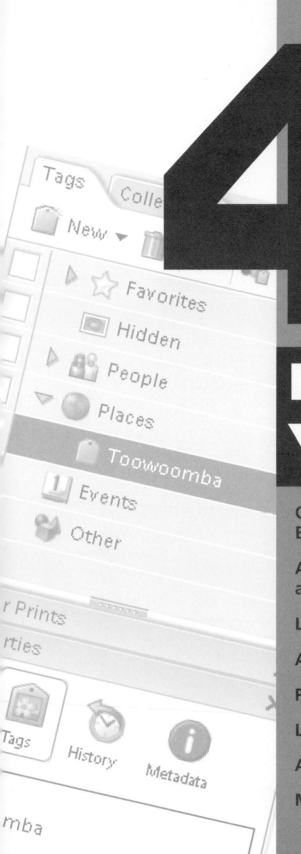

4

Managing Your Files

Organizing your photos with Photoshop Elements

Albums – the Elements way to group alike photos

Locating files

Attaching a Map Reference

Protecting your assets

Linking to Photoshop.com

Automating editing tasks

Multi-selection editing

79

ADOBE PHOTOSHOP ELEMENTS 7

With no film or processing costs to think about each time we take a picture, it seems that many of us are pressing the shutter more frequently than we did when film was king. The results of such collective shooting frenzies are hard drives all over the country full of photos. This is great for photography, but what happens when you want to track down that once in a lifetime shot that just happens to be one of thousands stored on your machine? Well, believe it or not, being able to locate your files quickly and easily is more a task in Organizer management, naming and camera setup than browsing through loads of thumbnails.

Organizing your photos with Photoshop Elements

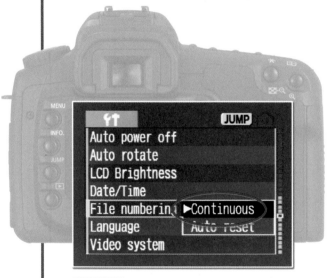

Figure 4.1 *Most cameras provide options for selecting the way in which files are numbered. The Continuous option ensures that a new number is used for each picture even if memory cards are changed in the middle of a shoot.*

It starts in-camera

Getting those pesky picture files in order starts with your camera setup. Most models and makes have options for adjusting the numbering sequence that is used for the pictures you take. Generally you will have a choice between an ongoing sequence, where no two photos will have the same number, and one that resets each time you change memory cards or download all the pictures. In addition, many models provide an option for adding the current date to the file name, with some including customized comments (such as shoot location or photographer's name) in the naming sequence or as part of the metadata stored with the file.

To adjust the settings on your camera search through the Set Up section of the camera's menu system for headings such as File Numbering and Custom Comments to locate and change the options. Ensure that number sequencing and date inclusion options are switched on and, where available, add these comments along with the photographer's name and copyright statement to the metadata stored within the picture file. See Figure 4.1.

And continues when downloading

As we have already seen Photoshop Elements includes the popular transfer utility that is designed to move pictures from your camera or memory card to the computer. Called the Adobe Photo Downloader, the feature is designed to detect when a camera or card reader is attached to the computer and then automatically transfer your pictures to your hard drive. As part of the download process, the user gets to select the location of the files, apply metadata, auto tag and stack, and select the way that the files are to be named and numbered. See Figure 4.2. For more details on the Adobe Photo Downloader go back to Chapter 3.

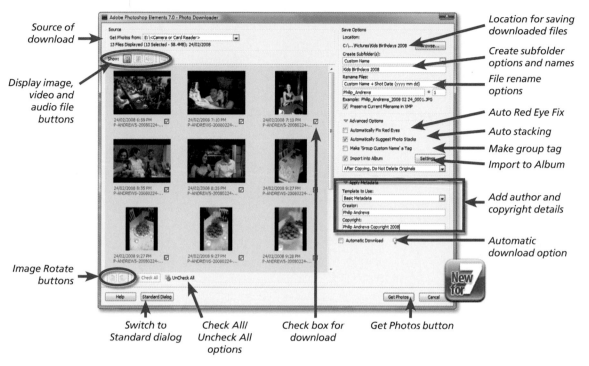

Source of download

Display image, video and audio file buttons

Image Rotate buttons

Location for saving downloaded files

Create subfolder options and names

File rename options

Auto Red Eye Fix

Auto stacking

Make group tag

Import to Album

Add author and copyright details

Automatic download option

Switch to Standard dialog

Check All/ Uncheck All options

Check box for download

Get Photos button

Figure 4.2 The Adobe Photo Downloader that comes bundled with Photoshop Elements allows the user to automatically apply naming changes and to determine the location where transferred files will be saved. In addition, in the Advanced mode (above) images can be auto stacked and tagged with a group name.

It is at this point in the process that you need to be careful about the type of folder or directory structure that you use. Most photographers group their images by date, subject, location or client, but the approach that you employ is up to you. Once you have selected a folder structure though, try to stick with it. Consistency is the byword of photo organization.

If your camera doesn't provide enough automatic Naming and Metadata options to satisfy your needs then use the Elements Photo Downloader feature to enhance your ability to distinguish the current images from those that already exist on your hard drive by setting the location, group tag, and filename of the picture files as you transfer them. It may also be useful to select the Auto Stack feature as a way of suggesting alike images which can be grouped into Albums or tagged together in the Organizer workspace. New for version 7 is the ability to add downloaded images directly to an album inside the Photoshop Elements Organizer. See Figures 4.3 and 4.4.

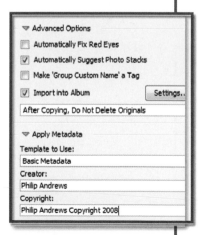

Figure 4.3 Use the options in the Photo Downloader to thoughtfully name, tag, stack and locate your digital photos.

Transferring files with the Photo Downloader

1   Start by connecting the memory card reader or camera/phone to your computer.

2   The Photo Downloader should auto launch when a camera or card reader is attached. If this doesn't occur then Select File > Get Photos > From Camera or Card Reader. Switch to the Advanced mode.

3   Choose the device where your photos are stored (camera or card reader) from the drop-down list in the Source section of the dialog (top left).

4   Scroll through the thumbnails that are displayed and select images to be transferred and deselect those to be left on the card using the check box on the bottom right of the thumbnail.

5   Choose the location and set the subfolder options in the Save Files section of the dialog.

6   Input a new title into the renaming options.

7   For photographs taken with a flash, select the Automatically Fix Red Eyes option to remove the crimson pupils in your portraits.

8   Click the Get Photos button to transfer the photos and automatically categorize them in the Organizer workspace.

9   Once the files have transferred successfully you will be offered the opportunity to delete the files from the card or camera, freeing up the device for taking more photos.

FEATURE SUMMARY

Advanced organization options with Adobe Photo Downloader

Gradually over the last few releases of Photoshop Elements, Adobe has been adding extra functionality to the Adobe Photo Downloader (APD) utility. The extra features added have been good news for photographers as they help organize your photos by automatically suggesting photo stacks, adding tags and now, with a new feature for version 7.0, even import images into an Elements Album. Let's look a little closer at each of these features which are located in the Advanced Dialog of the downloader.

Automatically Suggest Photo Stacks

Choosing the Automatically Suggest Photo Stacks in the Advanced Options of the APD instructs Elements to sort through the images as they are downloaded to your computer. What the program is looking for is similarities in picture content and proximity of capture. These photos are then presented back to the user in groups which can be stacked together by simply clicking a single button. So if you have a bunch of images of the same subject

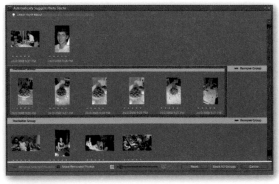

Figure 4.4 Group alike images when transferring your photos by selecting the Automatically Suggest Photo Stacks option in the Adobe Photo Downloader.

shot in quick succession, they will be grouped together and displayed as a possible Photo Stack in the Automatically Suggest Photo Stacks dialog.

Images can be added to or subtracted from groups by click-dragging the photos around the dialog. Alternatively, photos that you don't want stacked can be selected and removed from the process by clicking the Remove Group button. Once you are satisfied with the groupings, pressing the Stack All Groups option will create a Photo Stack in the Organizer workspace. See later in the chapter for more information on creating and using Photo Stacks.

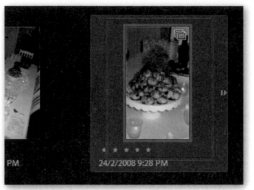

Figure 4.5 Once you have sorted the photos into groups, just press the Stack All Groups button to create Photo Stacks in the Organizer.

This option is also available when selecting the Get Photos and Videos > From Files and Folders option.

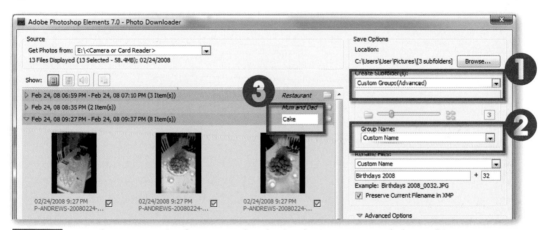

Figure 4.6 To use the group tagging feature start by selecting the Custom Groups (Advanced) item.

Make Group Custom Name a Tag

Another image management option available at the time of download is the ability to add a tag to groups of photos. Tags, which are also referred to as Keyword Tags in Photoshop Elements, are a set of descriptive words attached to pictures that can used to help locate specific photos in large Catalogs. Generally Tags are added to photos in the Organizer workspace (see the next section in this chapter for more details) but the Make 'Group Custom Name' a Tag option in APD allows you to add a tag when downloading. Using this feature is a three step process (see Figure 4.6):

1. Select the Custom Groups (Advanced) option in the Create Subfolders area. Use the slider control to adjust the number of photos included in each group.

2. Choose the Custom Name option from the Group Name drop down menu.

3. Ensure that the 'Make Group Custom Name a Tag' option is selected in the APD dialog.

4. Click on the tag name entry (called Custom Name by default) on the title bar of each group and type in a new Tag name. Click Get Photos to download the files and add the new Tag names to groups.

Individual photos can be excluded from the download and tagging process by unchecking the tickbox at the bottom right of the thumbnail. After setting up and selecting the Get Photos button, APD downloads the photos, creates new tag entries and then attaches these tags to the selected photos.

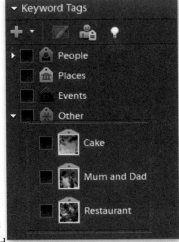

Figure 4.7 Tags are automatically added and applied using this feature.

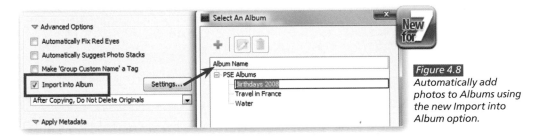

Figure 4.8 Automatically add photos to Albums using the new Import into Album option.

Import into an Album

New for Photoshop Elements is the ability to add photos to Albums as they are transferred from camera card to computer. After selecting the Import Into Album option in the Advanced dialog of the Adobe Photo Downloader, pressing the Settings button displays the Select an Album window where you can choose which Album to add the photos to. The window also contains buttons to add new tags, edit the name of tags and delete tags. The edit and delete options are only available when selecting empty Albums that have been added in the window. After setting up a new Album for the download, clicking OK will close the Settings window and Get Photos will download the pictures and add them to the new Album. See Figure 4.8.

Organizing and searching features

The Organizer workspace not only provides thumbnail previews of your photos but images can be categorized with different tags (keywords), notes and caption entries, split in different Albums (Collections) and then searched for based on the tags and metadata associated with each photo. Also, photos that are alike in appearance or subject matter can be stacked or grouped together. Unlike a traditional browser system, which is folder based (i.e. it displays thumbnails of the images that are physically stored in the folder), the Elements Organizer creates a catalog version of the pictures and uses these as the basis for searches and organization. With this approach it is possible for one picture to be a member of many different albums and to contain a variety of different keywords. See Figure 4.9.

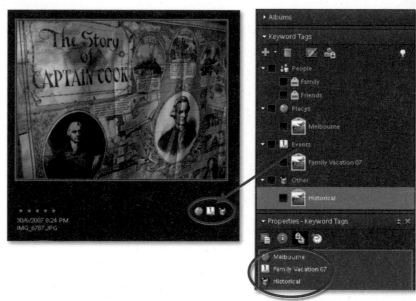

Figure 4.9 *Keyword Tags and Albums (previously called Collections) are used to organize the pictures in the Organizer workspace. One photo can belong to many different Albums and contain multiple tags but is only stored once in the catalog.*

Tagging your photos

From version 6, Keyword entries became Keyword Tags. As before, these simple descriptors can be added to your photos and used to help organize your images. The Keyword Tags panel stores the tags, provides an easy drag and drop approach to adding tags to selected photos, and sits to the right of the main thumbnail area in the Organizer workspace. The pane is grouped together with the Albums panel in the new Task pane (Window > Show Task Pane) and was previously called the Organize Bin. Tags are applied to a picture by selecting and dragging them from the panel onto the thumbnail or, alternatively, the thumbnail can be dragged directly onto the Tags pane. Multiple tags can be attached to a single picture by multi-selecting the tags first and then dragging them to the appropriate thumbnail.

1   To add a tag to a single image click and drag the tag from the Keyword Tags panel to the thumbnail image in the Organizer workspace.

2   To add a single tag to multiple thumbnails, multi-select the thumbnails in the images and then drag the tag from the Keyword Tags panel onto one of the selected thumbnails.

Creating new keyword tags

New keyword tags are created and added to the panel by selecting the New Tag option from the menu displayed after pressing the '+' button at the top left of the panel. Next, fill out the details of the new entry in the Create Keyword Tag dialog, select a suitable icon for the tag label and click OK. See Figure 4.10.

1   To create a new keyword tag, select the New Keyword Tag option from the '+' button menu at the top of the Tags panel.

2   In the Create Keyword Tag dialog select a category for the new tag, add in a name and include any explanatory notes.

3   Next, press the Edit Icon button and select a picture to include with the tag label before sizing and cropping the photo in the Edit Tag Icon dialog.

4   Click OK to close both dialogs and add the new keyword tag to the tag list.

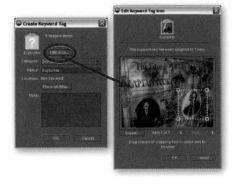

Figure 4.10 *You can add to the existing set of tags using the New Tag option. There is even an option to add your own pictures as the tag icon.*

Face Tagging technology

The ability to search through a group of photos and automatically select those that contain faces was first introduced in Elements 4.0. Using this feature makes it much easier to locate and tag photos of family and friends in the batches of pictures that you import. Start by selecting a group of photos from inside the Organizer workspace. Next, click the Find Faces for Tagging button in the Keyword Tags panel. The faces identified will be displayed in a new dialog box which also includes the Keywords Tags panel. See Figure 4.11. From here your tags can be quickly dragged onto individual or groups of selected face photos.

1   Multi-select a group of images from inside the Organizer workspace.

2   Either choose Find > Find Faces for Tagging or press the Find Faces for Tagging button at the top of the Keywords Tags panel.

3   Drag tags onto the pictures that are displayed in the Face Tagging dialog. Click Done to return to the Organizer workspace.

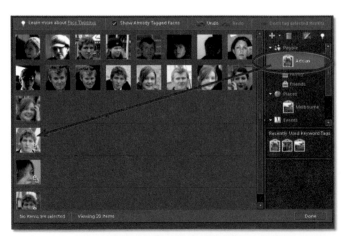

Figure 4.11
The Face Tagging option quickly scans a group of selected photos and identifies those pictures that contain faces and displays these in a separate dialog ready for tagging.

Book resources and video tutorials can be found at **www.photoshopelements.net**

Albums – the Elements way to group alike photos

Apart from tagging, Photoshop Elements also uses Albums (previously called Collections) as a way to organize your photos. Albums allows you to group images of a similar theme together in the one place, making it easier to locate these images at a later date. Another benefit is that the images contained in an album can also be ordered manually. After creating an album in the Albums pane, photos are simply dragged from

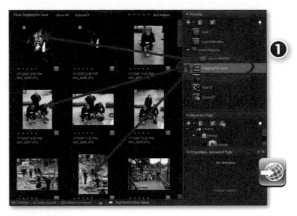

Figure 4.12 *Sort your pictures into groups of the same subject or theme using the Elements Albums feature. (1) Albums panel.*

the Photo Browser workspace to the Album heading to be added to the group. In Elements 7.0 you can share albums online, create photo books, burn them onto CD/DVD discs, email them to friends, and sync them online to photoshop.com.

The Albums feature allows you to allocate the same image to several different groups. Unlike in the old days with simple folders-based systems, this doesn't mean that the same file is duplicated and stored multiple times in different folders; instead, the picture is only stored or saved once and a series of Album associations is used to indicate its membership in different groups. When you want to display a group of images based on a specific subject, taken at a particular time or shot as part of a certain job, the program searches through its database of Album entries and only shows those images that meet your search criteria. The Albums panel is the pivot point for all your Album activities. Here you can view, create, rename and delete Album entries. See Figure 4.12.

Adding photos to an Album

To start using Albums make a new album first and then add it to your photos.

1   Start by making a new album by clicking on the '+' button in the Albums panel and selecting the New Album menu item.

2   In the Album Details dialog choose the group that the new album will belong to, add the name and include any explanation details for the group. Click OK.

3   Select the photos to be included in the album in the Organizer and drag them to the Items area in the Albums panel. Then click Done.

4   To view all the pictures contained in an album click on the Album heading in the Albums panel.

5   Single photos or even groups of pictures can be added to more than one album at a time by multi-selecting the album names first before dragging the images to the pane.

Smart Albums

Adobe introduced a new album type in Photoshop Elements 6 called Smart Albums. Images are included in a Smart Album based on one or more search criteria established at the time that the album is created. Each time the Smart Album entry is selected Elements automatically adds any new photos that meet the criteria to the group. Smart Albums are a great way to keep important collections of images up to date without the need to manually find and add images to the album. See Figure 4.13. You can create Smart Albums either via the New Smart Album entry in the new album pop-up menu (click the '+' button at the top of the panel to display), or by executing a search using the Find > By Details (Metadata) feature. Both avenues provide the user with the chance to choose the search criteria used for the basis of the Smart Album. With the Find > By Details option, it is necessary to select the Save this Search Criteria as Smart Album setting at the bottom of the dialog before starting the search. It should be noted that Smart Albums can't be synchronized.

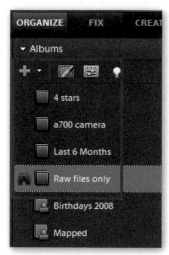

Figure 4.13 *After setting up, clicking the Smart Album entry will automatically search for, and include, any new images to the Album.*

Establishing search criteria

The idea of setting up specific search criteria as the basis of creating a Smart Album may seem a little daunting, but the range of possibilities included in the search dialog, either New Smart Album, or the Find by Details, makes the process as simple as selecting options from several drop-down menus. With the dialog open, start by choosing if the photos need to contain any, or all, of the search criteria to be included in the album. Obviously for single criteria searches this isn't an issue, but the dialog allows the user to add several criteria (click the '+' button at the right end of the criteria entry) for searching. Next, create the basis for the search by selecting the criteria. In the example in Figure 4.14 pictures are included if their rating is higher than three stars.

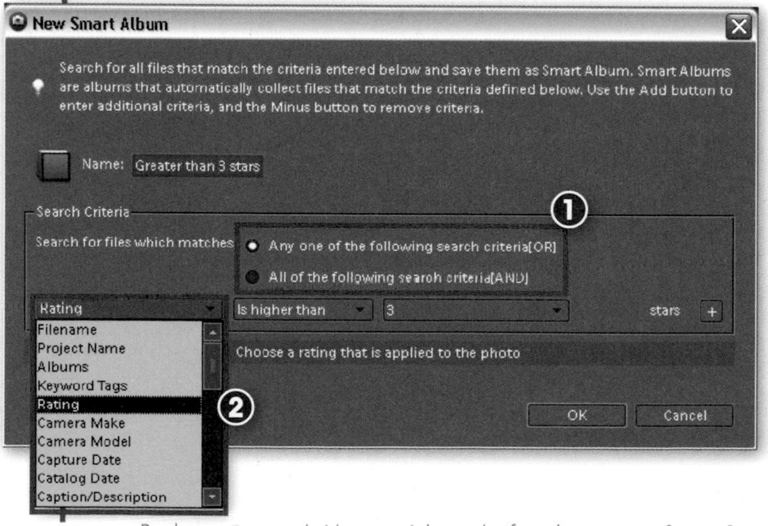

There are no less than 30 different criteria that can be used for the search. These include most camera settings (sometimes called EXIF data) such as lens, ISO, F-stop and Shutter Speed, individual photo details including file size, pixel dimensions

Figure 4.14 *To set up the search criteria used for a Smart Album pick the matching option first (1) and then the criteria from the drop-down menus (2).*

and filename as well as Elements-specific criteria like keyword tags, project name, version set, project type or even map location. Once you are comfortable with creating search criteria, the whole Smart Album system provides a very powerful and efficient way to locate groups of images in your catalog.

Creating a new Smart Album

There are three ways to create Smart Albums in Elements. The first is via the options in the Album panel. See Figure 4.15.

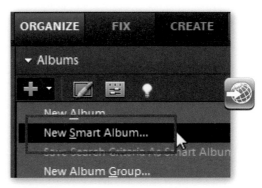

Figure 4.15 To create a Smart Album choose the New Smart Album from the menu access via the '+' button at the top of the Albums panel.

1 Start by selecting the New Smart Album entry from the menu displayed by clicking on the '+' button in the Albums panel.

2 Next, add in a name for the album in the text box at the top of the New Smart Album dialog.

3 Choose how the files will match the criteria. You can select between matching **any** of the criteria or **all** of the criteria.

4 Now start with the drop-down menu on the left of the dialog and select the criteria group to use for the search, i.e. Filename, Project Name, Keyword Tags, Camera Model, etc.

5 Depending which entry you choose in the first menu the number of menus (and their content) on the right will change accordingly. The entries in these menus are designed to refine the search. For instance, if you choose the Project Type as your main search criteria then you will have a second menu containing Gallery, Photobook and Slideshow.

6 With one criteria established you can add other criteria by clicking the '+' button on the right of the Search entry. This displays a new search criteria menu set.

Using Find to make Smart Albums

The second way to create Smart Albums in Elements is to use the search abilities in the Find > By Details (Metadata) .

1 Select the By Details (metadata) entry from the Find menu to display the Find by Details dialog. Input the match option and search criteria in the same way as outlined in steps 3–6 above.

2 Next, select the Save this Search Criteria as Smart Album option at the bottom of the dialog. This makes the Name text box active. Add a title for the New Smart Album here. See Figure 4.16.

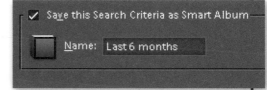

Figure 4.16 You can also create a new Smart Album using specific search criteria detailed in the Find > By Details (Metadata) feature.

Smart Albums via the new Search feature

The Adobe guys decided to include a new Search feature in the shortcuts bar at the top of the Organizer workspace. Like other such features typically found in computer operating systems this dedicated search box provides a speedy way to locate images based on a text entries associated with an image. This information may be stored in the filename, as a keyword or as part of the EXIF data for the photo.

Elements refines the results of the search as you type. Locating pictures in this way has the added bonus that the search term that you employed can be used to create a new Smart Album.

1   Start by typing the search term into the new text box located on the left of the Shortcuts bar. You may need to try a range of different search terms.

2   Once the correct photos are displayed in the Organizer workspace choose the Save Search Criteria As Smart Album entry from the Options menu, See Figure 4.17.

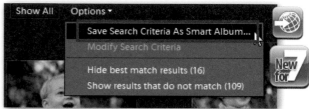

Figure 4.17 *Use the criteria input into the new search feature as the basis of a new Smart Album.*

Converting Keyword Tags to Smart Albums

The last way to create Smart Albums is to use existing Keyword Tags as the basis for creating a new Smart Album.

1   After clicking the Keyword Tag entry to display the images containing the tag, choose the Save Search Criteria As Smart Album entry from the Options menu at the top left of the workspace. See Figure 4.18.

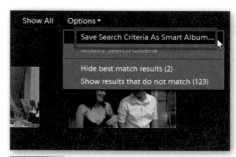

Figure 4.18 *Click onto the Keyword Tag entry to display the pictures with the associated keyword then choose the Save Search Criteria As Smart Album entry from the Options menu.*

Using Album Groups

Different albums (and the photos they contain) can also be organized into groups that have a common interest or theme. For instance, albums that contain pictures of the kids, family vacations, birthday parties and mother and father's days events can all be collated under a single 'Family' Album Group heading.

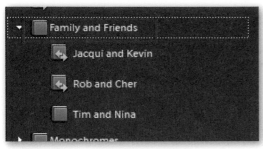

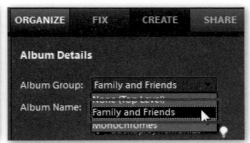

Figure 4.19 Album Groups are used to help organize Albums with common themes under one heading.

Figure 4.20 Add new Albums to existing Groups by selecting the Album Group entry in the Album Details pane.

Create an Album Group by selecting the New Album Group entry from '+' menu in the Albums panel. Next, click and drag existing album entries listed in the pane to the group heading. After creating an Album Group you can add any new Albums to the group by selecting the group entry from the Album Group drop down menu in the Album details pane. See Figures 4.19 and 4.20.

Album and Keyword Tagging strategies:

The best way that you choose to make use of the Tagging and Album features in Elements will depend a great deal on the way that you work, the pictures you take and the type of content that they include, but here are a few different proven methods that you can use as a starting point.

Subject:

Photos are broken down into subject groups using headings such as family, friends, holidays, work, summer, night shots, trip to Paris, etc. This is the most popular and most applicable approach for most readers and should be the method to try first.

Timeline:

Images are sorted and stored based on their capture date (when the picture was photographed), the day they were downloaded or the date that they were imported into the organizational package. This way of working links well with the auto file naming functions available with most digital cameras but can be problematic if you can't remember the approximate dates that important events occurred. Try using the

date approach as a subcategory for subject headings, e.g. Bill's Birthday > 2005.

File type:

Image groups are divided into different file type groups. Although this approach may not seem that applicable at first glance it is a good way to work if you are in the habit of shooting raw files which are then processed into PSD files before use.

Project:

This organizational method works well for the photographer who likes to shoot to a theme over an extended period of time. All the project images, despite their age and file type, are collated in the one spot, making for ease of access.

Client or Job:

Many working pros prefer to base their filing system around the way that their business works, keeping separate groups for each client and each job undertaken for each client.

Locating files

One of the great benefits of managing your pictures in the Organizer workspace is the huge range of search options that then becomes available to you. In fact there are so many search options that Adobe created a new menu heading 'Find' specifically to hold all the choices. See Figure 4.21. Here you will be able to search for your photos based on a selected date range, filename, caption, media type (video, photo, audio or creation), history (when an item was emailed, printed, received, imported, used in a creation project or even shared online) and even by the predominant color in the photo.

After selecting one of the Find menu options Elements either displays files that meet the search criteria in a new window (Find by Version Sets, Media Type, Untagged Items, Items not in a Album) or opens a new dialog where the user must enter specific details (dates, filenames, details, captions) which will be used to base the search. See Figure 4.21.

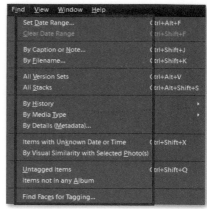

Figure 4.21 The Find menu in the Organizer workspace lists the many different ways to locate images within Elements.

Finding tagged photos or those contained in an Album

As well as the search options located in the Organizer: Find menu, you can make use of the Tags and Albums features to quickly locate and display sets of photos from your catalog.

To find tagged photos: Click the Keyword Tag entry in the Keyword Tags panel. See Figure 4.22.

To display all the images in an album: Click on the Album entry in the Albums panel.

To return the browser back to the original catalog of thumbnails: Click on the Show All button (previously Back to All Photos) at the top of the thumbnail group. See Figure 4.24.

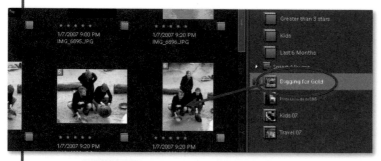

Figure 4.22 To display all images tagged with a specific entry click the Keyword Tag or Album name in the Keyword Tags or Albums panel.

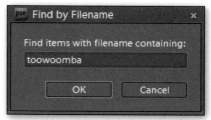

Figure 4.23 When choosing the Date Range, Caption or Note, Filename (see above), History and Details find options Elements displays a new dialog into which your search criteria can be entered.

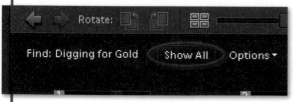

Figure 4.24 Press the Show All button (previously Back to All Photos) to return to displaying the images in the full catalog after conducting a search.

Find by details (metadata)

As we have already seen in passing, the Find option is designed to allow users to search the details or metadata that are attached to their picture files. Most digital cameras automatically store shooting details from the time of capture within the photo document itself. Called metadata, you can view this information by clicking the Metadata button inside the Properties palette.

The Find > By Details (Metadata) option displays a sophisticated search dialog that allows you to nominate specific criteria to use when looking within the metadata portion of the picture file. The dialog provides a section to input the text to search for as well as two drop-down menus where you can set where to look (Filename, Camera Make, Camera Model, Capture Date, etc.) and how to match the search text (Starts with, Ends with, Contains, etc.). See Figure 4.25.

Beyond camera-based metadata you can also use this dialog to search for any captions, notes, tags or albums that you have applied to your pictures.

1   Select Find > By Details (Metadata) from the Organizer workspace.

2   Select the match option – any or all.

3   Choose the type of details that you are looking for – Filename, Camera Make, Camera Model, etc. – from the drop-down list in the Find by Details dialog.

4   Enter the text you want to search for (if needed).

5   Enter how the search text should appear in the located files (contained, not contained, etc.)

6   Also included is the ability to save the Find settings that you input here as the search criteria for a Smart Album.

Figure 4.25 The Find by Details feature allows you to customize the search options used via settings within the dialog. Start by selecting how the criteria will be matched (1). Choosing the type of detail to look for from the drop-down list (2) determines the contents of the rest of the dialog. In this instance selecting 'Filename' displays a second list (3) describing how to match the text you input (4). Extra search criteria can be added or removed by pressing the Plus or Minus buttons to the right of the dialog (5). Also included is the ability to save the search criteria as a Smart Album (6).

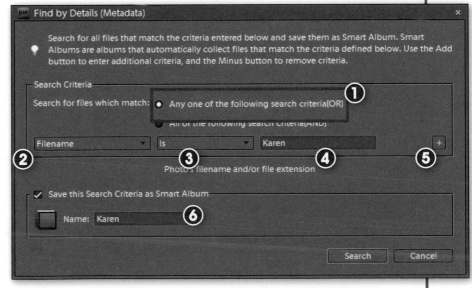

Attaching a Map Reference

First released in version 5.0 was the ability to link map references with the photos in your organizer catalog. This feature provides a new way to reference and locate your photos. See Figure 4.26. The mapping technology is provided in association with Yahoo and one of the ways that you can share your map referenced picture is via the company's popular photo sharing site www.flickr.com.

To create a map reference for a photo, drag and drop the thumbnail from the main Organizer workspace onto the Map pane (below left). If the Map panel is not shown then select the Show Map option from the Display menu on the right of the shortcuts bar. Or use the Place on Map command from the Context menu or Edit menu to type in a location. This approach can be more accurate than dragging the photo to a map. To reference a group of photos, tag these images first and then drag the tag to the map. Both these actions will place a pin on the map to indicate that there are photos linked with this area. To view photos associated with a map reference click on a pin with the Hand tool. Alternatively, to display all the photos associated with the current map, select the Limit Search to Map Area option in the tool bar below the map display.

The referenced maps you create, and their linked photos, can be shared online by uploading either to your own website using the Photo Galleries feature or to www.Flickr.com.

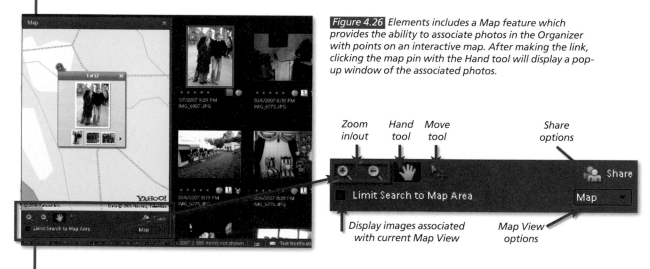

Figure 4.26 *Elements includes a Map feature which provides the ability to associate photos in the Organizer with points on an interactive map. After making the link, clicking the map pin with the Hand tool will display a pop-up window of the associated photos.*

Zoom in/out — Hand tool — Move tool — Share options

Limit Search to Map Area

Display images associated with current Map View — Map View options

Protecting your assets

Ensuring that you keep up-to-date duplicates of all your important pictures is one of the smartest work habits that the digital photographer can learn. Ask yourself 'What images can't I afford to lose – either emotionally or financially?' The photos you include in your answer are those that are in the most need of backing up. If you are like most image makers then every picture you have ever taken (good and bad) has special meaning and therefore is worthy of inclusion. So let's assume that you want to secure all the photos you have accumulated.

Making your first back up

Gone are the days when creating a back up of your work involved costly tape hardware and complex server software. Now you can archive your pictures from inside the very software that you use to enhance them – Photoshop Elements.

The Back up feature (Organizer: File > Back up Catalog to CD, DVD or Hard Drive) is designed for copying your pictures (and catalog files) onto DVD, CD or an external hard drive for archiving purposes. To secure your work simply follow the steps in the wizard. The feature includes the option to back up all the photos you currently have cataloged in the Photo Browser along with the ability to move selected files from your hard disk to CD or DVD to help free up valuable hard disk space. See Figure 4.27.

1   To start the back up process Select File > Back up Catalog to CD, DVD, or Hard Drive from the Photo Browser workspace.

2   Next, select Full Back up for first time archiving or Incremental Back up for all back ups after the first one. Click Next.

3   And, finally, select the place where you want the back up to be stored. This may be on a series of CDs or DVDs or on an internal drive, and then click Done to back up your files.

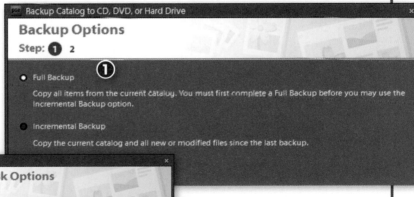

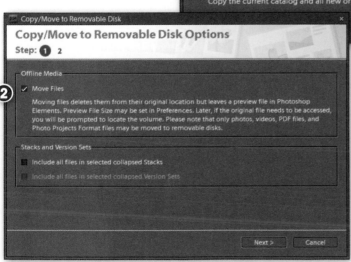

Figure 4.27 *Unlike the previous version of Elements, in versions 6 and 7 the backup files and Copy/Move Files functions have been separated into two different dialogs. To back up files select the File > Back up Catalog to CD, DVD, or Hard Drive option. To copy or move files choose the File > Copy/Move to Removable Disk entry.*

(1) Back up Catalog – This option provides a complete backup of all the files in your catalog and then the next time it is used allows you to add any files that have been changed or added since the last back up.

(2) Copy/Move Files – Use this selection to make copies of files that you have selected in the Photo Browser workspace or to permanently move files to another destination.

Multi-disk Back up

With the the Back up Catalog feature it is also possible to archive your catalog over a series of CD or DVD disks. Multiple disk options like this are sometimes referred to as 'disk spanning'.

In earlier versions, the Back up feature only allowed writing to a single disk and, even with the growing use of DVD-ROMs for archive scenarios, many digital photographers have a catalog of photos that far exceeds the space available on a single disk.

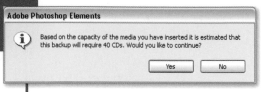

Figure 4.21 Elements includes the ability to back up the Organizer catalog across multiple disks.

The revised Back up feature estimates the space required for creating the backup copy of the catalog and, after selecting the drive that will be used for archiving, the feature also determines the number of disks required to complete the action. See Figure 4.21. During the writing process the feature displays instruction windows at the end of writing each disk and when you need to insert a new disk. All disks need to be written for the back up to be complete. To restore a catalog from a set of back up disks use the File > Restore Catalog option in the Organizer workspace.

Multi-session Back up

As well as providing the ability to back up large catalogs over multiple disks, the revised Back up feature also allows multi-session recording of archives. Multi-session DVD or CD-ROM recording means that you can add extra back up files to disks that you have already recorded to. This means that if you only fill a quarter of the storage space of a DVD disk when you first create a back up, you will be able to write to the non-used area in a later back up session. Most Elements users will find this useful when performing incremental back ups.

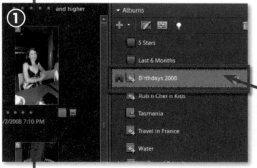
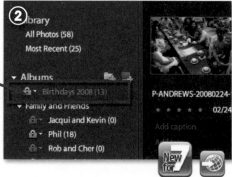

Figure 4.22 The new Backup/Synchronization feature in Elements stores exact copies of selected files on both the photoshop.com (2) website and in the Elements Organizer (1).

Online Backup and Synchronization

An online archive option was available in previous versions of Photoshop Elements. Called Online Back up (Organizer: File > Online Back up), the feature has now been replaced with a more sophisticated system linked with **photoshop.com**. Rather than provide a process that requires users to remember to backup their files on a regular basis, the Adobe guys have put in a place a synchronization model. This means that, once set up, the pictures you have sitting on your computer at home are duplicated on the photoshop.com website and vice-versa. Making a change to a picture either online using the website features or via Elements, results in an updated version being stored in both locations. See Figure 4.22. Cool!

Figure 4.23 Version 7 now includes the ability to synchronize the photos stored in Albums in Elements to space on the photoshop.com website. This feature is a sophisticated form of archiving which ensures that the albums on your computer are always the same as those stored online.

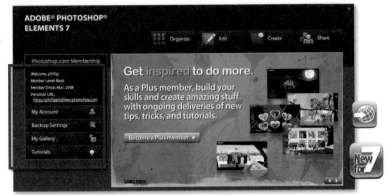

Rather than synchronizing your whole Photoshop Elements Catalog, the new synchronization system uses Albums which are common to both photoshop.com and the Organizer. As we have already seen in passing (in the last chapter) the Welcome screen in version 7 contains a series of new online options that are available to registered Elements users. One of these options is titled Backup Settings. See Figure 4.23. Clicking this entry will display the Backup/Synchronization section of the Elements' Preferences dialog. This window can also be displayed by selecting the Preferences entry from the Edit screen in the Organizer workspace or by clicking the Backup/Synchronization preferences button at the top of the Albums pane.

The settings contained here allow you to turn the synchronization feature on and off, choose for all new albums to synchronized online by default, options for resolving synchronization conflicts and scenarios when you delete photos online as well as maximum size files included in the synchronization process. The dialog also provides a visual summary of the albums that are currently stored in both locations and whether they are synchronized, a space usage meter and the option to upgrade your membership to access more backup space and exclusive Elements tips and techniques. See Figure 4.24.

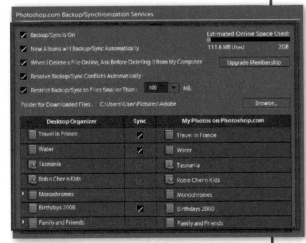

Figure 4.24 The options for the new backup feature are grouped together in the Backup/Synchronization Services section of the Photoshop Elements Preferences.

When the backup/synchronization feature is active on your computer a new icon is added to your system tray. Called the Sync Monitor, right-clicking on the icon will display several options

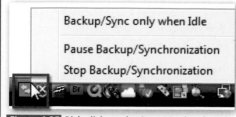

Figure 4.25 Rick-click on the Sync Monitor icon in the system tray to display settings for the feature.

which indicate the current status of the feature. If the Pause or Stop entries are shown, then the sync system is currently active. Choosing the Backup/Sync only when Idle option restricts update activity (which occurs via an active internet connection) to times when the connection is not being used by other programs such as a web browser or email program. See Figure 4.25. There is also another version of the Sync Monitor located in the bottom left of the Organizer workspace. Here there are options for viewing backup, not backed files as well as those that are waiting ('pending') to be backup. Chapter 12 contains more details about the features available at photoshop.com.

Back up glossary:

Multi-disk archive – A process, often called spanning, by which chunks of data that are larger than one disk can be split up and saved to multiple CD-ROMs or DVDs using spanning software. The files can be recompiled later using utility software supplied by the same company that wrote the disks.

Full back up – Duplicates all files even if they haven't changed since the last time an archive was produced.

Incremental – Backs up only those files that have changed since the last archive was produced. This makes for faster back ups but means that it takes longer to restore files as the program must look for the latest version of files before restoring them.

Restore – Reinstates files from a back up archive to their original state on your hard drive.

Back up hardware:

CD-ROM or DVD writer – This option is very economical when coupled with software that is capable of writing large numbers of files over multiple disks. The sets of archive disks can easily be stored off-site, ensuring you against theft and fire problems, but the back up and restore process of this approach can be long and tedious.

Internal hard drive – Adding an extra hard drive inside your computer that can be used for backing up provides a fast and efficient way to archive your files but won't secure them against theft, fire or even some electrical breakdowns such as power surges.

External hard drive – Connected via USB or Firewire these external self-contained units are both fast and efficient and can also be stored off-site, providing good all-round protection.

Back up regularly

There is no point having duplicate versions of your data if they are out of date. Base the interval between performing manual back ups on the amount of work you do. In heavy periods when you are downloading, editing and enhancing many images at a time back up more often; in the quieter moments you won't need to duplicate files as frequently. Most professionals back up on a daily basis or at the conclusion of a work session. Alternatively add the pictures used in your current projects to an Album with the Backup/Synchronization feature switched on. It should be noted that synchronization is not instantaneous, especially for large files.

Store the duplicates securely

In ensuring the security of your images you will not only need to protect your photos from the possibility of a hard drive crash but also from such dramatic events as burglary and fire. Do this by storing one copy of your files securely at home and an extra copy of your archive disks or external backup drives somewhere other than your home or office. Synchronised Albums account for such events by storing their contents both in Elements and also online.

Versioning your edits

Creating a good archival system goes a long way to making sure that the images you create are well protected, but what about the situation where the original photo is accidentally overwritten as part of the editing process? Embarrassing as it is, even I have to admit that sometimes I can get so involved in a series of complex edits that I inadvertently save the edited version of my picture over the top of the original. For most tasks this is not a drama as the edits I make are generally non-destructive (applied with adjustment layers and the like) and so I can extract the original file from inside the enhanced document but sometimes, because of the changes I have made, there is no way of going back. The end result of saving over the original untouched digital photo is equivalent to destroying the negative back in the days when film was king. Yep, photographic sacrilege!

So you can imagine my relief to find that in last few versions of Photoshop Elements Adobe featured a technology that protects the original file and tracks the changes made to the picture in a series of successively saved photos. The feature is called Versioning as the software allows you to store different versions of the picture as your editing progresses. What's more, the feature provides options for viewing and using any of the versions that you have previously saved. Let's see how this file protection technology works in practice.

Versions and Photoshop Elements

Versioning in Elements extends the idea of image stacks by storing the edited version of pictures together with the original photo in a special group or Version Set.

All photos enhanced in the Organizer space using tools like Auto Smart Fix are automatically included in a Version Set. Those images saved in the Quick and Full editor spaces with the Save As command can also be added to a Version Set by making sure that the Save with Original option is ticked before pressing the Save button in the dialog. See Figure 4.26.

Saving in this way means that edited files are not saved over the top of the original; instead, a new version of the image is saved in a Version Set with the original. It is appended with a file name that has the suffix '_edited' attached to the original name. This way you will always be able to identify the original and edited files. The two files are 'stacked' together in the Organizer with the most recent file displayed on top.

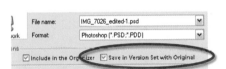

Figure 4.26 *To create a Version Set when saving an edited file from inside the Quick or Standard editor workspace make sure that the Save in Version Set with Original option is selected.*

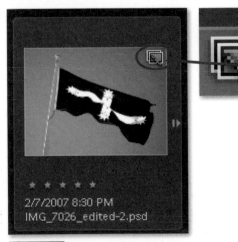

Figure 4.27 *The bundled photos icon at the top right of the thumbnail indicates that the photo is part of a Version Set.*

Book resources and video tutorials can be found at **www.photoshopelements.net**

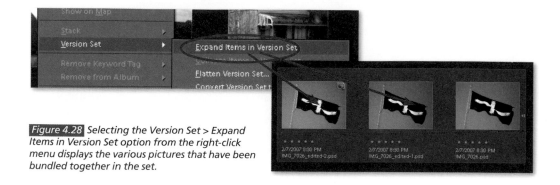

Figure 4.28 Selecting the Version Set > Expand Items in Version Set option from the right-click menu displays the various pictures that have been bundled together in the set.

When a photo is part of a Version Set, there is a small icon displayed in the top left of the Photo Browser thumbnail. The icon shows a pile of photos. See Figure 4.27 on previous page.

To see the other images in the version stack simply click the sideways arrow on the right of the thumbnail or right-click the thumbnail image and select Version Set > Expand Items in Version Set. See Figures 4.28 and 4.29. Using the other options available in this pop-up menu the sets can be expanded or collapsed, the current version reverted to its original form or all versions flattened into one picture. Version Set options are also available via the Photo Browser Edit menu. Only the top most photo in a version set is synchronized, but all photos in a stack are synchronized online.

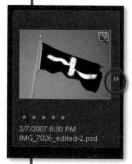

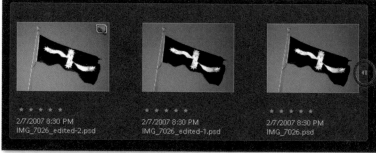

Figure 4.29 The Expand and Collapse buttons are positioned to the right of the thumbnail of standard image stacks as well as Version Sets.

Elements' photo stacks

A photo stack is slightly different from a Version Set as it is a set of pictures that have been grouped together into a single place in the Organizer workspace. Most often stacks are used to group pictures that have a common subject or theme and the feature is one way that Elements users can sort and manage their pictures. To create a version stack, multi-select a series of thumbnails in the workspace then right-click on one of the selected images to show the menu and from here select the Stack > Stack Selected Photos option. The photo you right-click on will be the top photo in the new stack. See Figure 4.30. You can identify stacked image groups by the small icon in the top right of the thumbnail. See Figure 4.31.

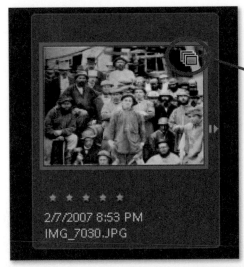

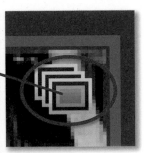

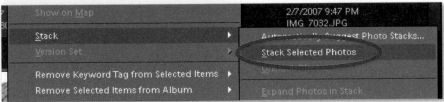

Figure 4.30 *Photo stacks use a layered photos icon in the top right of the thumbnail to indicate that the picture is one of several images that have been grouped together. All photos in a stack are synchronized.*

Figure 4.31 *To manually group alike photos into an photo stack, multi-select the pictures in the Photo Browser workspace before choosing Stack > Stack Selected Photos from the right-click menu.*

Auto stacking

The idea of grouping together alike photos in a single stack was introduced in version 3.0 of the program. Elements also contains the ability to auto stack images as they are downloaded from camera, imported into Elements from folders or even when displayed in the Organizer workspace. The feature looks for images that are visually similar, or were captured within a short time interval, when suggesting groups of images that are suitable for stacking.

You can employ the Elements Auto Stacking feature in a couple of different ways:

Photos in the Organizer – To auto stack pictures already in your catalog select a group of thumbnails and then choose Automatically Suggest Photo Stacks from either the Edit > Stack or the right-click pop-up menus. See Figure 4.32.

Photos being imported – To stack when importing choose the Automatically Suggest Photo Stacks option in the Get Photos and Videos dialog.

Either of these two options will then display a new window with alike pictures pre-grouped. Choosing the Stack All Groups button converts the groups to stacks.

The Remove Group button prevents the group of pictures being made into a stack.

MANAGING YOUR FILES

FEATURE SUMMARY

1 To automatically stack alike photos that have already been imported into the Organizer start by multi-selecting pictures from the Photo Browser.

2 Next right-click one of the thumbnails and choose Stack > Automatically Suggest Photo Stacks from the menu that is displayed.

3 Elements will then show you a new screen containing the groups of images that it suggests should be stacked. Click the Stack All Groups option to convert the groups to stacks.

4 To stop a set of pictures becoming a photo stack press the Remove Group button before conversion.

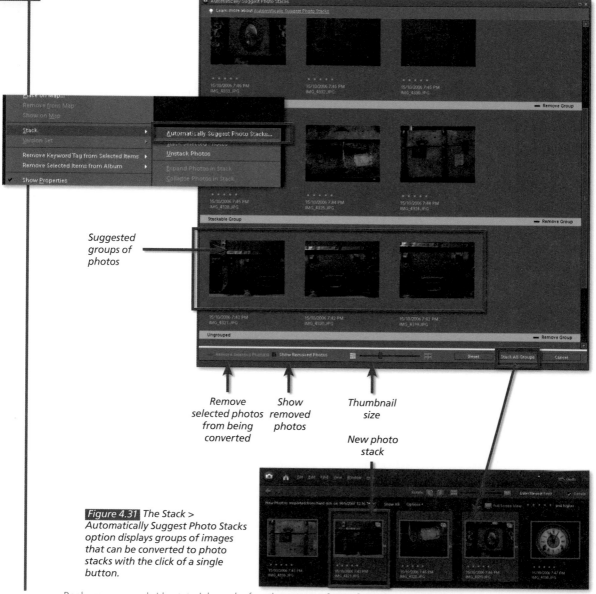

Suggested groups of photos

Remove selected photos from being converted

Show removed photos

Thumbnail size

New photo stack

Figure 4.31 The Stack > Automatically Suggest Photo Stacks option displays groups of images that can be converted to photo stacks with the click of a single button.

Book resources and video tutorials can be found at **www.photoshopelements.net**

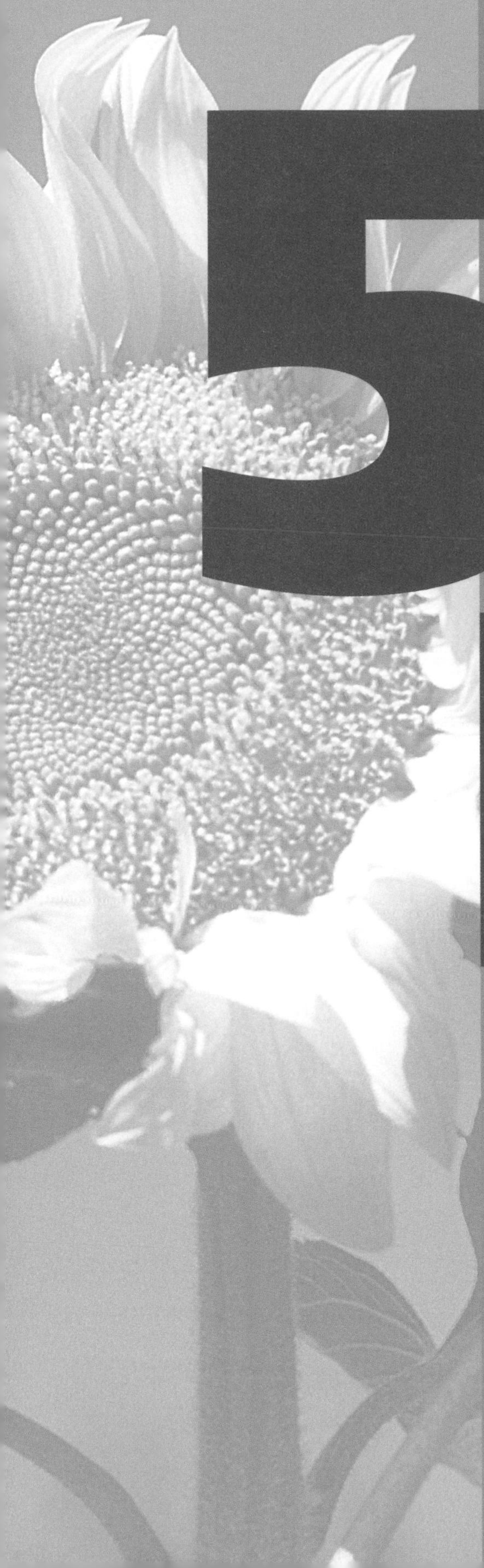

5

Simple Image Changes

Four levels of editing

Setting up your screen for Elements

Brightness and contrast changes

Dodge and Burn tools

Color corrections

Using filters and effects

The new Guided editing mode

Getting help with Elements

ADOBE PHOTOSHOP ELEMENTS 7

Four levels of editing

Photoshop Elements 7 provides a variety of edit and enhancement options for users to change and alter their digital photographs. The options can be grouped around four different approaches to the task. See Figure 5.1. Including four levels of editing features is Adobe's way of providing digital photographers with exactly the tools they need irrespective of their experience level and understanding. It also means that users can progress to more sophisticated tools as

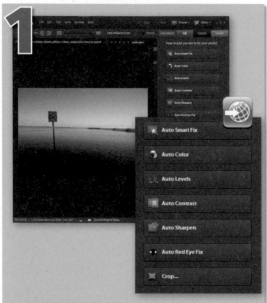

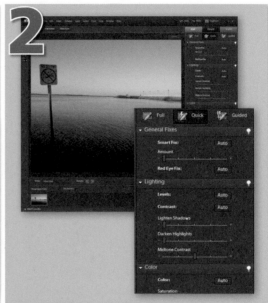

Automatic: The simplest tools are almost always fully automatic with the user having little control over the final results. These are the types of color, contrast and brightness controls that are available in the Organizer grouped in the Fix panel. Seven options (Auto Contrast, Auto Levels, Auto Color, Auto Sharpen, Crop, Auto Smart Fix and Auto Red Eye Fix) are available for use on the images displayed as thumbnails in the Organizer workspace.

This is the place to start if you are new to digital photography and want good results quickly and easily.

See Chapter 3 for more details.

Semi-Automatic: The second level of features sits in the middle ground between total user control and total program control over the Editing results. The tools in this group are primarily available in the Quick mode of the Editor workspace (previously called Quick Fix) but also encompass some of the more automatic or easy-to-use controls available in the Full edit mode.

Move to these tools once you feel more confident with the digital photography process as a whole (downloading, making some changes, saving and then printing) and find yourself wanting to do more with your pictures.

More details available in this chapter.

Figure 5.1 Photoshop Elements 6 has four different levels of editing and enhancement approach available to users: (1) Automatic, (2) Semi-Automatic, (3) Guided and (4) Manual. This means that you will have features that suit your skills level no matter how much digital photography experience you have.

their confidence and knowledge grow. This said, it can be a little confusing for those of you who are new to the program to know 'what tool to use when'. For this reason I have broken down the features into the four categories detailed below and have separated their introduction into different chapters in the book.

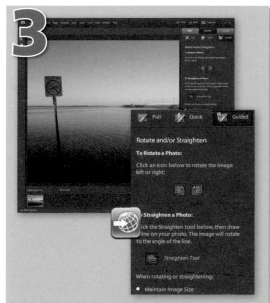

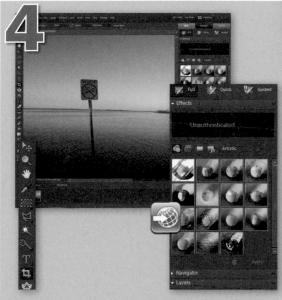

Guided: This approach to editing was introduced in Photoshop Elements 6 and provided a much needed synthesis of having the program perform enhancements automatically, with no user control, and the completely manual editing of the Full and Quick edit workspaces. Using a unique step-by-step approach, the Guided edit feature leads the new user through the processes involved in performing a specific technique. The techniques are grouped in a new Guided option found under the Edit panel. For some steps, duplicate controls are included in the Guided panel that directly manipulate their counterparts in the wider editing workspace. Guided is a great place to start learning more about how to use the powerful tools in the Edit workspaces. More details available in this chapter.

Manual: The final group of tools are those designed to give the user professional control over their editing and enhancement tasks. Many of the features detailed here are very similar to, and in some cases exactly the same as, those found in the Photoshop program itself. These tools provide the best quality changes available with Elements, but they do require a greater level of understanding and knowledge to use effectively. The extra editing and enhancement power of these tools comes at a cost of the user bearing all responsibility for the end results. Whereas the automatic nature of many of the features found in the other three groups means that bad results are rare, misusing or overapplying the tools found here can actually make your picture worse. This shouldn't stop you from venturing into these waters, but it does mean that it is a good idea to apply these tools cautiously rather than with a heavy hand. See Chapter 6 for more details.

Setting up your screen for Elements

In Chapter 3 we looked at how to download, crop, rotate, auto enhance, print and save images directly from the Photo Browser or Organizer workspace. Now you can try your hand at some simple changes courtesy of the editor components of Elements 7. It is here that you will start to see the power of the digital process. With a few clicks of the mouse you can perform basic picture adjustments and enhancements easier than ever before. This chapter will take you step by step through these changes and also show you how to use these techniques.

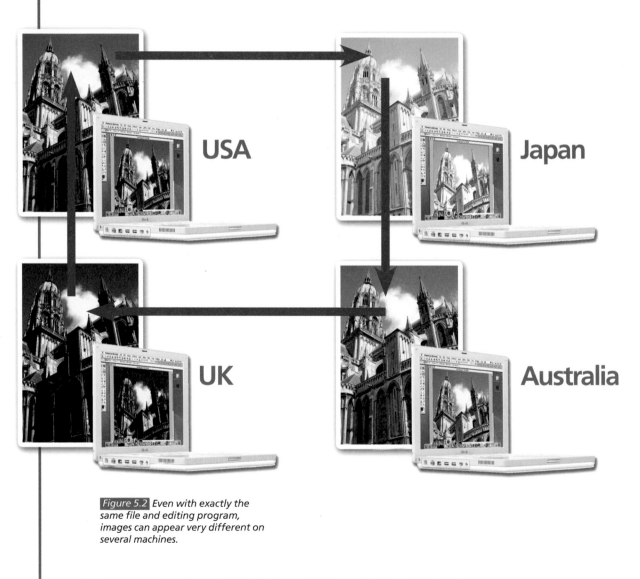

USA

Japan

UK

Australia

Figure 5.2 *Even with exactly the same file and editing program, images can appear very different on several machines.*

Popularity can be a problem

One of the truly amazing features of digital imaging is the diversity of people using the
technology. Many individuals in a range of occupations, using various brands of equipment, in
different countries across the world, use computer-based picture making as part of their daily
work or personal life. The popularity of the system is both its strength and, potentially, one of
its weaknesses. On the positive side it means that an image I make in Australia can be viewed
in the United Kingdom, enhanced in the United States and printed in Japan. Each activity
would involve importing my picture into a different computer, with a different screen, running
an image-editing package like Elements. This is where problems can occur. Even though the
program and image are exactly the same, the way that the computer is set up can mean that the
picture will appear completely different on each machine. On my computer the image exhibits
good contrast and has no apparent color casts. In the UK, however, it might look a little dark, in
the USA slightly blue and in Japan too light and far too green. See Figure 5.2.

Before you start

To help alleviate this problem Adobe has built into its imaging programs a color management
system that will help you set up your machine so that what you see will be as close as possible to
what others see. For this reason it is important that you set up your computer using the system
before starting to make changes to your images. The critical part of the process is ensuring that
your monitor is set up correctly. Most default profiles for screens are correctly set up at the time
that the installation CD/DVD is run, but if this isn't the case then use these following steps to
install the monitor profile manually:

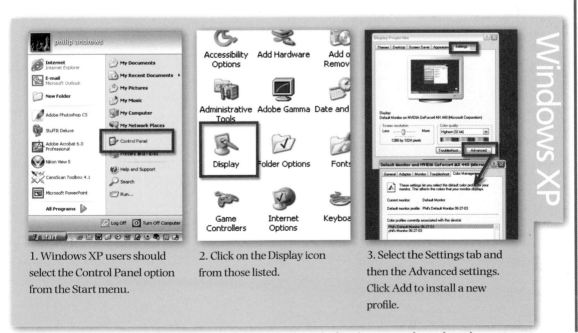

1. Windows XP users should
select the Control Panel option
from the Start menu.

2. Click on the Display icon
from those listed.

3. Select the Settings tab and
then the Advanced settings.
Click Add to install a new
profile.

Windows XP

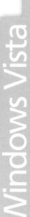

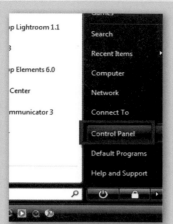
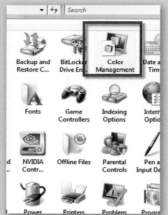
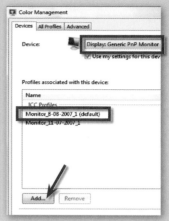

1. In Windows Vista select the Control Panel option from the Start Orb menu.

2. Click on the Color Management icon in the Control Panel.

3. Choose your monitor from the Device menu and then click the Add button to locate the ICC profile from the driver disk.

Hardware-based monitor calibration

The profile that is included with your screen drivers is based on the average characteristics of all the screens produced by the manufacturer. Individual screens will display slightly different characteristics even if they are from the same manufacturer and are the same model number. Add to this the fact that screens' display characteristics change as they age and you will start to see why some photographers who are interested in ensuring that their photos are displayed accurately on screen resort to using a hardware calibration solution such as the ones provided by X-RITE or ColorVision. See Figure 5.3.

The ColorVision option uses a seven-filter colorimeter attached to the screen during the calibration process. This piece of hardware samples a range of known color and tone values that the software displays on screen. The sampled results are then compared to the known color values, the difference calculated and this information is

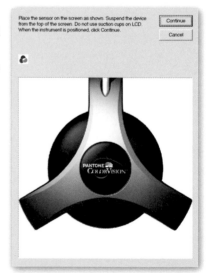

Figure 5.3 *For more accurate display of your photos calibrate your monitor with a hardware device such as the Spyder.*

then used to generate an accurate ICC profile for the screen. Unlike when using the the supplied profile, this method does require the purchase of extra software and hardware, but it does provides an objective way for the digital photographer to calibrate his or her screen.

Calibrate all screens and use color management wherever possible

Keep in mind that for the color management to truly work, all your friends or colleagues who will be using your images must calibrate their systems as well.

Brightness and contrast changes

As we saw in Chapter 1, a digital picture is made up of a grid of pixels, each with a specific color and brightness. The brightness of each pixel is determined by a numerical value between 0 and 255. The higher the number, the brighter the pixel will appear; the lower the value, the darker it will be. The extremes of the scale, 0 and 255, represent pure black and white, and values around 128 are considered midtones. In a correctly exposed image with good brightness and contrast, the tones will be spread between these two extremes. If an image is underexposed, then the picture will appear dark on screen and most of its pixels will have values between 128 and 0. In contrast, images that have been overexposed appear light on screen and the majority of their pixels lie in the region between 128 and 255. See Figure 5.4.

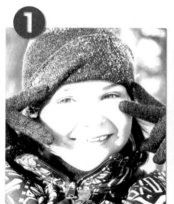
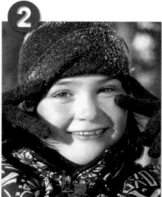
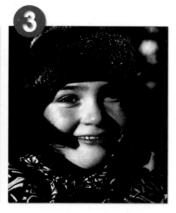

Figure 5.4 *A well-exposed photograph (2) will have good brightness and contrast, and will display a good spread of tones between black and white or shadow and highlight. An underexposed image (3) appears dark on screen whereas an overexposed image (1) appears light on screen.*

The best method for correcting these situations is for you to recapture the picture, changing the settings on your scanner or camera to compensate for the exposure problem. Good exposure not only ensures a good spread of tones, but also gives you the chance to capture the best detail and quality in your photographs. It is a misunderstanding of the digital process to excuse poor exposure control by saying 'it's okay, I'll fix it in Elements later'. You will not get the best quality pictures possible if you use Elements to correct shooting or scanning mistakes as vital detail has been lost forever in images that are either too dark or too light. See Figure 5.5. Sometimes, though, a reshoot is not possible or a rescan is not practical. In these circumstances, or in a situation where only slight changes are necessary, Elements has a range of ways to change the brightness and contrast in your photos.

SIMPLE IMAGE CHANGES

Highlight areas
with no details

Shadow details
much too light

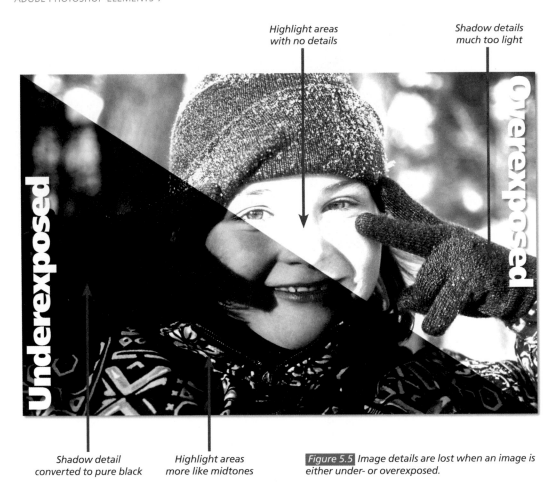

Shadow detail
converted to pure black

Highlight areas
more like midtones

Figure 5.5 *Image details are lost when an image is either under- or overexposed.*

Editor: Enhance > Adjust Lighting > Brightness/Contrast

In version 6.0: Enhance > Adjust Lighting > Brightness/Contrast

The Brightness/Contrast command helps you make basic adjustments to the spread of tones within the image. The feature was revamped for version 6 so that the changes it makes are less harsh. When opened you are presented with a dialog containing two slider controls. Click and drag the slider to the left to decrease brightness or contrast, or to the right to increase the value. Keep in mind that you are trying to adjust the image so that the tones are more evenly distributed between the extremes of pure white and black. Too much correction using either control can result in pictures where highlight and/or shadow details are lost. As you are making your changes, watch these two areas in particular to ensure that details are retained. See Figure 5.6.

FEATURE SUMMARY

1 Select Enhance > Adjust Lighting > Brightness/Contrast.

2 Move sliders to change image tones.

3 Left to decrease brightness/contrast, right to increase.

4 Click OK to finish.

Book resources and video tutorials can be found at **www.photoshopelements.net**

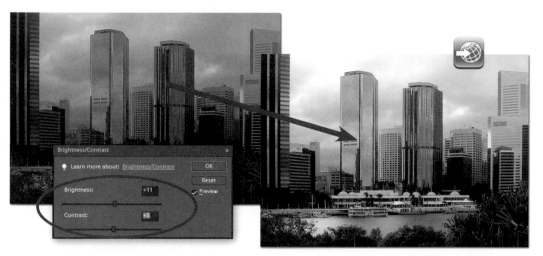

Figure 5.6 *The Brightness/Contrast feature is located under the Adjust Lighting section of the Enhance menu. After adjusting the brightness and contrast of an image, the picture will appear clearer and its tone will be spread more evenly.*

Editor: Enhance > Auto Contrast

In version 6.0: Enhance > Auto Contrast

The Auto Contrast command can be used as an alternative to the Brightness/Contrast sliders. In this feature Elements assesses all the values in an image and identifies the brightest and darkest tones. These pixels are then converted to white and black, and those values in between are spread along the full tonal range. Auto Contrast works particularly well with photographic images but can produce unpredictable results with graphic illustrations. This option is also available in the Fix panel in the Organizer workspace. See Figure 5.7.

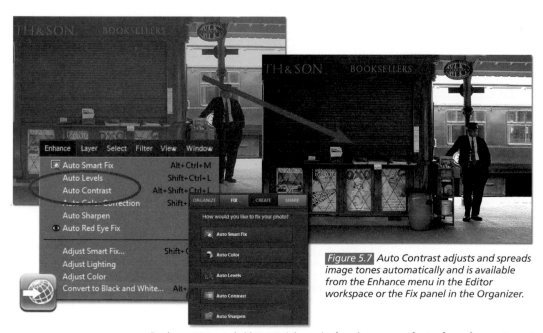

Figure 5.7 *Auto Contrast adjusts and spreads image tones automatically and is available from the Enhance menu in the Editor workspace or the Fix panel in the Organizer.*

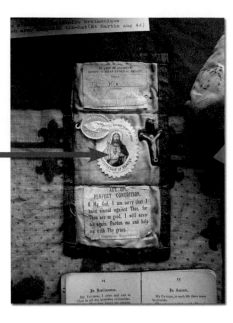

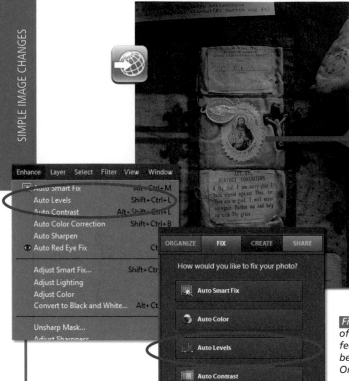

Figure 5.8 *Auto Levels adjusts and spreads the tones of each individual color channel. In some pictures this feature can help to reduce color casts. The feature can be found under the editor's Enhance menu or in the Organizers' Fix panel.*

Editor: Enhance > Auto Levels

In version 6.0: Enhance > Auto Levels

The Auto Levels command is similar to Auto Contrast in that it maps the brightest and darkest parts of the image to white and black. It differs from the previous technique because each individual color channel is treated separately. In the process of mapping the tones in the Red, Green and Blue channels, dominant color casts can be neutralized. See Figure 5.8. This is not always the case; it depends entirely on the make-up of the image. In some cases the reverse is true; when Auto Levels is put to work on a neutral image a strong cast results. If this occurs, undo (Edit > Undo) the command and apply the Auto Contrast feature instead. This option is also one of the Organizer's Fix panel enhancement options.

Editor: Enhance > Auto Smart Fix

In version 6.0: Enhance > Auto Smart Fix

The Auto Smart Fix feature enhances both the lighting and color in your picture automatically. The command is used to balance the color and improve the overall shadow and highlight detail. Most images are changed drastically using this tool. In some cases the changes can be too extreme, in which case the effect should be reversed using the Edit > Undo command and the more controllable version of the tool – Adjust Smart Fix – used instead. Auto Smart Fix can also be applied from inside the Organizer workspace. See Figure 5.9.

Editor: Enhance > Adjust Smart Fix

In version 6.0: Enhance > Adjust Smart Fix

The Adjust Smart Fix version of the feature provides the same control over color, shadow and highlight detail but with the addition of a slider control that determines the strength of the enhancement changes. Moving the slider from left to right will gradually increase the amount of correction applied to your picture. This approach provides much more control over the enhancement process and is a preferable way to work with all but the most general photos. The Auto button, also located in the dialog, automatically applies a fix amount of 100% and provides a similar result to selecting Enhance > Auto Smart Fix. See Figure 5.9.

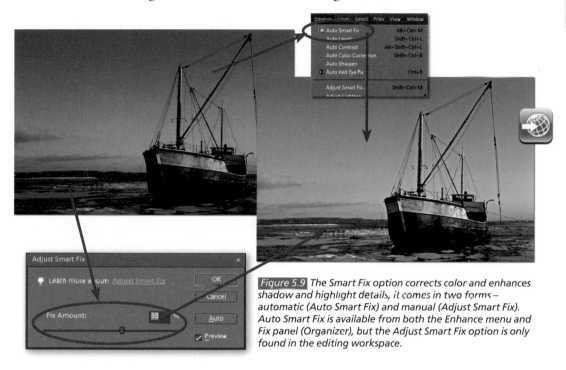

Figure 5.9 The Smart Fix option corrects color and enhances shadow and highlight details, it comes in two forms – automatic (Auto Smart Fix) and manual (Adjust Smart Fix). Auto Smart Fix is available from both the Enhance menu and Fix panel (Organizer), but the Adjust Smart Fix option is only found in the editing workspace.

The Quick Fix editor – 'quick change central'

The Quick Fix editor is home for many of the automatic or 'quick and easy' enhancement tools. You can access and apply the features via the menu system or take advantage of the controls displayed in the pane on the right of the workspace. Here you will find features that will enable you to quickly and easily adjust lighting, color, sharpening and, with the Smart Fix option included, highlight and shadow detail as well. You can let the program apply the changes for you by pressing the Auto button, or you can take control of the changes you apply by using the slider controls. Best of all, you can see the before and after results of your changes on screen via the zoomable previews.

In Elements 7.0 three new paint-on adjustment options have been added to the editor in a new Touch Up pane. Simply click on the entry that you want to use and then paint the effect onto your photo. The tools automatically anticipate the area that you want changed and apply the alteration before your eyes. Similar results can be obtained using the Smart Brush Tool in the Full Edit workspace.

There is no doubt that for making speedy adjustments of your favorite images in Elements, the Quick Fix editor is the best place to start. See Figure 5.10.

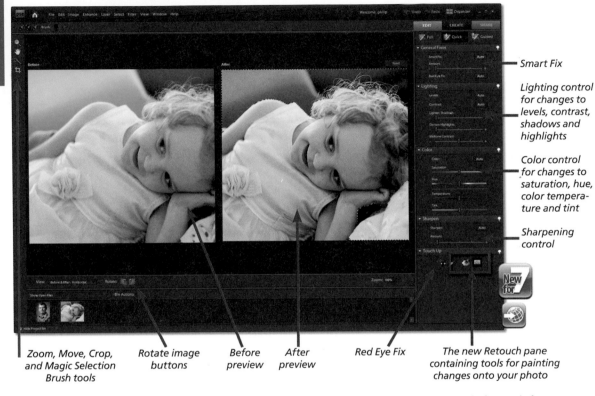

Smart Fix

Lighting control for changes to levels, contrast, shadows and highlights

Color control for changes to saturation, hue, color temperature and tint

Sharpening control

Zoom, Move, Crop, and Magic Selection Brush tools

Rotate image buttons

Before preview

After preview

Red Eye Fix

The new Retouch pane containing tools for painting changes onto your photo

Figure 5.10 *The Quick Fix editor combines the major automatic enhancing tools with great before and after preview pictures. In version 7.0 the Quick Fix editor also includes some paint on enhancement options which include Whiten Teeth, Make Dull Skies Blue and Black and White High Contrast.*

Altering a few tones only

Now that we have changed the brightness and contrast of the image so that the tones are more evenly spread between black and white, we can start to look at individual areas or groups of tones that need special attention.

For instance, when you are taking pictures on a bright sunny day, or where the contrast of the scene is quite high, the shadows in the image can become so dense that important details are too dark to see. A traditional method used by photographers to lighten the shadows is to capture the scene using a combination of existing light and a small amount of extra light from a flash. The flash illuminates the shadows, in effect 'filling' them with light, hence the name 'Fill Flash'. This is a great solution for a difficult problem.

Similarly, if the foreground or center section of a scene is dark, then the exposure system in a digital camera can overcompensate and cause the surrounding area to become too light. 'No problem', you say, as you adjust the brightness so that the whole picture is darker, but this action also affects the shadow and midtone areas of the picture, causing them to lose detail.

So how can we alter the brightness of just the shadow or only the highlight areas? Well, Adobe provided quite a clever solution to these problems in the earlier versions of the program, employing two features – Fill Flash and Adjust Backlighting. Version 3.0 replaced these with yet another feature called the Shadow/Highlight control. The tool combines two different controls that performed similar functions in previous versions of the product into one dialog.

Editor: Enhance > Adjust Lighting > Shadows/Highlights

In version 6.0: Enhance > Adjust Lighting > Shadows/Highlights

Designed as a replacement for both the Fill Flash and Adjust Backlighting controls, this one little dialog contains the same power as the previous two features in an easy-to-use format. The tool contains three sliders – the upper one is for Lightening Shadows, which replaces the Fill Flash tool, the control in the middle Darkens Highlights and is a substitute for the Adjust Backlighting tool, and the final slider adjusts Midtone Contrast.

Moving the Shadows control to the right lightens all the tones that are spread between the middle values and black. Sliding the Highlights control to the right darkens those tones between middle values and white. The beauty of this feature is that unlike the Brightness/Contrast tool, these changes are made without altering other parts of the picture. To fine-tune the tonal changes a third slider is also included in the dialog. Moving this Midtone control to the right increases the contrast of the middle values,

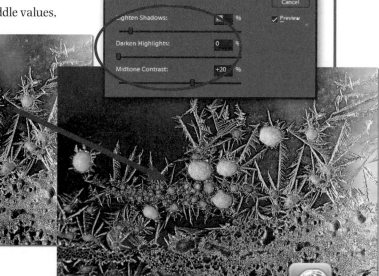

Figure 5.11 *The Shadows/Highlights feature (above) replaces both the Fill Flash and Adjust Backlighting tools available in earlier versions of Elements with the added advantage that the contrast of middle tones can be adjusted using the third slider.*

and movements to the left decrease the contrast, making the image 'flatter'. You can also use the Midtone Contrast slider in the Advanced options of the Adjust Color Curves dialog box to produce similar results. See Figure 5.11 on the previous page.

1 Select Enhance > Adjust Lighting > Shadows/Highlights.

2 Move all sliders so that their values are set to 0%.

3 Move the Lighten Shadows slider to the right to lighten the dark tones.

4 Move the Darken Highlights slider to the right to darken light areas.

5 Adjust the Midtone Contrast slider to restore any lost contrast to the picture.

Dodge and Burn tools

It is no surprise, given Adobe's close relationship with customers who are professional photographers, that some of the features contained in both Photoshop and Elements have a heritage in traditional photographic practice. The Dodge and Burn tools are good examples of this. Almost since the inception of the medium, photographers have manipulated the way their images have printed. In most cases this amounts to giving a little more light to one part of the picture and taking a little away from another. This technique, called dodging and burning, effectively lightens and darkens specific parts of the final print.

Adobe's version of these techniques involves two separate tools. See Figure 5.12. The Dodge tool's icon represents its photographic equivalent – a cardboard disk on a piece of wire. This device was used to shade part of the photographic paper during exposure. Having received less exposure, the area is lighter in the final print. When you select the digital version from the Elements toolbox, you will notice the cursor change to a circle which you can click and drag over your image to lighten the selected areas. The size and shape of the circle is based on the current brush size and shape. This can be changed via the palette in the options bar. Also displayed here are other options that allow you to lighten groups of tones like shadows, midtones and highlights independently. There are also controls to change the strength of the lightening process by adjusting the exposure. See Figures 5.12 and 5.13.

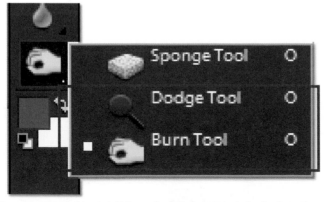

Figure 5.12 The Dodge and Burn tools are used to lighten and darken different parts of the picture.

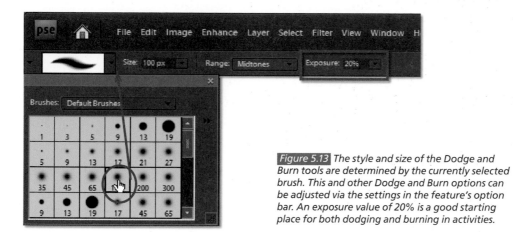

Figure 5.13 *The style and size of the Dodge and Burn tools are determined by the currently selected brush. This and other Dodge and Burn options can be adjusted via the settings in the feature's option bar. An exposure value of 20% is a good starting place for both dodging and burning in activities.*

FEATURE SUMMARY

1 Select the Dodge tool from the toolbox.

2 Choose the brush size from the palette in the options bar.

3 Select the group of tones to adjust – highlights, midtones or shadows.

4 Set the strength of the effect via the exposure value.

5 Click and drag the cursor over the image to lighten.

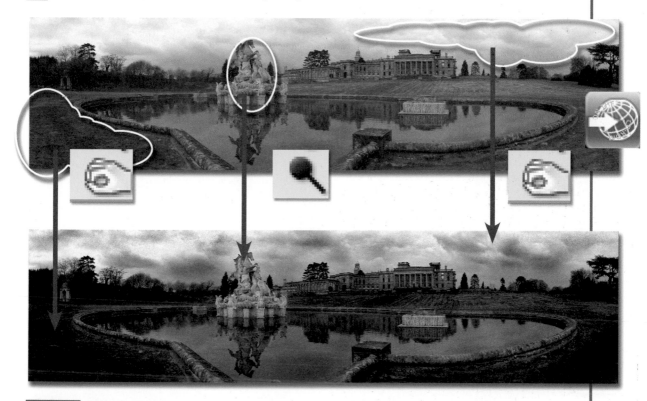

Figure 5.14 *Skillful dodging and burning can help improve the appearance of specific dark and light picture areas.*

The Burn tool's attributes are also based on the settings in the options bar and the current brush size, but rather than lightening areas this feature darkens selected parts of the image. Again, you can adjust the precise grouping of tones, highlights, midtones or shadows that you are working on at any one time. See Figure 5.15.

FEATURE SUMMARY

1 Select the Burn tool from the toolbox.

2 Choose the brush size from the palette in the options bar.

3 Select the group of tones to adjust – highlights, midtones or shadows.

4 Set the strength of the effect via the exposure value.

5 Click and drag the cursor over the image to darken.

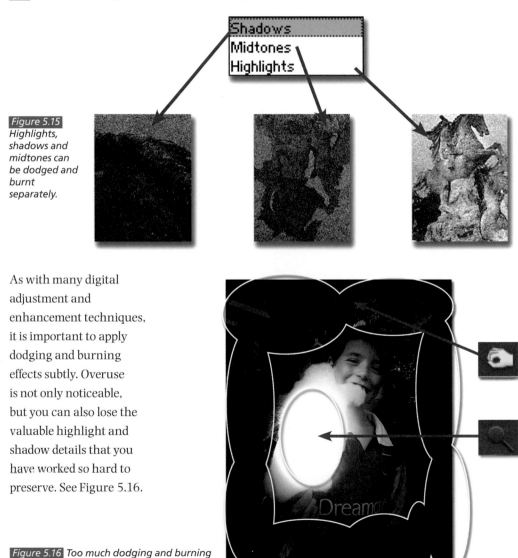

Figure 5.15
Highlights, shadows and midtones can be dodged and burnt separately.

As with many digital adjustment and enhancement techniques, it is important to apply dodging and burning effects subtly. Overuse is not only noticeable, but you can also lose the valuable highlight and shadow details that you have worked so hard to preserve. See Figure 5.16.

Figure 5.16 Too much dodging and burning is noticeable and can eventually degrade the image rather than improve it.

Color corrections

Our eyes are extremely complex and sophisticated imaging devices. Without us even being aware of it, they adjust to changes in light color and level. For instance, when we view a piece of white paper outside on a cloudy day, indoors under a household bulb or at work with fluorescent lights, the paper appears white. Our eyes adapt to each different environment.

Unfortunately, digital sensors, including those in our cameras, are not as clever. If I photographed the piece of paper under the same lighting conditions, the pictures would all display a different color cast. Under fluorescent lights the paper would appear green, lit by the household bulb it would look yellow, and when photographed outside it would be a little blue. See Figure 5.17.

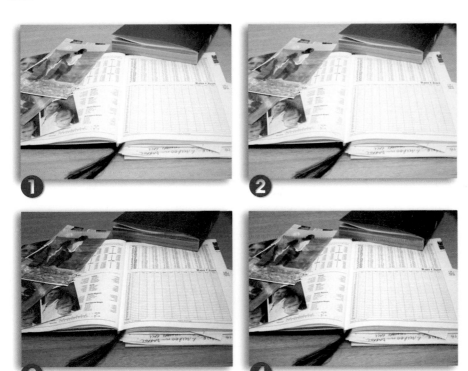

Figure 5.17 *The dominant color cast in an image changes when it is shot under different light sources.*
(1) Fluorescent.
(2) Household bulb.
(3) Candlelight.
(4) Daylight.

This situation occurs because camera sensors are generally designed to record images without casts in daylight. As the color balance of the light for our three examples is different from daylight – that is, some parts of the spectrum are stronger and more dominant than others – the pictures record with a cast. Camera manufacturers are addressing the problem by including Auto White Balance functions in their designs. These features attempt to adjust the captured image to suit the lighting conditions it was photographed under, but even so some digital pictures will arrive at your desktop with strange color casts. See Figure 5.18.

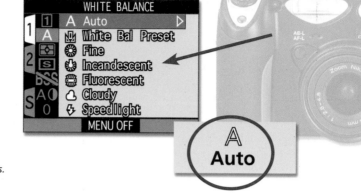

Figure 5.18 Some cameras include an Auto White Balance feature designed to compensate for different light sources.

Editor: Enhance > Auto Color Correction

In version 6.0: Enhance > Auto Color Correction

The Auto Color Correction feature, first seen in version 2.0 of the program, works in a similar way to tools like Auto Levels and Auto Contrast, providing a one-click fix for most color problems. As with all 'I'll let the computer decide' features, sometimes such automatic fixes do not produce the results that you expect. In these scenarios use the Undo (Edit > Undo) command to reverse the changes and try one of the manual tools detailed below. See Figure 5.19.

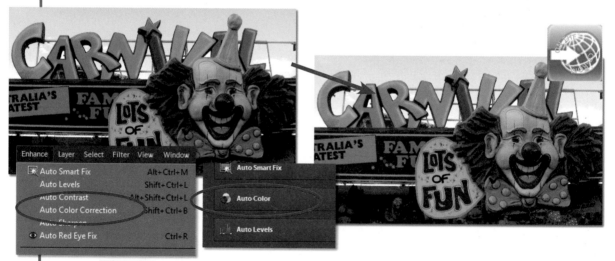

Figure 5.19 Auto Color Correction, known as just Auto Color in the Organizer's Fix panel, provides a one-click correction for most cast problems.

Editor: Enhance > Adjust Color > Remove Color Cast

In version 6.0: Enhance > Adjust Color > Remove Color Cast

To help provide a more selective solution to the color cast problem, Adobe included the Color Cast command in Elements. This function is designed to be used with images that have areas that are meant to be white, gray or black. By selecting the feature you can then click onto the neutral area and all the colors of the image will be changed by the amount needed to make the area free from color casts. This command works particularly well if you happen to have a gray or black area in your scene. See Figure 5.20. Some image makers include a gray card in the corner of scenes that they know are going to produce casts in anticipation of using Color Cast to neutralize the hues later.

FEATURE SUMMARY

1 Select Enhance > Adjust Color > Remove Color Cast.

2 Use the Eyedropper tool to click on a part of the image that is meant to be either a neutral white, gray or black.

3 If you are unhappy with the results, click the Reset button to start again or keep clicking until you get a suitable result.

4 Click OK when the cast has been removed.

Keep in mind that this command produces changes based on the assumption that what you are clicking with the Eyedropper is meant to be neutral – that is, the color should contain even amounts of red, green and blue. In practice, it is not often that images have areas like this. For this reason Elements contains another method to help rid your images of color casts.

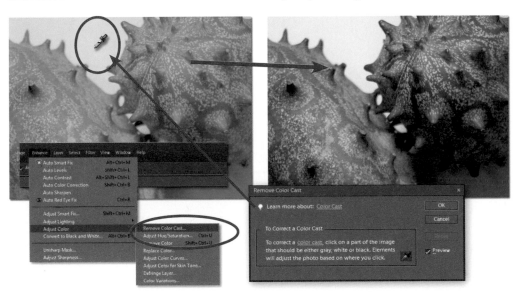

Figure 5.20 *The Remove Color Cast feature works when you select a portion of the picture that should be neutral (white, gray or black) but exhibits a cast. Elements then rebalances the rest of the hues in the image to ensure that this part of the picture is cast free.*

Editor: Enhance > Adjust Color > Color Variations
In version 6.0: Enhance > Adjust Color > Color Variations

An alternative to using the Remove Color Cast feature is the Color Variations command. From version 2.0 Elements has included a revised and simplified Color Variations dialog. Over the last few versions the color changing thumbnails have been rationalized so that users only have to make simple decisions about increasing or decreasing the red, green or blue components of their images. The Color Variations feature is now divided into four parts. See Figure 5.21. The top of the dialog contains two thumbnails that represent how your image looked before changes and its appearance after. The radio buttons in section 2 (middle left) allow the user to select the parts of the image they wish to alter. In this way, highlights, midtones and shadows can all be adjusted independently. The Amount slider in section 3 (bottom left) controls the strength of the color changes. The final parts, sections 4 and 5 (bottom), are taken up with six color and two brightness preview images. These represent how your picture will look with specific colors added or when the picture is brightened or darkened. Clicking on any of these thumbnails will change the 'after' picture by adding the color chosen. To add a color to your image, click on a suitably colored thumbnail. To remove a color, click on its opposite.

FEATURE SUMMARY

1 Select Enhance > Adjust Color > Color Variations.

2 Choose the tones you want to change (shadows, midtones or highlights) or alternatively select saturation.

3 Adjust the Amount slider to set the strength of each change.

4 Click on the appropriate thumbnails to make changes to your image.

5 Click OK to finish.

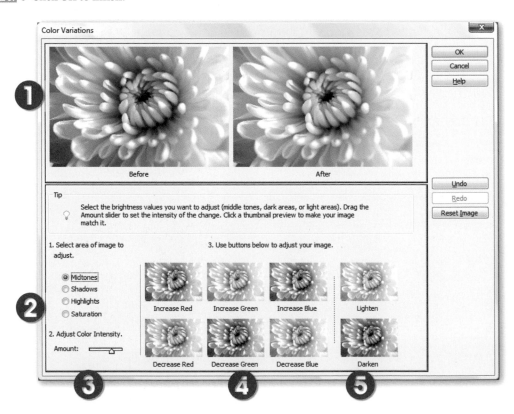

Figure 5.21 The Color Variations feature, as it appeared in version 6, gives the user more control over color changes in the image. (1) Before and after thumbnails. (2) Image area to change. (3) Color strength or intensity. (4) Color variation thumbnails. (5) Brightness thumbnails.

The Red Eye Removal tool

In version 6.0: Red Eye Removal tool

Using the built-in flash in your camera is a great way to make sure that you can keep photographing in any light conditions. One of the problems with flashes that are situated very close to the lens is that portrait pictures, especially when taken at night, tend to suffer from 'red eye'. The image might be well exposed and composed, but the sitter has glowing red eyes. This occurs because the light from the flash is being reflected off the back of the eye. Adobe recognized that a lot of small modern digital cameras have flashguns close to their lens – the major cause of this problem – and developed a specialist tool to help retouch these images. Called the Red Eye Removal tool since version 3.0 and the Red Eye Brush in previous releases, it changes the crimson color in the center of the eye to a more natural looking black.

To correct the problem is a simple process that involves selecting the tool and then clicking on the red section of the eye. Elements locates the red color and quickly converts it to a more natural dark gray. The tool's options bar provides settings to adjust the pupil's size and the amount that it is darkened. Try the default settings first and if the results are not quite perfect, undo the changes and adjust the option's settings before reapplying the tool. See Figure 5.22.

FEATURE SUMMARY

1 Select the Red Eye Removal tool from the toolbox.

2 Click on the red area of the eye or drag a marquee around the eye to apply the color change.

3 If the results are not perfect, Edit > Undo the changes and adjust the Pupil Size and Darken Amount settings in the options bar. Click on the red area to reapply the color change.

The Red Eye Removal tool is available in both the Quick Fix and Standard editing workspaces.

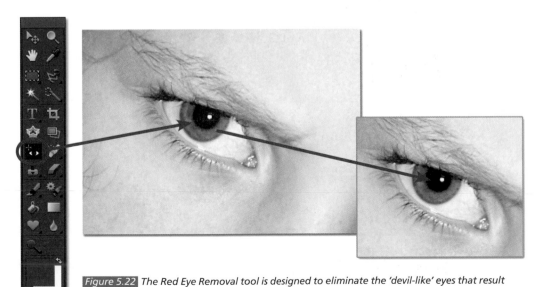

Figure 5.22 *The Red Eye Removal tool is designed to eliminate the 'devil-like' eyes that result from using the inbuilt flash of some digital cameras.*

Editor: Enhance > Adjust Color > Adjust Color for Skin Tone

In version 6.0: Enhance > Adjust Color > Adjust Skin Tone

The Adjust Color for Skin Tones feature is designed to allow you to adjust the hue of the skin tones within your picture.

Making changes is a two-step process. When the feature first opens you need to use the Eyedropper tool to select a typical section of skin within the photo. Next, you can adjust the color of the skin using the Tan and Blush sliders and the overall color of the picture with the Temperature control.

The picture can be reverted to its original hues by selecting the Reset button or the changes applied by pressing the OK button. See Figure 5.23.

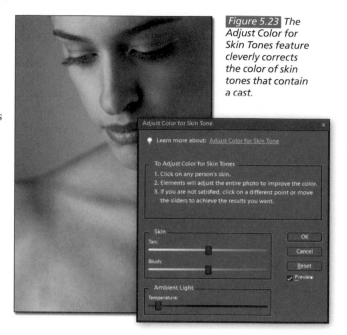

Figure 5.23 *The Adjust Color for Skin Tones feature cleverly corrects the color of skin tones that contain a cast.*

FEATURE SUMMARY

1 Select Enhance > Adjust Color > Adjust Skin Tone.

2 Use the Eyedropper tool to click on an area of typical skin in the picture.

3 Adjust the Skin and Blush sliders to alter skin color.

4 Change the Temperature slider to alter the color of the whole image.

5 Click Reset to remove changes or OK to finish.

As the Skin Tone tool averages tones as it works, multiple clicks around different parts of a person's face will often refine the results. Holding down the Ctrl key while clicking turns off averaging and will resample with each click.

Using filters and effects

Editor: Filters menu

In version 6.0: Filter > Filter Gallery or Window > Effects > Filters tab

The filters contained within image-editing programs are capable of producing truly stunning effects. Digital filters are based on the traditional photographic versions, which are placed in front of the lens of the camera to change the way the image is captured. Now, with the click of a button, it is possible to make extremely complex changes to our images almost instantaneously – changes that a few years ago we couldn't even imagine.

The filters in Adobe Photoshop Elements can be found grouped under a series of subheadings based on their main effect or feature in the Filter menu. Selecting a filter will apply the effect to the current layer or selection. Some filters display a dialog that allows the user to change specific settings and preview the filtered image before applying the effect to the whole of the picture. This can be a great time saver, as filtering a large file can take several minutes. See Figure 5.24.

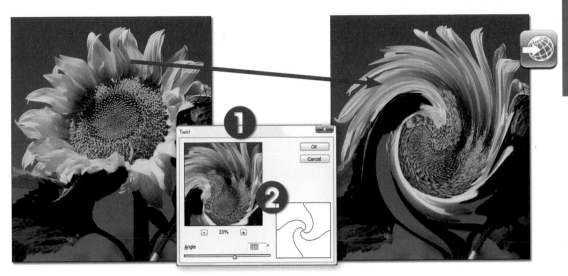

Figure 5.24 Most filters are supplied with a preview and settings dialog that allows the user to view changes before committing them to the full image. (1) Filter preview thumbnail. (2) Filter controls.

Editor: Filter > Filter Gallery

Most filters that don't work with their own dialog are incorporated into the Filter Gallery (Filter > Filter Gallery) feature which was first introduced in version 3.0. Designed to allow the user to apply several different filters to a single image it can also be used to apply the same filter several different times. The dialog consists of a preview area, a collection of filters that can be used with the feature, a settings area with sliders to control the filter effect and a list of filters that are currently being applied to the picture.

Multiple filters are applied to a picture by selecting the filter, adjusting the settings to suit the image and then clicking the New effect layer button at the bottom of the dialog. Filters are arranged in the sequence they are applied. Applied filters can be moved to a different spot in the sequence by click-dragging them up or down the stack. Click the eye icon to hide the effect of the selected filter from preview. Filters can be deleted from the list by selecting them first and then clicking the dustbin icon at the bottom of the dialog.

Most of the filters that can't be used with the Filter Gallery feature are either applied to the picture with no user settings or make use of the filter preview and settings dialog detailed in Figure 5.25.

If neither of these preview options is available then, as an alternative, you can make a partial selection of the image using the Marquee tool first and then use this to test the filter. Remember, filter changes can be reversed by using the Undo feature.

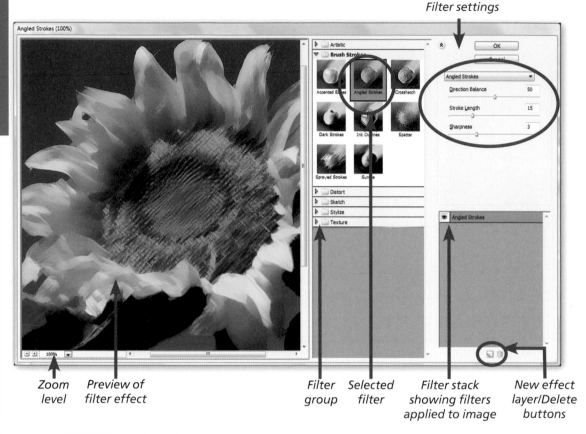

Zoom level   Preview of filter effect   Filter group   Selected filter   Filter stack showing filters applied to image   New effect layer/Delete buttons

Figure 5.25 *The Filter Gallery feature, first introduced in version 3.0, allows users to preview filter effects, alter filter settings and even apply several different filters to the same image interactively.*

Editor: Window > Effects

The number and type of filters available can make selecting which to use a difficult process. To help with this decision, Elements also contains a Filter Browser type feature that displays thumbnail versions of different filter effects. The browser is located with other thumbnail previews of shapes, graphics, themes, frames and layer styles in the Effects palette (Window > Effects), previously located in the Contents palette.

Double-clicking the filter preview thumbnail will either open the Filter Gallery or a filter dialog, where settings can be adjusted, or simply apply changes directly to your picture. The selection of filters previewed in the gallery at any one time can be changed by altering the selection in the pop-up menu at the top of the palette. See Figure 5.26.

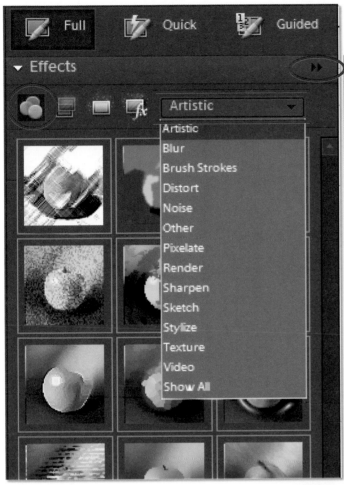

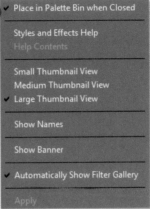

Full　　Quick　　Guided

▾ Effects

Artistic ▾

| Artistic |
| Blur |
| Brush Strokes |
| Distort |
| Noise |
| Other |
| Pixelate |
| Render |
| Sharpen |
| Sketch |
| Stylize |
| Texture |
| Video |
| Show All |

✓ Place in Palette Bin when Closed

Styles and Effects Help
Help Contents

Small Thumbnail View
Medium Thumbnail View
✓ Large Thumbnail View

Show Names

Show Banner

✓ Automatically Show Filter Gallery

Apply

Figure 5.26 The filter browser, located within the new Effects palette (previously the Artwork and Effects palette), gives users a good idea of the types of changes that a filter will make to an image when selecting a specific filter.

Let's get filtering

To give you a head start with your filtering, the next couple of pages contain some examples of the effects of a range of filters when applied to the same base image. See Figure 5.27. The results, along with the filter preview/settings and dialogs, are also included. See Figures 5.28 and 5.29. After that, the use and control of some of the selected filters are also featured in more detail.

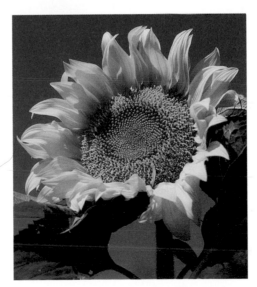

Figure 5.27 The base image used for all filter examples over the next few pages.

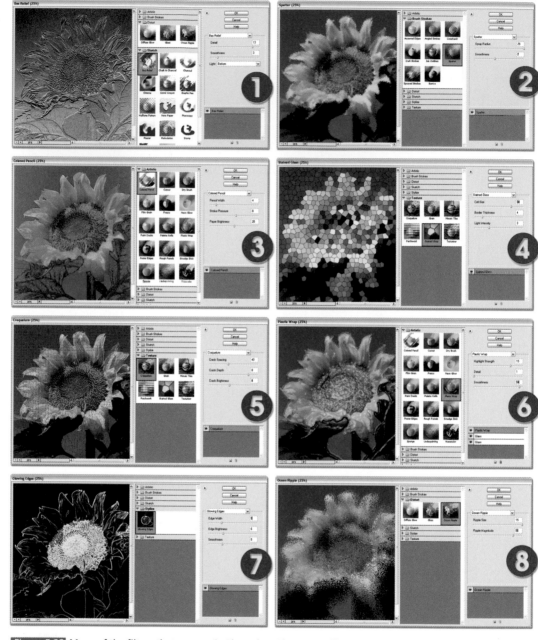

Figure 5.28 Many of the filters that you use in Photoshop Elements will open up via the Filter Gallery feature. This will give you the added ability to be able to combine filter effects and even reapply the same effect several times. Some of the filters that work with the Filter Gallery include:
(1) Filter > Sketch > Bas Relief.
(2) Filter > Brush Strokes > Spatter.
(3) Filter > Artistic > Colored Pencil.
(4) Filter > Texture > Stained Glass.
(5) Filter > Texture > Craquelure.
(6) Filter > Artistic > Plastic Wrap.
(7) Filter > Stylize > Glowing Edges, and
(8) Filter > Distort > Ocean Ripple.

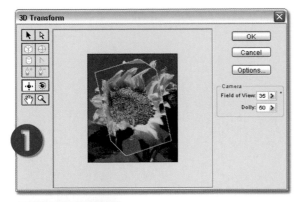

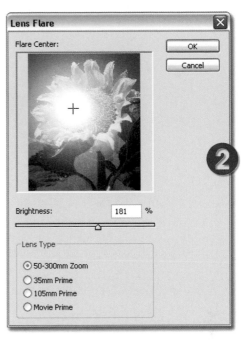

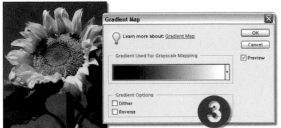

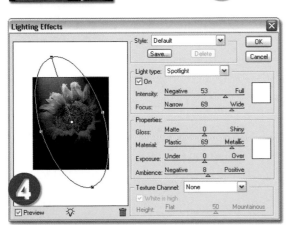

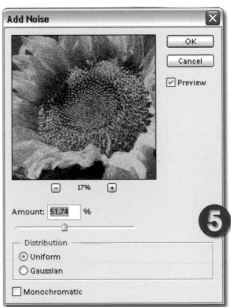

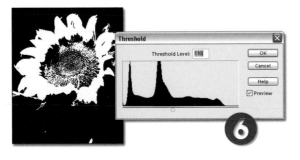

Figure 5.29 *Filters that are not included in the Filter Gallery often have their own preview and settings dialog. These include:*
(1) Filter > Render > 3D Transform.
(2) Filter > Render > Lens Flare.
(3) Filter > Adjustments > Gradient Map.
(4) Filter > Render > Lighting Effects.
(5) Filter > Noise > Add Noise, and
(6) Filter > Adjustments > Threshold.

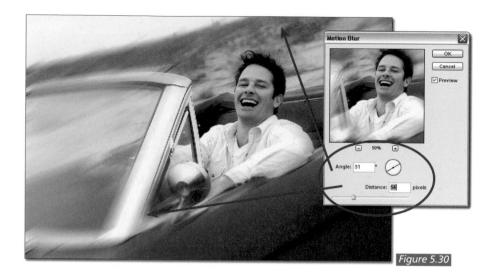

Figure 5.30

Editor: Filter > Blur > Motion Blur

The Motion Blur filter is great for putting back a sense of movement into action pictures that have been frozen by being photographed with a fast shutter speed. Used by itself, the filter produces photos that are very blurred and often lack any recognizable detail. Unless this is the effect you are looking for, it is best to apply this filter via a feathered selection to help retain sharpness in some picture parts whilst blurring others. See Chapter 7 for more details on selection techniques.

The filter dialog contains a single slider, a preview window and a motion direction (Angle) dial. The Angle dial determines the direction of the blur and should be set to simulate the natural direction of the subject. The Distance slider controls the amount of blur added to the picture – higher values create longer streaks and a more dramatic effect, smaller settings produce more subtle results. See Figure 5.30.

1 Before applying the filter we need to set up some controls over where the motion blur will be applied in our picture. To do this we start by selecting the area to remain sharp. Here I have used the Lasso tool to draw a freehand selection around the driver. Next, I invert the selection (Select > Inverse) so that the entire image except the driver is now selected.

2 To soften the transition between the sharp and blurred sections of the picture I applied a large feather (Select > Feather) to the selection. This replaces the normal sharp edge of the selection with a gradual change between selected and non-selected areas. I used a feathering of about 10% (100 pixels) of the total width of the picture.

3 Next, I hid the selection using the shortcut keys Ctrl + H (the selection is still active, you just cannot see the marching ants) and opened the Motion Blur dialog (Filter > Blur > Motion Blur). I adjusted the Angle and Distance settings to suit the picture. Make sure that the Preview option is selected so that you can see the results in the full image. Click OK to complete.

FEATURE SUMMARY

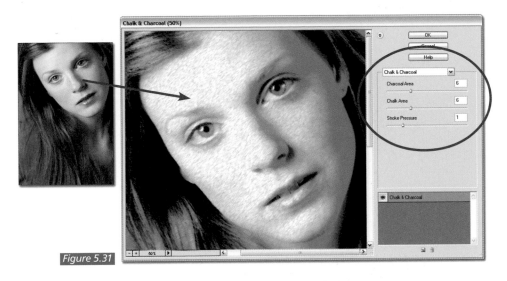

Figure 5.31

Editor: Filter > Sketch > Chalk & Charcoal

The Chalk & Charcoal filter is one of several drawing-like filters that can be found in the Sketch section of the Filter menu. The feature simulates the effect of making a drawing of the photograph with white chalk and black charcoal. The tones in the photograph that range from shadow to mid-gray are replaced by the charcoal strokes and those lighter values (from mid-gray to white) are 'drawn' in using the chalk color.

The filter dialog gives you control over the balance of the amount and placement of the charcoal and chalk areas as well as the pressure of the stroke used to draw the picture. Higher values for the Charcoal and Chalk Area sliders will increase the number and variations of tones that are drawn with these colors. High settings for the Stroke Pressure slider produce crisper transitions between tones and a more contrasty result. See Figure 5.31.

FEATURE SUMMARY

1 Set the foreground colors to default (foreground – black, background – white) by clicking the small black and white squares in the bottom left of the tool bar. The filter uses the foreground color as the 'charcoal' color and the background color as the 'chalk' color. If you have the same color set for background and foreground then a warning dialog will appear.

2 Select the Chalk & Charcoal filter from the Filter > Sketch menu. Using the preview window as a guide, adjust the Charcoal and Chalk Area sliders until you have situated the two tones in the positions most suited for the image. In the example I wanted to ensure that the shadow areas remained dark but still contained detail and that the skin tones were still fairly light.

3 Next, move your attention to the Stroke Pressure slider. Adjust the setting until you achieve a good balance of both detail and contrast. You may need to readjust the Chalk and Charcoal Area sliders to ensure a good spread of tones after the Pressure slider alterations.

SIMPLE IMAGE CHANGES

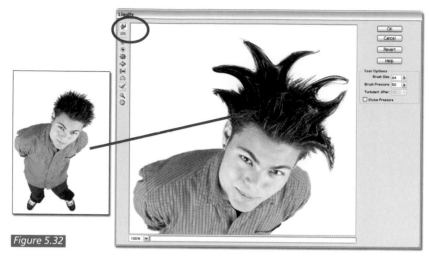

Figure 5.32

Editor: Filter > Distort > Liquify

The Liquify filter is a very powerful tool for warping and transforming your pictures. The feature contains its own sophisticated dialog box complete with a preview area and no fewer than eight different tools that can be used to twist, warp, push, pull and reflect your pictures with such ease that it is almost as if they were made of silly putty. See Figure 5.32.

1 Open an example image and then the Liquify filter (Filter > Distort > Liquify). The dialog opens and has a preview in the center, tools to the left and tool options to the right (use the Size, Pressure and Jitter options to control the effects of the tools). We will start with a simple manipulation designed to broaden the subject's smile. Select the Warp tool and drag the edge of the lips sideways and upwards. Make the brush smaller if too much of the surrounding detail is being altered as well.

2 Now let's exaggerate the perspective in the existing picture. Select the Pucker tool and increase the size of the Brush to cover the entire bottom of the figure. Click to squeeze in the subject's feet and legs. Now select the Bloat tool and place it over the upper portion of the subject; click to expand this area. If you are unhappy with any changes you can use the keyboard shortcuts for Edit > Undo (Ctrl + Z) to remove the last changes. If you want you can bloat the eyes as well.

3 To finish the caricature switch back to the Warp tool and drag some hair out and away from the subject's head. You can also use this tool to drag down the chin and lift the cheekbones. The picture can be selectively restored at any point by choosing the Reconstruct tool and painting over the changed area. Click OK to apply the changes that you have previewed to the fuller image. Depending on the size of the original this can take some time.

FEATURE SUMMARY

This is a fun tutorial, but it is also good to note that when doing more serious photo retouching the Liquify filter, subtly used, can actually be great for trimming someone down or removing a double chin.

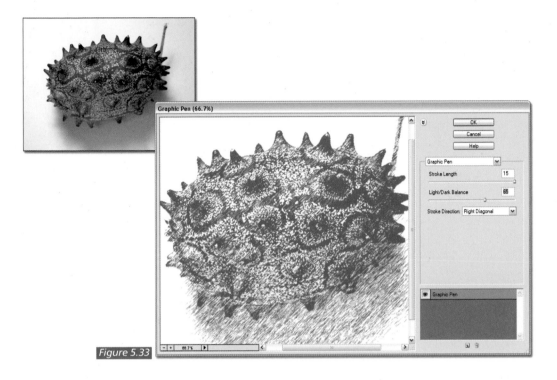

Figure 5.33

Editor: Filter > Sketch > Graphic Pen

The Graphic Pen filter is one of the group of Sketch filters. The feature simulates the effect of making a drawing of the photograph with a thin graphic arts pen. Close overlapping strokes are used for the shadow areas; midtones are represented by balancing strokes with the paper color showing through; and highlight details are drawn with a few sparse strokes.

The filter dialog gives you control over the balance of light and dark (paper and stroke) and the length of the pen stroke used to draw the picture. There is also a drop-down menu for selecting the direction of the pen strokes. See Figure 5.33.

1 Set the foreground colors to default (foreground – black, background – white) by clicking the small black and white squares in the bottom left of the tool bar. The Graphic Pen filter uses the foreground color as the 'ink' color and the background color as the 'paper' color.

2 Select the Graphic Pen filter from the Filter > Sketch menu. Using the preview window as a guide adjust the Stroke Length, Light/Dark Balance and Stroke Direction controls. Click OK to filter the picture.

3 To add a little more color to your Graphic Pen 'drawings' select colors other than black and white for the foreground and background values. Double-click each swatch to open the color swatch palette, where you can select the new color.

FEATURE SUMMARY

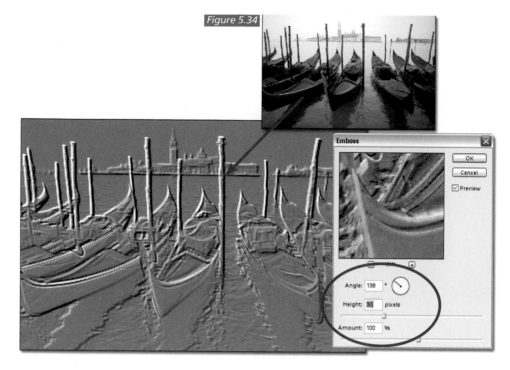

Figure 5.34

Editor: Filter > Stylize > Emboss

The Emboss filter converts your picture to flat areas of gray, fringed by lighter tones of various colors. The final result simulates an embossing effect, making the picture appear as though it has been beaten into a sheet of thin metal. See Figure 5.34.

The filter dialog contains two sliders, a preview window and a light direction (Angle) dial. The Angle dial determines the direction of the light used to produce the shadows and highlights that create the depth of the embossing effect. The Height slider controls the size of the edge outlines and adjusting the Amount slider determines the level of picture detail used in the final result.

1 With your picture open select the Emboss filter from the Stylize group in the Filter menu.

2 With the filter dialog open make sure that the Preview option is clicked and that the preview window is set to 100%. Turn the Angle dial to adjust the lighting direction used in the effect. Next, move the Height slider until the edges of the effect are the size you desire. Movements to the right increase the size of the edge lines.

3 Now turn your attention to the Amount slider. Move the control until the embossing effect is applied to the level of texture you desire. Movements to the right increase the detail in the result. If necessary, drag the visible area in the preview window to examine more closely the changes in other areas of the picture. Click OK to complete.

Third party filters

Ever since the early versions of Photoshop Elements, Adobe provided the opportunity for third party developers to create small pieces of specialist software that could plug into the program. The modular format of the software means that Adobe and other software manufacturers can easily create extra filters that can be added to the program at any time. In fact, some of the plug-ins that have been released over the years have became so popular that Adobe themselves incorporated their functions into successive versions of Elements. This is how the Photo filter, which made its first appearance in Elements 3.0, came into being.

Most plug-ins register themselves as extra options in the Filter menu, where they can be accessed just like any other Elements feature. The Digital SHO filter from Kodak, previously Applied Science Fiction, is a great example of plug-in technology. Designed to automatically enhance the shadow detail in digital photographs, when installed it becomes part of a suite of filters supplied by the company that are attached to the Filter menu. See Figure 5.35.

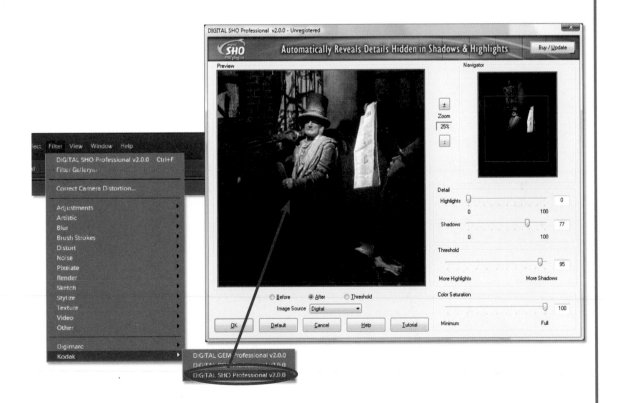

Figure 5.35 *Third party filters add extra functions to the main program.*

The 10 commandments for filter usage

1 Subtlety is everything. The effect should support your image not overpower it.

2 Try one filter at a time. Applying multiple filters to an image can be confusing.

3 View at full size. Make sure that you view the effect at full size (100%) when deciding on filter settings.

4 Filter a layer. For a change, try applying a filter to one layer and then using the Layer opacity slider to control how strongly the filter image shows through.

5 Print to check effect. If the image is to be viewed as a print, double-check the effect when printed before making final decisions about filter variables.

6 Fade strong effects. If the effect is too strong, try fading it. Apply the filter to a duplicate image layer that is above the original. Then reduce the opacity of this layer so the unfiltered original shows through.

7 Experiment. Try a range of settings before making your final selection.

8 Select then filter. Select a portion of an image and then apply the filter. In this way you can control what parts of the image are affected.

9 Different effects on different layers. If you want to combine the effects of different filters, try copying the base image to different layers and applying a different filter to each. Combine effects by adjusting the opacity of each layer.

10 Did I say that subtlety is everything?!

The Guided editing mode

In Photoshop Elements 6.0, the Adobe guys mixed together the explanations and instructions from the traditional Help entry with direct control over the enhancement process normally associated with feature dialogs. The result was the Guided edit mode. Located in the editing workspace, you can select the mode by clicking the Guided button in the Task pane (right-hand side of the window). See Figure 5.36.

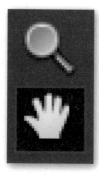

Like the Quick edit mode (Quick Fix), the Guided workspace contains a preview area which can be toggled between displaying just an After image or both a Before and After image. The preview can be enlarged or reduced with the Zoom tool located in the tool bar in the top left of the workspace or using the familiar shortcuts, Ctrl + to zoom in, and Ctrl −, to zoom out. The Hand tool, also located in the tool bar, can be used to navigate around a photo that has been enlarged beyond the boundaries of the preview space.

After selecting the Guided mode from the Edit panel you will see a list of technique headings. Clicking the sideways button next to a technique heading, on the left of the panel, will reveal the entries for this group. Selecting an individual entry will then display the steps for the technique.

Unlike a simple Help system entry, which explains the process involved for a given enhancement effect, many Guided edit entries also include a button, or slider control, with the instructions so that you can perform the editing action from inside the panel.

The Guided approach not only provides a great way to enhance photos, but also teaches the user the steps involved in the enhancement technique. For instance, the adjustments in the Lighten or Darken Guided entry target the brightness changes to shadow and highlight areas and contrast alterations to the midtones.

The same type of slider controls are available in the Shadows/Highlights feature (Enhance > Adjust Lighting > Shadows/Highlights). Once the user has a good understanding of how each slider works, and the changes it makes, it is possible for them to migrate from employing the Guided edit approach and go directly to the Shadows/Highlights feature for future enhancements of this type.

New for version 7.0 is the inclusion of a special Action Player feature to Guided editing workspace. Here you can select from a list of recorded editing sequences called Actions and apply the adjustments to your photos.

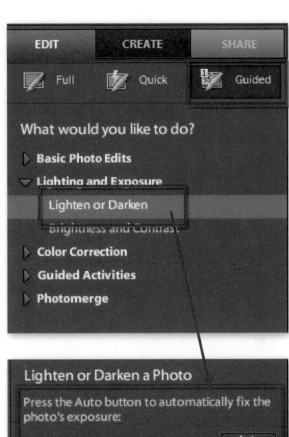

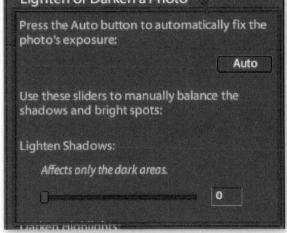

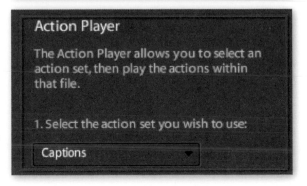

SIMPLE IMAGE CHANGES

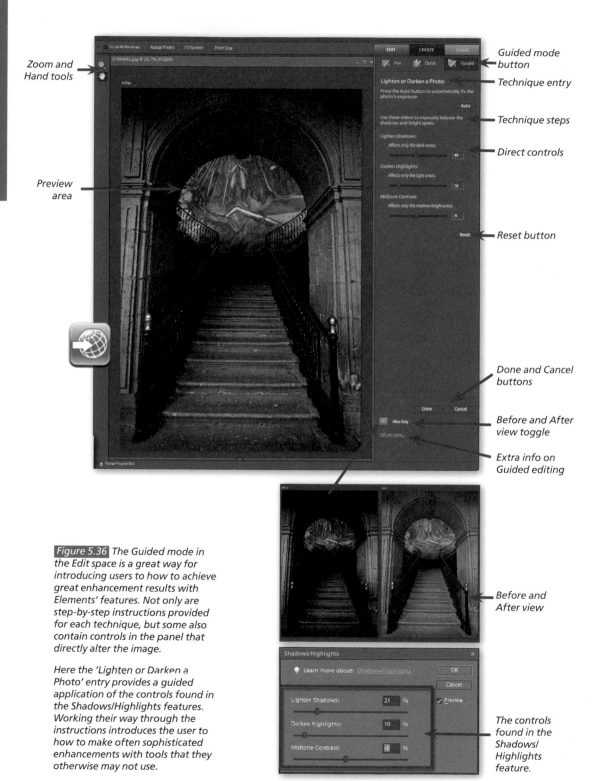

Zoom and Hand tools

Preview area

Guided mode button

Technique entry

Technique steps

Direct controls

Reset button

Done and Cancel buttons

Before and After view toggle

Extra info on Guided editing

Before and After view

Figure 5.36 *The Guided mode in the Edit space is a great way for introducing users to how to achieve great enhancement results with Elements' features. Not only are step-by-step instructions provided for each technique, but some also contain controls in the panel that directly alter the image.*

Here the 'Lighten or Darken a Photo' entry provides a guided application of the controls found in the Shadows/Highlights features. Working their way through the instructions introduces the user to how to make often sophisticated enhancements with tools that they otherwise may not use.

The controls found in the Shadows/ Highlights feature.

Automating editing tasks

It's true that shooting digitally has meant that many photographers have saved the time that they used to spend in the darkroom processing their images. The flip side to this coin is that now we while away the hours in on-screen production instead. Surely with all the power of the modern computer and flexibility of Elements there must be quicker ways to process files? Well yes there is!

Photoshop Elements users are able to automate a variety of editing functions with the Process Multiple Files feature located in the File menu of the Full editor workspace. The feature is like a dedicated batch processing tool that can name, size, enhance, label and save in a specific file format a group of photos stored in a folder or selected via the file browser. See Figure 5.37. The dialog's options include:

File source – Files to be processed can be stored in a single folder; the files currently open in the workspace; pictures in the Photo Bin or images multi-selected in the file browser.

File destination – Sets the location where processed files will be saved.

File naming – Options for naming or renaming of selected files including a range of preset naming styles.

Image sizing – Specify size and resolution changes after choosing the unit of measure to work with from the drop-down menu. Proportions can be constrained.

File type – Select the file format that processed files will be saved or converted to.

Quick Fix enhancement – Use the options here to apply automatic enhancement of the files being processed.

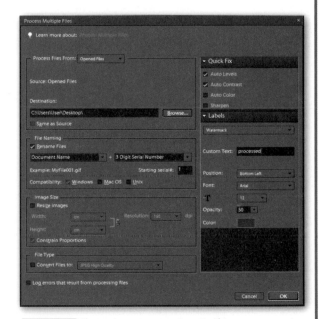

Figure 5.37 Elements users can automate the application of basic enhancement and editing features to a group of files using the Process Multiple Files feature located in the File menu of the Editor workspace.

Add labels – Add caption or filename labels to each of the processed files. Also contains an option for watermarking the pictures.

After setting the options for each of the sections in the dialog press the OK button to process the pictures.

Multi-selection editing

Another method of applying automatic changes to several photos at once is to multi-select photos in the Photo Browser workspace then choose an editing option from the right-click pop-up menu or the new Fix panel. There are a multitude of options available in this menu, with the Rotate, Auto Smart Fix and Auto Red Eye Fix features providing quick editing changes to the selected photos. For best results always apply critical edits and enhancements manually, but this technique is particularly useful if you want to process a bunch of files quickly. The added bonus is that the edited versions of the pictures are not saved over the original file but rather they are kept in a Version Set so that it is always possible to extract the original file if need be. See Figure 5.38.

Keystrokes for fast edits of multi-selected photos

Rotate Photos 90° Right – Ctrl + Right   **Auto Red Eye Fix** – Ctrl + R

Auto Smart Fix – Ctrl + Alt + M   **Rotate Photos 90° Left** – Ctrl + Left

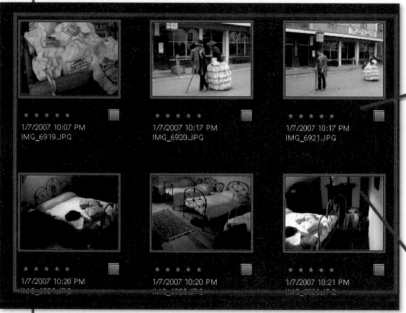

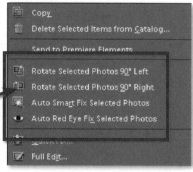

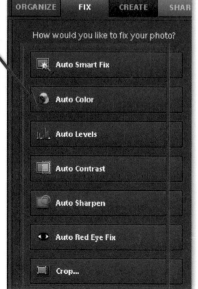

Figure 5.38 *The editing and enhancement options located on the menu that is displayed when you right-click a thumbnail in the Organizer workspace can be just as easily applied to several photos that have been multi-selected as to a single picture. This method is a quick and easy means of making automatic changes to a group of photos.*
The same approach can be applied using the options listed in the Fix panel. Here you are provided with more auto-fix options that can be applied to multi-selected photos than those listed on the right-click menu.

Getting help with Elements

In developing Elements, Adobe designed a range of learning aids that can help you increase your skills and understanding of the program. There is the usual Help menu complete with a dedicated window containing Contents, Topics, Search and Index listings for the whole program, but alongside this traditional approach Adobe also developed a couple of new Help devices – namely the tool and feature Hints and the Guided edit mode or tutorial system.

Hints

The Hints feature provides instant descriptions and help for the tool or feature that you are currently using. This information can be found by clicking the Help or hyperlink associated with the feature or tool. See Figure 5.39.

Figure 5.39 The Hints function is an extension of the Help system and offers the user a detailed explanation of the tool, menu or feature selected and is activated by clicking the hyperlink next to the tool or displayed in the feature's palette or dialog.

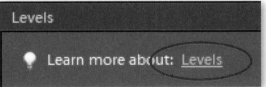
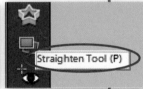

Help

The Photoshop Elements Help system was completely revamped for version 4.0 and since that time has been centered around the Help dialog (Help > Photoshop Elements Help). See Figure 5.40. From here you can search for, and more importantly, locate specific information on tools, menu items and program features from the vast array of Help files that accompany the program.

Figure 5.40 The Help feature in Elements provides a variety of ways to access the massive amount of Help files shipped with the package. You can browse through the Contents list, choose from Index headings, locate details in the Glossary or use the Search feature to hunt down the information you need.

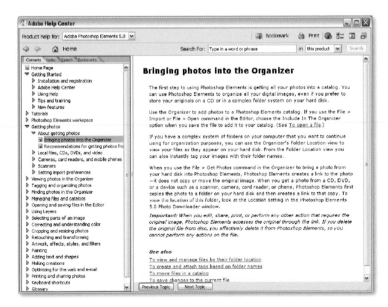

The Help system looks and works in the same way as the system found in other Adobe products such as Photoshop and InDesign. Rather than just providing information on how to use a specific tool or feature, the new design also includes ways for you to access extra support and product resources. The Help center also acts as a resource 'portal' providing direct access to tips and tutorials archive, support forums and training opportunities.

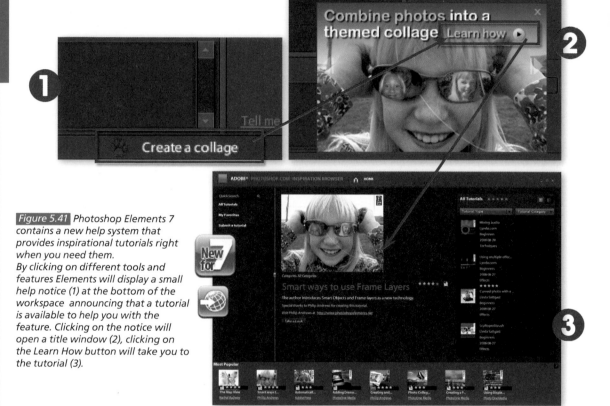

Figure 5.41 *Photoshop Elements 7 contains a new help system that provides inspirational tutorials right when you need them.*
By clicking on different tools and features Elements will display a small help notice (1) at the bottom of the workspace announcing that a tutorial is available to help you with the feature. Clicking on the notice will open a title window (2), clicking on the Learn How button will take you to the tutorial (3).

On the spot help

In a brand new system developed for version 7.0, Adobe has introduced 'intelligent' help for Elements users. When picking certain tools or using specific menu entries, the program pops up a little help notification at the bottom of the screen. When you click the notification a small window is displayed describing the type of help available. If you then click on the Learn How button within the window, the Inspirational Browser will be opened and the tutorial you selected displayed in the main workspace. See Figure 5.41.

The system draws its help and tutorial content from the online tips, tricks and tutorials which are also available from the Welcome Screen (if you are a registered for photoshop.com). This new way of finding help goes beyond what has been traditionally available as it provides tutorials by passionate Elements users (yes even me! see the example above) in a tutorial format right at the time that you need it.

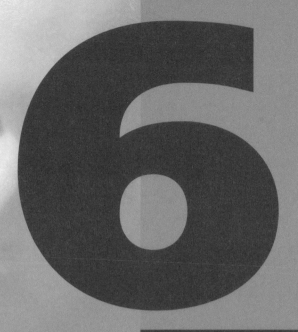

6

Hands on Techniques

Photoshop Elements has always been a software program that could produce professional results that go way beyond what you would expect given its modest price. I guess one of the main reasons for this is the fact that so many of the tools and features in the package are built on the same professional-level editing technology that gives Photoshop its strength. So it should come as no surprise when we come across tools and features that are very similar, and in some cases exactly the same, as those found in Photoshop. It is these very features, when coupled with a professional approach to their use, that will get you producing high quality digital photographs just like the pros (but at a fraction of the price!).

Elements 7 carries on this tradition by including plenty of great 'high-end' tools for us to play with. One of the most dramatic of these is the built-in Raw conversion utility (yes, just like Photoshop) as well as the ability to support 16 bits per channel color pictures. These features might not mean much to you now but this chapter will introduce these and other quality editing tools, techniques and ideas that will ensure that you produce the absolute best quality pictures possible.

Better digital capture

More and more medium- to high-end cameras are being released with the added feature of being able to capture and save your pictures in the raw format. Selecting Raw, instead of the usual JPEG, stops the camera from processing the color information from the sensor and reducing the image's bit depth, and saves the picture in this unprocessed file type. This means that the full description of what the camera 'saw' is saved in the image file and is available to you for use in the production of quality pictures. Many photographers call this type of file a 'digital negative' as it has a broader dynamic range, extra colors and the ability to correct slightly inaccurate exposures.

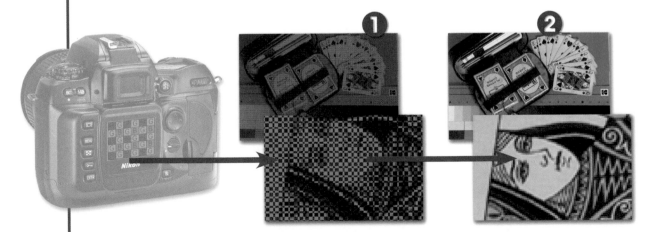

Figure 6.1 *Unlike TIFF and JPEG formats, raw files contain the unprocessed image and shooting data. In many cameras this visual information is laid out in the pattern (1) of the original sensor. The raw data needs to be interpolated to create the full color digital file we normally associate with camera output (2).*

Sounds great, doesn't it? All the quality of an information-rich image file to play with, but what is the catch? Well, raw files have to be processed before they can be used in a standard image-editing application. To access the full power of these digital negatives you will need to employ a special dedicated Raw editor. Photoshop Elements includes just such an editor built into the program. Called Adobe Camera Raw, this feature is designed specifically to allow you to take the unprocessed raw data directly from your camera's sensor and convert it into a usable image file format. The Elements Raw editor also provides access to several image characteristics that would otherwise be locked into the file format. Variables such as color depth, White Balance mode, image sharpness and tonal compensation (contrast and brightness) can all be accessed, edited and enhanced as part of the conversion process. Performing this type of editing on the raw data provides a better and higher quality result than attempting these changes after the file has been processed and saved in a non-raw format such as TIFF or JPEG. See Figure 6.1.

So what is in a raw file?

To help consolidate these ideas in your mind try thinking of a raw file as having three distinct parts:

Camera Data, usually called the EXIF or metadata, including things such as camera model, shutter speed and aperture details, most of which cannot be changed.

Image Data which, though recorded by the camera, can be changed in the Elements Raw editor and the settings chosen here directly affect how the picture will be processed. Changeable options include color depth, white balance, saturation, distribution of image tones and application of sharpness.

The Image itself. This is the data drawn directly from the sensor in your camera in a non-interpolated form. For most raw-enabled cameras, this data is supplied with a 16 bits per channel color depth, providing substantially more colors and tones to play with when editing and enhancing than found in a standard 8 bits per channel camera file. See Figure 6.2.

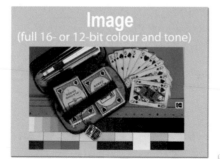

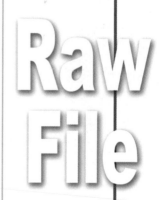

Figure 6.2 *The raw file is composed of three separate sections: Camera Data, Image Data and the Image itself. By keeping these components separate it is possible to edit variables like white balance and color depth, which are usually a fixed part of the file format, in the Raw file editor.*

Raw in action

When you open a raw file in Elements 7 you are presented with the Adobe Camera Raw editing dialog containing a full color interpolated preview of the sensor data. Using a variety of menu options, dialogs and image tools you will be able to interactively adjust image data factors such as tonal distribution and color saturation. Many of these changes can be made with familiar

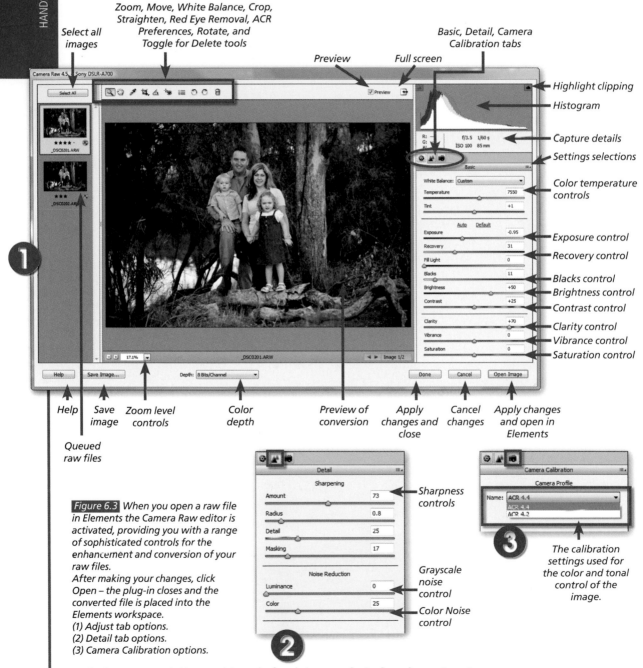

Select all images

Zoom, Move, White Balance, Crop, Straighten, Red Eye Removal, ACR Preferences, Rotate, and Toggle for Delete tools

Basic, Detail, Camera Calibration tabs

Preview

Full screen

Highlight clipping

Histogram

Capture details

Settings selections

Color temperature controls

Exposure control

Recovery control

Blacks control

Brightness control

Contrast control

Clarity control

Vibrance control

Saturation control

Help

Save image

Zoom level controls

Color depth

Preview of conversion

Apply changes and close

Cancel changes

Apply changes and open in Elements

Queued raw files

Sharpness controls

Grayscale noise control

Color Noise control

The calibration settings used for the color and tonal control of the image.

Figure 6.3 When you open a raw file in Elements the Camera Raw editor is activated, providing you with a range of sophisticated controls for the enhancement and conversion of your raw files.
After making your changes, click Open – the plug-in closes and the converted file is placed into the Elements workspace.
(1) Adjust tab options.
(2) Detail tab options.
(3) Camera Calibration options.

slider-controlled editing tools normally found in features like Levels and the Shadows/Highlights control. The results of your editing can be reviewed immediately via the live preview image and associated histogram graphs.

After these general image-editing steps have taken place you can apply some enhancement changes such as filtering for red-eye removal, straightening, cropping, sharpness, removing color noise and applying some smoothing. The final phase of the process involves selecting the color depth and image orientation. Clicking the Open Image button sets the program into action applying your changes to the raw file, whilst at the same time interpolating the Bayer data to create a full color image, and then opening the processed file into the full Elements workspace.

The raw advantage

The real advantages of editing and enhancing at the raw stage are that these changes are made to the file at the same time as the primary image data is being converted (interpolated) to the full color picture. Editing after the file is processed (saved by the camera in 8 bits per channel versions of the JPEG and TIFF format) means that you will be applying the changes to a picture with fewer tones and colors.

A second bonus for the dedicated raw shooter is that actions like switching from the White Balance option selected when shooting to another choice when processing are performed without any image loss. This is not the case once the file has been processed with the incorrect White Balance setting, as anyone who has inadvertently left the tungsten setting switched on whilst shooting in daylight can tell you.

Newly introduced ACR features

The Adobe Camera Raw utility that ships with Elements is in constant review. In fact the team that develops ACR are always making changes to keep up with photographer demand and new camera releases. For this reason the version of ACR that appears in versions 6 and 7 has some improvements over what was offered in previous releases.

The key differences are:

- The ability to work on more than one raw file at a time with the raw files queued as thumbnails on the left of the dialog.

- The inclusion of the Red Eye Removal, Straighten and Cropping tools.

- The option to increase the dialog to Full Screen mode with the new Full Screen toggle switch.

- A speciality saturation slider called Vibrance that concentrates on boosting the pastel colors in your photo.

- Moving the shadow and highlight clipping warning buttons to the top corners of the histogram.

- The addition of a new Clarity slider to help make the detail in photos stand out especially those taken under hazy conditions. In version 7.0 the slider is positioned in the middle at a 0 value providing the option to soften local contrast with a negative value.

- Substantially improved sharpening control growing the number of sliders in this area from one to four.

- The inclusion of the Camera Calibration tab to allow the user to select the latest calibration settings.

Processing with Photoshop Elements and Adobe Camera Raw (ACR)

Now that you have some basic understanding about raw files let's look at the process that you will use when bringing your raw images into the editing workspace in Photoshop Elements.

Opening

This seems like a simple step but just as there are many roads that lead to Rome so too are there a variety of ways to open a raw file in Adobe Camera Raw.

1. Opening the raw file in the Editor workspace

Once you have downloaded your raw files from camera to computer you can start the task of processing. Keep in mind that in its present state the raw file is not in the full color RGB format that we are used to, so the first part of all processing is to open the picture into Adobe Camera Raw. Selecting File > Open from inside Elements will automatically display the photo in this.

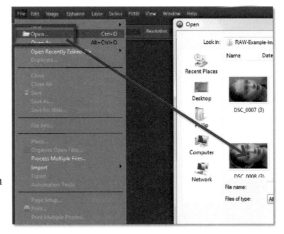

2. Starting with the PhotoBrowser

Starting in the PhotoBrowser or Organizer workspace simply right-click on the thumbnail of the raw file and select the any of the editing workspace options (Full Edit, Quick, Guided) from the pop-up menu to transfer the file to the Elements version of ACR in the Editor workspace.

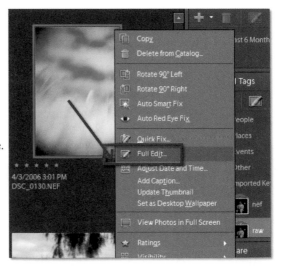

Book resources and video tutorials can be found at **www.photoshopelements.net**

Rotate, Crop and Straighten

3. Rotate Right (90° CW) or Left (90° CCW)

Once the raw photo is open in ACR you can rotate the image using either of the two Rotate buttons at the top of the dialog. If you are the lucky owner of a recent camera model then chances are the picture will automatically rotate to its correct orientation. This is thanks to a small piece of metadata supplied by the camera and stored in the picture file that indicates which way is up.

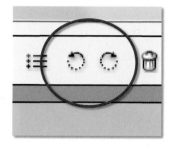

4. Straighten and Crop

The Straighten tool can automatically rotate a picture taken with the horizon slightly crooked. Simply drag the tool along the line in the image that is meant to be level and ACR will automatically rotate and crop the photo to realign the horizon.

Use the Crop tool to remove unwanted areas around your photo or to reshape the format of the image to fit a specific paper type. The tool can be click-dragged around the area you want to keep or a specific cropping format can be selected from the drop-down menu accessed via the small downward facing arrow in the bottom right of the Tool button.

Adjusting white balance

Unlike other capture formats (TIFF, JPEG) the White Balance settings are not fixed in a raw file. ACR contains three different ways to balance the hues in your photo.

5. Preset changes

You can opt to stay with the settings used at the time of shooting ('As Shot') or select from a range of light source specific settings in the White Balance drop-down menu of ACR. For best results try to match the setting used with the type of lighting that was present in the scene at the time of capture. Or choose the Auto option from the drop-down White Balance menu to get ACR to determine a setting based on the individual image currently displayed.

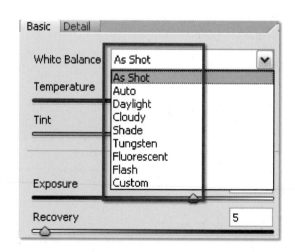

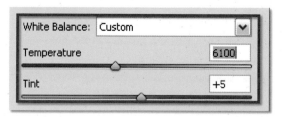

If none of the preset white balance options perfectly matches the lighting in your photo then you will need to fine tune your results with the Temperature and Tint sliders (located just below the Presets drop-down menu). The Temperature slider settings equate to the color of light in degrees Kelvin

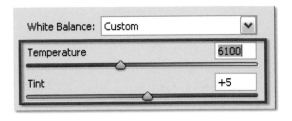

– so daylight will be 5500 and tungsten light 2800. It is a blue to yellow scale, so moving the slider to the left will make the image cooler (more blue) and to the right warmer (more yellow). In contrast the Tint slider is a green to magenta scale. Moving the slider left will add more green to the image and to the right more magenta.

6. The White Balance tool

Another quick way to balance the light in your picture is to choose the White Balance tool and then click on a part of the picture that is meant to be neutral gray or white. ACR will automatically set the Temperature and Tint sliders so that this picture part becomes a neutral gray and in the process the rest of the image will be balanced. For best results when selecting lighter tones with the tool ensure that the area contains detail and is not a blown or specular highlight.

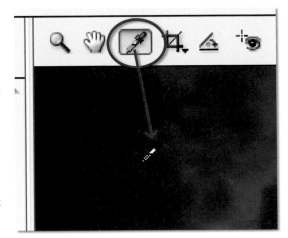

Tonal control

The next group of image enhancements alters the tones within the photo. There are nine different slider controls each dealing with a specific group of image tones. Each of the controls can be controlled automatically based on individual image content by clicking the Auto option just below the White Balance options. Use the following steps if you want a little more control.

7. Setting the white areas

To start, adjust the brightness with the Exposure slider. Moving the slider to the right lightens the photo and to the left darkens it. The settings for the slider are in f-stop increments with a +1.00 setting being equiva-

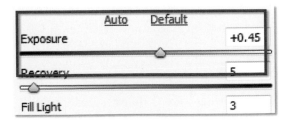

lent to increasing exposure by 1 f-stop. Use this slider to peg or set the white tones. Your aim is to lighten the highlights in the photo without clipping them (converting the pixels to pure white). To do this hold down the Alt/Option whilst moving the slider. This action previews the photo with the pixels being clipped against a black background. Move the slider back and forth until no clipped pixels appear but the highlights are as white as possible. The one exception to this advice is when your photo contains specular highlights (reflections from chrome, bright lights, etc.) which contain no detail. It is natural for these areas to be clipped when setting the white areas of your photo.

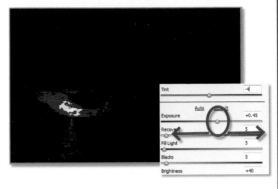

8. Adjusting the shadows (blacks)

The Blacks or Shadows slider performs a similar function with the shadow areas of the image. Again, the aim is to darken these tones but not to convert (or clip) delicate details to pure black. Just as with the Exposure slider, the Alt/Option key can be pressed whilst making Shadows adjustments to preview the pixels being clipped. Alternatively, the Shadow and Highlights Clipping Warning features (top left and right corners of the histogram) can be used to provide instant clipping feedback on the preview image. Shadow pixels that are being clipped are displayed in blue and clipped highlight tones in red.

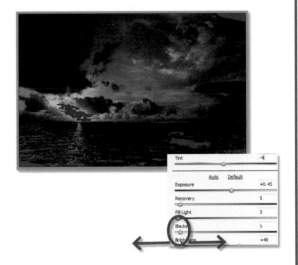

9. Brightness changes

The next control, moving from top to bottom of the ACR dialog, is the Brightness slider. At first the changes you make with this feature may appear to be very similar to those produced with the Exposure slider but there is an important difference. Yes, it is true that moving the slider to the right lightens the whole image, but rather than adjusting all pixels the same amount the feature makes major changes in the midtone areas and smaller jumps in the highlights. In so doing, the Brightness slider is less likely to clip the highlights (or shadows) as the feature compresses the highlights as it lightens

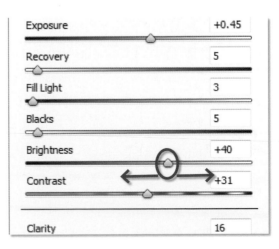

the photo. This is why it is important to set white and black points first with the Exposure and Shadows sliders before fine-tuning the image with the Brightness control.

10. Recovering Highlights and Shadow detail

If the highlights are still being clipped then use the Recovery slider to recreate detail in the problem area. Likewise, if the shadows areas are too dark then drag the Fill Light slider to the right to lighten these tones in the photo. Be careful with overapplication of either of these controls as it can make the image look low in contrast.

11. Increasing/Decreasing contrast

The last tonal control in the dialog, and the last to be applied to the photo, is the Contrast slider. The feature concentrates on the midtones in the photo with movements of the slider to the right increasing the midtone contrast and to the left producing a lower contrast image. Like the Brightness slider, Contrast changes are best applied after setting the white and black points of the image with the Exposure and Blacks sliders.

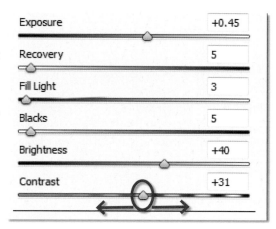

12. Local Contrast control

The Clarity slider is used to alter the local contrast or the contrast of details within the photo. It works well with photos that have been photographed with diffused light or on a cloudy day. Use Clarity and Contrast sliders together. In version 7.0 we have the option to use negative values for this control. This produces a lower contrast result around details in the photo and is good for softening the texture of skin tones.

Color strength adjustments

As one of the primary roles of the Adobe Camera Raw utility is to interpolate the captured colors from their Bayer mosaic form to the more usable RGB format, it is logical to include a couple of color strength controls in the process.

13. Vibrance adjustment

Unlike the Saturation slider which increases the strength of all colors in the photo irrespective of their strength in the first place, Vibrance targets its changes to just those colors that are desaturated. Use this control to boost the strength of colors in the photo with less risk of posterized results.

14. Saturation control

The strength or vibrancy of the colors in the photo can be adjusted using the Saturation slider. Moving the slider to the right increases saturation with a value of +100 being a doubling of the color strength found at a setting of 0. Saturation can be reduced by moving the slider to the left, with a value of -100 producing a monochrome image. Some photographers use this option as a quick way to convert their photos to black

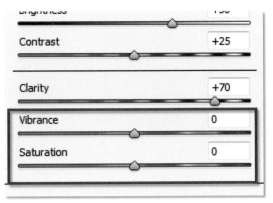

and white but most prefer to make this change in Elements proper where more control can be gained over the conversion process with features such as the Convert to Black and White.

Sharpness/Smoothness and Noise Reduction

With the tones and colors now sorted let's turn our attention to sharpening and noise reduction. Both these image enhancements can be handled in-camera using one of a variety of auto settings found in the camera setup menu, but for those image makers in pursuit of imaging perfection these changes are best left until processing the file back at the desktop.

15. To sharpen or not to sharpen

The latest version of ACR contains four separate sharpening controls. Use the Amount slider to determine the overall strength of the sharpening effect. The Radius is used to control the number of pixels from an edge that will be changed in the sharpening process. The Detail and Masking sliders are both designed to help target the sharpening at the parts of the

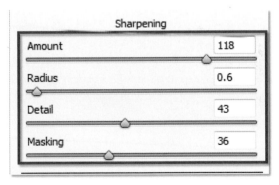

image that most need it (edges) and restrict the sharpening effects from being applied to areas that don't (skin tone and smooth graded areas). Moving the Detail slider to the right increases the local contrast surrounding edge areas and therefore enhances the appearance of details. Moving the slider to the left decreases the effect and also reduces the appearance of halos. The Masking control interactively applies a edge locating mask to the sharpening process. A setting of 0 applies no mask and therefore all detail in the photo is sharpened. Moving the slider to the right gradually isolates the edges within the photo until at a setting of 100 sharpening is only being applied to the most contrasty or dominant edges in the picture.

16. Reducing noise

ACR contains two different Noise Reduction controls. The Luminance Smoothing slider is designed to reduce the appearance of grayscale noise in a photo. This is particularly useful for improving the look of images that appear grainy. The second type of noise is the random colored pixels that typically appear in photos taken with a high ISO setting or a long shutter speed. This is generally referred to as chroma noise and is reduced using the Color Noise Reduction slider in ACR. The noise reduction effect of both features is increased as the sliders are moved to the right.

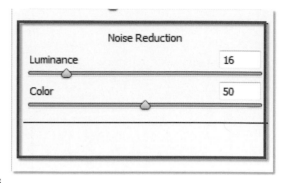

Output options

Now to the business end of the conversion task – outputting the file. The Photoshop Elements version of ACR contains only the Color Depth output option.

17. Controlling color depth/space and image size/resolution

The section below the main preview window in ACR contains the output options settings. Here, you can adjust the color depth (8 or 16 bits per channel) of the processed file. Earlier versions of Photoshop Elements were unable to handle 16 bits per channel images but the last two releases have contained the ability to read, open, save and make a few changes to these high color files.

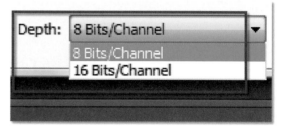

Save, Open or Done

The last step in the process is to apply the enhancement changes to the photo. This can be done in a variety of ways.

18. Opening the processed file in Photoshop Elements

The most basic option is to process the raw file according to the settings selected in the ACR

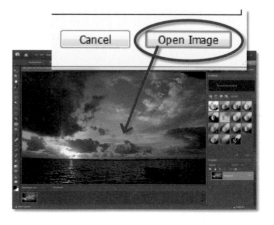

dialog and then open the picture into the Editor workspace of Photoshop Elements. To do this simply select the Open Image button. Select this route if you intend to edit or enhance the image beyond the changes made during the conversion.

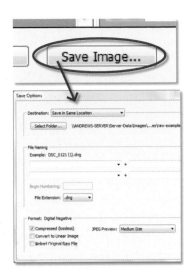

19. Saving the processed raw file

Users also have the ability to save converted raw files from inside the ACR dialog via the Save Image button. This action opens the Save Options dialog which contains settings for inputting the file name as well as file type specific characteristics such as compression. Use the Save option over the Open command if you want to process photos quickly without bringing them into the editing space.

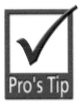

Pro's tip: Holding down the Alt/Option key whilst clicking the Save button allows you to store the file (with the raw processing settings applied) without actually going through the Save Options dialog.

20. Applying the raw conversion settings

There is also an option for applying the current settings to the raw photo without opening the picture. By Clicking the Done button (or Alt-clicking the OK button – holding down Alt/Option key changes the button to the Update button in previous versions of the dialog) you can apply the changes to the original file and close the ACR dialog in one step.

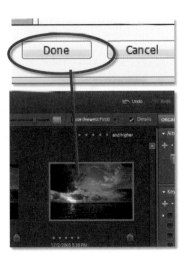

The great thing about working this way is that the settings are applied to the file losslessly. No changes are made to the underlying pixels, only to the instructions that are used to process the raw file.

When next the file is opened, the applied settings will show up in the ACR dialog ready for fine-tuning, or even changing completely.

Raw file queue

The thumbnail section of the Photoshop Elements ACR dialog appears when you select multiple raw files inside the Organizer workspace and then choose the Full Edit option from the right-click menu. The selected files are opened into the ACR dialog and listed on the left-hand side of the main workspace. This function first appeared in Photoshop Elements 6.

In general, only one image can be selected from the grouping, and displayed in the preview area, at a time. All changes made to the image settings are applied to the selected photo only. Users can move from image to image making the necessary enhancements before clicking the Done key to apply the changes without transferring the files, or the Open key to display the converted pictures in the Full edit workspace. But this is not the only way to work with the files. The Select All button at the top of the queued files can be employed for a more efficient workflow. Queued images can also be multi-selected by Shift-clicking or Ctrl-clicking the thumbnails. With this feature, enhancement changes made to a single photo can be applied across the whole range of images queued in the dialog.

Applying changes across rated raw files

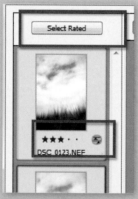
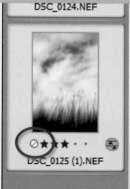

1. In addition to being able to apply image changes across all the queued files by choosing the Select All button, it is also possible to adjust just a subset of the files listed. Start by reviewing each of the queued files in turn by clicking onto the thumbnail on the left of the dialog.

2. During the review process rate those files that you want to adjust as a group. Do this by clicking the star rating section located under each thumbnail.

3. Once the review process is completed and all files to be enhanced as a group are rated hold down the Alt key and choose the Select Rated button at the top of the queued list. Notice that this action selects only those files with a star rating attached.

4. Now you can set about applying the changes to those selected as before.

5. If you want to remove an image from the Rated grouping simply click on the No Rating option under the thumbnail.

Applying changes across multiple raw files

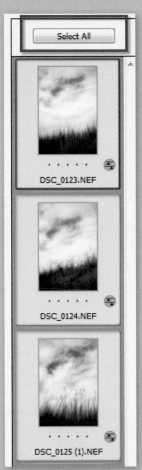

1. For best results, start by multi-selecting files from the Organizer space that have similar characteristics or were shot under the same lighting conditions.

2. Next, open the pictures in ACR by selecting one of the editing options from the right-click menu.

3. Now select a single photo from the queue that is indicative in tone and color of the whole group. With this photo displayed in the preview area, choose the Select All option from the top of the dialog.

4. Proceed to make enhancement changes to the previewed files as you would normally. Notice that these changes are also applied to the other photos in the queue.

5. The changes made to all the photos can then be fine-tuned to suit the characteristics of individual images (if needed) by selecting each picture in turn and adjusting the controls.

6. If no changes for individual files are necessary, then the selected photos can be saved, using the Save Images button, transferred to the Edit workspace with the Open Images option, or the enhancement settings applied by clicking the Done button.

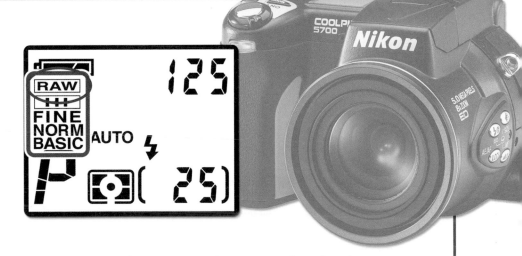

Figure 6.4 *If you want the best quality pictures always make sure that your scanner or camera captures in 16 bit per channel or 48-bit mode. On most cameras this is referred to as the 'TIFF' or 'Raw' setting.*

Color depth or 'What do you mean 8 bits per channel?'

Each digital file you create (capture or scan) is capable of representing a specific number of colors. This capability, usually referred to as the 'mode' or 'color depth' of the picture, is expressed in terms of the number of 'bits'. Most photos these days are created in 24-bit mode. This means that each of the three color channels (Red, Green and Blue) is capable of displaying 256 levels of color (or 8 bits per channel). When the three channels are combined, a 24-bit image can contain a staggering 16.7 million separate tones/hues.

This is a vast amount of colors and would be seemingly more than we could ever need, see or print, but many modern cameras and scanners are now capable of capturing up to 16 bits per channel or 'high-bit' capture in either raw or TIFF file formats. This means that each of the three colors can have as many as 65,536 different levels and the image itself, with all three channels combined, a whopping 281,474,976 million colors (last time I counted!). But why would we need to capture so many colors? See Figures 6.5 and 6.6.

More colors equals better quality

Most readers would already have a vague feeling that a high-bit file (16 bits per channel) is 'better' than a low-bit (8 bits per channel) alternative, but understanding why is critical for ensuring the best quality in your own work.

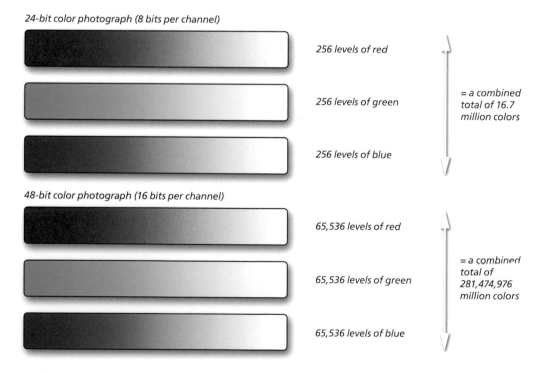

24-bit color photograph (8 bits per channel)

256 levels of red

256 levels of green

256 levels of blue

= a combined total of 16.7 million colors

48-bit color photograph (16 bits per channel)

65,536 levels of red

65,536 levels of green

65,536 levels of blue

= a combined total of 281,474,976 million colors

Figure 6.5 *The higher the bit depth of an image the more levels of tone and numbers of colors it can display.*

Here are the main advantages in a nutshell:

16-BIT OR HIGH-BIT ADVANTAGES

1 Capturing images in high-bit mode provides a larger number of colors for your camera or scanner to construct your image with. This in turn leads to better color and tone in the digital version of the continuous tone original or scene.

2 Global editing and enhancement changes made to a high-bit file will always yield a better quality result than when the same changes are applied to a low-bit image.

3 Major enhancement of the shadow and highlight areas in a high-bit image is less likely to produce posterized tones than if the same actions were applied to a low-bit version.

4 More gradual changes and subtle variations are possible when adjusting the tones of a high-bit photograph, using tools like Levels, than is possible with low-bit images.

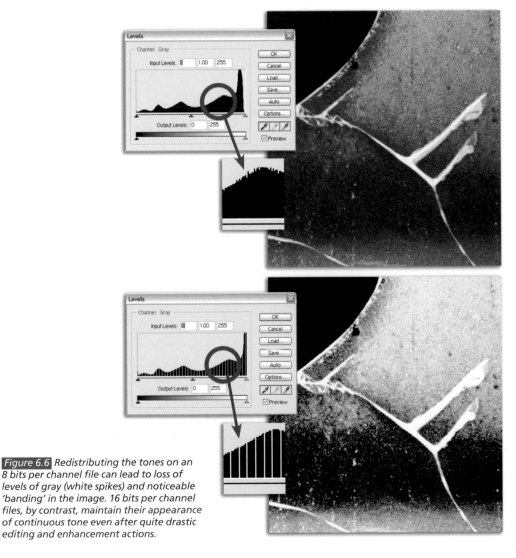

Figure 6.6 Redistributing the tones on an 8 bits per channel file can lead to loss of levels of gray (white spikes) and noticeable 'banding' in the image. 16 bits per channel files, by contrast, maintain their appearance of continuous tone even after quite drastic editing and enhancement actions.

Photoshop Elements is 16-bit enabled

But why all this talk about 16 bits per channel files (48-bit color in total)? Well, since the version 3.0 release of Elements the program has been 16-bit enabled. This means that if you have a camera or scanner that is capable of capturing in this mode you can now take advantage of the extra color and tone it provides. 'Fantastic!' you say. 'No more 8 bits per channel (24-bit image) tweaking for me, I'm a 16 bits per channel fanatic from here on in.' But there is a catch (you knew there had to be).

Despite the power and sophistication of Elements, only a subset of its features is available for working on 16-bit files. Of the tools, the Rectangular and Elliptical Marquee and Lasso, Eyedropper, Move, Crop and Zoom tools all function in this mode. In addition, you can rotate, resize, apply auto levels, auto contrast or auto color correct or use more manual controls such as Levels, Shadows/Highlights and Brightness/Contrast features. The Sharpen, Noise, Blur and Adjustment filter groups also work here. Does this mean that making enhancement changes in 16-bit mode is unworkable? No, you just need to use a different approach. Read on.

Global versus local enhancement

Because of the limitations when working with a 16 bits per channel file in Elements, some digital photographers break their enhancement tasks into two different sections – global and local.

Global, or those changes that are applied at the beginning of the process to the whole picture. These include general brightness and contrast changes, some color correction and the application of a little sharpening.

Local changes are those that are more specific and are sometimes applied to just sections of the picture. They may include dodging and burning in, removal of unwanted dust and scratches, the addition of some text and the application of special effects filters.

This separation of enhancement tasks fits neatly with the way that the 16-bit support works in Photoshop Elements. Global changes can be applied to the photograph whilst it is still in 16-bit mode; the file can then be converted to 8 bits per channel (Image > Mode > 8 Bits/channel) and the local alterations applied. This is the process that the professionals have been using for years and now Elements gives you the power to follow suit.

Common high-bit misconceptions

1 Elements can't handle high-bit images. Not true. Previous versions of the program couldn't handle high-bit pictures but since Elements 3.0 the program has contained a reduced feature set that can be used with 16 bits per channel images. And even with this limitation there are enough features available to ensure quality enhancement of your images.

2 High-bit images are too big for me to handle and store. Yes, high-bit images are twice the file size of 8-bit pictures and this does slow down machines with limited resources but, if this is

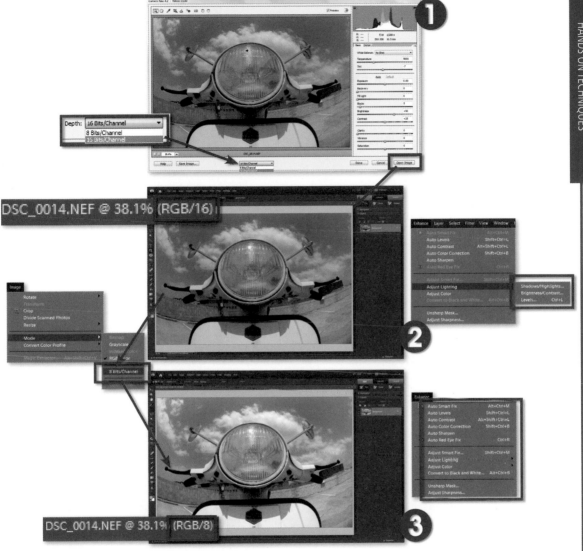

Figure 6.7 *Try to perform as many of your standard editing tasks on the 16-bit file as this will give you the best overall editing results. Once these changes have been made it is then time to convert the file to 8-bits per channel to finish your enhancement techniques. (1) Create 16-bit files from raw format pictures. (2) Perform all possible enhancement steps whilst the image is in 16-bit mode. (3) Convert to 8-bit mode and complete editing and enhancing the photo with tools and techniques that are only possible with 8-bit files.*

a concern, put up with the inconvenience of a slow machine whilst you make tonal and color changes then convert to a speedier 8-bit file for local changes.

3 I can't use my favorite tools and features in high-bit mode so I don't use high-bit images at all. You are losing quality in your images needlessly. Perform your global edits in 16-bit mode and then convert to 8-bit mode for the application of your favorite low-bit techniques. See Figure 6.7.

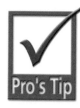

Ensure quality capture and enhancement with 16-bit and raw files

1 Capture all images in the highest color depth possible. This will help to ensure the best possible detail, tone and color in your pictures.

2 If you have a camera that can capture raw files then ensure that this feature is activated as well, as it provides the best quality files to work with.

Manual tonal control

The Brightness/Contrast feature that we looked at in the last chapter is a great way to start to change the tones in your images, but as your skill and confidence increase you might find that you want a little more control. Adobe included the Histogram feature and the Levels function from Photoshop in Elements for precisely this reason.

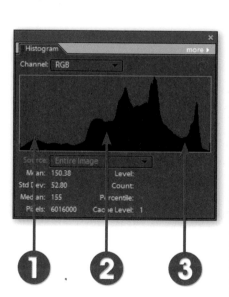

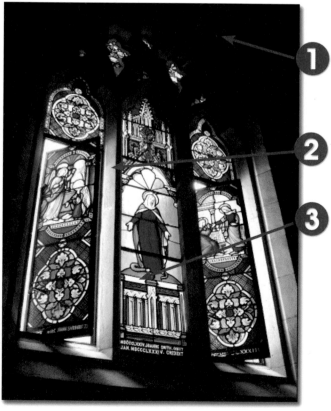

Figure 6.8 The Histogram provides graph-based information about the spread of pixel tones within your image so that you can see the number of pixels grouped in the shadows (1), midtones (2) and highlights (3) areas.

Editor: Window > Histogram

In version 6.0: Window > Histogram

The first step in taking charge of your pixels is to become aware of where they are situated in your image and how they are distributed between black and white points. The Histogram palette displays a graph of all the pixels in your image. The left-hand side represents the black values, the right the white end of the spectrum. As we already know, in a 24-bit image there are a total of 256 levels of tone possible from black to white – each of these values is represented on the graph. The number of pixels in the image with a particular brightness or tone value is displayed on the graph by height. See Figure 6.8.

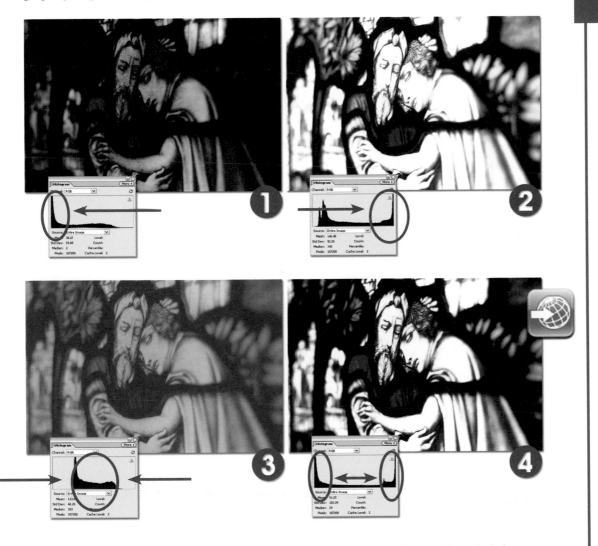

Figure 6.9 *You can diagnose the problems with your photos and predict the way that your picture looks by the shape of the graph in the Histogram palette and the Levels feature. (1) The pixels are bunched to the left end of the graph for underexposed images and (2) to the right end for overexposed ones. (3) Pixels are bunched together in the middle of the graph for flat images. (4) The pixels are spread right out to the left and right edges for contrast pictures.*

Knowing your images

After a little time viewing the histograms of your images, you will begin to see a pattern in the way that certain styles of photographs are represented. Overexposed pictures will display a large grouping of pixels to the right end of the graph, whereas underexposure will be represented by most pixels bunched to the left. Flat images or those taken on an overcast day will show all pixels grouped around the middle tones and contrasty pictures will display many pixels at the pure white and black ends of the spectrum. See Figure 6.9.

Previously in this book we have fixed these tonal problems by applying one of the automatic correction features, such as Auto Contrast or Auto Levels, found in Elements, or by using a simple slider control such as Brightness/Contrast. All of these tools remap the pixels so that they sit more evenly across the whole of the tonal range of the picture. Viewing the Histogram of a corrected picture will show you how the pixels have been redistributed. See Figure 6.10.

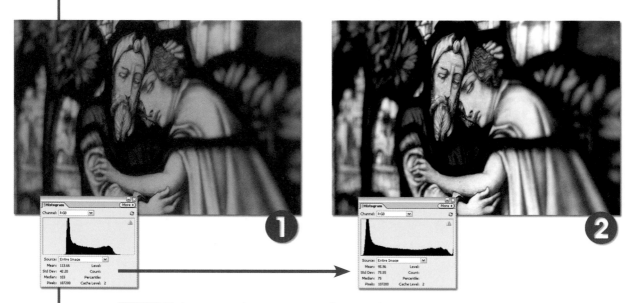

Figure 6.10 The Auto Levels or Auto Contrast feature redistributes pixels in the graph between the black and white points. (1) Before Auto Levels. (2) After Auto Levels.

Editor: Enhance > Adjust Lighting > Levels

In version 6.0: Enhance > Adjust Lighting > Levels

If you want to take more control of the process than is possible with the auto solutions, open the Levels dialog. Looking very similar to the Histogram, this feature allows you to interact directly with the pixels in your image. As well as a graph, the dialog contains two slider bars. The one directly beneath the graph has three triangular controls for black, midtones and white, and represents the input values of the picture. The slider at the bottom of the box shows output settings, and contains black and white controls only. See Figure 6.11.

Book resources and video tutorials can be found at **www.photoshopelements.net**

To adjust the pixels, drag the Input Shadow (left end) and Highlight (right end) controls until they meet the first set of pixels at either end of the graph. When you click OK, the pixels in the original image are redistributed using the new white and black points. Altering the Midtone control will change the brightness of the middle values of the image, and moving the output black and white points will flatten, or decrease, the contrast. Clicking the Auto button is like selecting Enhance > Auto Levels from the menu bar.

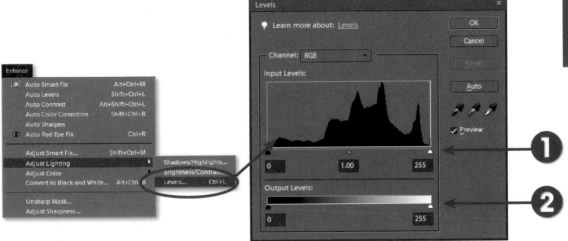

Figure 6.11 *The Levels control allows you to interactively control the spread of pixels within your image.*
(1) Input values. (2) Output values.

Pegging black and white points

On the right-hand side of the Levels dialog is a set of three Eyedropper buttons used for sampling the black, gray and white pixels in your image. Designed to give you ultimate control over the tones in your image, these tools are best used in conjunction with the Info palette (Window > Info). See Figure 6.12.

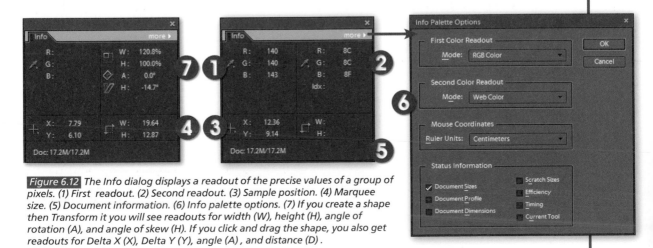

Figure 6.12 *The Info dialog displays a readout of the precise values of a group of pixels. (1) First readout. (2) Second readout. (3) Sample position. (4) Marquee size. (5) Document information. (6) Info palette options. (7) If you create a shape then Transform it you will see readouts for width (W), height (H), angle of rotation (A), and angle of skew (H). If you click and drag the shape, you also get readouts for Delta X (X), Delta Y (Y), angle (A), and distance (D).*

To use this technique, start by making sure that the Info palette is visible (Window > Info) and then select the black point eyedropper from the Levels dialog. Locate the darkest point in the picture by moving the dropper cursor over your image and watching the values in the Info palette. Your aim is to find the pixels with RGB values as close to 0 as possible. By clicking on the darkest area you will automatically set this point as black in your graph (and your picture). Next, select the white point eyedropper, locate the highest value and again click to set. With Highlight and Shadow values both pegged, all the values in the picture will be adjusted to suit. Note that the Info palette will show before and after values when making changes, for example 42/48 (before/after). When sampling white areas, you should avoid specular highlights such as the shine from the surface of a metallic object as these parts of the picture contain no printable details. See Figure 6.13.

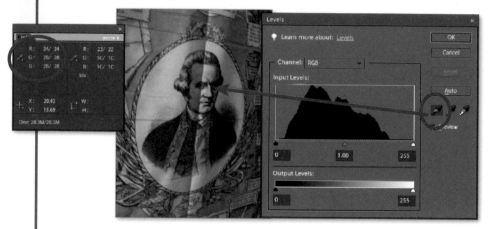

Figure 6.13 *With the aid of the details in the Info dialog locate the darkest and lightest points in your picture and peg these with the black and white point eyedroppers from the Levels feature.*

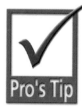

Color correction with the gray point eyedropper

The gray point eyedropper performs in a similar manner to the Color Cast command. With the tool selected, the user clicks on an area in the picture that should be a neutral gray. The color of the area is changed to neutral gray or equal amounts of red, green and blue, changing with it all the other pixels in the image. This tool is particularly useful for neutralizing color casts.

FEATURE SUMMARY

1 Select Window > Info.

2 Select Enhance > Adjust Lighting > Levels.

3 Peg highlights and shadow areas using the Levels' eyedropper tools and values in the Info palette.

4 Select OK to finish.

Make Levels changes in 16-bit mode

Levels changes can be performed and indeed should be performed when your photographs are in 16-bit mode. Adjusting your contrast and brightness here will give you much smoother gradation of tones and preserve more detail in your final picture.

Adjusting tones with Levels summary

Use the following guide to help you make tonal adjustments for your images using Levels:

1 *To increase contrast* – Move the Input black and white controls to meet the first group of pixels.

2 *To decrease contrast* – Move the Output black and white controls towards the center of the slider.

3 *To make middle values darker* – Move the Input midtone control to the right.

4 *To make middle values lighter* – Move the Input midtone control to the left.

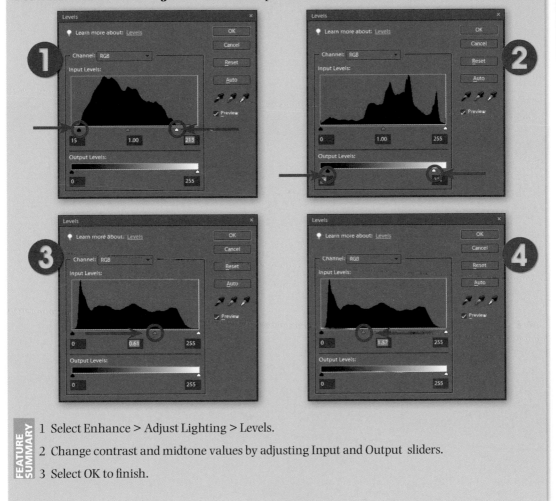

FEATURE SUMMARY

1 Select Enhance > Adjust Lighting > Levels.

2 Change contrast and midtone values by adjusting Input and Output sliders.

3 Select OK to finish.

Specialized color control

In traditional imaging it is very difficult to manipulate the hues in an image. Thankfully, this is not the case in digital picture making. Fine control over color intensity and location is an integral part of the new technology. Apart from the Variations and Color Cast features that we looked at in the last chapter, Elements also contains the Hue/Saturation command and the Auto Color feature.

Editor: Enhance > Auto Color Correction

In version 6.0: Enhance > Auto Color Correction

This feature works in a similar way to Auto Levels and Auto Contrast in that it identifies the shadows, midtones and highlights in an image and uses these as a basis for image changes. The feature adjusts the contrast of the image by remapping the shadows and highlights to black and white, and neutralizes any color casts by balancing the red, green and blue values in the picture's midtones. As with most Auto functions, this tool works well for the majority of images. For most users this is a good place to start to enhance and correct images, but for those occasions where Auto Color Correction produces poor results then my suggestion is to undo the automatic changes and rework the picture using either the Variations or Color Cast features. This option is also available in the Organizer's Fix panel. See Figure 6.14.

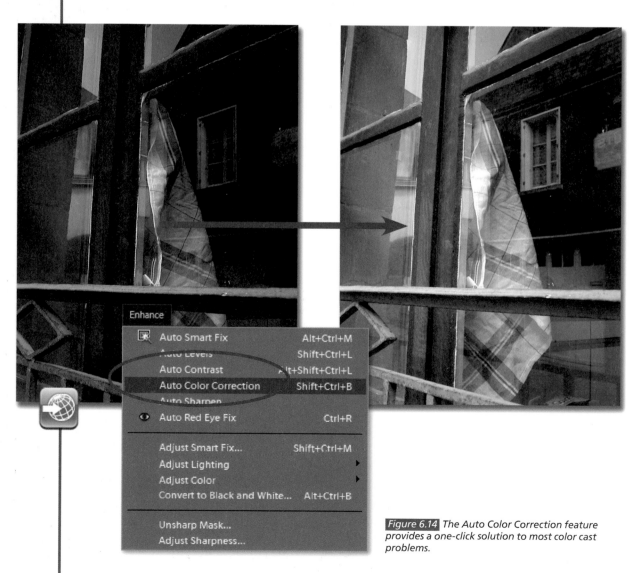

Figure 6.14 *The Auto Color Correction feature provides a one-click solution to most color cast problems.*

Editor: Enhance > Adjust Color > Adjust Hue/Saturation

In version 6.0: Enhance > Adjust Color > Hue/Saturation

To understand how this feature works you will need to think of the colors in your image in a slightly different way. Rather than using the three-color model (Red, Green, Blue) that we are familiar with, the Hue/Saturation control breaks the image into different components – Hue or color, Saturation or color strength, and Lightness (HSL). See Figure 6.15.

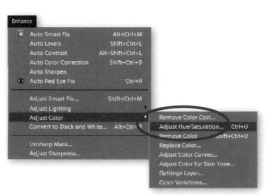 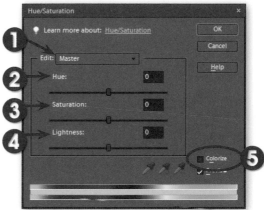

Figure 6.15 *The Hue/Saturation control provides control over the color within your image. (1) Target tones selected for adjustment. (2) Color slider. (3) Strength slider. (4) Lightness slider. (5) Colorize option.*

The dialog itself displays slider controls for each component, allowing the user to change each factor independently of the others. Moving the Hue control along the slider changes the dominant color of the image. From left to right, the hue's changes are represented in much the same way as colors in a rainbow. Alterations here will provide a variety of dramatic results, most of which are not realistic and should be used carefully. Moving the Saturation slider to the left gradually decreases the strength of the color until the image is reduced to just gray tones. In contrast, adjusting the control to the right increases the purity of the hue and produces images that are vibrant and dramatic. The Lightness slider changes the density of the image and works the same way as the Brightness slider in the Brightness/Contrast feature. You can use this feature to make slight adjustments when a color change darkens or lightens the midtones of the image, but more critical brightness changes should be made with the Levels feature.

By selecting the Colorize option and then moving the Hue control, it is possible to simulate sepia- or blue-toned prints. The option converts a colored image to a monochrome made up of a single dominant color and black and white. See Figure 6.16.

FEATURE SUMMARY

1 Select Enhance > Adjust Color > Hue/Saturation.

2 Select the Colorize option to make toned prints.

3 Change Hue, Saturation and Lightness by adjusting sliders.

4 Select OK to finish.

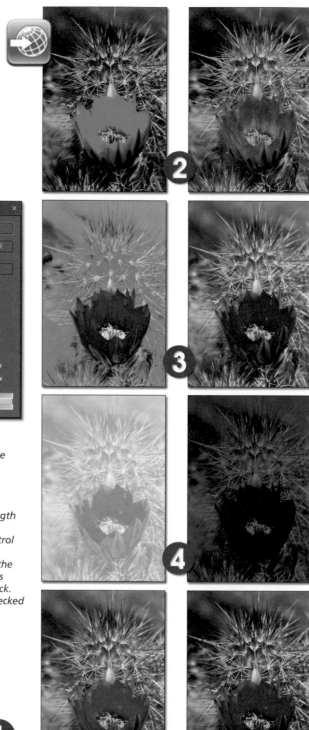

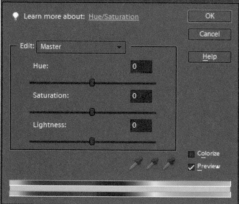

Figure 6.16 The Hue/Saturation feature provides you with the ability to change the color in your pictures in a variety of ways.
(1) Original picture.
(2) Moving the Hue slider changes the dominant colors in the image.
(3) The Saturation slider controls the strength or purity of colors in the picture.
(4) Movements of the Lightness slider control the brightness of the picture.
(5) Selecting the Colorize option changes the image to a monochrome, containing tones made up of one main color, white and black. Moving the Hue slider with this option checked produces 'toned' photographs.

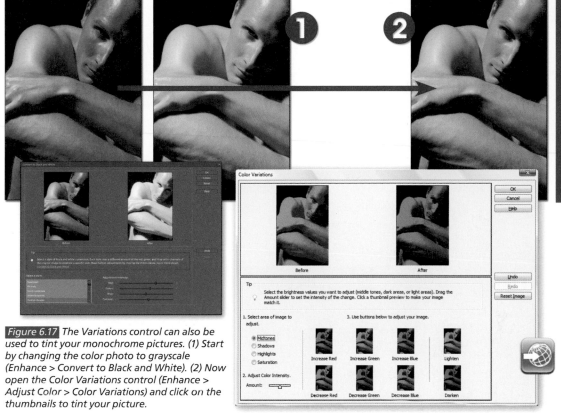

Figure 6.17 The Variations control can also be used to tint your monochrome pictures. (1) Start by changing the color photo to grayscale (Enhance > Convert to Black and White). (2) Now open the Color Variations control (Enhance > Adjust Color > Color Variations) and click on the thumbnails to tint your picture.

Editor: Enhance > Adjust Color > Color Variations

In version 6.0: Enhance > Adjust Color > Color Variations

The Variations command that we looked at in the last chapter can also be used to convert full color images to tinted monochromes. First, change your color image to grayscale using the brand new Enhance > Convert to Black and White feature. Your image will now appear to be a grayscale but the file is still in RGB mode so color can be added at any time. Open the Variations command (Enhance > Adjust Color > Color Variations) and tone your picture by clicking on the appropriate thumbnails. For some users this method might be a little easier to use than the Hue/Saturation command, as the results and color alternatives are previewed and laid out clearly. See Figure 6.17.

FEATURE SUMMARY

1 Open color image.

2 Select Enhance > Convert to Black and White using any of the Preset options.

3 Select Enhance > Adjust Color > Color Variations.

4 Adjust strength of the color changes using the Color Intensity slider.

5 Pick the thumbnails to change image color and check progress by viewing the Before and After thumbnails. Click OK to finish.

Editor: Enhance > Adjust Color > Adjust Color Curves

The Adjust Color Curves option provides another way that you can alter the brightness and contrast in your photo. Unlike the very basic Brightness/Contrast control, Adjust Color Curves provides separate controls for altering the brightness of highlights, shadows and midtones as well as a separate slider for changing midtone contrast. The feature has been revamped since its introduction in version 6.0 and now contains two separate sections – Style and Adjust Sliders. The features dialog contains both Before and After previews so that the effect of curve changes can be seen as you make them.

The **Style** area contains a series of preset curves settings for the most widely used enhancements, which include: Backlight, Darken Highlights, Default, Increase Contrast, Increase Midtone, Lighten Shadows, and Solarize.

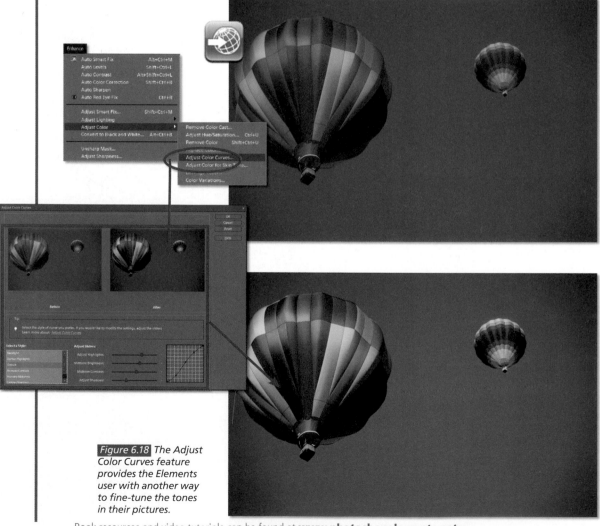

Figure 6.18 The Adjust Color Curves feature provides the Elements user with another way to fine-tune the tones in their pictures.

The **Adjust Sliders** section contains four slider controls plus a curves graph that plots the tonal relationships in the picture. Whereas the Samples thumbnails provided a one-click adjustment, the controls here allow multiple, additive, fine-tuning changes.

The best approach is to select a style of curve adjustment first, e.g. Lighten Shadows, and then fine-tune the results with the sliders. To reset the Curves feature back to its original position click the Default style entry or the Reset button in the top right of the dialog. See Figures 6.18 and 6.19.

FEATURE SUMMARY

1 Open color image and Select Enhance > Adjust Color > Adjust Color Curves.

2 Select the base curves adjustment style from the options on the left of the dialog.

3 Use the slider controls to fine-tune the results and then click OK to apply the changes or Reset to start again.

4 To reset the feature and remove any current adjustments click the Reset button.

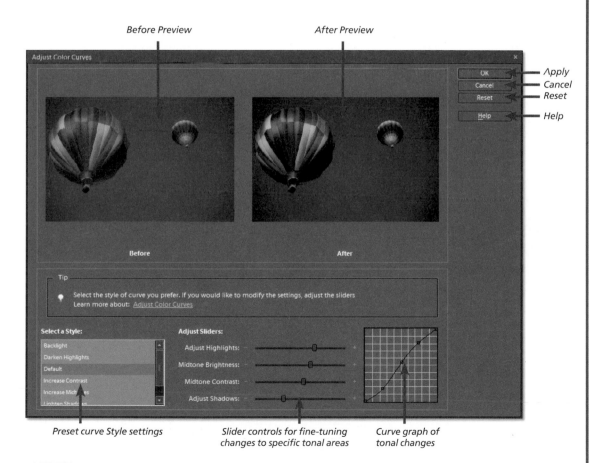

Before Preview   After Preview

Apply
Cancel
Reset
Help

Preset curve Style settings   Slider controls for fine-tuning changes to specific tonal areas   Curve graph of tonal changes

Figure 6.19 *The feature contains two different type of controls – thumbnail buttons for applying quick changes and sliders for fine-tuning the results.*

Sponge

It is possible to draw a viewer's attention to a particular part of an image by increasing its saturation. The difference in color (contrast) makes the saturated part of the picture a new focal point. The effect can be increased greatly by desaturating (reducing the color strength) the areas around the focal point. The Sponge tool is designed to make such saturation changes to the color within your photos. It can be used to saturate or desaturate and, in grayscale mode, it will even decrease or increase contrast. As with most other tools, size and mode can be changed in the options bar. Changing the Flow settings in the bar alters the rate at which the image saturates or desaturates. See Figure 6.20.

FEATURE SUMMARY

1 Pick the Sponge tool from the toolbox.

2 Select brush size, type and flow rate from the options bar.

3 Select the mode to use – Saturate or Desaturate.

4 Drag over the image part to change.

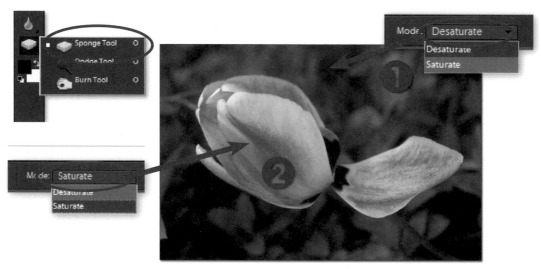

Figure 6.20 *The Sponge tool can be used to selectively increase or decrease the saturation of parts of the image. (1) Desaturate. (2) Saturate.*

Editor: Filter > Adjustments > Posterize

In version 6.0: Filter > Adjustments > Posterize

The Posterize feature reduces the number of color levels within an image. This produces a graphic design type illustration with areas of flat color from photographic originals. This type of image has very little graduation of tone; instead, it relies on the strength of the colors and shapes that make up the image for effect. The user inputs the number of tones for the images and Elements proceeds to reduce the total palette to the selected few. See Figure 6.21.

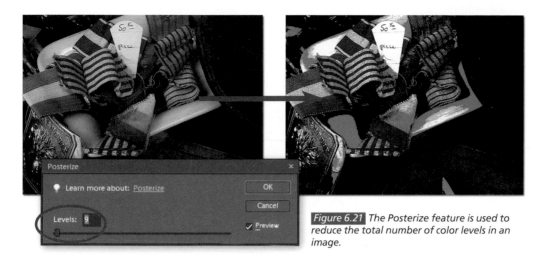

Figure 6.21 The Posterize feature is used to reduce the total number of color levels in an image.

FEATURE SUMMARY 1 Select Filter > Adjustments > Posterize.

2 Input the number of levels required.

3 Select OK to finish.

Editor: Filter > Adjustments > Invert

In version 6.0: Filter > Adjustments > Invert

The Invert command produces a negative version of your image. The feature literally swaps the values of each of the image tones. When used on a grayscale image the results are similar to a black and white negative. However, this is not true for a color picture as the inverted picture will not contain the typical orange 'mask' found in color negatives. See Figure 6.22.

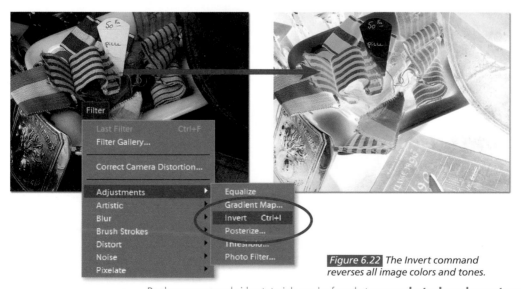

Figure 6.22 The Invert command reverses all image colors and tones.

Editor: Filter > Adjustments > Photo Filter

In version 6.0: Filter > Adjustments > Photo Filter

The Photo Filter was added to the feature line-up in Elements in version 3.0 after first appearing in the CS version of Photoshop. The tool applies a colored filter to your picture and simulates the effects that traditional photographers could achieve by screwing a colored piece of glass, or gel, to the front of their camera lenses. The change in color that this technique produces can be used for visual effect, such as making a cloudy day appear more sunny (by applying a warm-up filter) or to help correct color cast problems like those displayed in Figure 6.23. Here a Cooling Filter(82) is applied to the warm image to help eliminate the yellow cast.

Also included in the feature's dialog are areas for you to select the exact color of the filter applied, a Density slider that controls the strength of the filter, and the Preserve Luminosity check box which ensures that the overall tone of your picture doesn't darken or lighten with your filter changes.

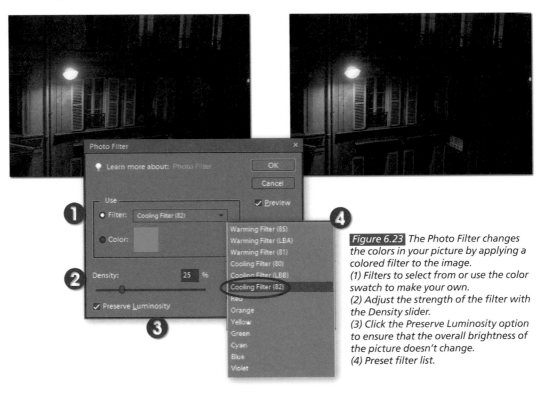

Figure 6.23 The Photo Filter changes the colors in your picture by applying a colored filter to the image.
(1) Filters to select from or use the color swatch to make your own.
(2) Adjust the strength of the filter with the Density slider.
(3) Click the Preserve Luminosity option to ensure that the overall brightness of the picture doesn't change.
(4) Preset filter list.

FEATURE SUMMARY

1 Select the Filter > Adjustments > Photo Filter.

2 Ensure that the Preview and Preserve Luminosity options are selected.

3 Pick the filter from the drop-down list or double-click the color swatch to pick the color more precisely.

4 Adjust the density of the filter to suit the image. Click OK to apply.

High quality sharpening techniques

Sometimes, during the image capture process, the picture loses some of the subject's original clarity. This can be especially true if you are scanning small prints or negatives at high resolutions. To help restore some of this lost clarity, it is a good idea to get into the habit of applying sharpening to images straight after capture (although ensure that your digital camera has not already done this as an automatic feature). I should say from the outset that although the specialist features in Elements will improve the appearance of sharpness in an image, it is not possible to use these tools to 'focus' a picture that is blurry. In short, sharpening won't fix problems that arise from poor camera technique; the only solution for this is ensuring that images are focused to start with. That said, let's get sharpening.

Adobe revamped the sharpening options offered in Elements 5.0. Whereas in previous releases all sharpening activity was based around the Filter menu, from version 5.0 the three sharpening options are grouped under the Enhance menu. The Unsharp Mask filter from previous releases is now joined with the Auto Sharpen and Adjust Sharpness features. These together with the specialized Sharpening tool provide a variety of methods for adding extra clarity to your pictures.

Editor: Enhance > Auto Sharpen
Version 4.0: Filter > Sharpen > Sharpen
Most digital sharpening techniques are based on increasing the contrast between adjacent pixels in the image. When viewed from a distance, this change makes the picture appear sharper. The new Auto Sharpen feature applies basic sharpening to the whole of the image. See Figure 6.24.

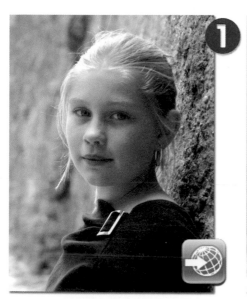
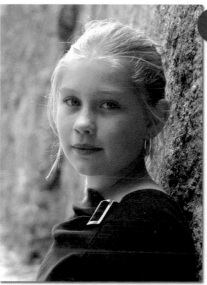

*Figure 6.24 The two basic sharpening filters provide automatic sharpening of all the pixels in your photographs.
(1) No sharpening.
(2) With Auto Sharpen applied.*

Editor: Enhance > Unsharp Mask

Version 4.0: Filter > Sharpen > Unsharp Mask

This feature is based on an old photographic technique for sharpening images that used a slightly blurry mask to increase edge clarity. The digital version offers the user control over the sharpening process via three sliders – Amount, Radius and Threshold. By careful manipulation of the settings of each control the sharpness of images destined for print or screen can be improved. Beware though – too much sharpening is very noticeable and produces problems in the image, such as edge haloes, that are very difficult to correct later. See Figure 6.25.

Before using the Unsharp Mask filter, make sure that you are viewing your image at 100%. If you intend to print the sharpened image, make test prints at different settings before deciding on the final values for each control. Repeat this exercise for any pictures where you want the best quality, as the settings for one file might not give the optimum results for another picture that has a slightly higher or lower resolution.

The Unsharp Mask controls

The **Amount** slider controls the strength of the sharpening effect. Values of 50–100% are suitable for low-resolution pictures, whereas settings between 150% and 200% can be used on images with a higher resolution. See Figure 6.26.

The **Radius** slider value determines the number of pixels around the edge that is affected by the sharpening. A low value only sharpens edge pixels. Typically, values between 1 and 2 are used for high-resolution images, and settings of 1 or less for screen images. See Figure 6.27.

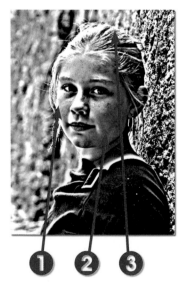

The **Threshold** slider is used to determine how different the pixels must be before they are considered an edge and therefore sharpened. A value of 0 will sharpen all the pixels in an image, whereas a setting of 10 will only apply the effect to those areas that are different by at least 10 levels or more from their surrounding pixels. To ensure that no sharpening occurs in sky or skin tone areas, set this value to 8 or more. See Figure 6.28.

1 Select Filter > Sharpen > Unsharp Mask.

2 Adjust Amount slider to control strength of filter.

3 Adjust Radius slider to control the number of pixels surrounding an edge that is included in the effect.

4 Adjust Threshold slider to control what pixels are considered edge and therefore sharpened.

FEATURE SUMMARY

Figure 6.25 Overuse of the Unsharp Mask filter can lead to irreversible problems.
(1) Too much contrast.
(2) Coarse skin tones.
(3) Haloes.

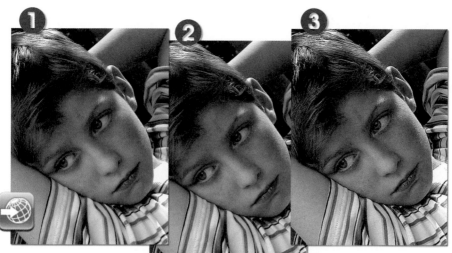

Figure 6.26
The Amount slider controls the strength of the sharpening effect.
(1) Amount = 50%.
(2) Amount = 150%.
(3) Amount = 500%.

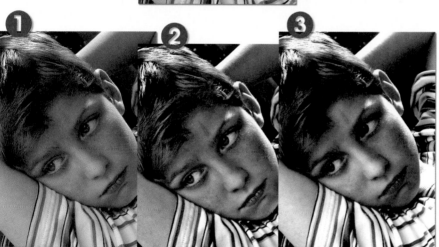

Figure 6.27
The Radius slider determines the number of edge pixels that are sharpened.
(1) Radius = 1.0 pixels.
(2) Radius = 20 pixels.
(3) Radius = 250 pixels.

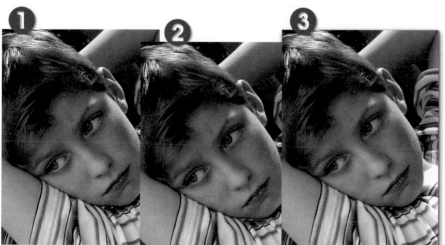

Figure 6.28
The Threshold slider controls the point at which the effect is applied.
(1) Threshold = 0 levels.
(2) Threshold = 8 levels.
(3) Threshold = 100 levels.

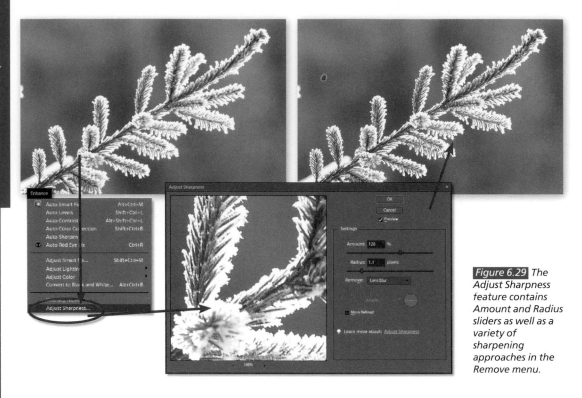

Figure 6.29 The Adjust Sharpness feature contains Amount and Radius sliders as well as a variety of sharpening approaches in the Remove menu.

Editor: Enhance > Adjust Sharpness

The Adjust Sharpen feature provides all the control that we are familiar with in the Unsharp Mask dialog plus better edge detection abilities, which leads to better results and in particular less apparent sharpening haloes. The feature's dialog contains a zoomable preview, two slider controls, a drop-down menu to choose the sharpening approach used and a More Refined option. See Figure 6.29.

The user can control the sharpening effect with the following settings:

Amount – Strength of sharpening effect.

Radius – Determines the extent of sharpening. Higher values equal more obvious edge effects.

Remove – Determines sharpening algorithm used. Gaussian Blur uses the same approach as the Unsharp Mask filter. Lens Blur concentrates on sharpening details and produces results with fewer haloes. Motion Blur reduces the effects of blur caused by camera shake or subject movement.

Angle – Sets Motion Blur direction.

More Refined – Longer processing for better results.

For best results, choose the Remove setting first. The Lens Blur option provides a good balance between sharpening effects and minimal sharpening artifacts. Enlarge the preview to at least 100%. Next, select a low Radius value – 1 or 2 for high-resolution images and 1 or less for low-resolution photos. Now gradually move the Amount slider from left to right, stopping occasionally to check the results of the sharpening. When you reach a setting that provides good sharpening, but doesn't create halo artifacts, click OK to apply.

To see the results of your sharpening being reflected in the Elements document itself, make sure that the Preview option is selected.

Applying sharpening makes permanent and irreversible changes to your photos so it is always a good idea to keep an unsharpened copy of your image as an original.

Elements' sharpening tools

In addition to using a filter to sharpen your image, it is also possible to make changes to specific areas of the picture using one of the two sharpening tools available. The Blur and Sharpen tools are located in the Elements toolbox. See Figure 6.30.

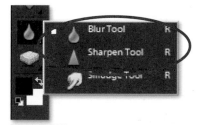

Figure 6.30 The Blur and Sharpen tools can be used to apply sharpening to specific areas within an image.

The size of the area they change is based on the current brush size. The intensity of the effect is controlled by the Strength value found in the options bar.

As with the Airbrush tool, the longer you keep the mouse button down the more pronounced the effect will be. These features are particularly useful when you want to change only small parts of an image rather than the whole picture. See Figure 6.31.

1 Select the Blur or Sharpen tool from the toolbox.

2 Adjust the size and style of the tool with the Brush palette in the options bar.

3 Change the intensity of the effect by altering the Strength setting.

4 Blur or sharpen areas of the image by clicking and dragging the tool over the picture surface.

5 Increase the change in any one area by holding the mouse button down.

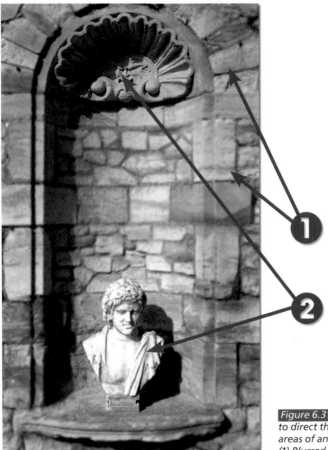

Figure 6.31 The Sharpen/Blur tools can be used to direct the eye of the viewer by making some areas of an image more prominent than others. (1) Blurred area. (2) Sharpened area.

Retouching techniques

Used for more than just enhancing existing details, these techniques are designed to rid images of visual information, like dust and scratches, which can distract from the main picture.

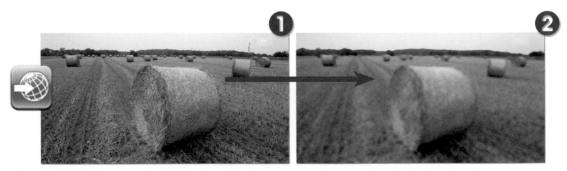

Figure 6.32 Too much Dust & Scratches filtering can destroy image detail and make the picture fuzzy. (1) Original picture. (2) Photo after too much Dust & Scratches filtration.

Editor: Filter > Noise > Dust & Scratches

In version 6.0: Filter > Noise > Dust & Scratches

It seems that no matter how careful I am, my scanned images always contain a few dust marks. The Dust & Scratches filter in Elements helps to eliminate these annoying spots by blending or blurring the surrounding pixels to cover the defect. The settings you choose for this filter are critical if you are to maintain image sharpness whilst removing small marks. Too much filtering and your image will appear blurred, too little and the marks will remain. See Figure 6.32.

To find settings that provide a good balance, first try adjusting the Threshold setting to zero. Next, use the Preview box in the Filter dialog to highlight a mark that you want to remove. Use the zoom controls to enlarge the view of the defect. Now drag the Radius slider to the right. Find, and set, the lowest Radius value where the mark is removed. Next, increase the Threshold value gradually until the texture of the image is restored and the defect is still removed. See Figure 6.33.

FEATURE SUMMARY

1 Select Filter > Noise > Dust & Scratches.

2 Move preview area to highlight a mark to be removed.

3 Zoom the preview to enlarge the view of the mark.

4 Ensure that the Threshold value is set to zero.

5 Adjust the Radius slider until the mark disappears.

6 Adjust Threshold until texture returns and the mark is still not visible.

7 Click OK to finish.

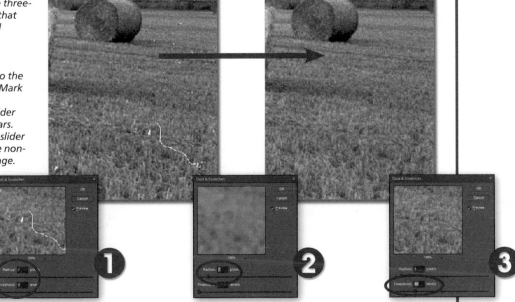

Figure 6.33 Follow the three-step process to ensure that you choose the optimal settings for the Dust & Scratches filter.
(1) Set both sliders to minimum (all the way to the left). Preview the Dust Mark area.
(2) Adjust the Radius slider until the mark disappears.
(3) Raise the Threshold slider to regain texture in the non-marked area of the image.

Clone Stamp

In some instances the values needed for the Dust & Scratches filter to erase or disguise picture faults are so high that it makes the whole image too blurry for use. In these cases it is better to use a tool that works with the problem area specifically rather than the whole picture surface.

The Clone Stamp tool samples an area of the image and then paints with the texture, color and tone of this copy onto another part of the picture. This process makes it a great tool to use for removing scratches or repairing tears or creases in a photograph. Backgrounds can be sampled and then painted over dust or scratch marks, and whole areas of a picture, can be rebuilt or reconstructed using the information contained in other parts of the image. See Figure 6.34.

Using the Clone Stamp tool is a two-part process. The first step is to select the area that you are going to use as a sample by Alt-clicking the area. See Figure 6.35. Now move the cursor to where you want to paint, and click and drag to start the process. See Figure 6.36.

The size and style of the sampled area are based on the current brush and the Opacity setting controls the transparency of the painted section.

FEATURE SUMMARY

1 Pick the Clone Stamp tool from the toolbox.

2 Adjust the brush size via the Brush palette in the options bar.

3 Set the opacity for the painted area.

4 Position the mouse cursor on a part of the image you want to sample and Alt-click.

5 Move the tool to the area of the image you want to use the sample to cover and click and drag to paint.

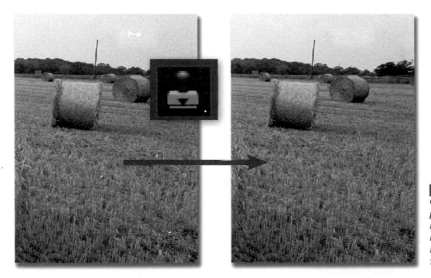

Figure 6.34 The Clone Stamp tool is perfect for retouching the marks that the Dust & Scratches filter cannot erase.

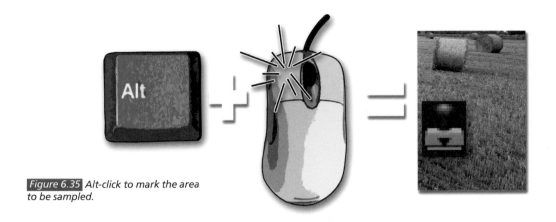

Figure 6.35 *Alt-click to mark the area to be sampled.*

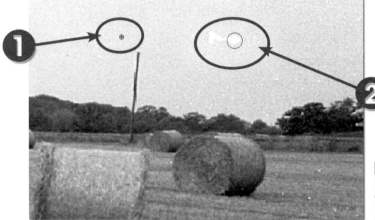

Figure 6.36 *Move the cursor over the mark and click to paint over with the sampled texture. (1) Sample point. (2) Retouching area.*

Spot Healing Brush

In recognition of just how tricky it can be to get seamless dust removal with the Clone Stamp tool, Adobe decided to include the Spot Healing Brush in Elements. After selecting the tool you adjust the size of the brush tip using the options in the tool's option bar and then click on the dust spots and small marks in your pictures. The Spot Healing Brush uses the texture that surrounds the mark as a guide to how the program should 'paint over' the area. In this way, Elements tries to match color, texture and tone whilst eliminating the dust mark. The results are terrific and this tool should be the one that you reach for first when there is a piece of dust or a hair mark to remove from your photographs. See Figure 6.37.

FEATURE SUMMARY

1 Locate the areas to be repaired.

2 Adjust the brush size to suit the size of the mark.

3 Click on the spot to repair.

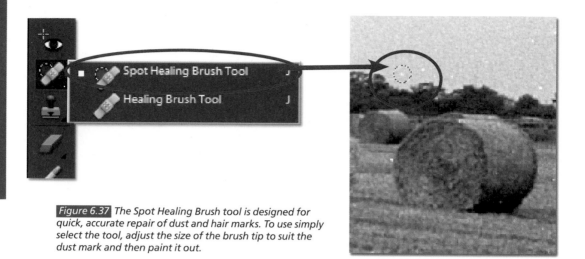

Figure 6.37 *The Spot Healing Brush tool is designed for quick, accurate repair of dust and hair marks. To use simply select the tool, adjust the size of the brush tip to suit the dust mark and then paint it out.*

Healing Brush tool

The Clone Stamp tool is good, but the best way to remove unwanted detail from your pictures is with the amazing Healing Brush tool. Designed to work in a similar way to the Clone Stamp tool, the user selects the area (Alt-click) to be sampled before painting and then proceeds to drag the brush tip over the area to be repaired. The tool achieves such great results by merging background and source area details as you paint. Just as with the Clone Stamp tool the size and edge hardness of the current brush determine the characteristics of the Healing Brush tool tip.

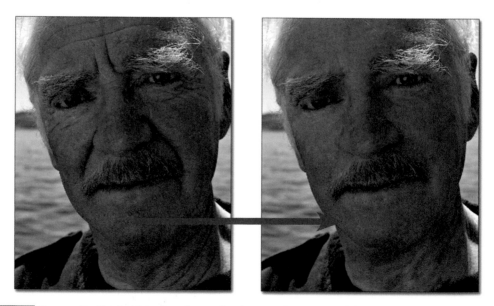

Figure 6.38 *The new Healing Brush tool works wonders for removing unwanted details. It can even provide a little digital plastic surgery when required.*

One of the best ways to demonstrate the sheer power of the Healing Brush is to remove the wrinkles from an aged face. Though I'm not sure of the ethics of such an action it is a request that is often put to me. In Figure 6.38, the deep crevices of the fisherman's face have been easily removed with the tool. The texture, color and tone of the face remain even after the 'healing' work is completed because the tool merges the new areas with the detail of the picture beneath.

FEATURE SUMMARY

1 The first step is to locate the areas of the image that need to be retouched.

2 Hold down the Alt key and click on the area that will be used as a sample for the brush. Notice that the cursor changes to cross hairs to indicate the sample area.

3 Move the cursor to the area to heal and click and drag the mouse to 'paint' over the problem picture part. After you release the mouse button Elements merges the newly painted section with the image beneath. See Figure 6.39.

You can remove wrinkles on a duplicate layer and then fade the opacity of this layer to create a more natural appearance, where wrinkles are softened and not completely removed.

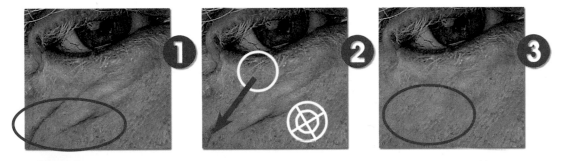

Figure 6.39 (1) Locate the areas to be healed. (2) Alt-click the source that you will use in the repairs. (3) Drag the brush tip over the area to be repaired.

Editor: Filter > Noise > Reduce Noise

In version 6.0: Filter > Noise > Reduce Noise

Many new digital cameras have a variety of ISO settings to choose from. When shooting in sunny or bright conditions you generally use values of 100 or 200, giving sharp and noise-free results, but when you select a higher value such as 1600 for use at night, or in low light, the resultant pictures can become very noisy. Camera manufacturers often include Noise Reduction features as part of the camera functions but sometimes the length of time the camera takes to process the file means that it is almost impossible to take a series of night-time pictures rapidly. If this is your requirement then you are stuck with grainy photographs because you have had to shoot with the Noise Reduction feature turned off.

With just this sort of problem in mind, the Adobe engineers included a new Noise Reduction filter (Filter > Noise > Reduce Noise) in version 3.0 of Elements. The feature includes a preview window, a Strength slider, a Preserve Details control and a Reduce Color Noise slider. As with the Dust & Scratches filter you need to be careful when using this filter to ensure that you balance removing noise whilst also retaining detail.

The best way to guarantee this is to set your Strength setting first, ensuring that you check the results in highlights, midtone and shadow areas. Next, gradually increase the Preserve Details value until you reach the point where the level of noise that is being reintroduced into the picture is noticeable and then back off the control slightly (make the setting a lower number). For photographs with a high level of color noise (random speckles of color in an area that should be a smooth flat tone) you will need to adjust this slider at the same time as you are playing with the Strength control. See Figure 6.40.

FEATURE SUMMARY

1 Open the noisy image and select the Filter > Noise > Reduce Noise filter.

2 Drag the Preserve Details slider to the left and then gradually move the Strength slider to the right until the noise is at an acceptable level.

3 Now slowly move the Preserve Details slider to the right until there is an acceptable balance between detail and noise in your picture.

4 To reduce the appearance of JPEG compression select the Remove JPEG Artifact check box in the feature's dialog.

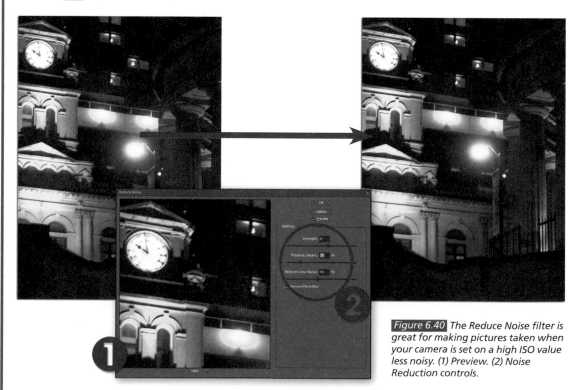

Figure 6.40 The Reduce Noise filter is great for making pictures taken when your camera is set on a high ISO value less noisy. (1) Preview. (2) Noise Reduction controls.

Adding texture to an image

At first, the idea of making a smooth, evenly graduated image more textured seems to be at odds with the general direction that digital technology has been heading over the last few years. Research scientists and technicians have spent much time and money ensuring that the current crop of cameras, scanners and printers is able to capture and produce images so that they are in effect textureless or grainless. The aim has been to disguise the origins of the final print so that the pixels cannot be seen.

For me to introduce to you at this stage a few techniques that intentionally add noticeable texture to your image may seem a little strange but, despite the intentions of the manufacturers, many digital image makers do like the atmosphere and mood that a 'grainy' picture conveys. See Figure 6.41. All the techniques use filters to alter the look of the image. Filter changes are permanent, so it is always a good idea to keep a copy of the unaltered original file on your hard drive, just in case.

Editor: Filter > Noise > Add Noise

In version 6.0: Filter > Noise > Add Noise
The Add Noise filter is one of four options contained under the Noise heading in the Filter menu. Using this feature adds extra contrasting pixels to your image to simulate the effect of high-speed film. See Figure 6.42. When the filter is selected, you are presented with a dialog that contains several choices. A small zoomable thumbnail window is provided so that you can check the appearance of the filter settings on your image. There is also the option to preview the results on the greater image by ticking the Preview box. The strength of the effect is controlled by the Amount slider and the type of noise can be switched from Uniform, a more even effect, to Gaussian, for a speckled appearance. The Monochromatic option adds pixels that contrast in tone only and not color to the image. See Figure 6.43.

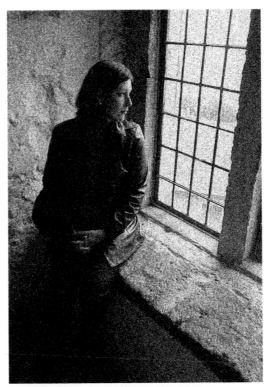

Figure 6.41 *Despite all the techniques in the previous section, which were designed to reduce the marks in our pictures, there are many photographers who like texture and who regularly use other techniques to intentionally put back desirable textures into their photographs.*

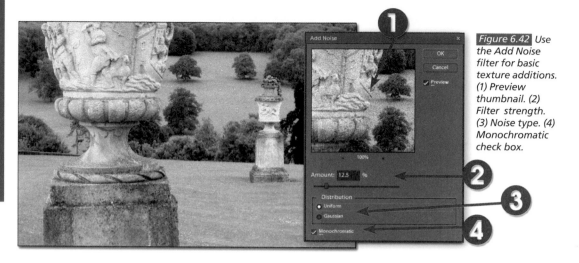

Figure 6.42 Use the Add Noise filter for basic texture additions. (1) Preview thumbnail. (2) Filter strength. (3) Noise type. (4) Monochromatic check box.

FEATURE SUMMARY

1 Select the Add Noise filter from the Noise section of the Filter menu.

2 Adjust thumbnail preview to a view of 100% and tick the Preview option.

3 Select Uniform for an even distribution of new pixels across the image, or pick Gaussian for a more speckled effect.

4 Tick the Monochromatic option to restrict the effect to changes in the tone of pixels rather than color.

5 Adjust the Amount slider to control the strength of the filter, checking the results in both the thumbnail and full image previews.

6 Click OK to finish.

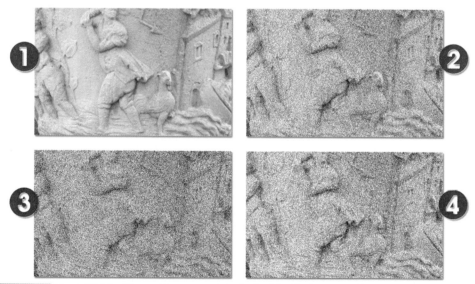

Figure 6.43 The Add Noise filter settings control the look of the final texture. (1) Original non-filtered picture. (2) Uniform Distribution selected. (3) Gaussian Distribution selected. (4) Uniform Distribution and Monochrome setting selected.

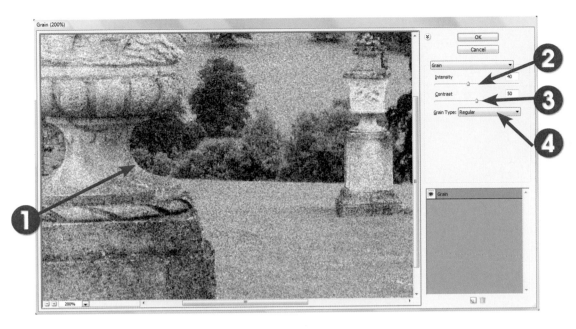

Figure 6.44 The Grain filter provides a little more control over the type of texture that is added to your images. (1) Preview thumbnail. (2) Filter strength. (3) Effect contrast. (4) Grain style.

Editor: Filter > Texture > Grain

In version 6.0: Filter > Texture > Grain

Found under the Texture option in the Filter menu, the Grain filter, at first glance, appears to offer the same style of texture changes as the Add Noise feature, but the extra controls in the dialog give users the chance to add a range of different texture types to their images. See Figure 6.44.

The dialog provides a thumbnail preview of filter changes. The Intensity slider controls the strength of the effect and the Contrast control alters the overall appearance of the filtered image. The Grain Type menu provides 10 different choices of the style of texture that will be added to the image. By manipulating these three settings, it is possible to create some quite different and stunning texture effects. See Figure 6.45.

FEATURE SUMMARY

1 Select the Grain filter from the Texture section of the Filter menu.

2 Adjust thumbnail preview to a view of 100%.

3 Select Grain Type from the menu.

4 Adjust the Intensity slider to control the strength of the filter, checking the results in the thumbnail preview.

5 Alter the Contrast slider to change the overall appearance of the image.

6 Click OK to finish.

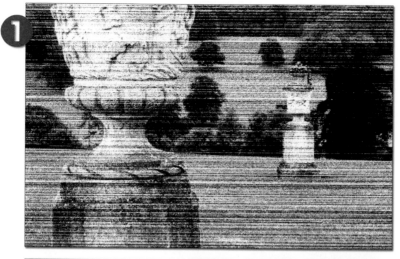

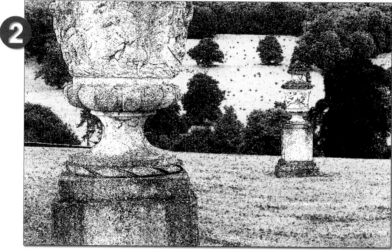

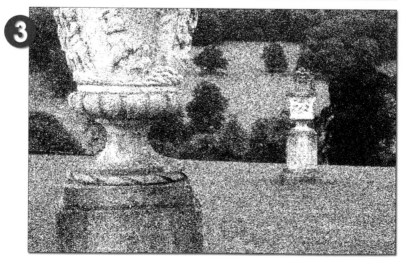

Figure 6.45 The Grain
filter with a range of
options selected.
(1) Horizontal option set.
(2) Speckle option set.
(3) Stippled option set.

Book resources and video tutorials can be found at **www.photoshopelements.net**

Editor: Filter > Texture > Texturizer

In version 6.0: Filter > Texture > Texturizer

The Texturizer filter provides a slightly different approach to the process of adding textures to images. With this feature much more of the original image detail is maintained. The picture is changed to give the appearance that the photo has been printed onto the surface of the texture. The Scaling and Relief sliders control the strength and visual dominance of the texture, whilst the Light direction menu alters the highlight and shadow areas. See Figure 6.46. Different surface types are available from the Texture drop-down menu. See Figure 6.47. The feature also contains the option to add your own files and have these used as the texture that is applied by the filter to the image.

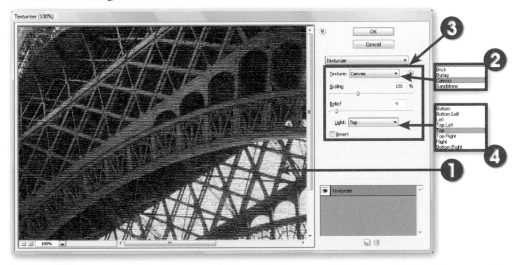

Figure 6.46 The Texturizer filter changes the image so that It appears to have been printed onto a textured surface. (1) Preview thumbnail. (2) Texture type. (3) Texture settings. (4) Light direction.

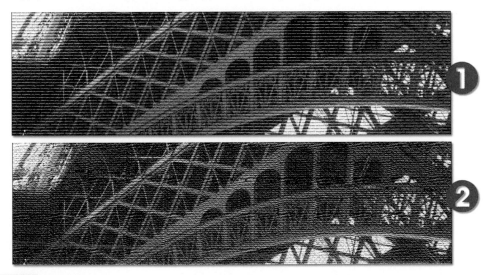

Figure 6.47 The example is textured using the Texturizer filter with (1) Brick surface selected and (2) Burlap surface selected.

1 Select the Texturizer filter from the Texture section of the Filter menu.

2 Adjust thumbnail preview to a view of 100%.

3 Select texture type from the drop-down menu.

4 Move the Scaling slider to change the size of the texture.

5 Adjust the Relief slider to control the dominance of the filter.

6 Select a Light direction to adjust the highlights and shadow areas of the texture.

7 Tick the Invert box to switch the texture position from 'hills' to 'valleys' or reverse the texture's light and dark tones.

8 Click OK to finish.

Making your own textures

Being able to make your own texture files is the real bonus of the Texturizer filter. This ability gives the user the chance to extend the available surface options by adding customized Elements files that have been designed, or captured, especially for the purpose. Any Elements or Photoshop file (.PSD) can be loaded as a new texture via the Load Texture option in the side-arrow menu, in the top right of the Texturizer dialog. Simply locate the file using the browsing window and then adjust the Scaling, Relief and Lighting controls as you would for any of the built-in surface options.

1 Shoot, scan or design a texture image and save as an Elements or Photoshop file (.PSD). See Figure 6.48.

2 Select the Texturizer filter from the Texture options of the Filter menu.

3 Pick the Load Texture item from the drop-down list in the Texture menu. See Figure 6.49.

4 Browse folders and files to locate texture file.

5 Click File name and then Open to select.

6 Once back at the Texturizer dialog, treat like any other surface option. See Figure 6.50.

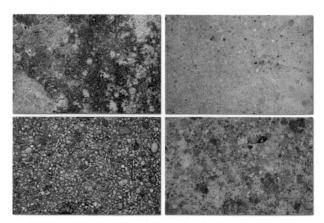

Figure 6.48 Shoot your own texture photos and save the images as an Elements or PSD file.

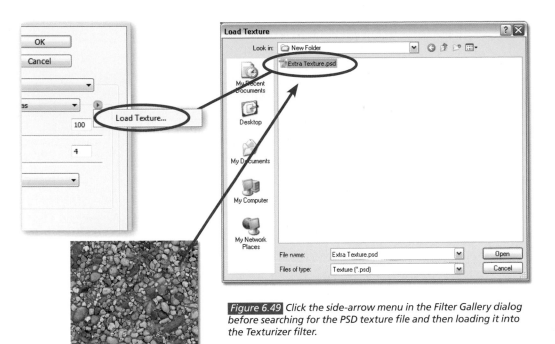

Figure 6.49 Click the side-arrow menu in the Filter Gallery dialog before searching for the PSD texture file and then loading it into the Texturizer filter.

Figure 6.50 Apply the new texture to your image.

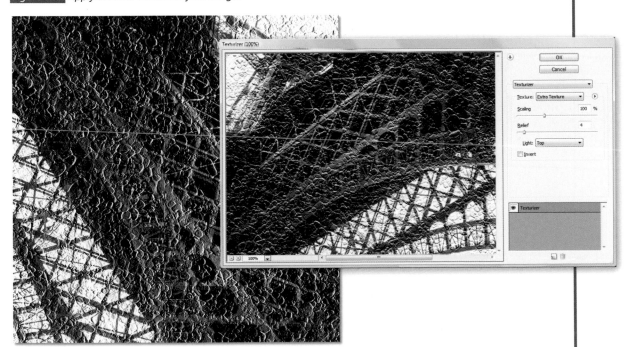

Changing the size of your images

As we have seen in earlier chapters, the size of a digital image is measured in pixel dimensions. These dimensions are determined at the time of capture or creation. Occasionally, it is necessary to alter the size of your digital photograph to suit different output requirements. For instance, if you want to display an image on a website that was captured in high resolution, you will need to reduce the pixel dimensions of the file to suit.

Grouped under the Resize option of the Image menu, Elements provides a couple of sizing features which can be used to alter the dimensions of your picture. PROCEED WITH CAUTION. Increasing or decreasing the dimensions of your images directly affects the quality of your files, so my suggestion is that until you are completely at home with these controls always make a backup file of your original picture before starting to resize.

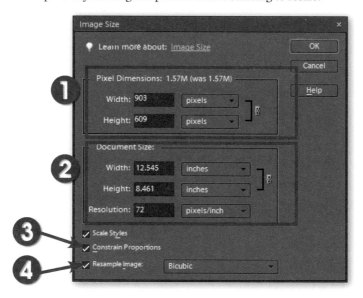

Figure 6.51 The Image Size dialog controls the dimensions and resolution of your pictures.
(1) Pixel Dimensions section.
(2) Document Size section.
(3) Constrain Proportions check box.
(4) Resample Image check box and drop-down menu.

Editor: Image > Resize > Image Size

In version 6.0: Image > Resize > Image Size

The Image Size dialog provides several options for manipulating the pixels in your photograph. At first glance the settings displayed here may seem a little confusing, but if you can make the distinction between the Pixel Dimensions of the image (shown in the topmost section of the dialog) and the Document Size (shown in the middle), it will be easier to understand. See Figure 6.51.

Pixel Dimensions represent the true digital size of the file.

Document Size is the physical dimensions of the file represented in inches (or centimeters) based on using a specific number of pixels per inch (resolution or ppi).

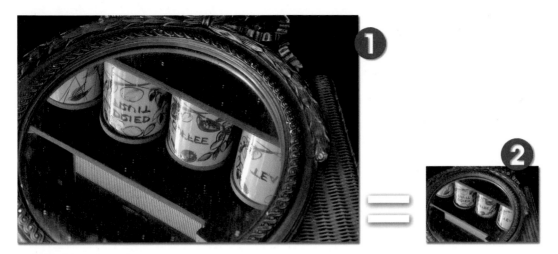

Figure 6.52 *The example image contains 1800 × 1200 pixels and can be output to a print that is 6 inches × 4 inches or 1.8 inches × 1.2 inches, depending on how the pixels are spread (resolution).*
(1) 6 × 4 inches @ 300 dpi = 1800 × 1200 pixels. (2) 1.8 × 1.2 inches @ 1000 dpi = 1800 × 1200 pixels.

Non-detrimental size changes

A file with the same pixel dimensions can have several different document sizes based on altering the spread of the pixels when the picture is printed (or displayed on screen). In this way you can adjust a high-resolution file to print the size of a postage stamp, postcard or a poster by only changing the dpi or resolution. This type of resizing has no detrimental quality effects on your pictures as the original pixel dimensions remain unchanged. See Figure 6.52.

To change resolution, open the Image Size dialog and uncheck the Resample Image option. Next, change either the resolution, width or height settings to suit your output. See Figure 6.53.

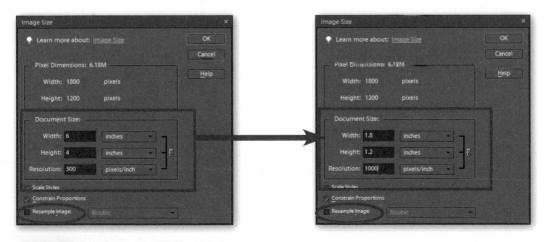

Figure 6.53 *Non-detrimental size changes, or the changes that don't lose picture quality, can be made to your image if the Resample Image option is always left unchecked.*

HANDS ON TECHNIQUES

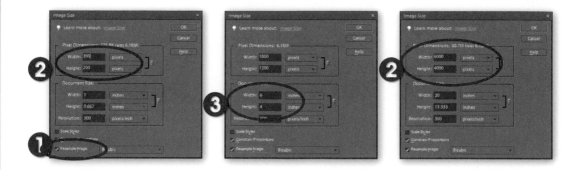

Figure 6.54 *With the Resample Image option selected, it is possible to increase and decrease the total number of pixels in your image. (1) Resample Image option ticked. (2) New pixel dimensions. (3) New document size.*

Upsizing and downsizing

This said, in some circumstances it is necessary to increase or decrease the number of pixels in an image. Both these actions will produce results that have less quality than if the pictures were scanned or photographed at precisely the desired size at the time of capture. If you are confronted with a situation where you are unable to recapture your pictures, then Elements can increase or decrease the image's pixel dimensions. Each of these steps requires the program to interpolate, or 'make up', the pixels that form the resized image. See Figure 6.54. To increase the pixels or upsize the image, tick the Resample Image check box and then increase the value of any of the dimension settings in the dialog. To decrease the pixels or downsize the image, decrease the value of the dimension settings.

Image Size dialog settings

To keep the ratio of width and height of the new image the same as the original, tick the Constrain Proportions check box.

Interpolation quality and speed are determined by the options in the drop-down menu next to the Resample Image check box. Bicubic is the best setting for photographic images.

FEATURE SUMMARY

1 Select Image Size from the Resize option under the Image menu.

2 Tick the Resample Image check box for changes to the pixel dimensions of your image.

3 Uncheck the Resample Image option for changing image resolution.

4 Adjust the dimension settings to suit your output requirements.

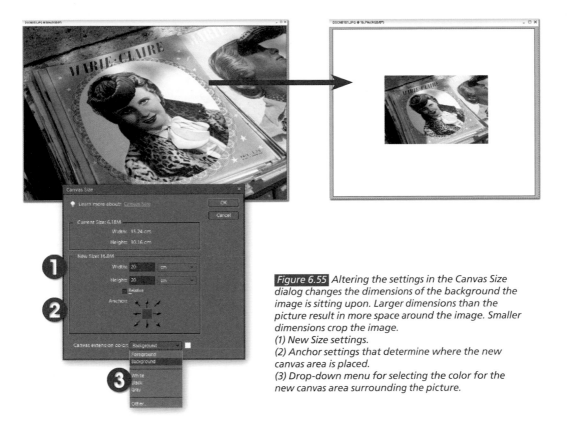

Figure 6.55 Altering the settings in the Canvas Size dialog changes the dimensions of the background the image is sitting upon. Larger dimensions than the picture result in more space around the image. Smaller dimensions crop the image.
(1) New Size settings.
(2) Anchor settings that determine where the new canvas area is placed.
(3) Drop-down menu for selecting the color for the new canvas area surrounding the picture.

Editor: Image > Resize > Canvas Size

In version 6.0: Image > Resize > Canvas Size

Just to add a little more complexity to the picture size discussion, Elements also provides the ability to change the size of the canvas that your photograph is sitting upon. Alterations here result in no change to the size of the image itself, but the overall canvas size does change, which means that the total dimensions of the document change as well.

This feature is particularly useful if you want to add several images together. Increasing the canvas size will mean that each of the extra pictures can be added to the newly created space around the original image.

To change the canvas size, select Canvas Size from the Resize option of the Image menu and alter the settings in the New Size section of the dialog. You can control the location of the new space in relation to the original image by clicking one of the sections in the Anchor diagram. Leaving the default setting here will mean that the canvas change will be spread evenly around the image. See Figure 6.55.

FEATURE SUMMARY

1 Select Canvas Size from the Resize option under the Image menu.

2 Alter the values in the New Size section of the dialog.

3 Set the anchor point in the Anchor diagram.

4 Click OK to complete.

Increasing the canvas size with the Crop tool

Pros use the Crop tool to quickly increase the size of the canvas that the picture sits in. First, zoom out from the picture so that it sits smaller in the workspace, then select the Crop tool and drag a marquee around the whole image. After releasing the mouse button, click on one of the side or corner handles and drag the crop marquee outwards until it is the size and shape of the new canvas. Double-click to complete the canvas resize. The new canvas will be the color of the current background color. See Figure 6.56.

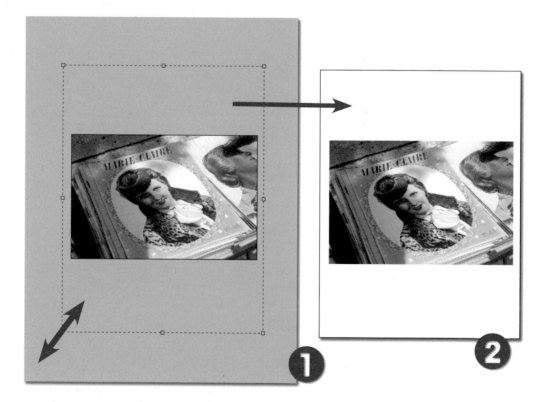

Figure 6.56 *The Crop tool can be used to increase the size of the canvas by dragging the crop marquee outside the dimensions of the picture. (1) Make the crop marquee larger than the picture. (2) Double-click inside the crop marquee to increase the canvas size.*

7

Using Selections and Layers

Selection basics

Modifying drawn and color-based selections

Selections in action

Smart Brush tool

Layers and their origins

For those users who are a little familiar with both selections and layers, it might seem a bit strange to group these features together, but to my mind they both deal with a similar idea – isolating specific sections of an image to make them easier to manipulate. They also represent two Elements features that are central to many advanced manipulation and enhancement techniques.

Selection basics

Until now, we have assumed that any changes being made to an image will be applied to the whole of the picture, but before too long it will become obvious that there are many imaging scenarios that would benefit from being able to restrict alterations to a specific part of a picture. For this reason, most image-editing packages contain features that allow the user to isolate small sections of an image that can then be altered independently to the rest of the picture.

When a selection is made, the edges of the isolated area are indicated by a flashing dotted line, which is sometimes referred to as the 'marching ants'. See Figure 7.1. When a selection is active, any changes made to the image will be restricted to the isolated area. See Figure 7.2. To resume full image-editing mode, the area has to be deselected by choosing Select > Deselect or pressing the Esc key.

The selection features contained in Elements can be divided into three groups:

- *Drawing selection tools*, or those that are based on selecting pixels by drawing a line around the part of the image to be isolated.

- *Color selection tools*, or those features that distinguish between image parts based on the color or tone of the pixels, and

- the *Quick Selection tool* (replacing the Magic Selection Brush) and *Magic Extractor,* which combine both drawing and color selection by using an approach that automatically creates selections based on the areas that the user has painted.

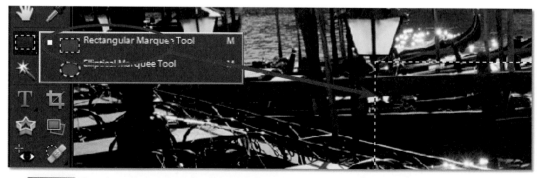

Figure 7.1 *The edges of an active selection are indicated using a flashing dotted line or 'marching ants'.*

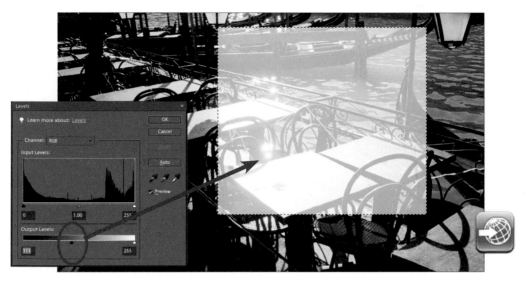

Figure 7.2 *Image alterations made when a selection is active are restricted to the area of the selection.*

Drawing selection tools (see Figures 7.3 and 7.4)

The Selection Brush tool that was first introduced in Elements 3.0, along with the tools contained in the Marquee and Lasso tool sets, are used to draw around the pixels in an image.

Marquee tools

By clicking and dragging the Rectangular or Elliptical Marquees, it is possible to draw rectangle- and oval-shaped selections. Holding down the Shift key whilst using these tools will restrict the selection to square or circular shapes, whilst using the Alt key will draw the selections from their centers. The Marquee tools are great for isolating objects in your images that are regular in shape, but for less conventional shapes you will need to use one of the Lasso tools.

Lasso tools

The normal Lasso tool works like a pencil, allowing the user to draw freehand shapes for selections. In contrast, the Polygonal Lasso tool draws straight edge lines between mouse-click points. Either of these features can be used to outline and select irregular-shaped image parts. See Figure 7.5.

A third tool, the Magnetic Lasso, helps with the drawing process by aligning the outline with the edge of objects automatically. See Figure 7.6. It uses contrast in color and tone as a basis for determining the edge of an object. The accuracy of the 'magnetic' features of this tool is determined by three settings in the tool's options bar. See Figure 7.7. Edge Contrast is the value that a pixel has to differ from its neighbor to be considered an edge. Width is the number of pixels either side of the pointer that are sampled in the edge determination process and Frequency is

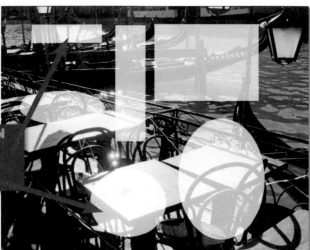

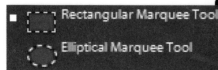

Figure 7.3 *The Elliptical and Rectangular Marquee tools are used for making selections in these shapes.*

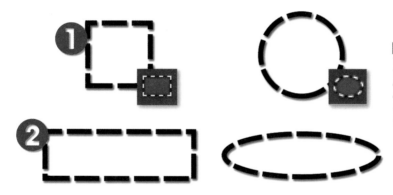

Figure 7.4 *Holding down the Shift key when using the Marquee tools will constrain the selection to either a square or a circle. (1) Constrained. (2) Unconstrained.*

how often fastening points are added to the outline. For most tasks, the Magnetic Lasso is a quick way to obtain accurate selections, so it is good practice to try this tool first when you want to isolate specific image parts.

Selection Brush tool

Responding to photographers' demands for even more options for making selections, Adobe included the Selection Brush for the first time in version 2.0 of Elements. The tool lets you paint a selection onto your image. The size, shape and edge softness of the selection are based on the brush properties you currently have set. These can be altered in the Brush Presets pop-up palette located in the options bar. See Figure 7.8. In versions 6.0 and 7.0 the Selection Brush tool is nested in the tool bar with the Quick Selection tool.

The tool can be used in two modes – Selection and Mask.

Image courtesy of www.ablestock.com

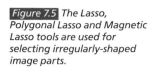

Figure 7.5 *The Lasso, Polygonal Lasso and Magnetic Lasso tools are used for selecting irregularly-shaped image parts.*

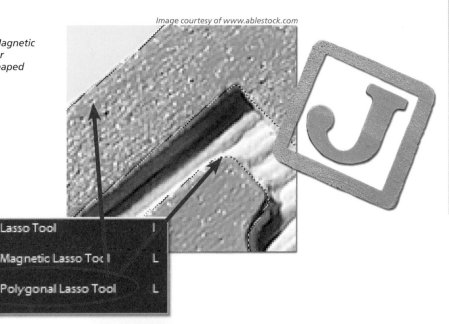

Figure 7.6 *The Magnetic Lasso snaps to the edge of contrasty objects.*

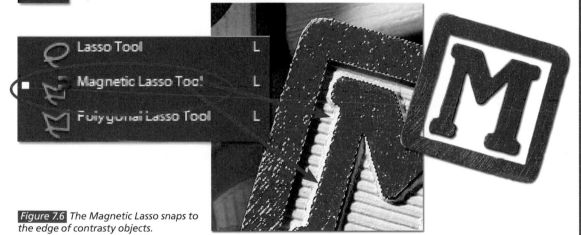

Figure 7.7 *The settings in the Magnetic Lasso's options bar alter how the tool snaps to the outline of particular image parts.*

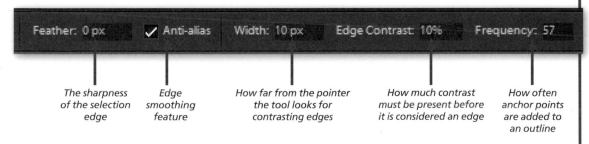

| Feather: 0 px | ✔ Anti-alias | Width: 10 px | Edge Contrast: 10% | Frequency: 57 |

The sharpness of the selection edge | Edge smoothing feature | How far from the pointer the tool looks for contrasting edges | How much contrast must be present before it is considered an edge | How often anchor points are added to an outline

- The *Selection mode* is used to paint over the area you wish to select.

- The *Mask mode* works by reverse painting in the areas you want to 'mask from the selection'. It is particularly well suited for showing the soft or feathered edge selections made when painting with a soft-edged brush.

Holding down the Alt (Windows) keys whilst dragging the brush switches the tool from adding to the selection to taking away from the area. Alternatively you can also switch between Add and Subtract modes using the settings in the options bar. See Figure 7.9.

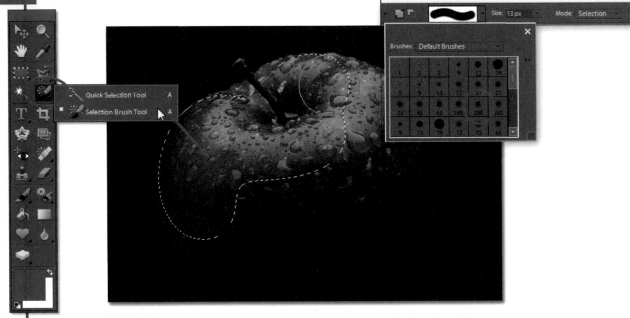

Figure 7.8 *The Selection Brush tool allows the user to create selections by painting directly onto the picture surface.*

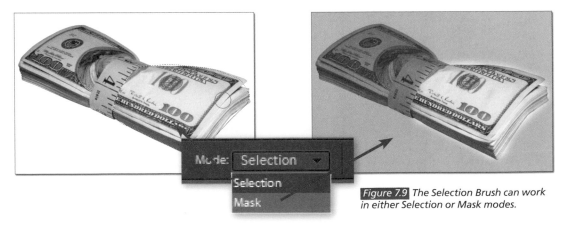

Figure 7.9 *The Selection Brush can work in either Selection or Mask modes.*

Drawing selection tool summaries

Rectangular and Elliptical Marquee tools

1 After selecting the tool, click and drag to draw a marquee on the image surface.

2 Hold down the Shift key whilst drawing to restrict the shape to either a square or a circle.

3 Hold down the Alt (Windows) key to draw the shape from its center.

4 Hold down the Spacebar to reposition the marquee.

Lasso tool

1 After selecting the tool, click and drag to draw the selection area by freehand.

2 Release the mouse button to join the beginning and end points and close the outline.

Polygonal Lasso tool

1 After selecting the tool, click and release the mouse button to mark the first fastening point.

2 To draw a straight line, move the mouse and click again to mark the second point.

3 To draw a freehand line, hold down the Alt (Windows) key and click and drag the mouse.

4 To close the outline, either move the cursor over the first point and click or double-click.

Magnetic Lasso tool

1 After selecting the tool, click and release the mouse button to mark the first fastening point.

2 Trace the outline of the object with the mouse pointer. Extra fastening points will be added to the edge of the object automatically.

3 If the tool doesn't snap to the edge automatically, click the mouse button to add a fastening point manually.

4 Adjust settings in the options bar to vary the tool's magnetic function.

5 To close the outline, either double-click or drag the pointer over the first fastening point.

Selection Brush tool

1 After selecting the tool, adjust the settings in the options bar to vary the brush size, shape and hardness (edge softness).

2 To make a selection, change the mode to Selection and paint over the object with the mouse pointer.

3 To make a mask, change the mode to Mask and paint over the area outside the object with the mouse pointer.

4 Holding down the Alt (Windows) whilst painting will change the action from adding to the Selection/Mask to taking away from the Selection/Mask.

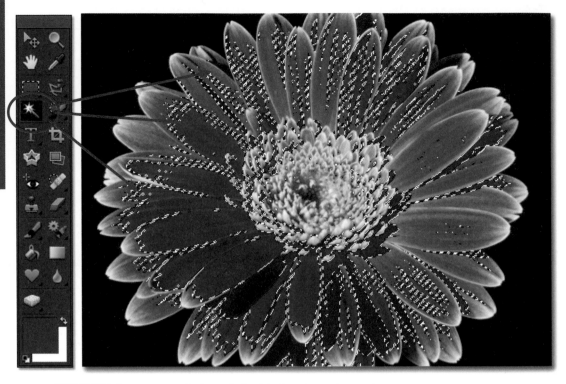

Figure 7.10 *The Magic Wand selects pixels of similar color and tone.*

Color selection tools

Unlike the Lasso and Marquee tools, the Magic Wand makes selections based on color and tone. See Figure 7.10. When the user clicks on an image with the Magic Wand tool, Elements searches the picture for pixels that have a similar color and tone. With large images this process can take a little time, but the end result is a selection of all similar pixels across the whole picture.

How identical a pixel has to be to the original to be included in the Magic Wand selection is determined by the Tolerance value in the options bar. See Figure 7.11. The higher the value here, the less alike the two pixels need to be, whereas a lower setting will require a more exact match before a pixel is added to the selection. Turning on the Contiguous option will only include the pixels that are similar and are adjacent to the original pixel in the selection. See Figures 7.11 and 7.12.

1 With the Magic Wand tool active, click onto the part of the image that you want to select.

2 Modify the Tolerance of the selection by altering this setting in the options bar, then deselect, then click the tool again to reselect with the new Tolerance settings.

3 Constrain the selection to adjacent pixels only by checking the Contiguous option.

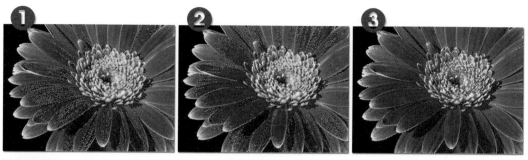

Figure 7.11 *The Tolerance setting determines how alike pixels need to be before they are included in the selection. (1) Tolerance setting 10. (2) Tolerance setting 50. (3) Tolerance setting 130.*

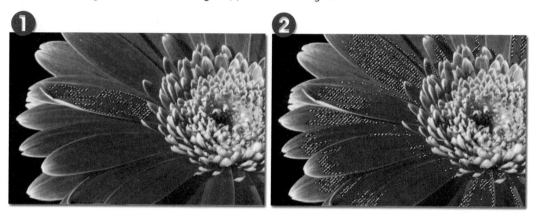

Figure 7.12 *The Contiguous option restricts the selection to those pixels adjacent to where the tool was first clicked on the image surface. (1) A selection made with the Contiguous option turned on. (2) A selection with the option turned off.*

Modifying drawn and color-based selections

With some complex images, no one selection technique will be able to isolate all the pixels required; instead, a combination of tools is needed to make the final outline. To aid with this, Adobe has included several selection possibilities in the options bar of the previous tools. See Figure 7.13.

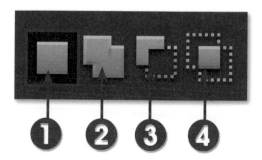

Figure 7.13 *The choices in the selection tools' options bar determine how the new selection interacts with the existing one.*
(1) New selection.
(2) Add to selection.
(3) Subtract from selection.
(4) Intersect with selection.

With these options, it is possible to 'add to', or 'subtract from', an existing selection or even use the 'intersection' of two separate selections as the basis for a third. Simply choose a different selection option when using a new tool. For those users who prefer to use keyboard shortcuts, holding down the Shift key whilst using a selection tool will add to an existing outline, whereas using the Alt key will subtract from it. See Figures 7.14 and 7.15.

All of this may seem a little complex to start with, but it is important to persevere, as good selecting skills are critical for a lot of advanced editing techniques and, besides, after some practice, making multi-tool complex selections will become second nature to you.

FEATURE SUMMARY

1 Add to a selection by either holding down the Shift key whilst using another selection tool or clicking the Add to Selection button in the options bar.

2 Subtract from a selection by either holding down the Alt key whilst using another selection tool or clicking the Subtract from Selection button in the options bar.

3 Use the intersection of a new and existing selection to form a third outline by clicking the Intersect with Selection button in the options bar before making a new selection.

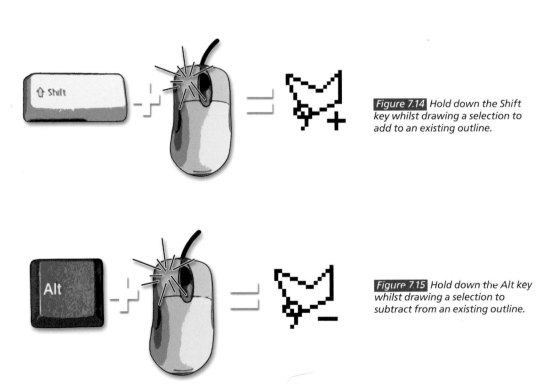

Figure 7.14 Hold down the Shift key whilst drawing a selection to add to an existing outline.

Figure 7.15 Hold down the Alt key whilst drawing a selection to subtract from an existing outline.

The Quick Selection tool (previously the Magic Selection Brush)

Along with the Selection Brush tool, the Quick Selection tool (previously the Magic Selection Brush) provides Elements users with a unique approach to creating and modifying selections. As we have seen, when using the Selection Brush the user must paint over the area to be encompassed by the selection. The accuracy of this painting step determines the accuracy of the final selection. For example, painting over an edge accidentally will result in the creation of a selection that goes beyond this picture part.

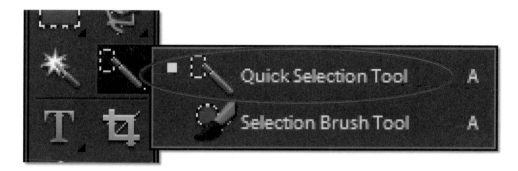

Figure 7.16 *The Quick Selection tool is coupled with the Selection Brush in the Elements 6 and 7 tool bar.*

The Quick Selection tool provides a quicker, easier and, in most cases, more accurate way to make selections by combining both the drawing and color selection approaches of the other tools we have covered. To make a selection choose the tool from the tool bar. If it is hidden from view click the small arrow at the bottom right of the Selection Brush button to reveal the tool. See Figure 7.16. The Quick Selection tool doesn't require you to scribble or place some dots on the picture parts that you want to select as was the case with the Magic Selection Brush. Instead Elements creates the selection as you paint over specific picture areas. You don't have to be too careful with your initial painting as the program registers the color, tone and texture of the

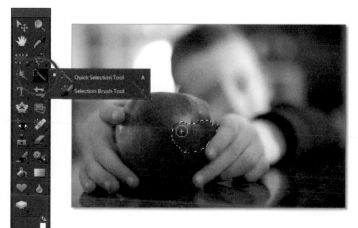

Figure 7.17 *As you are drawing with the Quick Selection tool Elements automatically generates a selection of all the adjacent areas in the picture that have similar color, texture or tone.*

picture parts and then intelligently searches for other similar pixels to include in the selection. See Figure 7.17.

Fine-tuning the areas selected with Quick Selection tool

Although this tool does a pretty good job of selecting alike areas, there will always be occasions when either too much or too little of the picture has been included. Just like the other tools we have looked at, the Quick Selection tool allows you to easily modify the selections it makes.

To include other areas in the selection, click the Add to Selection button in the tool's options bar (the cursor will change to include a small +) and paint over a new picture part. This step will cause Elements to regenerate the selection to include your changes. To remove an area from the selection, click on the Subtract from Selection button (cursor changes to the brush tip and a small - sign), and paint over the part to eliminate. Again, Elements will regenerate the selection to account for the changes. The Shift and Alt keys can be used whilst drawing to change modes on the fly and add to or subtract from the selection. See Figure 7.18.

The Quick Selection tool is available in both the Full and Quick Fix editor workspaces.

FEATURE SUMMARY

1 With the Quick Selection tool active, paint over the areas to select.

2 After the first selection area is drawn, the tool's mode automatically changes to Add to Selection so that you can include extra areas in the selection.

3 Subtract from the selection by painting over new areas after switching to the Subtract from Selection mode.

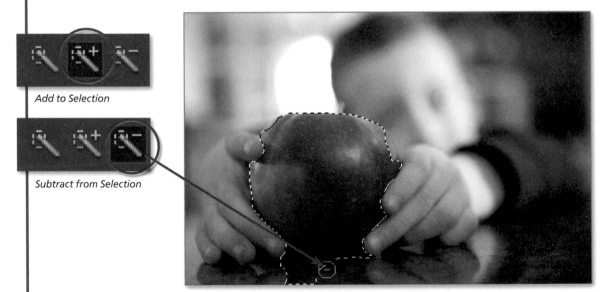

Add to Selection

Subtract from Selection

Figure 7.18 The options bar of the Quick Selection tool contains several modes that can be used for altering or refining the selection created by the tool. You can add other picture parts to a selection by clicking on the Add to Selection button and then painting over the new area. Parts already selected can be removed by changing to the Subtract from Selection mode and painting on these areas.

Book resources and video tutorials can be found at **www.photoshopelements.net**

The new Smart Brush tool

One of the major changes introduced in Photoshop Elements 7.0 is the ability to select and make changes with the one tool. The new Smart Brush tool brings a whole new level of ease to the process of changing specific areas of your photo. By combining the selecting abilities of the Quick Selection tool and the enhancement options available via adjustment layers, the Adobe engineers have created a new way to change the look of your photos.

Unlike the traditional way of applying adjustments where the user must first make a selection and then apply the adjustment, the Smart Brush Tool creates the selection and applies the adjustment as the user paints over the image. You can select the type of adjustment that will be applied with the tool from a list of over 65 that ships with Elements. These presets are grouped under general headings in the Preset Chooser located in the options bar. Here you will find options for altering image characteristics such as color, tone and saturation as well as subject based enhancements such as brightening teeth or making a dull sky bluer and, of course, a bunch of special effects changes. Preset entries can be displayed in a list or thumbnail form by selecting one of the options displayed when pressing the double sideways arrows in the top left of the Presets window. See Figure 7.18.

The Smart Brush Tool is only available in Full editor workspace.

1 With the Smart Brush tool active, go to the Options Bar and select the type of enhancement

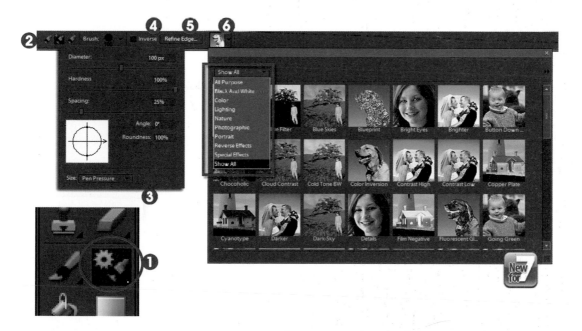

Figure 7.18 *The Smart Brush tool sits aside the Brush tool in the Photoshop Elements toolbar (1). The tool's options bar contains three brush mode buttons on the left - new selection, add to selection and subtract from selection (2), the familiar brush presets to adjust brush tip qualities (3), an Inverse check box to flip the enhancement to the non-selected part of the photos (4), a Refine Edge button to open the feature (5) and the Preset Chooser (6) which displays a preview of the different adjustment presets available with the tool.*

from the Preset Chooser pop-up menu.

2 Now paint over the areas that you wish to select and enhance. See Figure 7.19.

3 After the first selection area is drawn, the tool's mode automatically changes to Add to Selection so that you can include extra areas in the selection.

4 Subtract from the selection by painting over new areas after switching to the Subtract from Selection mode using the buttons in the Options Bar or the floating palette at the top right of the photo.

FEATURE SUMMARY

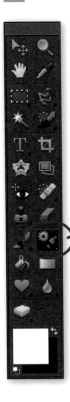

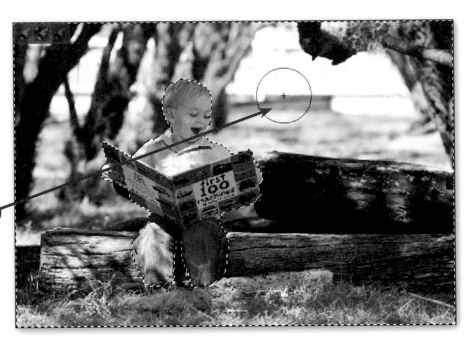

Figure 7.19 *After selecting the enhancement type, here I used one of the convert to black and white options, all you need to do is paint over the parts of the photo that you want to change. If the tool selects too much of the photo, switch to the Subtract from Selection mode (hold down the Alt key) and paint over the unwanted change to remove it.*

Fine-tuning Smart Brush selections

Just like the other selection tools we have seen it is possible to add to, or take away from, an existing selection. This gives you the chance to fine-tune the areas of the photo that the Smart Brush Tool has changed. You can switch between selection modes in three different ways:

1. By choosing an entry from the mode buttons on the left of the options bar.

2. By using one of the shortcut keys – Shift to add, Alt to subtract,

3. By choosing one of the mode entries from the buttons displayed in the new floating palette located at the top left of the open photo. See Figure 7.20.

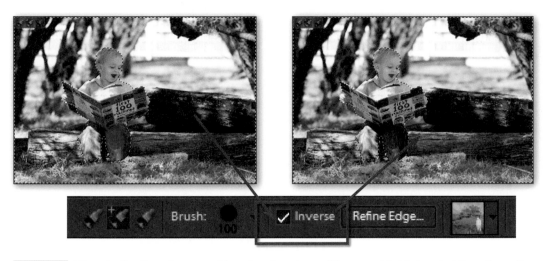

Figure 7.20 *After selecting the enhancement type, here I used one of the convert to black and white options, all you need to do is click the Inverse option to switch the adjustment from the selected area to the non-selected area.*

Choosing what not to change

We have already seen that sometimes it is easier to select what you don't want to change, rather than what you do. Imagine trying to select every small branch and twig of a bare winter-time tree against a blue sky. It would be easier to use the Magic Wand tool to select all of the blue sky and then Invert the selection to isolate the tree. With this in mind the Options Bar of the new Smart Brush Tool contains an Inverse check box. Selecting this option after painting on a change to your photo will remove the adjustment from the selected area and paste it onto the non-selected area. See Figure 7.20. Some presets have the Inverse option built in so painting on an object will apply the effect to all picture parts except the object.

Adjusting Smart Brush Tool effects

When you paint on a photo with the Smart Brush Tool, Elements creates a new Adjustment Layer and adds it to the layer stack with a mask based on the painted selection. Now without going into too much detail about adjustment layers or their masks (this will be handled later in this chapter), it is important to realise that making an change to your photo in this way has two important benefits over applying changes directly:

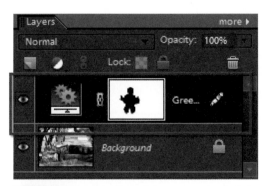

Figure 7.21 *Smart Brush Tool changes are applied via a masked adjustment layer. Here you can see the entry for the convert to black and white changes made seen in Figure 7.19.*

- Firstly, the adjustments are made non-destructively. Which means that the original photo's pixels are left untouched as the changes are made in a separate layer that sits above the background (picture) layer. See Figure 7.21. You can easily hide the effect applied with the

Smart Brush Tool by simply clicking on the 'eye' icon situated to the left of the layer entry. Clicking the 'eye' a second time will reapply the changes.

- Secondly, the way that the Smart Brush Tool effect alters your photo can be modified by adjusting how the adjustment layer interacts with the picture layer, and, in some cases, by changing the settings for the effect itself.

So Smart Brush Tool adjustments can be modified. Great, but how? Well again some of these concepts will be better explained later in the chapter but let's look at a simplified version here while the whole idea of this new way of altering our photos is fresh in our mind.

To alter the strength of a Smart Brush Effect: Changing the strength of the effect is a simple matter of selecting the Smart Brush Tool entry in the layers palette and then adjusting the Opacity slider at the top right of the palette. The lower the opacity number the more subtle the effect. See Figure 7.22.

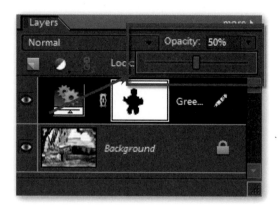

Figure 7.22 The Opacity slider at the top right of the Layers palette controls how transparent the layer content is. In the case of a Smart Brush Tool entry you can use the Opacity slider to control the strength of the effect. Here a setting of 50% will display a mixture of the original (background image) and the Smart Brush Tool effect.

To change how the effect combines with the picture: Photoshop Elements has many different ways to control how the contents of two layers are mixed together. This interaction is called layer blending and is controlled by a setting called the layer Blend Mode. By default the content of upper layers obscure the content of layers beneath. This is the Normal Blend Mode, but Elements offers

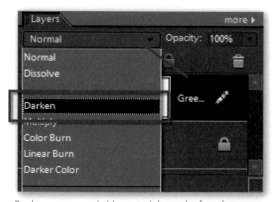

Figure 7.23 Changing the Blend Mode option of the Smart Brush Tool layer will alter the way that the effects interact with the image or background layer.

many more choices about how the Smart Brush Tool layer can interact with the background or image layer. To change Blend Modes just select a new entry from the drop down list at the top left of the layers palette. See the Blend Modes section later in the chapter for more details on Blend Modes and their effects. See Figure 7.23. It is also worth noting that many Smart Brush presets use blend modes other than Normal by default.

To change the settings of the effect itself: One of the great things about Adjustment layers is that you can alter the settings used at any time by double-clicking on the Layer Thumbnail (on the left) to display a dialog box complete with all the controls that you used originally to make the change. Now as all Smart Brush Tool effects are based on masked adjustment layers, to change the style of the effects, it should be possible to double-click on the layer thumbnail and simply change the settings in the dialog that appears. For most Smart Brush Tool adjustments this is true (check out the Lighting options) as they are built upon Elements Adjustment Layers, but this is not always the case as some effects are based on features that are only available in Photoshop itself. See Figure 7.24. If you try to adjust these you will get a warning notice saying that it is not possible to tweak the settings.

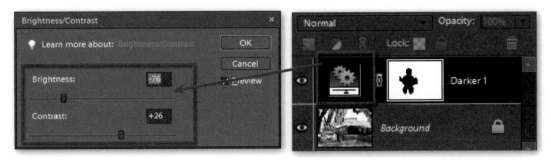

Figure 7.24 With some Smart Brush Tool entries the actual settings used for making the image adjustments can be edited. In this example, the 'Darker' preset was applied to parts of the photo with the Smart Brush Tool. A new Smart Brush Tool layer was added to the Layers palette as a result. By double-clicking on the thumbnail on the left of the entry, the Brightness/Contrast dialog is displayed. This is the feature used to make the changes you applied with the brush. In the dialog you can change the settings used for the adjustment. Clicking OK will apply the changes to your photo.

That said, for those entries based on Elements features, double-clicking the layer thumbnail will display the feature's dialog allowing the user to fine-tune the effects applied. You can also display the adjustment dialog, when you have the Smart Brush Tool selected by double clicking on the Smart Brush Tool icon on the photo. Single clicking the icon reselects the area originally isolated by the brush and makes the Smart Brush Tool layer active (in the Layers palette). See Figure 7.25.

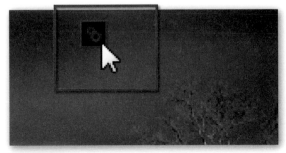

Figure 7.25 To reselect the adjustment area marked out by the Smart Brush Tool, when you have the tool selected, single click the icon on the photo. Double-clicking will open the associated adjustment dialog as long as it is an Elements feature.

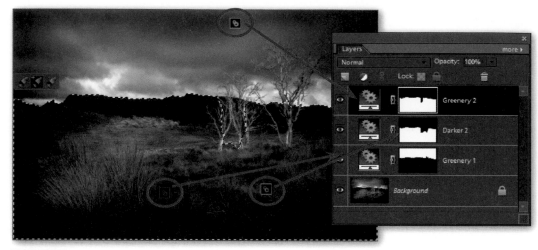

Figure 7.26 *Multiple Smart Brush Tool effects can be applied to a photo. Each effect will have a separate entry in the Layers palette as well as an icon that is displayed on the surface of the photo when the tool is selected.*

Adding multiple Smart Brush Tool adjustments

The 'paint on' nature of Smart Brush Tool adjustments will mean that this new feature will be one that you reach for often when wanting to tweak specific parts of your photo. This scenario will, undoubtedly, lead to you wanting to apply more than one adjustment to a single image. Thankfully, this is not a problem as each time you apply a Smart Brush Tool adjustment a new layer is added to the layer stack. This means that each change is independent and can be hidden from view (turn off the 'eye' icon) or tweaked (Opacity and Blend Mode). Along with the new layer entries, Elements also places new icons on the photo for each additional Smart Brush Tool adjustment. These are colored different hues so that you can distinguish them from each other. See Figure 7.26.

FEATURE SUMMARY

1 After making a initial Smart Brush Tool, click onto the New Select mode button in the Options Bar or the floating palette to tell Elements that you want to create a new adjustment selection.

2 Go to the Options Bar and select the type of enhancement from the Preset Chooser pop-up menu.

3 Now paint over the areas that you wish to select and enhance.

4 After the first selection area is drawn, the tool's mode automatically changes to Add to Selection, so to add another adjustment you must click the New Selection button once again.

5 To reselect an existing adjustment area, make sure that the Smart Brush Tool is selected and then click onto the colored icon associated with the selected area. Now you can add to the existing selection by painting over new areas or change to the Subtract from Section mode and remove selection parts.

Select > Refine Edge

A new way to modify the edges of the selections you create was introduced in Photoshop Elements 6. Called the Refine Edge feature it is accessed either via the button now present in all the selection tools' options bars, or via the Select > Refine Edge menu entry. The feature brings together three different controls for adjusting the edges of the selection with two selection edge preview options. The edge controls previously existed as separate entries in either the Select or Select > Modify menu. Bringing them together in the one dialog, and then providing live preview options as well, means that the refining activity will be a lot more accurate, as you will be able to see the results of the changes made to any of the controls reflected in the image itself.

The feature's dialog contains a Preview toggle, and Zoom and Move tools which can be used for navigating around enlarged images to check the properties of the selection edge. See Figure 7.27. The edge controls themselves come in the form of the following three sliders:

Smooth – This option removes stepped or jagged selection edges.

Feather – Softens the edge of the selection by a given pixel value. You can use this setting to provide a gradual transition between selected and non-selected areas.

Contract/Expand – Increase or decrease the size of the area outlined by the selection by the percentage value selected.

The Preview modes buttons at the bottom of the dialog provide a range of different ways to view the selection on your picture. The left button displays a standard selection edge superimposed on the photo. The edge is outlined using the familiar 'marching ants' line.

The other button previews the selection as a mask, with the selected area displayed clear of color and the non-selected area colored with a specific color overlay. The color and transparency of the mask overlay can be altered by double-clicking the preview button. See Figures 7.28 and 7.29.

Selecting the Mask option provides a much better way of viewing the quality of the selection edge as it is possible to preview the sharpness of the edge as well as how

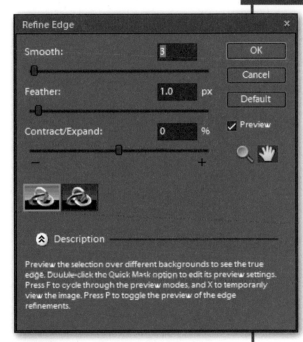

Figure 7.27 *The new Refine Edge dialog brings together all the controls used for altering the characteristics of the selection's edge into a single dialog. The feature also includes two edge preview options.*

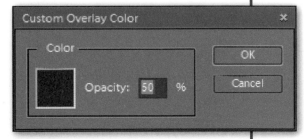

Figure 7.28 *By double-clicking the Mask Preview option you can alter the color and opacity of the mask.*

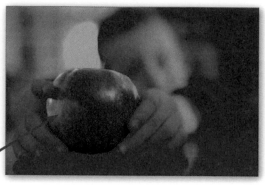

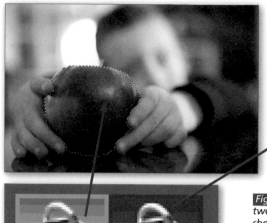

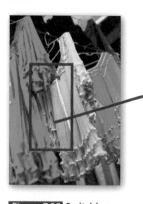

Figure 7.29 *The Quick Selection tool contains two preview modes. The standard option (left) shows the traditional marching ants outlining the selected area and the Mask view (right) displays a colored mask over the non selected areas.*

transparent the overlap is between selected and non-selected areas (feathering). For best results, use the Mask option in conjunction with the Zoom and Move tools to inspect an enlarged preview of the selection edge, as you make changes to the dialog's slider controls. See Figure 7.30.

Press the 'P' key to turn off the preview of the current Refine Edge settings and the 'X' key to temporarily display the Full Image view.

FEATURE SUMMARY

1 With the Quick Selection tool active, paint over the areas to select.

2 Add to the selection by painting over new areas after switching to the Add to Selection mode.

3 Subtract from the selection by painting over new areas after switching to the Subtract from Selection mode.

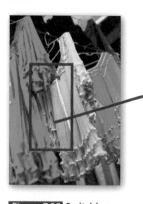

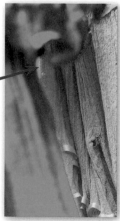

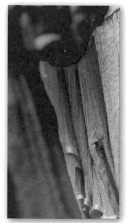

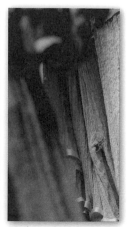

Figure 7.30 *Switching between the standard and Mask views of an enlarged image allows you to see more accurately where the selection is being applied.*

Standard preview   Mask preview   Mask preview showing feathered edge

The Magic Extractor feature

The Magic Extractor feature quickly removes the background of a picture whilst retaining the subject in the foreground. The Magic Extractor works by marking, with a scribbled line or a series of dots, the foreground (to be kept) and the background (to be removed) parts of the picture. Elements then automatically finds all the background parts in the picture and removes them from the document, replacing it with transparency and previewing it with your choice of black, gray, white or transparency.

The Magic Extractor works within its own window, which includes a zoomable preview area, a set of tools for marking the foreground and background parts of a photo, touch-up options to refine extraction results as well as settings to select the background area once it is removed. See Figure 7.31.

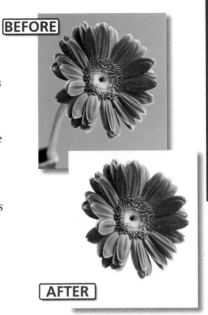

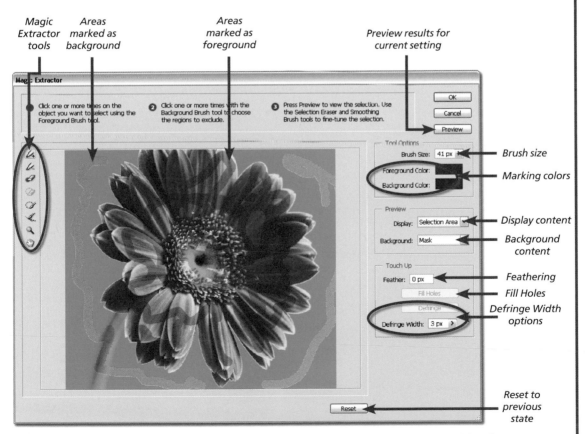

Magic Extractor tools

Areas marked as background

Areas marked as foreground

Preview results for current setting

Brush size

Marking colors

Display content

Background content

Feathering

Fill Holes

Defringe Width options

Reset to previous state

Figure 7.31 *The Magic Extractor isolates and removes background picture parts based on the user identifying foreground and background details with painted dots or scribbles.*

Using the Magic Extractor tool is a three-step process. You start by selecting the Foreground Brush tool and scribbling or placing dots over the areas that you want to retain. Next, you switch to the Background Brush tool and scribble over the areas to be removed. See Figures 7.32 and 7.33.

1 Display the Magic Extractor option by choosing the Magic Extractor option from the Image menu.

2 Next, select the Foreground Brush and paint, scribble or place dots on the areas to be kept.

3 Now select the Background Brush tool and paint over the picture parts that will be deleted as part of the extraction process.

4 To check the accuracy of the extraction press the Preview button.

5 To add extra sections to the extracted area reselect the Foreground Brush, switch the Preview Display option to Original Photo and paint over the extra parts.

6 To remove unwanted parts from the selection do the same thing but using the Background Brush instead.

7 Finally, to clean up the edges of the extraction select the Smoothing Brush tool and drag it over the edges of the extraction.

8 Click OK to process the extraction and return the completed results to the main editing workspace.

FEATURE SUMMARY

Pro's Tip When adding or removing parts from your extraction click the 'X' key toggle between the Preview and Extracted views.

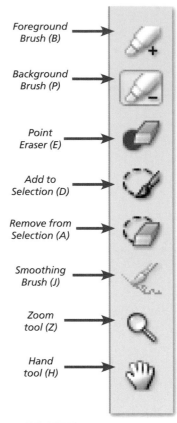

Foreground Brush (B)

Background Brush (P)

Point Eraser (E)

Add to Selection (D)

Remove from Selection (A)

Smoothing Brush (J)

Zoom tool (Z)

Hand tool (H)

Figure 7.32 The tool bar in the Magic Extractor contains the brushes that are used for painting on foreground and background picture parts as well as tools for adjusting the extraction results and altering the view.

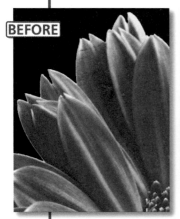

BEFORE

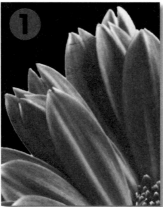

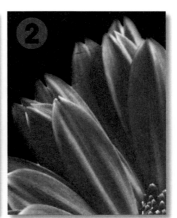

Figure 7.33 The Defringe option in the Magic Extractor feature removes any stray background colored pixels from the edge of an extracted foreground detail (1), whereas the Feather option softens the edge of the detail (2).

Selections in action
Advanced dodging and burning

Previously, we have used the Dodge and Burn tools to adjust the tones in our images. Now, using carefully made selections, it is possible to darken, or lighten, whole areas of your pictures.

1 To start, use the Lasso or Selection Brush tool to select a portion of your image.

2 Next, open the Levels dialog (Enhance > Adjust Lighting > Levels).

3 Move the Midtone Input slider to the left to lighten the selected tones, or to the right to darken them. Notice that the Levels changes have successfully dodged, or burned, the image. There is one problem with the results though – the changes are noticeable because of the sharp edge of the selection. A little modification is needed.

4 Undo (Edit > Undo) the Levels adjustment and then, with the selection still active, apply a Feather (Select > Feather) to its edge. This command will soften the edge of the selection and make the change between areas that have been altered, and sections that have been left unchanged, more gradual. The amount of feather required depends on the image's resolution. Higher settings can be used with higher resolution images. See Figures 7.34 and 7.35.

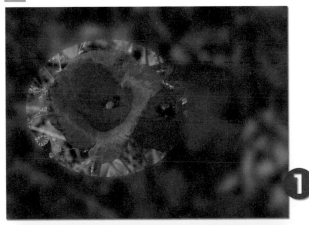

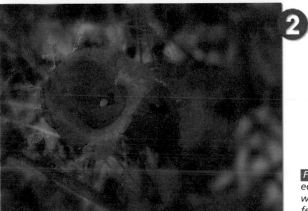

Figure 7.34 Changes made with a sharp-edged selection (1) are more obvious than when they are applied to a selection with a feathered edge (2).

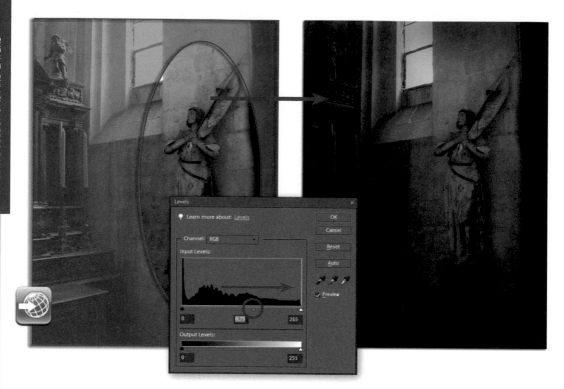

Figure 7.35 Using a feathered edge selection it is possible to easily lighten or darken whole areas of an image.

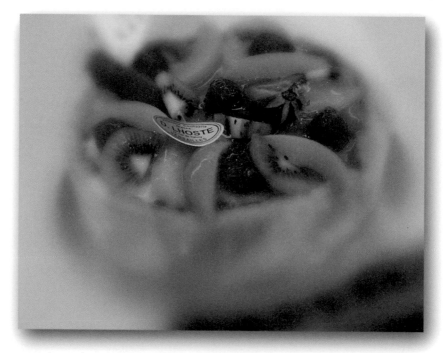

Figure 7.36 Shallow depth of field effects are the current picture fashion for food photographers.

Artificial depth of field

These days it is difficult to open the color magazine from a weekend paper without being confronted by a shallow depth of field picture. It seems that this photographic technique is very popular with food photographers in particular; the majority of the image is blurry, save for a single small and sharply focused portion. See Figures 7.36 and 7.37.

A similar effect can be created digitally using simple selection techniques.

FEATURE SUMMARY

1 Again, start the process by making a feathered selection of the part of your image that you want to remain sharp.

2 Next, invert (Select > Inverse) the selection so that the rest of the image is now isolated.

3 Using the Gaussian Blur filter (Filter > Blur > Gaussian Blur), change the sharpness of the selection until the desired effect is achieved.

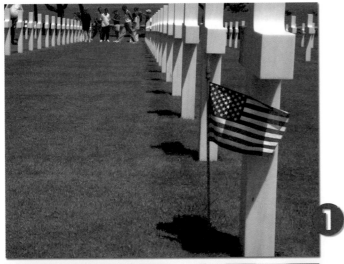

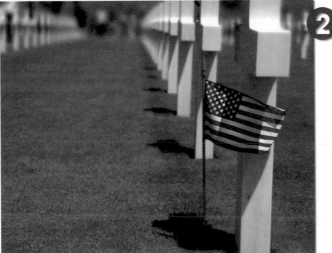

Figure 7.37 You can create a digital look-alike version of shallow depth of field effects by combining a feather selection and the Gaussian Blur filter.
(1) Before depth of field technique.
(2) After depth of field technique.

Filtering a selection

In Chapter 5 we looked at some of the dramatic ways that we can change the look of an image using the filters that are supplied with Photoshop Elements. You can gain more control over where and how the filters are applied to your pictures by combining their use with carefully created selections.

FEATURE SUMMARY

1 By selecting a portion of the picture first, it is possible to restrict the effects of a filter to this one section of the image.

2 Feathering the selection before applying the filter will help blend the changes into the rest of the image. See Figure 7.38.

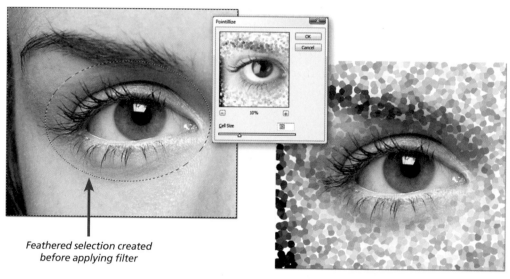

Feathered selection created
before applying filter

Figure 7.38 *The effects of filters can be restricted to specific areas of a picture by making a selection first and then applying the filter.*

Selective saturation changes

Color, as well as tone, texture and focus, can direct the viewer's eye within a picture. Burning and dodging and depth of field effects are designed to control the way that the audience sees an image and, more importantly, which parts of the picture become the points of focus. Using the selection tools, as well as the Hue/Saturation control, Elements provides a further option for helping to establish focal points within your pictures.

The result is a photograph where the viewer's eye is drawn to the saturated area of the image. Remember, complete desaturation will result in a grayscale image. Making this degree of change to the inverted selection would produce a dramatic picture that is both black and white and color. See Figure 7.39.

FEATURE SUMMARY

1 Start by making a selection of the most visually important part of the picture.

2 Next, open the Hue/Saturation feature (Enhance > Adjust Color > Hue/Saturation) and increase the saturation of this part of the picture.

3 Finally, invert (Select > Inverse) the selection so that the rest of the image is now selected and, using the Hue/Saturation control again, reduce the saturation.

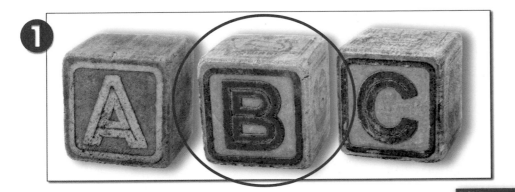

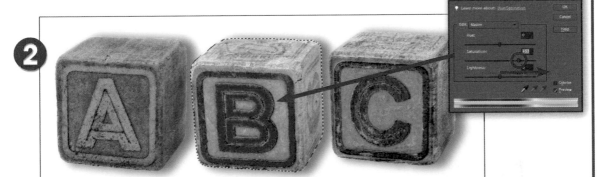

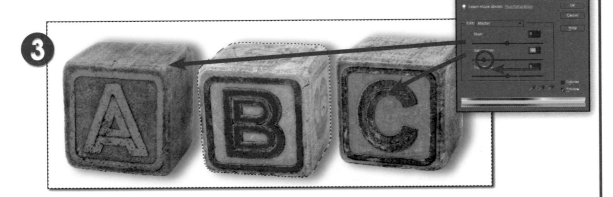

Figure 7.39 *Focal points can be created in an image by saturating a selection and desaturating the inverse selection. (1) Select the focal point. (2) With the selection active, saturate this portion of the picture. (3) Inverse the selection and desaturate the rest of the picture.*

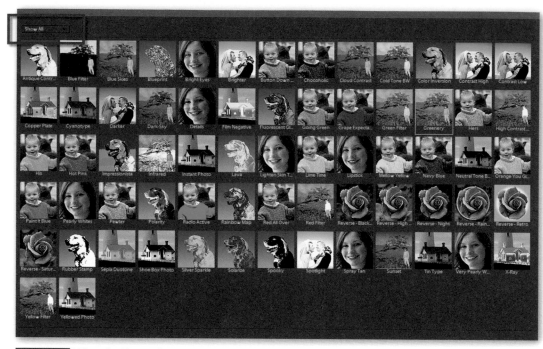

Figure 7.40 *When the Show All option is selected in the Preset Chooser, the user is presented with a series of thumbnails representing the different adjustments available to use with the Smart Brush Tool.*

Paint on selective changes

As we have already seen Photoshop Elements 7.0 contains a brand new way to select and apply adjustments in one step using the Smart Brush Tool. The feature ships with over 65 preset adjustments that can be used to alter the look of your photos. See Figure 7.40. There is also the ability to add extra presets, so don't be too surprised if these become available to download and install, either from photoshop.com or other Elements websites. Of those that ship with Elements, I have selected a few here to demonstrate the different effects that can be achieved using the tool. See Figure 7.41.

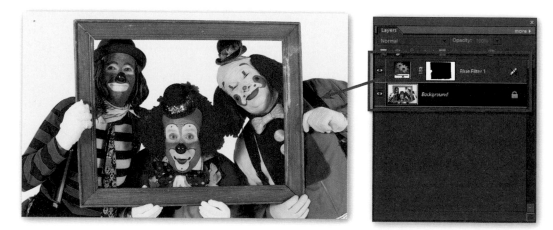

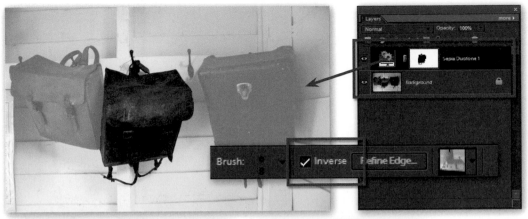

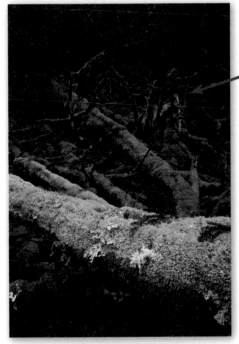

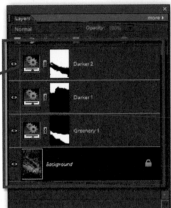

Figure 7.41 The Smart Brush Tool is capable of producing changes that range from the dramatic to the subtle. There are presets that will help enhance landscapes, portraits and candid photos. The examples on this and the previous pages show both the enhanced or after image and the Smart Brush Tool layer entries needed to create them.

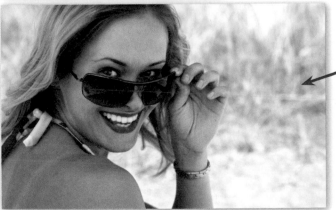

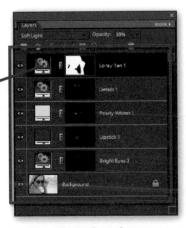

Layers and their origins

The first image-editing programs used a flat file format. See Figure 7.42. All the information for the file was contained in a single plane and all changes made to the image were permanently and irreversibly stored in this file. It did not take users and software manufacturers long to realize that a more efficient and less frustrating way to work was to build an image from a series of picture parts each contained on its own layer.

The concept was not entirely new; the cell animation industry has used the idea for years. Each character and prop was painted onto a transparent plastic sheet, which was then layered together over a solid background. When seen from above, the components and the background appeared to be a single image.

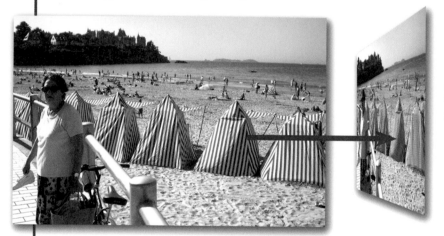

Figure 7.42 A flat file contains all the image information in a single plane.

In Photoshop and Photoshop Elements, Adobe has based its layers system on this idea. See Figure 7.43. When an image is first created and opened in the editing package, it becomes the background by default. Any other images that are copied and pasted onto the image, or text that is added to the picture, become a layer that sits on top of this background. Just as with the animation version, the uppermost layer is viewed first and the other layers and background then show through the transparent areas of each other layer.

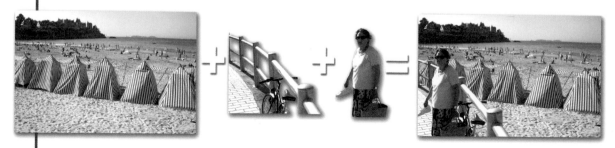

Figure 7.43 Multi-layered image files are used by most editing programs as a way to separate different picture components whilst keeping them available for editing and enhancement purposes.

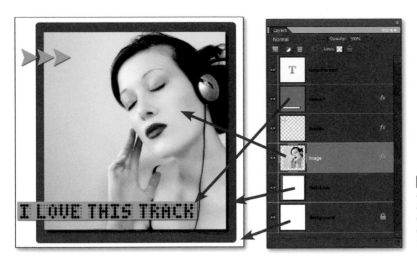

Figure 7.44 The Layers palette in Elements shows the content and position of each layer within the stack.

The Layers palette

Undoubtedly this whole idea might seem a little confusing to the new user, but the benefits of a system that allows picture parts to be moved and adjusted independently far outweigh the time it will take to understand the concept. To help visualize the setup, Elements contains a specialized Layers palette that shows each of the individual layers, their position in the layer stack and a small thumbnail of their contents. See Figure 7.44.

A transparent area is represented by a checkerboard gray and white pattern that surrounds any image parts that are smaller than the background. The eye, sitting to the left of the thumbnail, shows that the layer is visible. Clicking on this icon will make the eye disappear and visually remove the image part from the whole picture. Only one layer in the stack can be edited at a time and for this reason it is called the working layer. See Figure 7.45. This layer will be colored differently to the others in the stack. Clicking on a different layer in the area to the right of the thumbnail will make this layer the new working layer. See Figure 7.46.

When the full image is saved as an Elements file in PSD format, all the individual layers are maintained and can be manipulated individually when the picture is opened next. This is not true if the image is saved in other formats like standard JPEG. Here, the information contained in each layer is merged together at the time of saving to form one flat file.

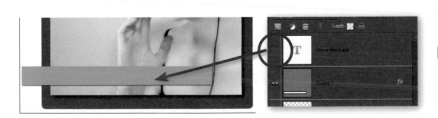

Figure 7.45 Clicking the eye icon removes that layer from view in the image.

Layer types

Image layers

Several different types of layers can be added to an Elements image; of these the most simple, and probably the most obvious, is the image layer. When an image part is copied and pasted it automatically makes a new layer. This is true whether the picture part came from the original image or from another picture that is already opened. When this new layer is selected as the working layer it can be moved around the image surface using the Move tool. The contents can also be changed in size and shape using one of the four options found in the Transform menu (Image > Transform > Free Transform or Skew or Distort or Perspective). See Figure 7.47. These features allow you to manipulate the layer to fit the other components of the image.

The background layer is a special image layer. Its dimensions define the image size. It is also locked by default, meaning that it cannot be moved. You can restrict the movement of other key layers by clicking the lock icon in the top part of the Layers palette. Ticking the Transparency option located next to the lock icon will not allow any changes made to the layer to impinge on the transparent area.

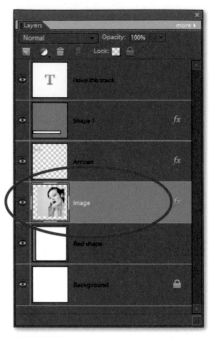

Figure 7.46 *The active or working layer is a different color to the others in the stack.*

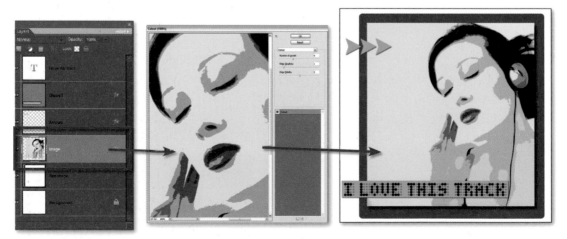

Figure 7.47 *Individual image layers can be manipulated independently of other layers in the stack.*

Type layers

Type layers do not show a thumbnail of their contents in the Layers palette. See Figure 7.48. A large 'T' is positioned in its place and the first few words of the text are used as the layer's name. Unlike other packages, Elements' type layers remain editable even after they have been saved, provided that the file has been saved in the PSD, TIFF or PDF formats.

Shape layers

Drawing with any of the shape tools creates a new vector-based shape layer. The layer contains a thumbnail for the shape as well as the color of the layer. Shape layers need to be simplified or changed to a standard image layer before they can be enhanced or filtered.

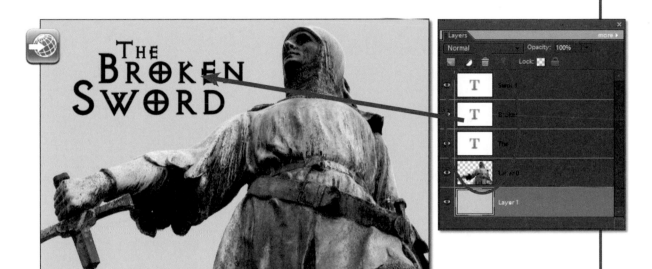

Figure 7.48 *Elements uses editable type layers for any text that is added to images.*

Adjustment layers

Adobe added adjustment layers to Elements as a way for users to change the look of images whilst retaining the integrity of the image file. Familiar image-change features, such as Levels and Hue/Saturation, are available as adjustment layers and, depending on where they are placed in the layer stack, will alter either part, or all, of the image. See Figure 7.49.

Adjusting your images using these types of layers is a good way of ensuring that the basic picture is not changed in any way. The other advantage is that the settings in the adjustment layers can be edited and changed at a later date, even after the file has been saved. Users can access the original settings used to make the alteration by double-clicking the dialog icon on the left-hand side of the adjustment layer.

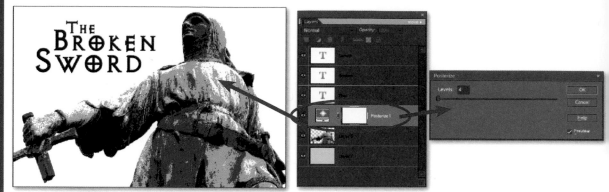

Figure 7.49 Adjustment layers alter the look of all layers that are positioned beneath them in the stack, unless they are grouped with the layer beneath by holding the Alt key down and clicking the dividing line between each layer in the Layers palette.

As we have already seen, version 7.0 contains a new feature called the Smart Brush Tool, which automatically enters a new adjustment layer in the layers palette when used. This extends the functionality of Adjustment Layers and makes their use much easier than ever before. Keep in mind that you can change the whole of the image by adding an adjustment layer without using the Smart Brush Tool. However if you want the adjustment layer effects to be restricted to just one portion of the photo then either make a selection first before adding the layer or use the Smart Brush Tool to paint on the changes.

If you create an Adjustment layer manually, that is select an entry from the Layer > Adjustment Layer menu, then it will be treated like a Smart Brush layer when that tool is selected.

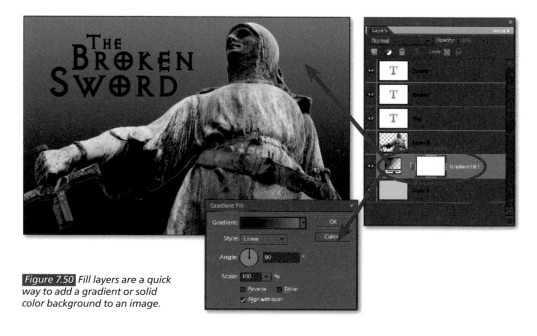

Figure 7.50 Fill layers are a quick way to add a gradient or solid color background to an image.

Fill layers

Users can also apply a Solid Color, Gradient or Pattern to an image as a separate layer. These three selections are available as a separate item (Layer > New Fill Layer) under the Layer menu or grouped with the adjustment layer options via the Quick button at the bottom of the Layers palette. See Figure 7.50.

Frame layers

A new layer type was introduced in Elements 5.0 to coincide with the release of the Photo Layout creation project (see Chapter 10 for more details). Called the Frame layer, its role is to store both the frame and the picture that sits within it. This would not be a difficult task if, once the frame and picture were combined, both parts became one entity, but this approach would not provide much room for fine-tuning later. So, instead, the development team created the Frame layer, borrowing some of the technology from the Smart Object Layer feature in Photoshop.

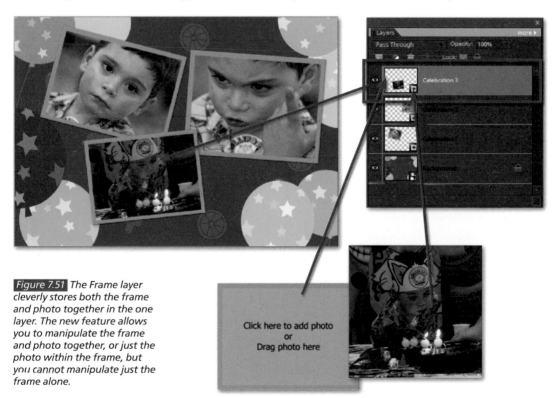

Figure 7.51 *The Frame layer cleverly stores both the frame and photo together in the one layer. The new feature allows you to manipulate the frame and photo together, or just the photo within the frame, but you cannot manipulate just the frame alone.*

In Frame layers both the component parts remain as separate individual images despite being stored as one layer. What does this mean in day-to-day editing? Well, it means that you can do things like change the size, shape and orientation of either the frame, or the picture, independently of each other. This level of flexibility is a godsend for those photographers who

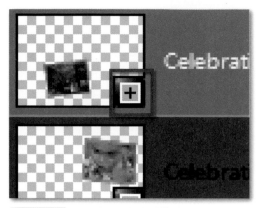

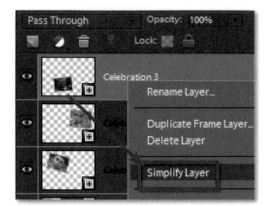

Figure 7.52 Frame layers look different from other layer types because they have a small plus symbol at the bottom right of the layer thumbnail.

Figure 7.53 Like shape and text layers, Frame layers are resolution independent and so need to be simplified before you can edit them directly.

regularly compose album or scrapbook pages. Individual photos and their frames can be pushed, pulled, twisted and sized until the composition is just right. See Figure 7.51.

In Photoshop Elements 6 and 7 Frame layers are used in the production of photo projects options including Photo Collages, Photo Books, Greeting Cards, CD or DVD Jackets and CD/DVD Labels.

Frame layers appear like a standard image layer except they have a small plus sign in the bottom right-hand corner of the layer thumbnail to distinguish them from other layer types. Like text and shape layers, Frame layers are also resolution independent. See Figure 7.52.

The upside of this characteristic is that the frame and photo content can be up- or downsized many times with minimal or no damage to picture components. This is not the case for a standard image layer where such changes over time cause the photo to become less clear. The downside, you knew there had to be one, is that because of this basic structure you cannot edit or enhance the pixels in a Frame layer directly. Any attempt to adjust brightness, color, contrast or even filter the photo or the frame meets with a warning dialog that states that you must Simplify the Frame layer first. Simplifying the layer means converting it from its resolution-independent 'frame plus photo' state to a standard pixel-based image layer. See Figure 7.53. For more details on Frame layers and how to use then go to Chapter 10.

Layer transparency

Until this point we have assumed that the contents of each layer were solid. When a layer is placed on top, and in front, of the contents of another layer, it obscures the objects underneath completely. And for most imaging scenarios this is exactly the way that we would expect the layers to perform, but occasionally it is desirable to allow some of the detail, color and texture of what is beneath to show through. To achieve this effect, the Transparency of each layer can be interactively adjusted via the Opacity slider control in the top right-hand corner of the palette.

See Figure 7.54. Keep in mind that making the selected layer less opaque will result in it being more transparent.

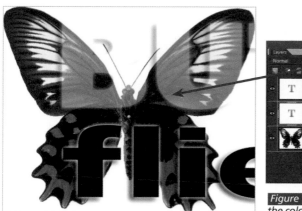
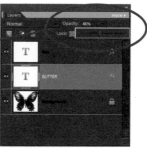

Figure 7.44 Altering the opacity of a layer allows the color, texture and tone of the image beneath to show through.

Layer blend modes

The layer blending modes extend the possibilities of how two layers interact. See Figures 7.55 and 7.56 . Twenty-three different mode options are available in the drop-down menu to the left of the Opacity slider in the Layers palette. For ordinary use the mode is kept on the Normal selection, but a host of special effects can be achieved if a different method of interaction, or mode, is selected. The mode options are the same ones available for use with tools like the Paintbrush and

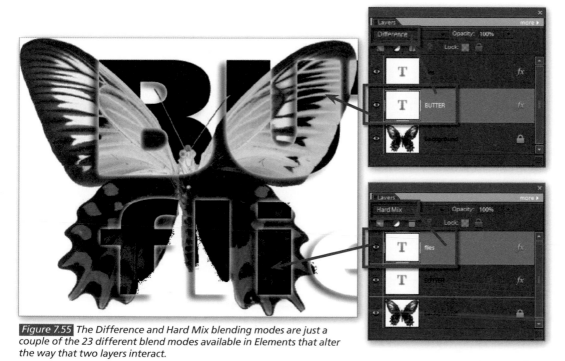

Figure 7.55 The Difference and Hard Mix blending modes are just a couple of the 23 different blend modes available in Elements that alter the way that two layers interact.

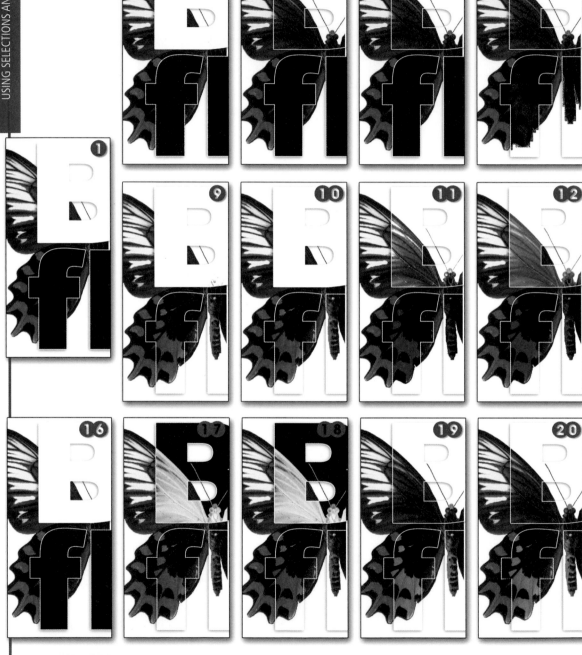

Figure 7.56 Layer blending modes control the way that two separate layers interact. The examples above indicate the different effects that are possible when selecting one of the 23 that are available. (1) Normal. (2) Dissolve. (3) Darken. (4) Multiply. (5) Color Burn. (6) Linear Burn. (7) Lighten. (8) Screen. (9) Color Dodge. (10) Linear Dodge. (11) Overlay. (12) Soft Light. (13) Hard Light. (14) Vivid Light. (15) Linear Light. (16) Pin Light. (17) Difference. (18) Exclusion. (19) Hue. (20) Saturation. (21) Luminosity. (22) Hard Mix. (23) Color.

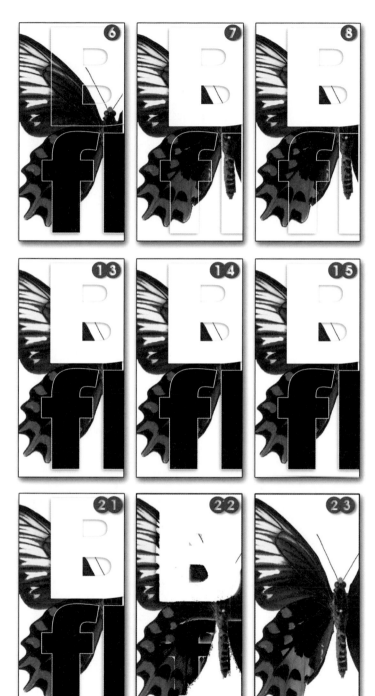

Pencil, and some advanced editing or enhancement techniques are based on their use. Experimenting with different modes will help you understand how they affect the combining of layers and will also help you to determine the best occasions to use this feature.

Layer Styles

Early on in the digital imaging revolution, users started to place visual effects like drop shadows or glowing edges on parts of their pictures. A large section of any class teaching earlier versions of Photoshop was designated to learning the many steps needed to create these effects. With the release of packages like Elements, these types of effects have become built-in features of the program. Now, it is possible to apply an effect like a 'drop shadow' to the contents of a layer with the click of a single button. See Figure 7.57.

Adobe has grouped all these layer effects under a single heading 'Special Effects' in the palette called Effects (previously Artwork and Effects). As with many features in the program, a thumbnail version of each style provides a quick reference to the results of applying the effect. To add the style to a selected layer, simply click on the thumbnail and then press the Apply button.

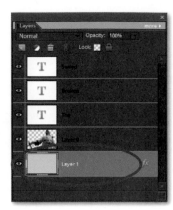

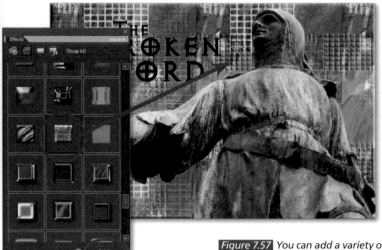

Figure 7.57 *You can add a variety of effects to the contents of your layers with the Layer Styles feature.*

Multiple styles can be applied to the one layer and the settings used to create the effect can be edited by double-clicking the starburst icon on the selected layer in the palette. Remove a layer style by selecting Layer > Layer Style > Clear Layer Style whilst selecting the layer with the style applied.

Customizing of layer styles

In Elements 5.0 it became easier to customize the layer styles in your Elements documents with the controls in the Style Settings dialog. To fine-tune your styles select a layer in the Layers palette and then choose Layer > Layer Style > Style Settings. The Style Settings dialog groups together a variety of sliders and settings that control the look of the style. Here you can not only adjust the settings of the applied style but you can also apply other styles. The settings and controls listed depends on the style applied to the layer. See Figure 7.58.

Pro's Tip: Double clicking on the effects icon on the layer entry in the layers palette is a quicker way to access this dialog.

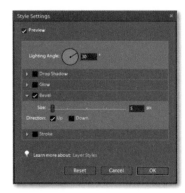

Figure 7.58 *Customize the look of the layer styles in your documents by changing the values in the Style Settings dialog.*

Adding Elements' Layer Styles

If you spread your styles wings a little further there are many sites on the web that offer free downloadable styles that can be added to your library. Usually, the files are downloaded in a compressed form such as a zip. The file needs to be extracted and then saved to the Adobe\Photoshop Elements 7\Presets\Styles folder before use. The next time you start Elements you will have a smorgasbord of new styles to apply to your images. See Figure 7.59.

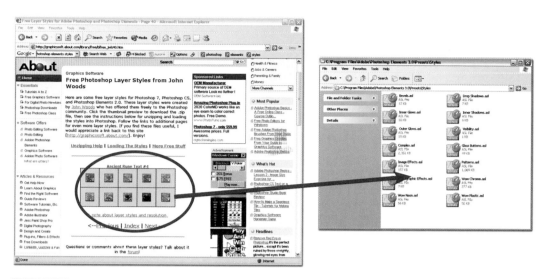

Figure 7.59 Extending the library of styles you have available to you is as simple as downloading new examples from the Net and installing them in the Elements Styles folder.

Organizing layers

Moving

Layers can be moved up and down the layer stack by click-dragging them to a new position. Moving a layer upwards will mean that its picture content may obscure more of the details in the layers below. Moving downwards progressively positions the layer's details further behind the picture parts of the layers above. You can reposition the content of any layers (except background layers) using the Move tool.

Linking

Two or more layers can be joined together so that when the content of one layer is moved the other details follow precisely. This process is called linking and preserves the content of each layer but allows them to be moved as if they were just one entity.

Adobe provided a new way to link layers in Elements 5.0. Firstly, the layers are multi-selected using Shift-click to select layers that are consecutive and Ctrl-click to choose random layers to link. The selected layers will change to the active layer color – gray in use in Figure 7.60. After selecting, the layers are linked by clicking the chain icon at the top of the Layers palette. To unlink reverse these steps.

Before these changes in the new release, you simply clicked on the box on the right of the eye symbol in the Layers palette to link them together. When linked the box is filled with a chain symbol to indicate that this layer is now linked with others in the palette.

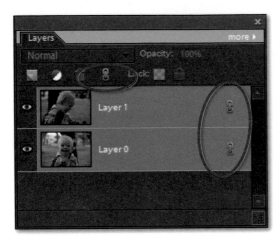

Figure 7.60 *Layers are linked by multi-selecting first and then clicking the chain icon in the Layers palette.*

Merging

The content of multi-selected layers can be combined into a single layer using the Merge Layers option in the Layer menu. In a similar way, a layered document can be flattened into a picture that only contains a background via the Layer > Flatten Image command. Merging or flattening layers are not steps that are recommended though, as both actions remove the ability of editing the content or position of each layer individually.

Deleting

Unwanted layers can be deleted by dragging them to the dustbin icon at the bottom of the Layers palette or by selecting the layer and clicking the icon.

Quick guide to Layer shortcuts

1 To display Layers palette – Choose Windows > Layers
2 To access layer options – Click the More button in the upper right of the Layers palette
3 To change the size of layer thumbnails – Choose Palette options from the Layers palette menu and select a thumbnail size
4 To make a new layer – Choose Layer > New > Layer
5 To create a new adjustment layer – Choose Layer > New Adjustment Layer and then select the layer type
6 To create a new fill layer – Choose Layer > New > New Fill Layer and select the layer type
7 To add a style or effect to a layer – Select the layer and click on a thumbnail in the Styles and Effects palette

8

Having a great time... wishing...

Combining Text with Your Images

Creating simple type

Creating paragraph text

Basic text changes

Creating and using type masks

Reducing the 'jaggies'

Warping type

Applying styles to type layers

New text alternatives

Debunking some type terms

Digital imaging has blurred the boundaries between many traditional industries. No longer does the image maker's job stop the moment the illustration or photograph hits the art director's desk. With the increased abilities of software like Photoshop Elements has come the expectation that not only are you able to create the pictures needed for the job, but you are also able to perform other functions like adding text. See Figure 8.1.

Combining text and images is usually the job of a graphic designer or printer, but the simple text functions that are now included in most desktop imaging programs mean that more and more people are trying their hand at adding type to pictures. Elements provides the ability to input type directly onto the canvas rather than via a Type dialog. This means that you can see and adjust your text to fit and suit the image beneath. Changes of size, shape and style can be made at any stage by selecting the existing text and applying the changes via the options bar. As the type is saved as a special type layer, it remains editable even when the file is closed, so long as it is saved and reopened in the Elements PSD format. See Figure 8.2.

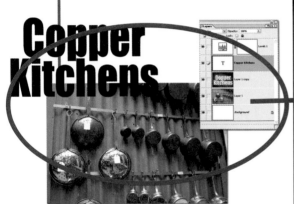

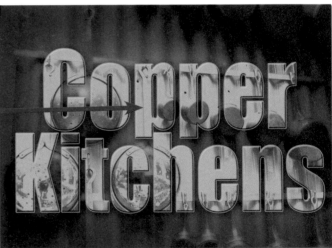

Figure 8.1 *Elements has a range of sophisticated text features built right into the main program. This means that combining text and images in the one document has become a task that is easier to complete than ever before.*

Paragraph text

In earlier versions of Elements text was entered one line at a time. The user needed to press the Enter key at the end of each line in order to start a new line of text underneath. From version 4.0 this way of working was no longer necessary. Now text entered in Paragraph mode will automatically wrap when the cursor reaches the text box edge. See Figure 8.3.

WYSIWYG font previews

Present since version 5.0, is the WYSIWYG (What You See Is What You Get) preview that is displayed on the Text tool font menu. With this feature it is possible to see an example of how the letter shapes for each font family appear right in the menu itself. See Figure 8.4.

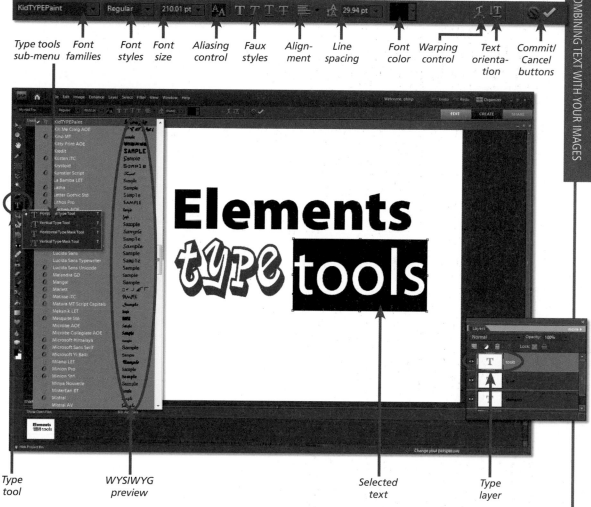

Type tools sub-menu · Font families · Font styles · Font size · Aliasing control · Faux styles · Align-ment · Line spacing · Font color · Warping control · Text orienta-tion · Commit/Cancel buttons

Type tool · WYSIWYG preview · Selected text · Type layer

Figure 8.2 The advanced Type tools in Elements' Editor workspace allow the user to enter (and edit) text directly in the Editor workspace.

The paragraph text feature in Pho-toshop Elements automatically wraps text lines when they reach the boundaries of a text box

Figure 8.3 Paragraph text automatically wraps from one line to the next.

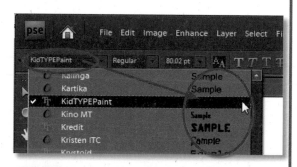

Figure 8.4 The font family menu (Text tool options bar) displays a WYSIWYG example of the font.

Creating simple type

In version 7 you can select from four different type tools including the Horizontal and Vertical Type tool options, as well as Horizontal and Vertical Type Mask tools. Of the standard Type tools (non-mask varieties), one is used for entering text that runs horizontally across the canvas and the other is for entering vertical type. See Figure 8.5. To place text onto your picture, select the Type tool from the toolbox. Next, click onto the canvas in the area where you want the text to appear. Do not be too concerned if the letters are not positioned exactly, as the layer and text can be moved later. Once you have finished entering text you need to commit the type to a layer. Until this is done you will be unable to access most other Elements functions. To exit the Text editor, either click the tick button in the options bar or press the Control + Enter keys in Windows. See Figure 8.6.

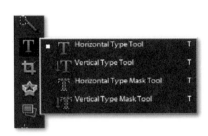

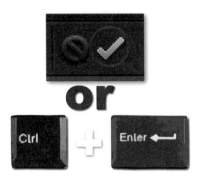

Figure 8.5 Four text options are available via the Type tool selection in the toolbox.

Figure 8.6 Any text entered must be 'committed' to a type layer before other tools or menu choices can be used. As well as pressing the Commit button you can click another tool, or apply a Layer Style or menu command. The type will then auto-commit.

Creating paragraph text

In version 4.0 Adobe introduced the Paragraph Text options to the simple Type ones detailed above. To create a paragraph, select the Type tool and then click and drag a text box on the surface of the picture. Automatically Elements positions a cursor inside the box and creates a new layer to hold the contents. Typing inside the box will add text that automatically wraps when it reaches the box edge. When you have completed entering text, either click the tick button in the options bar, or press the Control + Enter keys.

You can resize or even change the shape of the box at any time by selecting a Type tool and then clicking onto the area where the paragraph text has been entered. This action will cause the original text box to display. The box can then be resized by moving the cursor over one of the handles (small boxes at the corners/edges) and click-dragging the text box marquee to a new position. The text inside the box will automatically rewrap to suit the new dimensions.

Basic text changes

All the usual text changes available to word processor users are contained in Elements. It is possible to alter the size, style, color and font of your type using the settings in the options bar. See Figure 8.7. You can either make the selections before you input your text or later by highlighting (clicking and dragging the mouse across the text) the portion of type that you want to change. In addition to these adjustments, you can also alter the justification or alignment of a line or paragraph of type. After selecting the type to be aligned, click one of the Justification buttons on the options bar. Your text will realign automatically on screen. After making a few changes, you may wish to alter the position of the text; simply click and drag outside of the type area to move it around. If you have already committed the changes to a text layer then select the Move tool from the toolbox, making sure that the text layer is selected (just roll the mouse over text until you see the blue outline and click), then click and drag to move the whole layer. See Figure 8.8.

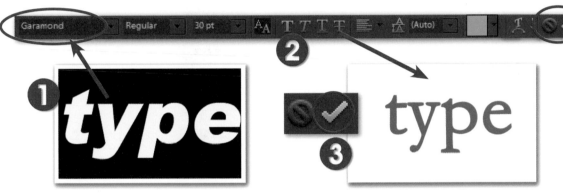

Figure 8.7 *The text options bar contains a number of settings for altering the style, font, color, aliasing, alignment and size of the type entered. To change the settings of your type, (1) select the text, (2) make the changes in the Type tool options bar and then (3) commit the changes by clicking the tick icon in the bar.*

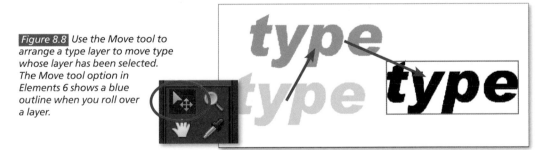

Figure 8.8 *Use the Move tool to arrange a type layer to move type whose layer has been selected. The Move tool option in Elements 6 shows a blue outline when you roll over a layer.*

Creating and using type masks

The Type Mask tools are used to provide precise masks or selections in the shape and size of the text you input. Rather than creating a new text layer containing solid colored text, the mask tools produce a selection outline. From this point on the text mask can be used as you would use any other selection. See Figure 8.9.

FEATURE SUMMARY

1 Choose the Type tool from the toolbox. To change between Type tools, click and hold on the tool to reveal the hidden options.

2 Click on the picture surface to position the start of the text or click-drag to create a text box.

3 Make changes to font type, size, style, justification and color by altering the settings in the options bar.

4 Enter your text using the keyboard or by pasting sections (Edit > Paste) from a copied word processing document.

5 For non-masked text, click and drag to move the text over the image background.

6 Commit entered text or changes to a type layer by clicking 'tick' in the options bar or by pressing Control + Enter.

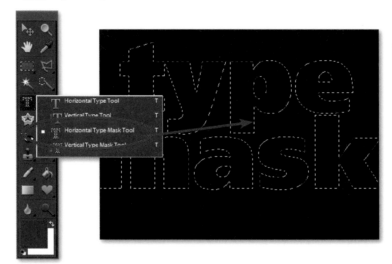

Figure 8.9 The Type Mask tools are used to make text-shaped selections.

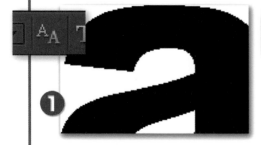
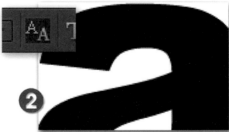

Figure 8.10 The Anti-aliasing setting helps smooth out the edges of 'jagged' text. (1) Anti-aliased feature off. (2) Anti-aliased feature on.

Reducing the 'jaggies'

One of the drawbacks of using a system that is based on pixels to draw sharp-edged letter shapes is that circles and curves are made up of a series of pixel steps. Anti-aliasing is a system where the effects of these 'jaggies' are made less noticeable by partially filling in the edge pixels. This technique produces smoother looking type overall and should be used in all print circumstances and web applications. See Figure 8.10. The only exception is where file size is critical, as anti-aliased web text creates larger files than the standard text equivalent. Anti-aliasing can be turned on and off by clicking the Anti-aliased button or checking the box (version 1.0) in the options bar.

FEATURE SUMMARY

1 Turn anti-aliasing on by clicking the Anti-aliased button in the options bar, or by selecting Layer > Type > Anti-Alias On.

2 Turn anti-aliasing off by reclicking the button, unchecking the box (version 1.0) in the options bar or by selecting Layer > Type > Anti-Alias Off.

Warping type

One of the special features of the Elements type system is the Warping feature. This tool forces text to distort to one of a range of shapes. An individual word, or even whole sentences, can be made to curve, bulge or even simulate the effect of a fish-eye lens. See Figure 8.11. The strength and style of the effect can be controlled by manipulating the Bend and Horizontal and Vertical Distortion sliders.

This feature is particularly useful when creating graphic headings for posters or web pages. See Figure 8.12.

FEATURE SUMMARY

1 Choose a completed type layer.

2 Select Layer > Type > Warp Text or pick the Type tool from the toolbox and click the Warp button in the options bar.

3 Choose the warp style from the drop-down menu.

4 Adjust the Bend, Horizontal Distortion and Vertical Distortion sliders.

5 Click OK to finish.

Applying styles to type layers

Elements' Layer Styles can be applied very effectively to type layers and provide a quick and easy way to enhance the look of your text. Everything from a simple drop shadow to complex surface and color treatments can be applied using this single-click feature. See Figure 8.13. A collection of included styles can be found under the Layer Styles heading in the Effects palette (previously called the Artwork and Effects palette). A variety of different Style groups are available from the drop-down list and small example images of each style are provided as a preview of the effect. See Figure 8.14. Additional styles can be downloaded from websites specializing in resources for Elements users. These should be installed into the Adobe\Photoshop Elements\Presets\Styles folder. The next time you start Elements, the new styles will appear in the Styles and Effects palette. Extra type effects are also located in the Effects group of the Styles and Effects palette.

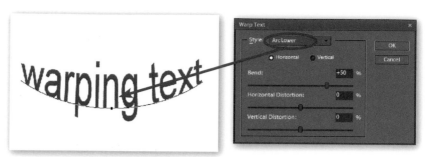

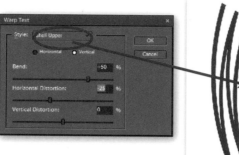

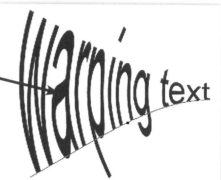

Figure 8.11 The Warp feature is used to twist and squeeze text into a range of shapes. The style of the warping can be selected from the drop-down menu in the feature's dialog.

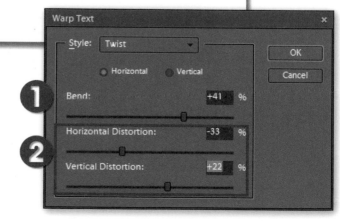

Figure 8.12 The degree of bend (1) and distortion (2) of the text can be altered using the settings in the Warp Text dialog.

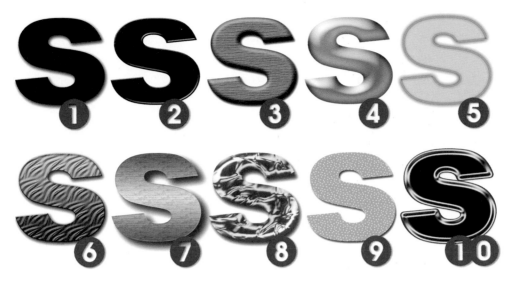

Figure 8.13 The look of text can be changed with a single click using Layer Styles. (1) Drop shadow. (2) Inner Ridge Bevel. (3) Wood Grain. (4) Pink Glass. (5) Purple Neon. (6) Waves. (7) Brushed Metal. (8) Molten Gold. (9) Cactus. (10) Chrome Fat.

To apply a style to a section of type, make sure that the text layer is currently active. Do this by checking that the layer is highlighted in the Layers palette. See Figure 8.15. Next, open and view the Layer Styles section in the Effects palette. Click on the thumbnail of the style you want to apply to the text and then click the Apply button at the bottom of the palette.

The changes will be immediately reflected in your image. See Figure 8.16. Multiple styles can be applied to a single layer and unwanted effects can be removed by using the Step Backward button (Undo) in the shortcuts bar or the Undo command (Edit > Undo Apply Style).

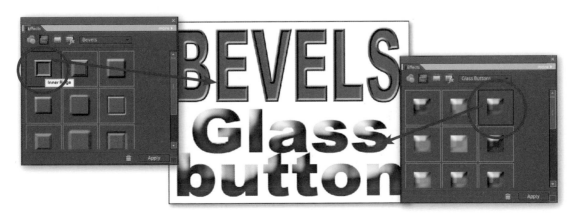

Figure 8.14 Layer styles are grouped in menus around a common theme such as Drop Shadows, Bevels and Glass Buttons. In versions 6 and 7 layer styles are grouped with other effects and filters in the Effects palette which was called the Artwork and Effects palette in Photoshop Elements 5.0.

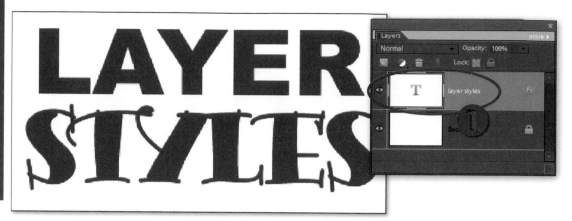

Figure 8.15 *Make sure the type layer is selected before applying a layer style. (1) Active text layer.*

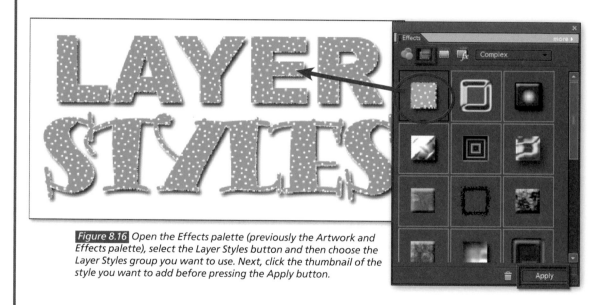

Figure 8.16 *Open the Effects palette (previously the Artwork and Effects palette), select the Layer Styles button and then choose the Layer Styles group you want to use. Next, click the thumbnail of the style you want to add before pressing the Apply button.*

The settings of individual styles can be edited by double-clicking on the star icon in the text layer and adjusting one or more of the Style settings. See Figure 8.17.

FEATURE SUMMARY

1 Ensure that the text layer is selected.

2 View the Layer Styles group by clicking the Special Effects tab in the Effects palette and then choosing the Layer Styles option from the drop-down menu.

3 Choose the group and style to apply to your text from the drop-down list and thumbnails.

4 Edit Style Settings by double-clicking the '*fx*' symbol in the text layer.

5 Remove effects by selecting Edit > Undo Layer Styles or by clearing Layer Styles.

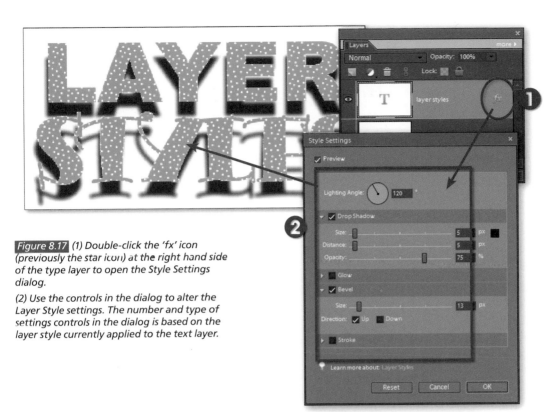

Figure 8.17 (1) Double-click the 'fx' icon (previously the star icon) at the right hand side of the type layer to open the Style Settings dialog.

(2) Use the controls in the dialog to alter the Layer Style settings. The number and type of settings controls in the dialog is based on the layer style currently applied to the text layer.

Other ways to add text

In the last couple of versions of Photoshop Elements Adobe created a couple of new ways to handle the text in your photos. In version 7 these option are accessed by clicking the Create tab on the right of the Edit workspace. Located in the Content palette in the Artwork pane is a Text section which contains thumbnail previews of a variety of text effects.

On the simplest level the design options listed here can be used in much the same way as the Layer Style entries we looked at in the previous section. To change the look of existing text layers, select the layer in the Layers palette first and then choose the text style by clicking one of the thumbnails. Add the style to the layer by pressing the Apply button at the bottom of the palette. The 'fx' icon is added to the text layer to indicate that it now has a style associated with it. See Figure 8.18.

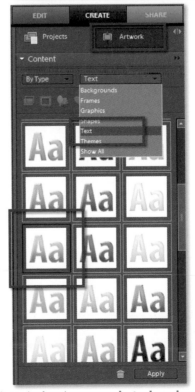

Figure 8.18 The Text section of the Effects palette contains a range of text styles that can be added to the type in your photos. In version 7 the Artwork palette is located in the Create tab of the Edit workspace.

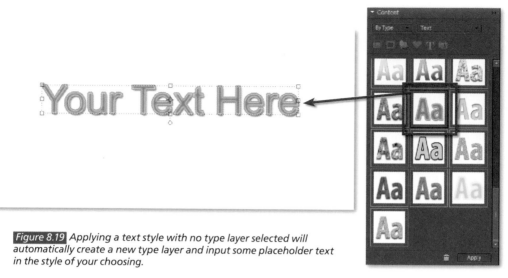

Figure 8.19 Applying a text style with no type layer selected will automatically create a new type layer and input some placeholder text in the style of your choosing.

Editing or customizing the style is as simple as double-clicking the '*fx*' icon to display the Styles Settings dialog and then altering the controls for each style characteristic (drop shadow, glow, bevel, stroke).

If you have not yet created the text layer then there is no need to add it first before selecting the style. Just click on the thumbnail style of your choice and then press the Apply button. This action will automatically create a new text layer in your document and input some placeholder text, 'Your Text Here', with the style applied. From this point on it is a simple matter to replace this generic text with your own. Just double-click on the text with the Move tool; Elements will then switch tools to the Type tool and select all of the placeholder text. Now type in the new text to complete the replacement. Alternatively, you can click on the text and then choose Edit Text from the Move tool's context menu. See Figure 8.19.

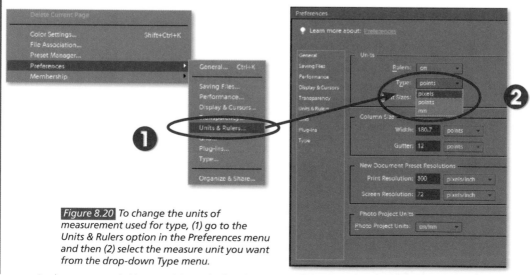

Figure 8.20 To change the units of measurement used for type, (1) go to the Units & Rulers option in the Preferences menu and then (2) select the measure unit you want from the drop-down Type menu.

Debunking some type terms

Font size

The size of the text you place in your image files is measured as pixels, millimeters or points. I find the pixel setting most useful when working with digital files, as it indicates to me the precise size of my text in relationship to the whole image. Millimeter and points values, on the other hand, vary depending on the resolution of the picture and the resolution of the output device. Some of you might be aware that 72 points approximately equals 1 inch, but this is only true if the picture's resolution is 72 dpi. At higher resolutions the pixels are packed more closely together and therefore the same 72 point type is smaller in size.

FEATURE SUMMARY

To change the unit of measurement used for text in Elements:

1 Windows users, select Edit > Preferences > Units & Rulers.

2 Then alter the unit of measurement for Type. See Figure 8.20.

Font family and style

The font family is a term used to describe the way that the letter shapes look. Most readers would be familiar with the difference in appearance between Arial and Times Roman. These are two different families each containing different characteristics that determine the way that the letter

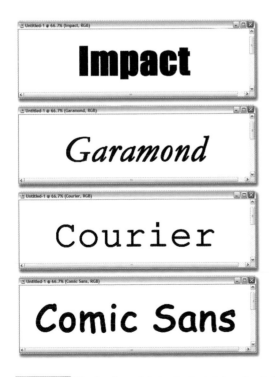

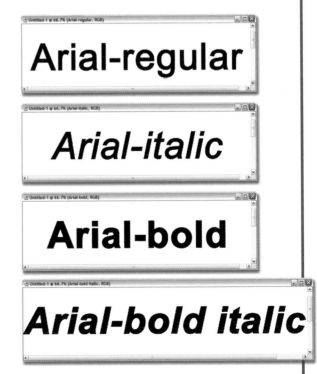

Figure 8.21 *The family and style of a font determine its look.*

shapes appear. The font style refers to the different versions of the same font family. Most fonts are available in regular, italic, bold and bold italic styles. See Figure 8.21.

You can download new fonts from specialist websites to add to your system. Some families are available free of charge, others can be purchased online. After downloading, the fonts should be installed into the Fonts section of your system directory. Windows and Macintosh users will need to consult their operating system manuals to find the preferred method for installing new fonts on their computer.

Alignment and justification

These terms are often used interchangeably and refer to the way that a line or paragraph of text is positioned on the image. The Left Align, or Left Justify, feature will arrange all text to the left of the picture. When applied to a group of sentences, the left edge of the paragraph is organized into a straight vertical line whilst the right-hand edge remains uneven or ragged. Right align works in the opposite fashion, straightening the right-hand edge of the paragraph and leaving the left ragged. Selecting the Center Text option will align the paragraph around a central line and leave both left and right edges ragged. See Figure 8.22.

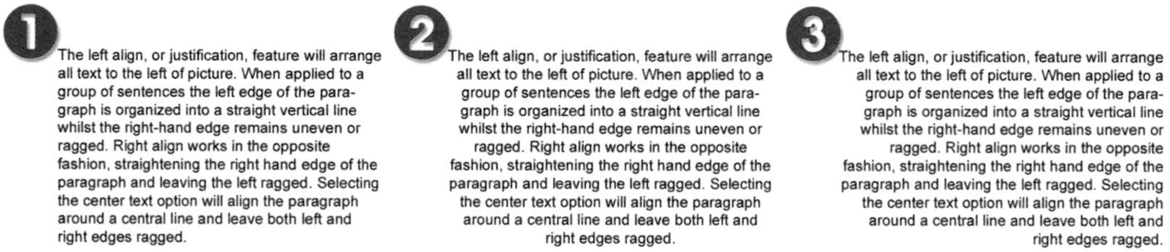

1 The left align, or justification, feature will arrange all text to the left of picture. When applied to a group of sentences the left edge of the paragraph is organized into a straight vertical line whilst the right-hand edge remains uneven or ragged. Right align works in the opposite fashion, straightening the right hand edge of the paragraph and leaving the left ragged. Selecting the center text option will align the paragraph around a central line and leave both left and right edges ragged.

2 The left align, or justification, feature will arrange all text to the left of picture. When applied to a group of sentences the left edge of the paragraph is organized into a straight vertical line whilst the right-hand edge remains uneven or ragged. Right align works in the opposite fashion, straightening the right hand edge of the paragraph and leaving the left ragged. Selecting the center text option will align the paragraph around a central line and leave both left and right edges ragged.

3 The left align, or justification, feature will arrange all text to the left of picture. When applied to a group of sentences the left edge of the paragraph is organized into a straight vertical line whilst the right-hand edge remains uneven or ragged. Right align works in the opposite fashion, straightening the right hand edge of the paragraph and leaving the left ragged. Selecting the center text option will align the paragraph around a central line and leave both left and right edges ragged.

Figure 8.22 Type alignment controls how the text is arranged in the image. (1) Left align. (2) Center. (3) Right align.

Leading

Originally referring to the small pieces of lead that were placed in between lines of metal type used in old printing processes, nowadays it is easier to think of the term referring to the space between lines of text. Unlike earlier versions of the program, Elements now includes the ability to alter the leading of the type input in your documents. Start with a value equal to the font size you are using and increase or decrease from here according to your requirements. See Figure 8.23.

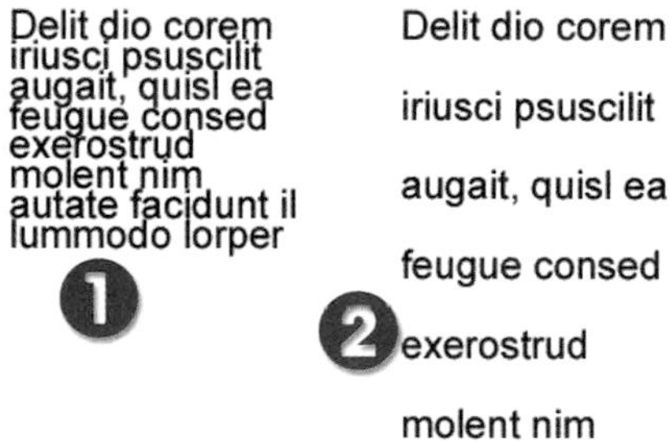

1 Delit dio corem iriusci psuscilit augait, quisl ea feugue consed exerostrud molent nim autate facidunt il lummodo lorper

Delit dio corem

iriusci psuscilit

augait, quisl ea

feugue consed

2 exerostrud

molent nim

Figure 8.23 Leading is the space between lines of text. 24 pixel type with: (1) 18 pixel leading and (2) 48 pixel leading.

9

Using Elements' Painting and Drawing Tools

Cookie Cutter tool

Painting tools

Better with a tablet

Painting tools in action

Drawing tools

At some point during your imaging life you will need, or want, to create an image from scratch. Until now, we have concentrated on editing, adjusting and enhancing images that have been generated using either a camera or scanner; now we will look at how to use Elements' painting and drawing tools to create something entirely new.

Although the names are the same, the tools used by the traditional artists to paint and draw are quite different from their digital namesakes. The ***painting*** tools (the Paint Brush, Pencil, Eraser, Paint Bucket and Airbrush) in Elements are pixel based. That is, when they are dragged across the image they change the pixels to the color and texture selected for the tool. These tools are highly customizable and, in particular, the painting qualities of the Brush tool can be radically changed via the brush More Options palette.

The ***drawing*** tools (the Shape tool), in contrast, are vector or line based. The objects drawn with these tools are defined mathematically as a specific shape, color and size. They exist independently of the pixel grid that makes up your image. They produce sharp-edged graphics and are particularly good for creating logos and other flat colored artwork. See Figure 9.1.

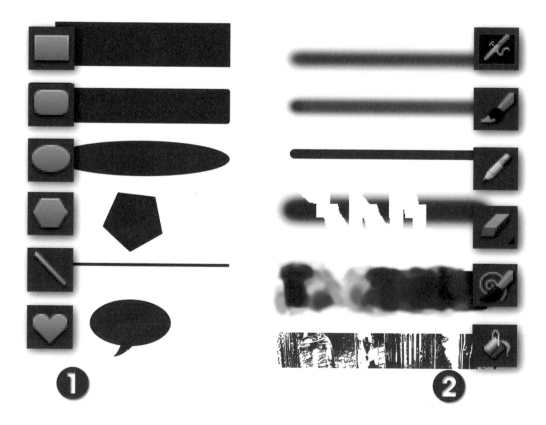

Figure 9.1 Drawing and painting tools are used to add non-photographed information to your images. (1) Drawing tools. (2) Painting tools.

Cookie Cutter tool

Also included in this vector type (hard-edged) Drawing tools group is the Cookie Cutter tool. Though not strictly a drawing tool, the feature works in a very similar way to the Custom Shape tool as it too allows users to select and draw a range of predesigned shapes in the workspace. It is after the drawing step that the two tools differ. The shape drawn with the Cookie Cutter is used to define the edges of the current image. In this way the feature functions as a fancy Crop tool, providing a range of graphic designs that can be used to stamp out the edges of your pictures. See Figure 9.2.

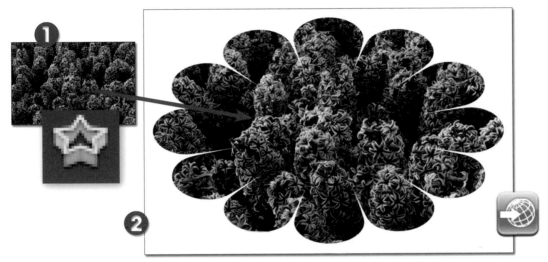

Figure 9.2 *The Cookie Cutter tool that was first introduced in Elements 3.0 functions much like a fancy cropping feature, allowing users to remove the edges of their pictures in a range of graphic hard-edged shapes. Adding a feather value via the options bar softens the edge of the crop, producing smoother transitions between the filled shape and the background. (1) Original photo. (2) Photo cropped with the Cookie Cutter tool.*

Painting tools

Paint Brush

The four main painting tools all apply color to an image in slightly different ways.

The Paint Brush lays down color in a similar fashion to a traditional brush. The size and shape of the brush can be selected from the list in the Brush Presets list (versions 2.0 – 6) or Brush palette (version 1.0) in the options bar. Changes to the brush characteristics can be made by altering the settings in the options bar and the More Options palette. See Figure 9.3.

In addition to changes to the size, painting mode and opacity of the brush, which are made via the options bar, you can also alter how the Paint Brush behaves. The Brush Dynamics palette (displayed by pressing the brush icon on the right end of the options bar) is used to creatively control your brush's characteristics, or brush dynamics as it is sometimes called.

The More Options palette

- **Spacing** determines the distance between paint dabs measured in brush diameters, with high values producing dotty effects.

- The **Fade** setting controls how quickly the paint color will fade to nothing. Low values fade more quickly than high ones.

- **Hue Jitter** controls the rate at which the brushes' color switches between foreground and background hues. High values cause quicker switches between the two colors.

- **Hardness** sets the size of the hard-edged center of the brush. Lower values produce soft brushes.

- The **Scatter** setting is used to control the way that strokes are bunched around the drawn line. A high value will cause the brush strokes to be more distant and less closely packed.

- **Angle** controls the inclination of an elliptical brush.

- The **Roundness** setting is used to determine the shape of the brush tip. A value of 100% will produce a circular brush, whereas a 0% setting results in a linear brush tip. See Figure 9.4.

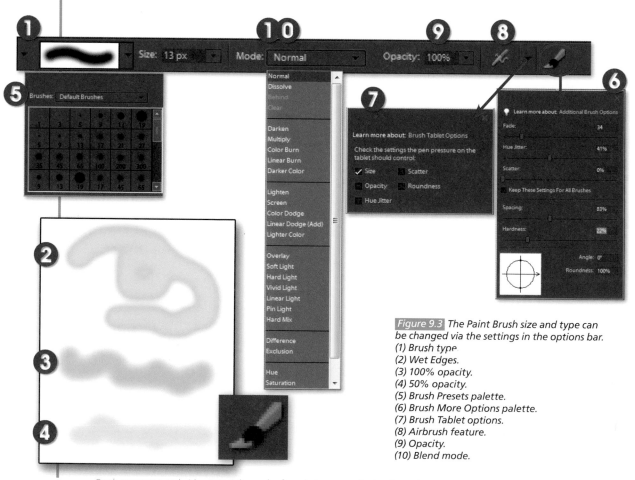

Figure 9.3 The Paint Brush size and type can be changed via the settings in the options bar.
(1) Brush type.
(2) Wet Edges.
(3) 100% opacity.
(4) 50% opacity.
(5) Brush Presets palette.
(6) Brush More Options palette.
(7) Brush Tablet options.
(8) Airbrush feature.
(9) Opacity.
(10) Blend mode.

In previous versions users had a more limited set of brush controls that were accessed by clicking the thumbnail of the currently selected brush or pressing the More Options button. Thankfully Elements 6 and 7 have a wide range of brush options and completely new brushes can be added to the palette by selecting the side-arrow in the Brush palette and choosing the New Brush option. For the truly creative among us, extra custom-built brush sets are available for download and installation from websites specializing in Photoshop Elements resources.

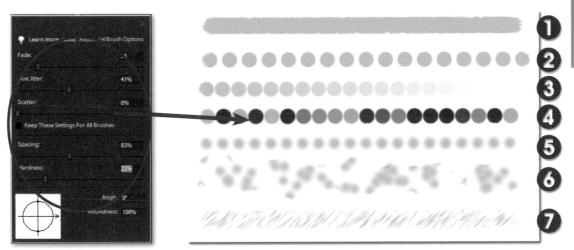

Figure 9.4 *The Elements brush engine provides a range of Brush Dynamics settings that allow users to completely control the behavior and characteristics of their brushes. (1) Normal. (2) Spacing increased. (3) Fade introduced. (4) Hue Jitter increased. (5) Hardness decreased. (6) Scatter increased. (7) Angle = 45°, Roundness = 0%.*

Airbrush

The Airbrush tool, located in the options bar of the Brush tool, sprays the paint color over the surface of the image. Although the size and style of the spray are determined by the selected brush (in the options bar), the edge of the area painted with this tool is a lot softer than the equivalent paint brush. Holding the mouse button down in one spot will build up the color in much the same way as paint from a spray can. See Figure 9.5.

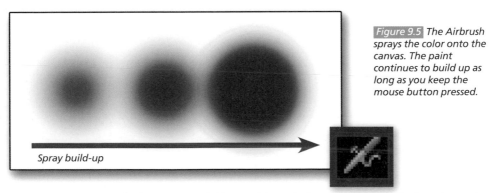

Figure 9.5 *The Airbrush sprays the color onto the canvas. The paint continues to build up as long as you keep the mouse button pressed.*

Spray build-up

Pencil

The Pencil differs from the other tools we have looked at so far in that it paints freehand lines. The thickness of these lines is dependent on the selected brush size and the lines drawn with the pencil have hard edges with no anti-aliasing. By clicking and dragging the mouse, the user can create free form lines just as if you were using a pencil and a piece of paper. Using the tool in conjunction with the Shift key means that you can draw straight lines by clicking at the beginning and end points.

Don't confuse the Pencil with the line version of the Shape tool. The Pencil draws with pixels; the Line tool defines a beginning and end point to a mathematical pixel-free line that is drawn only at the time that it is printed. See Figure 9.6.

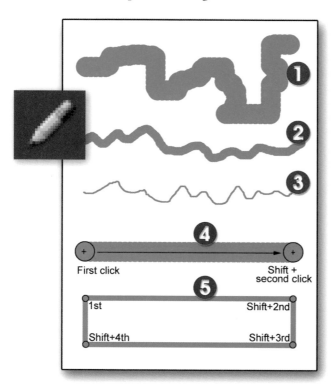

Figure 9.6 *The Pencil tool draws hard-edged lines.*
(1) 70 pixel pencil.
(2) 30 pixel pencil.
(3) 8 pixel pencil.
(4) To draw a straight line click to start the line and hold down the Shift key and click the mouse button a second time to mark the end of the line.
(5) The shift + click technique is used to draw a rectangle.

Paint Bucket

The Paint Bucket, though not usually considered a painting tool, is included here because its main role is to apply color to areas of the image. The best way to describe how it functions is to imagine a Magic Wand tool that selected areas based on their color and then filled these selections with the foreground tint. In this way, the Paint Bucket selects and fills in a one-step action. See Figure 9.7.

Just like the Magic Wand, the Paint Bucket makes its selection based on the Tolerance value in the options bar. Higher Tolerance values mean pixels with greater difference in tone and color will be marked for color changes by the tool. The Anti-aliased, Contiguous and Use All Layers settings also work in the same was as they do for the Magic Wand.

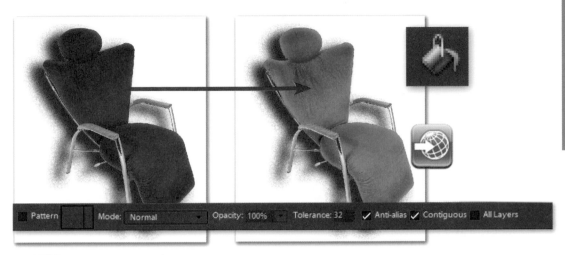

Figure 9.7 *The Paint Bucket tool selects and fills an area in the image based on pixel colors.*

In addition to applying color to selected areas, the Paint Bucket can also fill the area with a pattern. See Figure 9.8. After selecting the Pattern option you can choose from the included patterns displayed in the drop-down menu. Alternatively you can create your own using the following steps.

1 Select an area of an image using the Rectangular Marquee.

2 With the selection still active, select Define Pattern from Selection in the Edit menu.

3 Enter a name in the New Pattern dialog.

4 The new pattern is now available for use from the Pattern palette of the Paint Bucket tool.

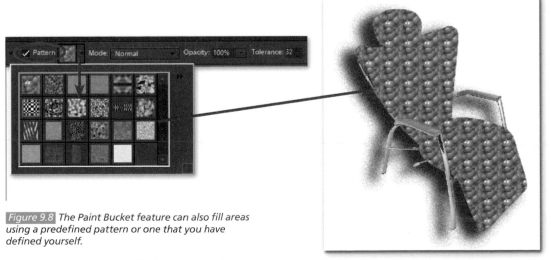

Figure 9.8 *The Paint Bucket feature can also fill areas using a predefined pattern or one that you have defined yourself.*

Choosing my paint colors

The color of the paint for all tools is based on the foreground color selected in the toolbox. To change this hue you can double-click the swatch and select another color from the palette or you can use the Eyedropper tool to sample a color already existing in your image. See Figure 9.9.

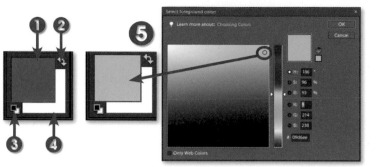
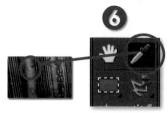

Figure 9.9 *All brushes paint with the color that is selected in the foreground/background swatches. (1) Foreground color. (2) Switch colors. (3) Default colors. (4) Background color. (5) Changing color using the Color Picker. (6) Changing color using the Eyedropper tool to sample a new hue from a picture. With the Color Picker selected, if you move the cursor over the image, it will turn into the Eyedropper tool, allowing you to sample color directly from the image.*

Painting tools summary

1 Pick foreground color (painting color).

2 Select the Painting tool from the toolbox.

3 Click the down arrow next to the sample brush in the options bar to select brush type.

4 Adjust brush opacity.

5 Adjust other options for a particular tool.

6 Drag brush over image surface to paint.

The Impressionist Brush tool

In addition to these standard painting options, Elements has a specialist Impressionist Brush tool that allows you to repaint existing images with a series of stylized strokes. By adjusting the special paint style, Area, Size and Tolerance options, you can create a variety of painterly effects on your images. See Figure 9.10.

1 Pick Impressionist Brush from the toolbox (hidden under the Brush tool in Versions 6, 5.0, 4.0, and 3.0).

2 Select brush size, mode and opacity from the options bar.

3 Set the style, area and Tolerance values from the More Options palette.

4 Drag the brush over the image surface to paint.

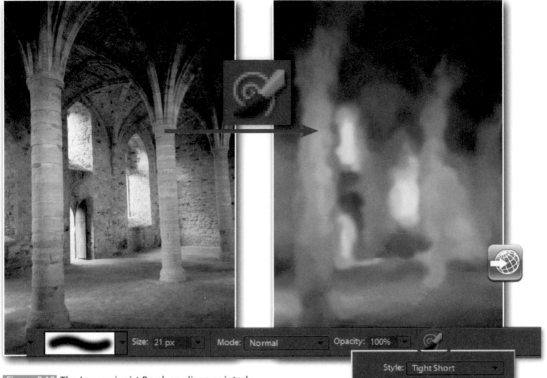

Figure 9.10 *The Impressionist Brush applies a painterly effect to the picture as you brush over the surface.*

Color Replacement tool

The Color Replacement tool locates and replaces a specific color in an image with one of your choosing. In this way it works a little like a more sophisticated version of the Red Eye Removal tool in that you can choose both the color to be replaced as well as its substitute hue. See Figure 9.11.

1 Pick the Color Replacement tool from the toolbox (hidden under the Brush tool).

2 Select brush size and set mode to Hue, sampling to Background Swatch and limits to Discontiguous in the options bar.

3 Using the Eyedropper tool select the color from the picture that you want to replace as the foreground color swatch.

4 Switch foreground and background swatches.

5 Double-click on the foreground swatch and select a replacement color.

6 Click and drag the Color Replacement brush over the image surface to substitute the colors.

FEATURE SUMMARY

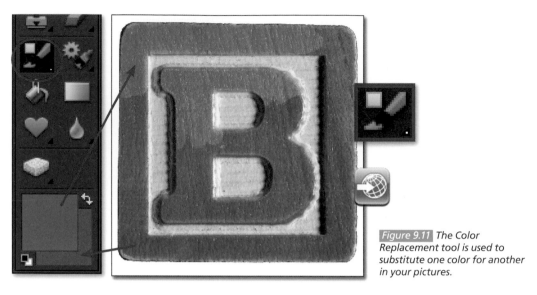

Figure 9.11 The Color Replacement tool is used to substitute one color for another in your pictures.

Erasing

The Eraser tool changes image pixels as it is dragged over them. If you are working on a background layer then the pixels are erased or changed to the background color. In contrast, erasing a normal layer will convert the pixels to transparent, which will let the image show through from beneath. See Figure 9.12.

As with the other painting tools, the size and style of the eraser is based on the selected brush. But unlike the others the eraser can take the form of a paint brush, pencil or block. Setting the opacity will govern the strength of the erasing action. Apart from the straight Eraser tool, two

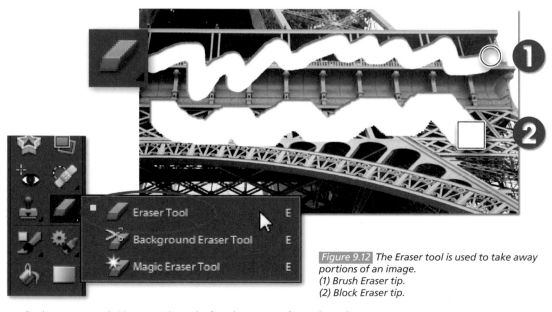

Figure 9.12 The Eraser tool is used to take away portions of an image.
(1) Brush Eraser tip.
(2) Block Eraser tip.

other versions of this tool are available – the Background Eraser and the Magic Eraser. These extra options are found hidden under the eraser icon in the toolbox.

The *Background Eraser* is used to delete pixels around the edge of an object. This tool is very useful for extracting objects from their backgrounds. The tool pointer is made of two parts – a circle and a cross hair. The circle size is based on the brush diameter. To use the tool, the cross hair is positioned and dragged across the area to be erased, whilst at the same time the circle's edge overlaps the edge of the object to be kept. The success of this tool is largely based on the contrast between the edge of the object and the background. The greater the contrast, the more effective the tool. Again, a Tolerance slider is used to control how different pixels need to be in order to be erased. See Figure 9.13.

The *Magic Eraser* uses the selection features of the Magic Wand to select similarly colored pixels to erase. This tool works well if the area of the image you want to erase is all the same color and contrasts in tone or color with the rest of the image. See Figure 9.14.

Both tools replace the background color with transparency and in the process create a new image layer if the tool was applied to a background layer.

FEATURE SUMMARY

1 Pick the Eraser tool type from the toolbox.

2 For the Eraser tool – select a brush size and style and choose the form that the tool will take.

3 For Magic Eraser and Background Eraser – set Tolerance and Contiguous values.

4 Drag over or click on the image to erase.

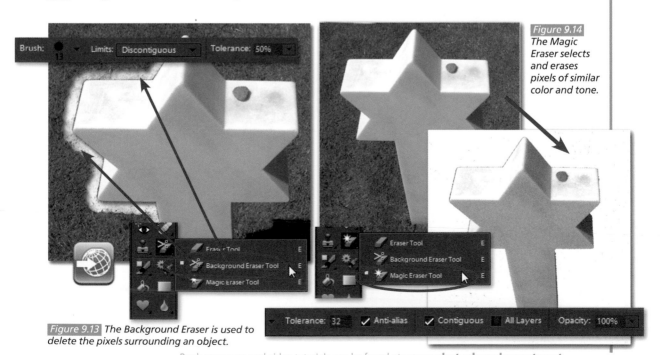

Figure 9.14 The Magic Eraser selects and erases pixels of similar color and tone.

Figure 9.13 The Background Eraser is used to delete the pixels surrounding an object.

Smart erasing

As we have seen in Chapter 6, one of the great technologies included in more recent versions of Elements is the Magic Extractor feature (Image > Magic Extractor). In this release the feature's selecting powers have been boosted so that your results will be more accurate than ever. The tool automatically erases some picture parts whilst retaining others. The user marks the areas in the photo that are to be retained or erased by painting over these sections with dots or scribbles of different colors. Elements then goes to work intelligently erasing and retaining parts throughout the photo. It is this intelligent erasing power that warrants the feature's inclusion in this part of the text. See Figure 9.15.

Used carefully, the Magic Extractor has both the power and fine-tuning abilities to make it a regular part of your erasing toolset. For more details on how to use the feature turn to the selection section in Chapter 6.

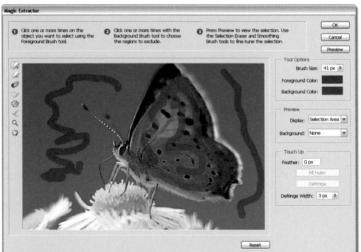

Figure 9.15 *The Magic Extractor feature acts as an intelligent Eraser tool by allowing the user to mark (scribble or dot) picture parts to be retained (foreground) and areas to be erased (background).*

Better with a tablet

Many professionals prefer to work with a stylus and tablet when working with complex drawing tasks. The extra options provided by the pressure sensitivity of the stylus, along with the familiar 'pencil and paper' feeling, make using this approach more intuitive and often faster than using a mouse. When a stylus and tablet are installed on your machine you will be able to access the extra pen or stylus options available through the program. See Figure 9.16.

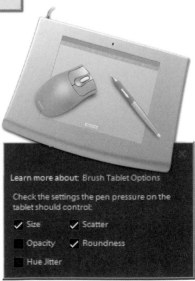

Figure 9.16 *Elements contains support for pressure-sensitive devices such as Wacom Stylus and Tablets. Elements enables the user to link specific settings to the Pressure setting of the stylus.*

Painting tools in action

Hand coloring black and white photos

In this technique, we will use the Elements Brush tool to apply a color tint to a photograph. But to ensure that the detail from the image shows through the coloring we must modify the way the hue is added. By switching the Brush mode (this is similar to the Layers blend mode options) from its Normal setting to a specialized Color setting the paint starts to act more like traditional watercolor paint. When the hue is applied the detail is changed in proportion to the tone beneath. Dark areas are changed to a deep version of the selected color and lighter areas are delicately tinted. See Figure 9.17.

1 With your image open in Elements check to see what Color mode the picture is stored in. Do this by selecting Image > Mode and then locate which setting the tick is next to. For most black and white photographs the picture will be in Grayscale mode. If this is the case change it to RGB Color (Image > Mode > RGB Color).

2 You will not notice any difference in the picture as a result of its mode change but now the image is capable of holding colors (not just grays). Now double-click on the foreground swatch in the toolbox and select a color appropriate for your picture. Here I chose a dark green for the leaves.

3 Now select the Paint Brush tool from the toolbox and adjust its size and edge softness using the settings in the options bar. Start to paint onto the surface of the picture. You will notice straight away that the paint is covering the detail of the picture beneath. This is because the brush is still in Normal mode. Use Ctrl + Z to undo your painting.

4 In order for the brush to just color the picture (keeping the details from beneath) the tool must be in the Color mode. To make the change click on the Mode drop-down menu in the options bar and select the Color option towards the bottom of the list.

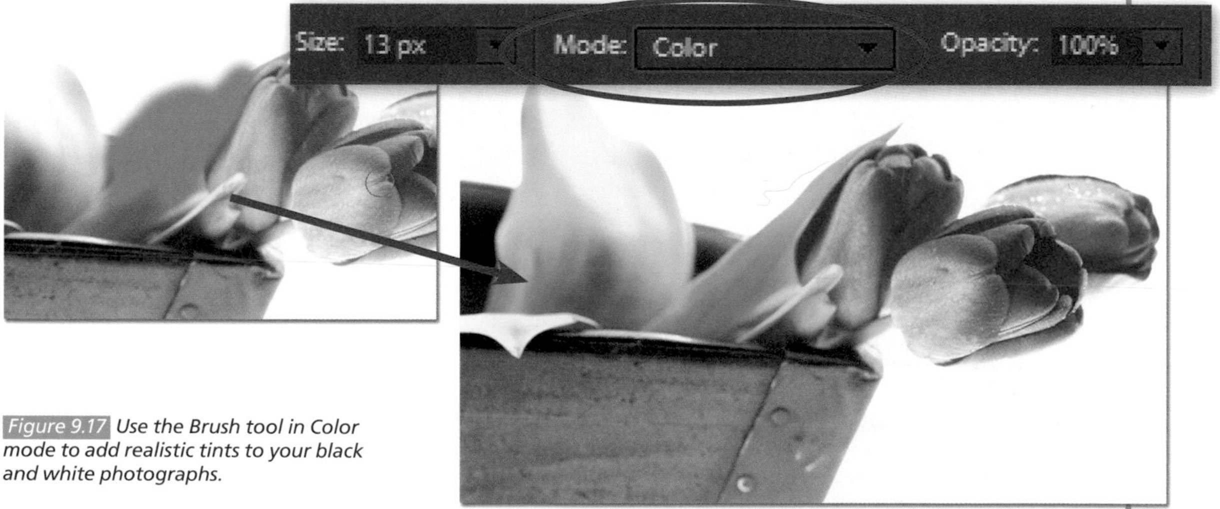

Figure 9.17 Use the Brush tool in Color mode to add realistic tints to your black and white photographs.

FEATURE SUMMARY

5 With the Color mode now selected start to apply the color again. Immediately you will notice the difference. The brush is now substituting the color for the gray tones in the picture and it is doing so proportionately: dark gray = dark green, light gray = light green.

6 Once the leaves and stems have been colored, select new colors for the flowers and finally the bucket. The amount and areas of the picture that you choose to color is up to you. Some photographs look great with only one colored section and the rest black and white.

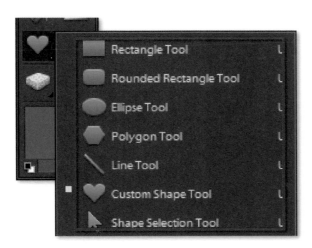

Figure 9.18 *Only one Shape tool is shown in the toolbox, but others can be viewed by clicking and holding the mouse over the small triangle in the bottom right corner of the button or by repeatedly pressing the tool's hotkey (U).*

Drawing tools

With the Shape tool it is possible to draw lines, rectangles, polygons and ellipses, as well as creating your own custom shapes. After selecting the tool and picking the fill color, you can draw the shape by clicking and dragging the mouse. Although only one Shape tool is visible in the toolbox at any time, you can select a different option by clicking and holding the mouse button down over the tool icon and then selecting the new tool from the list as it appears. See Figures 9.18 and 9.19.

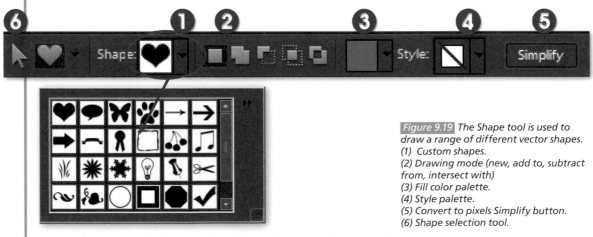

Figure 9.19 *The Shape tool is used to draw a range of different vector shapes.*
(1) Custom shapes.
(2) Drawing mode (new, add to, subtract from, intersect with)
(3) Fill color palette.
(4) Style palette.
(5) Convert to pixels Simplify button.
(6) Shape selection tool.

A new shape layer is opened automatically when you select a tool and draw a new shape. Double-clicking the shape thumbnail in the Layers palette allows you to change the color. See Figure 9.20.

When you create multiple shapes on a single layer you have the opportunity to decide how overlapping areas interact. Two or more different shapes can be added to form a third and the intersection of shapes can be added or subtracted from the image. At first the Shape tool can seem a little confusing, but with practice you will be able to build up complex images by gradually adding and subtracting shapes. See Figure 9.21.

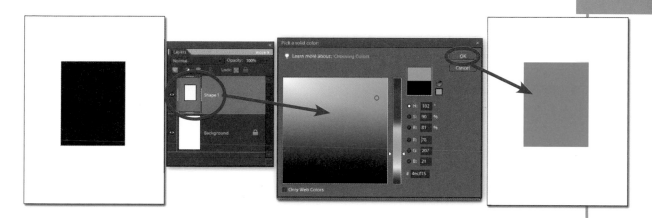

Figure 9.20 *The fill color of a shape can be changed by double-clicking the shape in the shape's layer or the color icon (earlier versions of Elements).*

1 Pick the Shape tool you require from the toolbox. Click and hold down the mouse button to reveal hidden options.

2 For a new shape pick the Create New Shape Layer option. For adding to an existing shape layer, select the layer and select the Shape Area option that suits your needs. You can pick from Add, Subtract, Intersect and Exclude.

3 Click on the color swatch to specify the fill color for the shape.

4 Click and drag on the image surface to draw the shape.

Even more shapes

Elements comes supplied with a vast range of shapes. New shape sets can be added to those already visible as thumbnails by clicking the side-arrow button in the Custom Shape Picker palette. If you can't find a favorite here then why not try some of the extra shape sets that can be downloaded from specialist Elements resources websites?

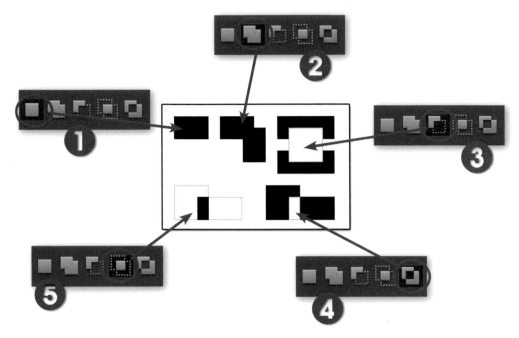

Figure 9.21 *The way that successively drawn custom shapes interact can be customized via buttons on the options bar. (1) Single new shape. (2) Add shape to existing shape. (3) Subtract shape from existing shapes. (4) Subtract overlapping areas of existing shapes. (5) Use the intersection of the areas as a new shape.*

Cookie Cutter tool

The Cookie Cutter tool is a two-step feature that crops your pictures in the shape of one of many 'cookie' designs that Elements is shipped with. The feature is a great way to add interesting edge effects to your pictures. See Figure 9.22.

1 Open an image to crop and select the Cookie Cutter tool from the toolbox.

2 Click the Shape button in the options bar to reveal the pop-up menu of cookie shapes. Select the shape to use.

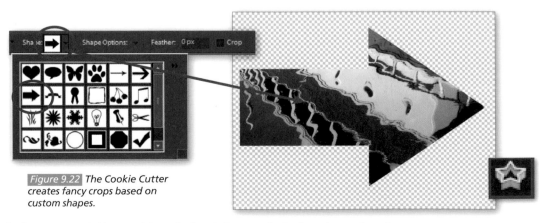

Figure 9.22 *The Cookie Cutter creates fancy crops based on custom shapes.*

FEATURE SUMMARY

3 To soften the edge of the cookie cutter crop, add a Feather value in the options bar before you drag the shape.

4 Optional – Select the Crop option if you want the image cropped to the edge of the shape.

5 Click and drag the tool over the surface of the picture. Let the mouse button go and click and drag the edge handles to adjust the size of the cookie shape to suit the picture.

6 Double-click inside the cookie shape or click the tick icon in the options bar to crop.

Shapes and graphics in the new Effects palette

Photoshop Elements 5.0 first introduced the concept of grouping together visual content in the Artwork and Effects palette. In versions 6 and 7 this grouping has been fine-tuned slightly with the Artwork content now available in the Artwork > Content palette located under the Create module in the editing workspace. This is a central location for storing frames, backgrounds, and themes options and is a key place to look for small picture elements to add to compositions when you are creating Photo Layouts. In versions 6 and 7, Layer Styles and Filters are stored in the Effect palette.

In addition, you will also find a variety of shapes and graphics stored in the palette. Both groups of picture elements are vector based (resolution independent) and so can be scaled, rotated, twisted and distorted to fit your compositions with no loss in quality. Unlike the Custom Shape tool though, you do not need to draw the shape onto the canvas surface; simply click on the thumbnail of your choice and then press Apply at the bottom of the palette. See Figure 9.23.

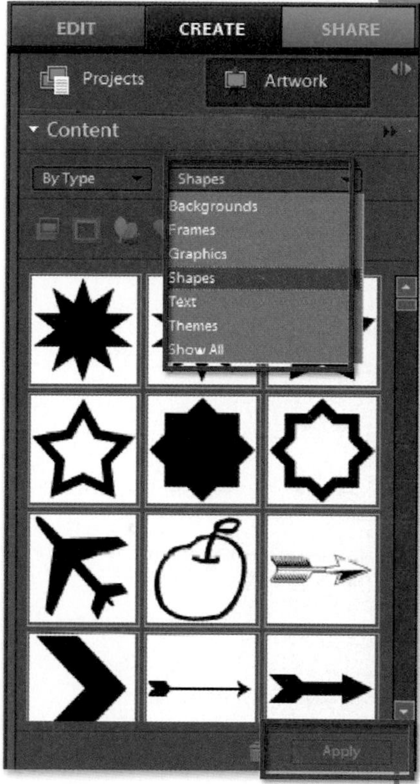

Elements automatically creates a new layer and places the picture element on the canvas. From this point you can rotate, size and distort the shape/graphic using the handles situated on its edges. Apply the changes by clicking the green tick or Commit button that appears at the bottom edge.

Figure 9.23 You can also draw shapes and add graphics to your Photo Layouts by dragging them from the Artwork tab of the Create section.

To scale proportionately – Click and drag a corner handle.

To squish or stretch non-proportionately – Click and drag a side handle.

To scale or squish from the center – Hold down the Alt key whilst dragging a handle.

To rotate – Click and drag the rotate handle located in the middle of the bottom edge of the graphic/shape. Alternatively, move the mouse cursor outside the edges of the graphic and then click-drag to rotate.

To distort or twist – Ctrl-click side or corner handles to distort or change perspective.

Shapes added to the document from the Content palette (Window > Content) are stored in a standard shape layer whereas graphics are stored in a new Smart Object layer. The Smart Object layer is similar to a Frame layer in that it is resolution independent and must be simplified before you can edit it directly. Simplifying the layer loses its ability to be scaled and distorted non-destructively.

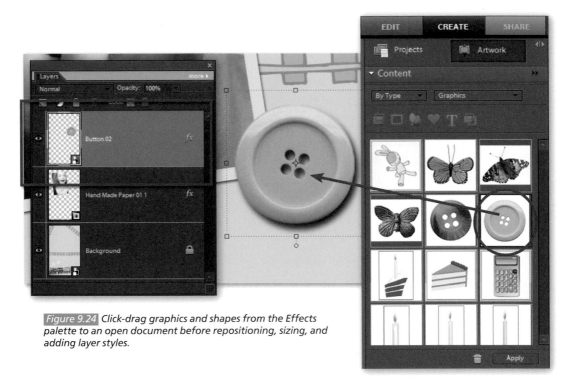

Figure 9.24 Click-drag graphics and shapes from the Effects palette to an open document before repositioning, sizing, and adding layer styles.

Adding shapes or graphics from the new Effects palette is an easy task. Follow the steps below to place, size and position one of these picture elements. See Figure 9.24.

1 Display the Content palette by selecting Window > Content or choosing the Create module heading and then the Artwork tab.

2 Select the By Type entry from the drop-down menu on the left and then the Graphics or Shapes option menu on the right.

3 With the thumbnails displayed, either click and drag the shape/graphic from the palette onto the open document or select the thumbnail and press the Apply button at the bottom of the palette or double-click the thumbnail.

4 To move the shape/graphic around the canvas, move the mouse cursor onto the picture element and click and drag to a new position.

5 To resize, click and drag a corner or side handle. To pivot, click and drag the rotate handle.

10

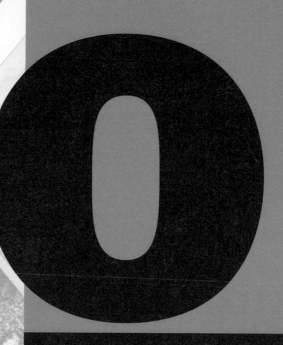

Creating Albums and Scrapbooks

Five steps to creating an Elements Photo Book

Edit an existing design

Adding, replacing and removing photos

Adding, moving and deleting pages

The Artwork panels

The Photo Layout feature first appeared in Elements 5.0 but owes much of its heritage to the album page creation wizards of previous versions of the program. The feature has been revamped since then and now is broken into two main categories – Photo Books and Photo Collages. The Photo Book option is designed to help create professional quality photo albums and scrapbooks containing between 20 and 80 pages. This option combines the template-like production of the original Elements feature along with some unique, newer, Elements features which include:

- the ability to auto place and size a series of selected photos,

- a special Frame layer type that can store, and provide, edit options for both an image and its frame, and a Smart Object layer that is used for storing image content such as photos (when dragged from the Project Bin), graphics and shapes,

- a unique multi-page document format called the Photo Creation or .PSE document,

- the option to apply frames, backgrounds and whole themes (a combination of frames and backgrounds) to photo projects. See Figure 10.1,

- a series of new or revamped Photo Creation wizards (see Figure 10.2), and

- the ability to add text, graphics, shapes and special effects to the project from those listed in the Content palette.

Photo Books are a real bonus for all those users who regularly want to produce a series of pages containing multiple photos. The scrapbooking fraternity will certainly find plenty to love as the feature provides more ease of use, flexibility and customization than was previously available. General photographers too will find the whole book production process truly infectious. The Photo Collage option takes a slightly different approach resulting in one, or more, pages of montaged images that can be printed individually rather than output as a whole book.

In this chapter we will take a closer look at Photo Books and Collages, work step by step through the creation of an initial multi-page document, and then look at how to customize an existing design.

Edit pictures before adding them to a Photo Book or Collage

The production of Photo Books, Collages, or any of the other Photo Creation projects in Photoshop Elements, is essentially a presentation exercise for photos that have already been

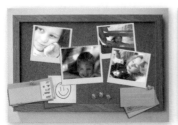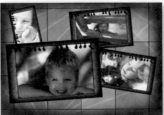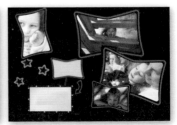

Figure 10.1 *The Photo Book and Photo Collage features in Photoshop Elements can be used to quickly create a series of photo album pages using photos selected in the Organizer workspace. A variety of layout designs is shipped with the program, with other variations promised as downloads in the future.*

enhanced. For this reason it is a good idea to complete any preliminary editing work such as color and tonal correction, spotting and retouching changes and the application of sharpening before including the picture in a new photo project.

This is especially true when working with the special framed picture elements of a Photo Book or Collage, as these visual components are stored in a special Frame layer which has to be simplified before it can be edited. The act of simplification, which is also called rasterization, converts the Frame layer to a standard image layer and in the process removes the layer's ability to scale, rotate and distort repeatedly without image quality loss.

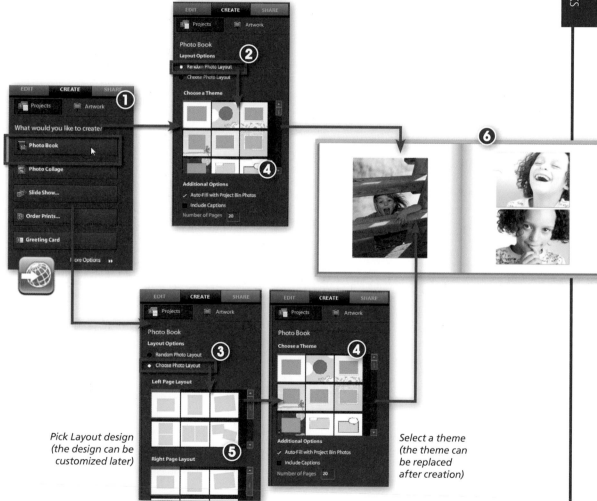

Pick Layout design (the design can be customized later)

Select a theme (the theme can be replaced after creation)

Figure 10.2 *The Photo Book panel groups together the options that govern the way that your multi-page Photo Layout document is created. The first step is to select the option from the Create pane (1). From this point there are two ways to proceed based on whether you select the Random Photo Layout (2) or Choose Photo Layout (3) option. Either way will provide the chance to select a theme (4) for the book pages, but selecting the Choose Photo Layout route will also allow the user to pick different layout styles for left and right pages (5). With the settings selected clicking the Done button creates the book document and displays the pages in the workspace. The multi-page book documents created with this process are editable later inside the Full edit workspace where extra images, text, graphics, effects and pages can be added or removed.*

Five steps to creating an Elements Photo Book

Using the Photo Book feature in Elements is a simple five-step process with the creation options centered around the Projects panel in the Create module of the Organizer and Editor workspaces.

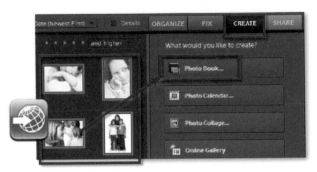

Step 1: Select the images to include

The process of creating a Photo Book will generally start in the Organizer workspace. Here you can multi-select the photos that will be used in the layout. To choose a series of images click on the first thumbnail and then hold down the Shift key and click the last picture in the series. To pick non-sequential photos, select the first one and then hold down the Control key whilst clicking on other thumbnails to be included in the selection. With the images highlighted, the next step is to choose the Create module (top right of the Organizer workspace) and then the Photo Book option from the projects listed.

Alternative starting options

Using an Elements Album (previously called a Collection) as a starting point means that you can alter the order or sequence in which the photos appear in the multi-page document. After rearranging the position of photos in the Album, multi-select those to be included in the layout. Alternatively a blank document can be created in the Editor workspace by selecting the Create module, the Projects heading and then the Photo Book option. Open images can then be dragged into the blank document from the Project Bin area of the Editor. Images grouped in Albums can be easily displayed in the Project Bin by selecting the Album entry from the bin's Show File menu.

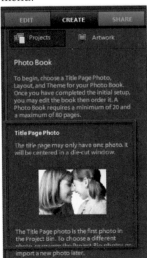

Step 2: Create a title page

If you are using Elements in a country that provides online book production then after choosing the Photo Book option in the Organizer, Elements opens the Editor workspace, switches the display to the Create module and shows the title page instructions in the Panel area (right of the main workspace). The title page of any Photo Book is treated as a special page because when the book is printed the front cover contains a hole through which the contents of this page can be seen. For this reason, it is important that the picture displayed here is a good example of the photos included in the book. Alternatively you can use a specially created title design (saved as an Elements document and included in the files selected for the project) that includes text and sample images from the book. The first image on the left of the Project Bin is always inserted into the title page automatically, but this selection can be changed by click-dragging a new photo to this position in the bin. The title page preview in the panel updates automatically with your new selection. Alternatively another image can be substituted once the multi-page document has been created. See the 'Edit an existing design' section later in the chapter. Click the Next button at the bottom of the panel to move to the next step in the process. This step doesn't appear if you are unable to order books online.

Step 3: Adjusting the look of the book pages

Clicking the Next button changes the contents of the Photo Book panel to display the layout options. Each book page is created based on two style characteristics – the **Theme** and the **Layout**. Themes in Elements refer to matched frame designs and background image combinations created to provide a uniform look to your multi-page documents. Layouts, on the other hand, control the number and general position of the pictures on the document pages.

The first decision in this part of the book making process is to choose the layout of the pages. The options are listed at the top of the panel (1) and are **Random Photo Layout** or **Choose Photo Layout**.

Random Photo Layout

Selecting the Random Photo Layout route will instruct Elements to create the pages in the book using a variety of the default layout options. With the layouts for each page being handled by the program, all you need to do to complete the book creation is to choose the theme (2) used for the pages from the thumbnail list, make sure the Auto Fill with Project Bin Photos is selected, and choose the numbers of pages to include before pressing Done. This is the fastest way to create a Photo Book and, if need be, the layouts and theme selection can be tweaked, or adjusted, after the book is created.

Choose Photo Layout

Selecting the Choose Photo Layout option adds an extra step to the process outlined above. As soon as this option is selected, the contents of the panel change to display the Layout choices (3) for both the right and left pages of the book. After selecting the design (image number and placement) for each page, clicking the Next button will switch panel contents again to display the Theme selection group of thumbnails, Auto-fill and Total page number options.

Whichever route you choose, extra pages and images can be added or removed after the Photo Book has been created from inside the Editor workspace. The frames, backgrounds and themes can also be changed by applying an alternative design from those listed in the Content palette.

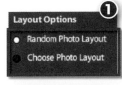

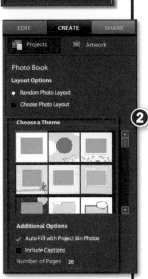

Tool bar

Photo

Frame

Background

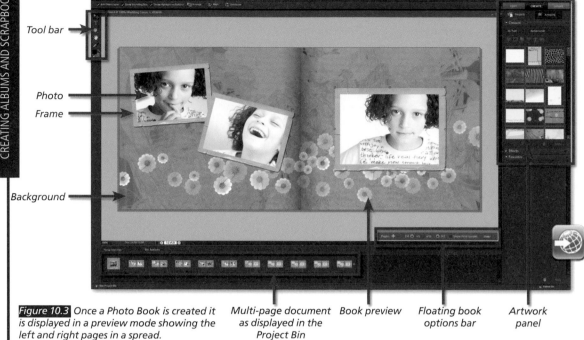

Figure 10.3 *Once a Photo Book is created it is displayed in a preview mode showing the left and right pages in a spread.*

Multi-page document as displayed in the Project Bin

Book preview

Floating book options bar

Artwork panel

Step 4: Create the Photo Book

Once the Layout, Theme and other Photo Book options are set then clicking the Done button at the bottom of the panel will instruct Elements to create the multi-page document. This process can take a little while as the program creates the pages and then sources, sizes and inserts the pictures into the new pages and layouts.

Each photo is stored on a separate Frame layer which is indicated by a small plus icon in the bottom right of the layer's thumbnail. Frame layers are unlike other image layers in that they contain both the photo as well as its surrounding frame. These picture parts are stored separately and remain editable even though they appear as a single layer. When the creation process is finished, the book is displayed in a new book preview mode complete with its own tool bar (top left) and floating book options bar (bottom right of the window). The tool bar contains a subset of the tools found in the regular Edit workspace and includes Move, Type, Zoom, Hand and Eyedropper tools as well as the foreground and background color swatches. The book's floating options bar contains + and − buttons, to add or delete pages, and Next, Previous, Last and First page navigation buttons. Order Book, to place an order for the selected Photo Book with an online publisher, and Show Print Guide options are also included.

The completed pages are displayed in a book form that is new for Element 6 and 7. Here you can flip between pages by clicking on the Next (or Previous) page buttons in the options bar. Also, the contents of the Create panel change from Project to Artwork allowing the user to immediately start to add special effects, graphics, shapes, text or swap themes, backgrounds or frame designs.

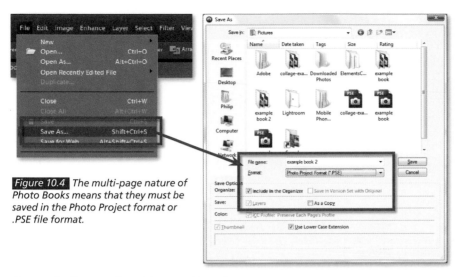

Figure 10.4 The multi-page nature of Photo Books means that they must be saved in the Photo Project format or .PSE file format.

Step 5: Save the Photo Book

Unlike the album pages in earlier versions of Elements, Photo Books and their contents remain editable after they have been saved and reopened. To enable this new ability, Adobe created a completely new file format for the multi-page editable documents. Called the Photo Project format (previously Photo Creation Format) it has an extension of .PSE as opposed to the .PSD that is associated with standard Photoshop and Photoshop Elements documents. See Figure 10.4. When saving a newly created Photo Book the file format in the Save dialog automatically changes to .PSE. By default the Include in the Organizer option is also selected ensuring that the new document is cataloged and displayed in the Organizer space. A small multi-page icon is displayed at the top right of the thumbnail of each Photo Book document and double-clicking the thumbnail displays a special book preview complete with page navigation buttons that allow the user to flick through the pages they need to open the book into the Editing space. See Figure 10.5.

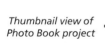

Thumbnail view of Photo Book project

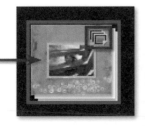

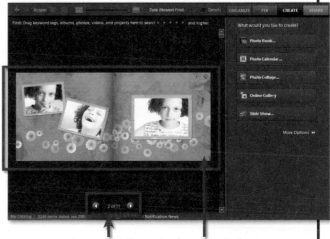

Figure 10.5 When the Include in the Organizer option is selected in the Save dialog the document is shown as a thumbnail in the Content area. Double-clicking the thumbnail will preview the book and all its pages without having to open the file into the editing workspace.

Page navigation buttons

Book preview in the Organizer workspace

Edit an existing design

As we have seen, the Photo Book feature creates a multi-page document complete with photos in frames on a background. In producing this design Elements will make decisions about the size and position of the frames and the pictures within them. On many occasions you will probably want to use the pages the feature produces with no alterations, but there will be times when you will want to tweak the results. At these times use the following techniques to edit the automatically produced designs.

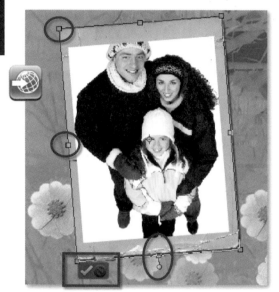

Figure 10.6 The frame and its contents can be edited using either the handles on the edge or options in the right-click menu.

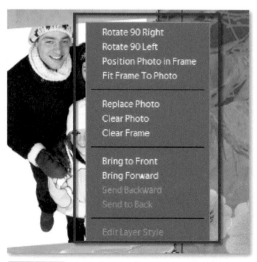

Figure 10.7 Right-clicking the picture when the frame is selected produces the menu above.

Adjusting the frame and picture

To move the picture and frame combination to a new position on the canvas just click and drag the combination. The size and orientation of the frame/picture can be altered by clicking on the picture and frame first, to select it, and then using the corner, edge and rotate handles to scale or pivot. Click on the Commit button (green tick) at the bottom of the selected picture to apply the changes. To disregard the changes click the Cancel button (red circle with diagonal line through it) instead. See Figure 10.6.

Other adjustment options are available via the right-click menu when the Move tool is selected. See Figure 10.7. Selections in this menu allow you to:

Rotate 90° Right or Left – Pivot the frame and picture by a set amount.

Position Photo in Frame – Switch to Picture Select mode to allow scaling, rotating and moving the photo within the frame.

Fit Frame to Photo – Automatically adjust the frame size to accommodate the dimensions and format of the placed photo. Use this option if you don't want to crop the photo with the edges of the frame.

Replace Photo – Displays a file dialog where you can select a new photo for the frame.

Clear Photo – Removes the photo but keeps the frame.

Clear Frame – Removes the frame but keeps the photo.

Bring to Front/Bring Forward – Moves the frame and photo up the layer stack.

Send to Back/Send Backward – Moves the frame and photo down the layer stack.

Edit Layer Style – Displays the Style Settings dialog when a style is applied to the frame.

Adjusting the picture

As well as being able to alter the characteristics of the frame by selecting the photo you can perform similar changes to the picture itself. Double-clicking or choosing the Position Photo in Frame option from the right-click menu selects the photo and displays a marquee around the picture. A small Control Panel is also displayed at the top of the marquee. See Figure 10.8.

To move the position of the photo in the frame simply click and drag on the image, releasing the mouse button when the picture is correctly placed.

You can alter the size of the photo within the frame by moving the Scale slider (in the control panel) or by dragging one of the handles of the marquee. Moving a corner handle will scale the photo proportionately, whereas dragging a side handle will squish or stretch the image.

The picture can be rotated in 90 degree increments (to the left) by clicking the Rotate button in the control panel. Alternatively, you can rotate the image to any angle using the rotate handle (middle of the bottom edge of the marquee) or by click-dragging the cursor outside the boundaries of the marquee.

The photo can be replaced with a new picture by clicking the Replace button in the control panel and then selecting the new picture from the file dialog that is displayed.

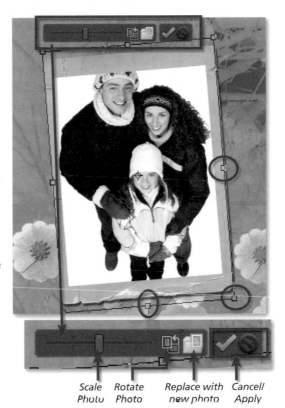

Scale   Rotate   Replace with   Cancel/
Photo   Photo   new photo   Apply

Figure 10.8 *The picture inside the frame can be scaled and rotated independent of the frame by firstly double-clicking the photo (to select the picture without the frame) and then click-dragging the side, corner or rotate handles. Alternatively you can scale, rotate 90° left, replace the current picture with a new one and apply or cancel the changes with the buttons in the new pop-up control that appears at the top of the picture border.*

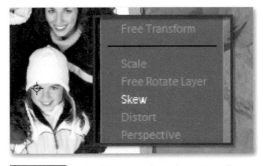

Figure 10.9 *Right-clicking a selected picture will also display a range of adjustment options.*

Extra image adjustment options are available from the right-click menu. See Figure 10.9 on the previous page. These include the ability to switch the default action of dragging a marquee handle from scaling, as it is in the Free Transform mode, to alternatives such as Skew or Distort. To return to the default action choose Free Transform from the right-click menu. The actions available are:

Free Transform – The default mode where dragging the corner of the marquee scales proportionately, and dragging the edges, squashes or stretches the picture. The following keys alter the action of dragging a handle when in this mode:

- **Shift + corner handle** to scale proportionately,
- **Ctrl + any handle** to distort the picture,
- **Ctrl + Shift + middle edge handle** to skew the picture, and
- **Ctrl + Alt + Shift + corner handle** to apply perspective.

Scale – Resizes in the same manner as the Free Transform mode.

Free Rotate Layer – Rotates the image when click-dragging outside of the marquee.

Skew – Skews the photo when dragging an edge handle.

Distort – Distorts the picture when moving any handle.

Perspective – Applies a perspective effect when dragging a corner handle.

Adding, replacing and removing photos

Photo Books do not become static documents once they are created. In the previous section we saw how it is possible to adjust the size, position and orientation of both the photos and frames that were added during the initial creation process, but the feature's flexibility doesn't end there. You can also add new photos, replace existing pictures with alternative choices and even remove images that you no longer want to keep. Here's how.

Adding new photos

All editing of Photo Books occurs in the Full Edit Editor workspace. So to add new photos to an existing layout you need to add a new blank frame to the composition. Do this by clicking on the selected frame in the Artwork section of the Artwork panel and pressing the Apply button. See Figure 10.10. A new frame will be created on the current page of the document.

To add a photo to the frame, click-drag a thumbnail from the Project Bin to the frame

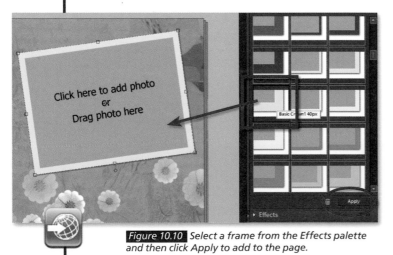

Figure 10.10 Select a frame from the Effects palette and then click Apply to add to the page.

Book resources and video tutorials can be found at **www.photoshopelements.net**

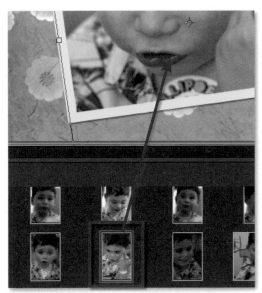

or click the text in the empty frame and select a photo from the file browser that opens. Using this approach you can add a photo without it first having to be open in the Project Bin. When moving the photo make sure that the frame is highlighted with a blue rectangle before releasing the mouse button to insert the picture. See Figure 10.11

The last part of the process is to fine-tune the picture by adjusting size, orientation and position within the frame. Use the techniques in the previous section to make these alterations.

Figure 10.11 *Click-drag a new photo to the blank frame.*

Replacing existing photos

It is just as easy to replace existing photos with different images whilst still retaining the frame. Select the frame first and then click-drag a picture from the Project Bin to the frame. This action swaps the two pictures but you will need to have the replacement image already open in the Full edit workspace beforehand. If this isn't the case, then an alternative is to select the Replace Photo entry from the right-click menu and choose a new picture via the file dialog that is displayed. See Figure 10.12.

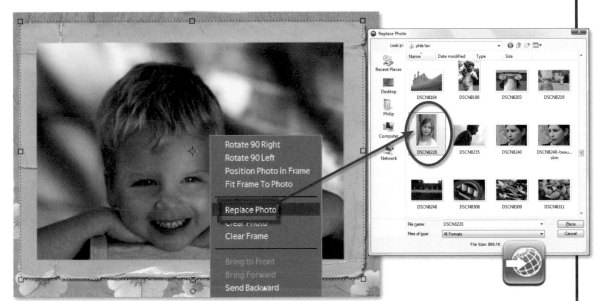

Figure 10.12 *To replace a photo either drag a new image from the Project Bin to the frame or select the Replace Photo option from the right-click menu.*

CREATING ALBUMS AND SCRAPBOOKS

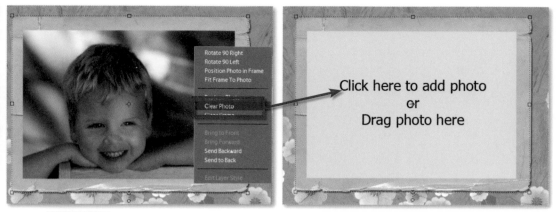

Figure 10.13 *To remove a picture but leave the frame in place select the Clear Photo option from the right-click menu. To remove both frame and photo select the frame, press the Delete key and then answer Yes to the Delete Selected Layers warning.*

Removing photos

Pictures inserted into frames can be removed whilst still retaining the frame by selecting the Clear Photo option from the right-click menu. The frame will then revert back to a blank state providing the opportunity to add a new image to the composition. See Figure 10.13.

If you want to remove both the frame and the photo it contains then select the frame first and click the Delete key. A warning window will display asking you if you want to delete Selected Layers. Answer Yes to remove the frame and picture from the composition.

Adding, moving and deleting pages

If you selected the Auto Fill option when first creating your Photo Book then Elements will have generated enough pages to insert the photos that were initially included. If you want to add images, some text or graphics later on then you will need to add some extra pages. The new Photo Creation file format (.PSE) was developed especially to handle multi-page documents and to ensure that tasks such as adding, deleting and moving pages were as easy as possible.

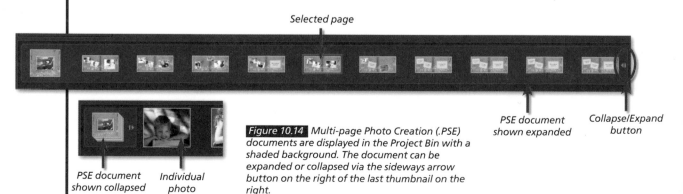

Figure 10.14 *Multi-page Photo Creation (.PSE) documents are displayed in the Project Bin with a shaded background. The document can be expanded or collapsed via the sideways arrow button on the right of the last thumbnail on the right.*

Selected page

PSE document
shown collapsed

Individual
photo

PSE document
shown expanded

Collapse/Expand
button

All page management activities are centered around the PSE document in the Project Bin. The document can be displayed collapsed, where all the pages are grouped together on top of each other, or expanded, where each of the thumbnails representing a single page can be viewed separately. See Figure 10.14.

Adding pages

All new pages in a PSE document are added after the current selected page. So start by expanding the multi-page document in the Project Bin and then select the thumbnail of the page before the position where the new page is to be created.

In Elements you have two options for creating new pages:

Add Blank Page – Use this option to add a white page with no frames, backgrounds or themes present. Once the page is created then text, graphics, shapes, frames, backgrounds and special effects can be added from the Effects palette.

Add Page Using Current Layout – This feature duplicates the Layout settings of the selected page when creating the new one. Use this option to add new pages to a group of pages that already contain a background and frames as it will help to keep the look of the whole document consistent.

To add a new page choose either the Add Blank Page or Add Page Using Current Layout option from the Edit menu. The new page is then added to the document and a new thumbnail is displayed in the Project Bin to the right of the selected page. These Add Page options are also available from the right-click menu when you select a page in the Project Bin. See Figure 10.15.

Moving pages

The position of pages (from left to right) in the Expanded view of a multi-page document in the Project Bin indicates the page's location in the production. The first page in the document is the

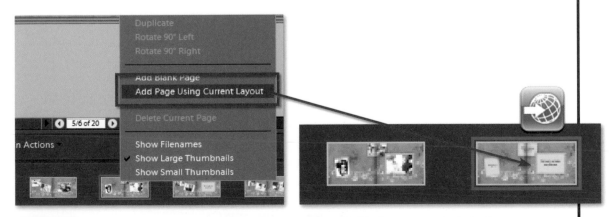

Figure 10.15 *Pages are added to a PSE document by selecting the page before the new entry in the Project Bin and then choosing the Add Page option either from the Edit menu or the right-click menu.*

one positioned furthest to the left, the second page is the next one along to the right, and so on. Changing the position of the page thumbnail in the Project Bin preview alters the page's actual position in the document. Moving pages is a simple task – just click on the page to move and drag it to a new location in the document, release the mouse button and the page is relocated. See Figure 10.16.

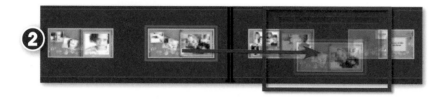

Figure 10.16 To relocate a page in a PSE document select the page (1) in the Expanded view in the Project Bin and click-drag it to a new location (2). Releasing the mouse button will insert the page in the new location (3).

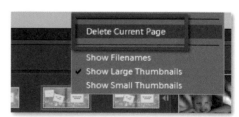

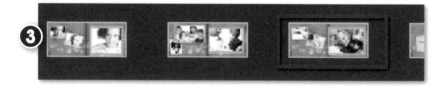

Deleting pages

Pages, and the frames and photos they contain, can be deleted from a multi-page document by selecting the page thumbnail in the Project Bin and then choosing Edit > Delete Current Page. Alternatively, the Delete Current Page entry can also be selected from the right-click menu. See Figure 10.17.

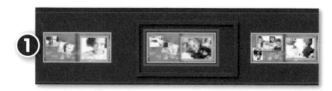

Figure 10.17 Delete pages and their contents by right-clicking the page thumbnail in the Project Bin and then selecting Delete Current Page from the menu.

Viewing pages

Navigate between the different pages of your PSE document by selecting the thumbnail of the page that you want to display from the Project Bin. Alternatively, you can move from one page to the next using the Forward and Back buttons located at the bottom of the document window or in the floating Photo Book options bar. See Figure 10.18.

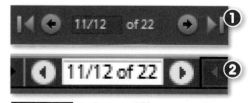

Figure 10.18 Navigate to different pages by clicking the Forward and Back buttons in the floating Photo Book Options bar (1), at the bottom of the document window (2) or selecting a different page thumbnail in the Project Bin.

The Artwork panels

The Artwork panel in the Create module replaces the Artwork and Effects palette of version 5.0 and is the central place for the storage of a variety of design components that can be used to enhance the look of your Photo Book compositions. Once a multi-page document is created it is the various components that are housed in this palette that can be used to add to or alter the look and feel of your design. The palette contains three sections – **Content**, **Effects** and **Favorites** which are accessed by clicking the section headings in the panel. See Figure 10.19.

The **Content** section contains backgrounds, frames, graphics, text, shapes and themes. Many of the frame and theme options featured in these sections are also available in the Photo Book dialogs. The **Effects** group includes filters, layer styles, and photo effects. The **Favorites** group holds user-selected favorites chosen from the other areas. See Figure 10.20.

To add a theme, frame, background or any other entry from the palette select the entry and then choose the Add to Favorites option from the right-click menu. Alternatively you can drag the thumbnail from the Content or Effects panels to the Favorites panel.

To apply a style, effect or add artwork to a document select the Panel entry and click the Apply button. Extra palette options and preferences are available via the double sideways arrows buttons at the top right of the panel.

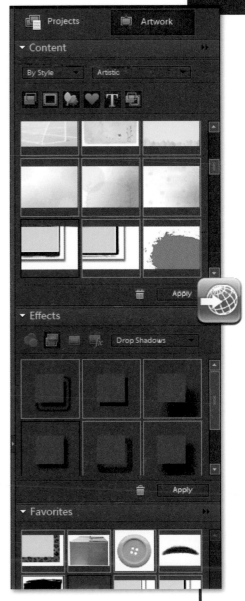

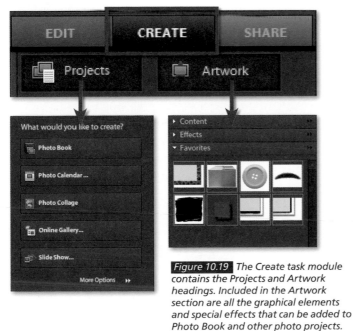

Figure 10.19 The Create task module contains the Projects and Artwork headings. Included in the Artwork section are all the graphical elements and special effects that can be added to Photo Book and other photo projects.

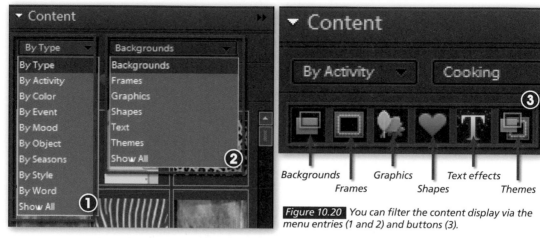

Figure 10.20 You can filter the content display via the menu entries (1 and 2) and buttons (3).

Create > Artwork > Content

As we have already seen, the Artwork section of the Create task module contains three panels – Content, Effects and Favorites. The Content panel itself contains backgrounds, picture frames, graphics, shapes, text effects and themes that can be added to your layouts.

In Photoshop Elements there are many ways to locate individual content pieces from the many listed. The top of the panel contains two drop-down menus. The right side menu contains options for filtering the thumbnails listed in the panel by the content type. This selection can be further refined with the other options listed in the second menu on the right of the panel. The entries listed here change depending on the entry selected in the first menu (left). In addition to filtering using the menu options you can also filter via the buttons located just below the menu entries at the top of the panel. The buttons filter the content to display backgrounds, frames, graphics, shapes, text effects and themes and are available with all menu entry headings except 'By Type' and 'By Word', See Figure 10.20.

Backgrounds, graphics and shapes

Backgrounds, graphics, text and shapes all create their own layers when added. Frames, on the other hand, are applied to existing layers. To add a piece of artwork click on the thumbnail in the palette and then press the Apply button. To add a picture to a frame drag the image from another open document to the frame. All artwork except backgrounds can be scaled and rotated via the corner, middle edge and rotate handles. Click the image layer to activate the handles.

Themes

The Themes section lists a variety of predesigned backgrounds and matched frame sets that can be applied to your Elements document. In the previous version of Elements a document was only able to have one theme at a time so trying to apply a second theme would replace the existing background and frames throughout the book. Thankfully this has changed in recent versions of Elements and now it is possible for each double-page spread to have a different theme applied. See Figure 10.21.

Themes are a great place to start when you want to provide a consistent look and feel to your album or scrapbook pages. Commencing you project with themes doesn't mean that you can't add other frames, graphics, shapes or text later. Just choose and apply the frame from the Effects palette as you would normally.

You can also change the theme's background without altering the frames by picking and applying a new background. Different frame styles can be substituted by dragging the new style over the existing frame and letting go when the layer border turns blue.

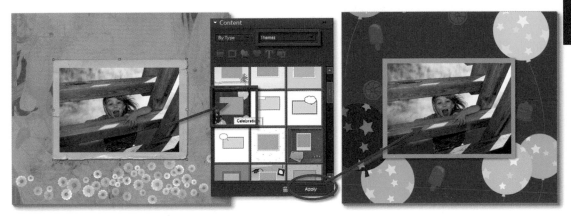

Figure 10.21 *Themes are design sets that contain matching frames and backgrounds. You can apply a theme to page spreads in a document by selecting the theme thumbnail in the Artwork panel and then clicking the Apply button at the bottom of the panel.*

Text

The Text section in the Content panel contains a variety of styled text effects that you can apply to your Photo Book documents. The effects include bevels, drop shadows, glows and gradients, and only work with text layers. You can apply a text effect to an existing type layer by selecting the type and then the thumbnail of the effect that you want to add, before finally clicking the Apply button. In addition you can also click Apply with no type selected to create a new type layer. Like Layer Styles the attributes of the text effects (size of drop shadow, color of stroke, etc.) can be adjusted via the Edit Layer Style option in the right-click menu. Text effects can be removed by selecting the Clear Layer Style entry from the right-click menu. See Figure 10.22.

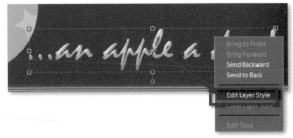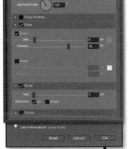

Figure 10.22 *The attributes of the text effects or Layer Styles can be adjusted using the Style Settings dialog which is displayed by selecting the Edit Layer Style option from the menu that is displayed when right-clicking the type object.*

Create > Artwork > Effects

The Effects panel is available in both the Edit and Create task modules in Photoshop Elements. The panel is displayed when you are working on a project that you have created using the Photo Book option. The palette groups together Filters, Layer Styles and Photo Effects options, but of these only the Layer Styles entries are available when working with Photo Book documents. Layers styles add effects such as drop shadows, outer glows and strokes to selected book objects such as framed images, text entries and graphics. After selecting the object in the composition, the effect is selected from the panel and added by pressing the Apply button. The characteristics of the styles can be customized by right-clicking the object and then selecting the Edit Layer Style entry from the menu that appears. Individual style characteristics are then altered with the controls in the Style Settings dialog.

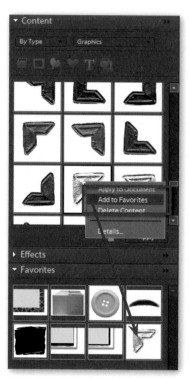

Create > Artwork > Favorites

The Favorites panel in the Artwork section of the Create task module lists all the artwork, effects, themes and styles that you have nominated as favorites. This area is a great place to store the Artwork entries that you use time and time again. For instance when you find a layer style or text effect that you particularly like, rather than have to search for it each time you want to use it, simply right-click on the entry and select the Add to Favorites option from the pop-up menu. See Figure 10.23. Remove items from the Favorites panel by right-clicking on the thumbnail of the Favorites entry and selecting Remove from Favorites entry in the pop-up menu or clicking the Dustbin button at the bottom of the Favorites panel.

Figure 10.23 *Effects, graphics, frames or themes that you use regularly can be added to the Favorites panel by right-clicking on the thumbnail and choosing the Add to Favorites entry from the menu. Alternatively you can drag the thumbnail to the open Favorites panel to create a new entry.*

Bringing it all together

Using the features and techniques described over the last few pages it is possible to build a very sophisticated Photo Book document. As we have seen, Photoshop Elements cleverly provides both the multi-page structure that is necessary to underpin the whole project and the frames, graphics, shapes, text options, effects and backgrounds needed for quality presentation, but the story doesn't stop there. Once you have created your photo album, or digital scrapbook, you then have the ability to print the Photo Book either with your own desktop machine, or have the document professionally printed and bound by an online provider. See Figure 10.24.

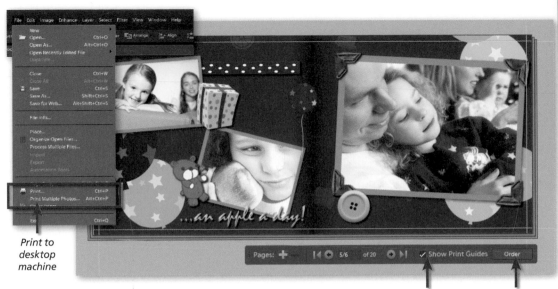

Print to desktop machine

Show print guides for online output

Order online printing and binding

Figure 10.24 *Once the Photo Book document is completed it can be printed via a desktop machine or professionally printed and bound using the special Order button located in the floating Photo Book options bar.*

Online printing and binding (available in some countries only)

The easiest and, arguably, the most professional looking results are obtained when printing and binding online. The features of the Photo Book project, and in particular the way that the file is set up at the beginning of the process, is specifically designed to suit this method of producing your book. The position and size of the image on the title page, for instance, matches precisely with the window in the hard cover of the completed bound book. This close linking of the production of the multi-page document, and its online output, is the prime reason why many photographers will bypass printing and binding the title themselves.

To start the online production process just click the Order button located in the floating Photo Book options bar. A warning window will appear letting you know that the process required to prepare the book for uploading can take between 5 and 20 minutes to complete. Obviously placing an order for a Photo Book online requires an Internet connection and you won't be able to proceed from this point if one is not available. Next, you will see the Kodak Photo Book wizard display. See Figure 10.25. If you haven't used the service before you will need to register before proceeding. Work your way through each of the screens choosing cover material and color and adding recipient and billing details before finally uploading the

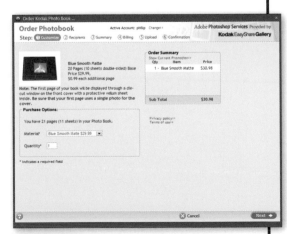

Figure 10.25 *Kodak uses an online wizard to step you through the Photo Book ordering process.*

book file and confirming the order. With the order process completed the book file will be printed and bound and then returned to you in the post or by courier.

Printing at home

The alternative to online production is printing your Photo Book project via a desktop inkjet printer. The multi-page document is designed for producing book pages 9 × 10.25 inches (23 × 26 cm), so make sure that you have paper either equal to these dimensions, or greater, and a printer capable of outputting to this size sheet. Alternatively, you can use standard paper sizes and simply select the Scale to Fit option (in the Print dialog) to squeeze your book pages to suit.

To get the look and feel of a traditionally printed book some photographers, who regularly produce their own albums or scrapbooks, use paper that can be printed on both sides. After printing one side the sheet is reinserted into the printer to print the reverse. When bound these pages replicate a professionally printed page.

With the paper and printer organized, outputting the file is a simple matter of selecting the Print entry from the File menu. Elements will then display the Print dialog. See Figure 10.26. Here you can select the printer, adjust the size and position of the book page on the paper and choose how the color will be managed. For more details about the settings in the Print dialog turn to Chapter 12. With all the settings selected press Print to start the output process.

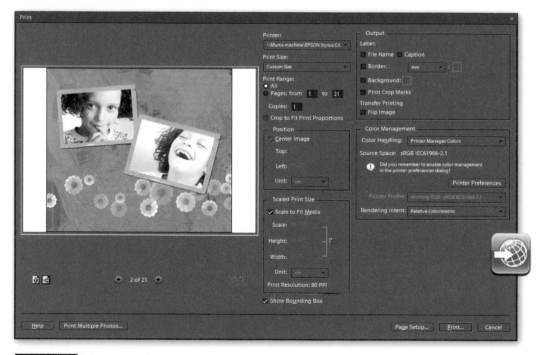

Figure 10.26 *When outputting Photo Book pages to a desktop printer using the File > Print feature you can adjust the size and position of the page on the paper in the Photoshop Elements Print dialog.*

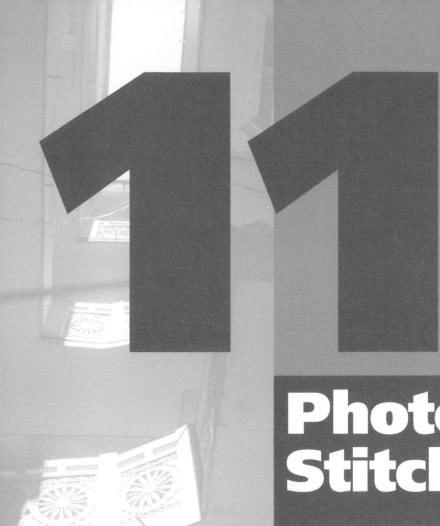

11
Photomerge Stitching

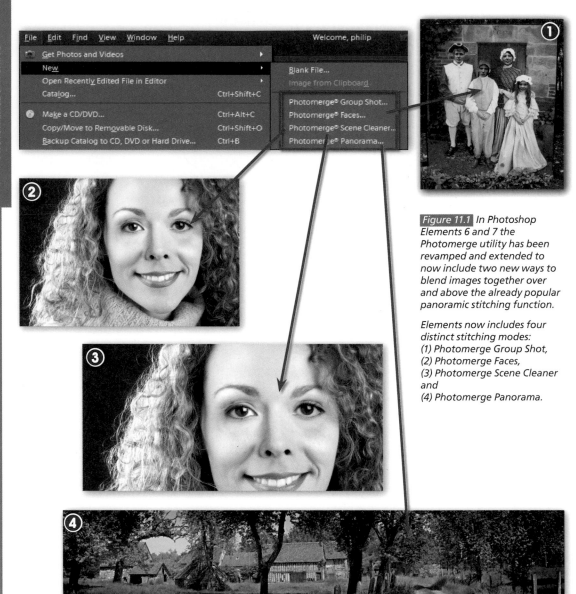

Figure 11.1 *In Photoshop Elements 6 and 7 the Photomerge utility has been revamped and extended to now include two new ways to blend images together over and above the already popular panoramic stitching function.*

Elements now includes four distinct stitching modes: (1) Photomerge Group Shot, (2) Photomerge Faces, (3) Photomerge Scene Cleaner and (4) Photomerge Panorama.

hotomerge is Adobe's very own stitching technology designed, initially, to blend together several overlapping images to form a panoramic photograph. In Photoshop Elements 6 and 7, the utility has received a complete overhaul and can now be used for other stitching tasks as well. The tasks are broken down into four distinct ways of using the utility – **Photomerge Group Shot**, **Photomerge Faces,** the new **Photomerge Scene Cleaner** and **Photomerge Panorama**. See Figure 11.1. Over the next few pages we will look at each feature in turn.

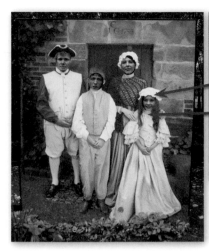
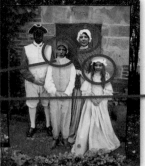
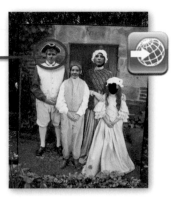

Figure 11.2 *The Photomerge Group Shot option combines the elements of two or more photos to create a montaged result.*

Photomerge Group Shot

Ever tried taking a group photo where all the members were facing the right direction and had their eyes open at the same time? If you have, then you will know that it is not an easy task. Often photographers will capture multiple frames in the hope that one photo will be perfect. Well, the Group Shot feature is designed to help with this problem. It is still necessary to shoot several images of the group but, rather than having to capture one perfect photo, you can combine the best elements of several (maximum 10) into a single picture. The feature is accessed via the Photomerge entry in the Guided edit panel in the Editor workspace. The dialog uses an interface design with a side-by-side preview of the source and final images. Think of the final image as the base of the composite photograph. It should be the photo where most of the group members are looking good. The source image, on the other hand, is the photo (or photos) that you will use to overlay corrected areas for group members that are blinking in the final photo.

If you are using a series of photos, taken in the same location, then the feature is clever enough to automatically align the common elements in both the source and final pictures. Alternatively, you can use the Alignment tool in the Advanced options of the panel to position three alignment points on the common areas of the source and final images. Then it is just a matter of using the Pencil tool to draw over the Source areas and Photomerge will automatically (and seamlessly) paint them over the same area in the final image. Hey presto, blinks be gone. See Figure 11.2.

Photomerge Faces

The Faces feature is used to mix, or blend, facial characteristics from two or more (maximum 10) different images to create a single, montaged, caricatured face as the end result. Like the Group shot option, the feature is assessed by clicking the Photomerge > Faces entry in the Guided edit panel (right side of the interface) or File > New > Photomerge Faces in either workspace, and then following the directions in the panel. Unlike other features involving the Project Bin where all the images are used, Faces and Group Shot both require you to multi-select the images to use

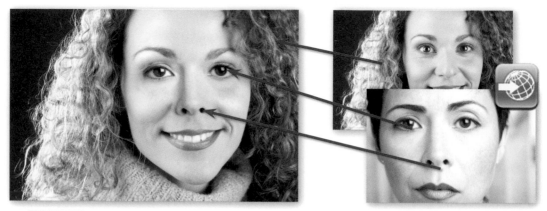

Figure 11.3 *The Photomerge Faces option provides the ability to merge the characteristics of two or more face photos together into a single photo.*

before invoking the feature. To help match facial characteristics, the feature also contains an Align option, where three points (eyes and mouth) are pin pointed on both the final and source files and then the source image is distorted to match the size and shape of the face in the Final Image section of the dialog. After alignment, the Pencil tool is used to draw over the parts of the source photo that you want to appear in the final image. See Figure 11.3.

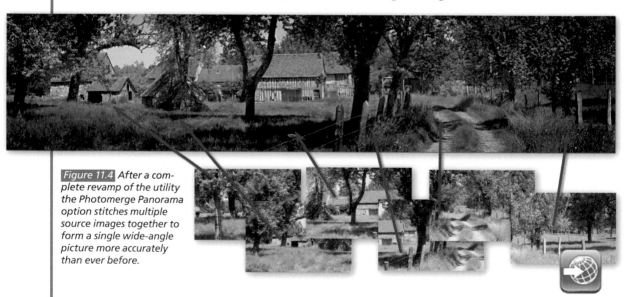

Figure 11.4 *After a complete revamp of the utility the Photomerge Panorama option stitches multiple source images together to form a single wide-angle picture more accurately than ever before.*

Photomerge Panorama

You may think that given the additional Photomerge options listed above that the panoramic stitching component of the feature has seen little change since version 5.0, but you would be wrong. The Photomerge Panorama feature has been completely revised and now contains four auto stitching modes as well as the manual alignment workspace that was present in previous releases. As well as the extra modes, the fancy mathematics that help align and blend the separate images to form a wide-angle vista have been rewritten and now create more accurate results with a wider range of source photos than before. See Figure 11.4.

With these changes in mind let's look at each of the Photomerge options in action.

Photomerge Group Shot

Designed for those times when you are unable to get all the participants in a photo to look in the same direction at the same time, the Group Shot option mixes and matches parts of several images and pastes them seamlessly onto a single photo which is used as a background. In the example below, not having a tripod handy is not a problem when it comes time to capture a portrait of the whole family on holidays. Simply take two photos of the same scene, swapping the family member who is acting as the photographer, and then use the Photomerge Group Shot utility to merge the best part of both photos. Here's how:

1   Start by locating the source files that you will use to create your montaged image in the Organizer workspace.

2   Multi-select the pictures and then transfer the photos to the Guided edit workspace by choosing File > New > Photomerge Group Shot. This action will open the pictures into the Group Shot panel and select the Group Shot instructions. See Figure 11.5.

3   Alternatively, if the images are already open in the Editor workspace then click on the Edit heading in the Task pane and then choose the Guided option. When the Guided edit entries are displayed select the Photomerge > Group Shot heading.

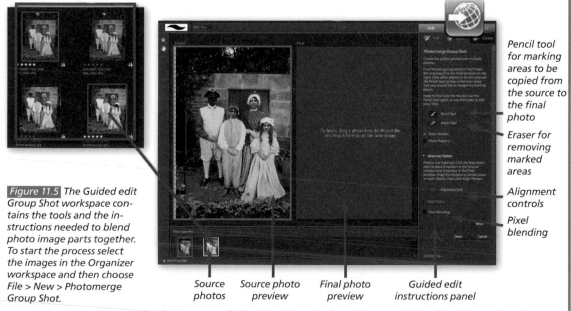

Pencil tool for marking areas to be copied from the source to the final photo

Eraser for removing marked areas

Alignment controls

Pixel blending

Figure 11.5 *The Guided edit Group Shot workspace contains the tools and the instructions needed to blend photo image parts together. To start the process select the images in the Organizer workspace and then choose File > New > Photomerge Group Shot.*

Source photos   Source photo preview   Final photo preview   Guided edit instructions panel

4   Automatically Elements will position one of the images in the Source preview (left). Drag the best photo from the Project Bin to the Final preview space. This will act like a background to which you will add other image parts.

5   Now click onto the Pencil tool in the Group Shot panel and paint over the picture parts from the source file that you want to add to the final image. Here are the faces. Adjust the pencil size with the Size control in the options bar. Use the Eraser tool to remove pencil marks and refine the size and shape of the Source area used for the montage. To see the area in the final photo affected by the change, click the Show Regions option. This will display regions that are tinted the same color as the source photo. See Figure 11.6.

6   If you have more than one source image in the Project Bin, click onto alternative photos to display them in the Source preview area and then use the Pencil tool to draw over the areas to add to the final picture. The highlight color around the edge of the source image in the Project Bin matches the color of the pencil strokes in the Source area so that you always know which photo is the source.

7   For the best results it is important for the Source pictures to be aligned with the final image. If the photos weren't aligned in the transfer process from the Organizer space then manually align them by selecting the Alignment tool in the Group Shot workspace. Position the three alignment markers on similar positions in both the source and final photos and then click the Align Photos button to line the images up.

8   The Pixel Blending option softens the edges of the source and final picture parts and often creates a smoother transition between the elements. Deselecting this option leaves the pasted source picture parts with a hard edge. Click the Done button to create the montage.

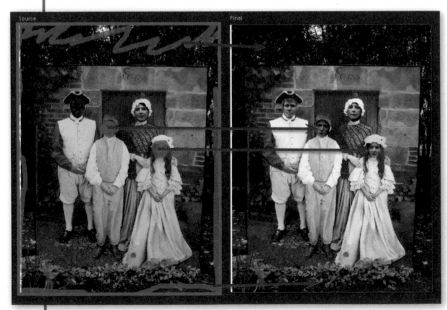

Figure 11.6 The Pencil tool is used to draw over the areas in the source photo that are to pasted into the final image. The Eraser can be used to refine these areas by changing the shape and size of the pencil marks.

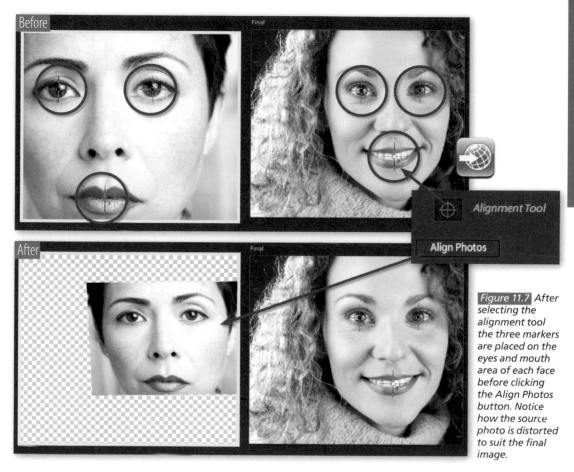

Figure 11.7 *After selecting the alignment tool the three markers are placed on the eyes and mouth area of each face before clicking the Align Photos button. Notice how the source photo is distorted to suit the final image.*

Photomerge Faces

Like the Group Shot feature, Photomerge Faces is also all about merging the characteristics of two or more images. In this case, however, the workspace has been tweaked to be used with portrait photos. The process is the same; align the photos using the Alignment tool (this time the three markers are positioned over the eyes and mouth) and then draw over the picture parts in the source image that are to pasted into the final photo. See Figure 11.7.

FEATURE SUMMARY

1   Find the source files that you will use to create your montaged image in the Organizer workspace. Multi-select the photos (you can use up to 10) and then choose File > New > Photomerge Faces. The images will be opened into the Guided edit workspace and the Photomerge Faces tutorial will be displayed in the right-hand panel.

2   Drag the photo you want to use as a base, the one that you want to use as a backdrop for the composition, from the Project Bin to the Final preview area.

3   Select the Alignment tool and place the three markers on the eyes and mouth of the Source picture and the Final image. Click the Align Photos button. The source image will distort to match the position of the eyes and mouth in the final image.

4   Now select the Pencil tool and draw over the facial features in the source image that you want to overwrite in the final photo. Elements will automatically copy and blend the details from the source to the final image. Use the Show Regions option to see regions and their associated source files.

5   If you have more than one source image in the Project Bin then click on an alternate photo, realign and draw over other image areas to copy these parts to the final photo. The areas drawn from different source photos will be marked in different colors and the source photo will be outlined in the same color in the Project Bin. This makes identifying which source files are link to specific picture parts an easy task.

6   The Eraser tool can be used to refine the size and shape of the Source areas. Clicking the Show Regions setting will display a color coded overlay on the final image that shows which source images are being used for which parts of the final composite.

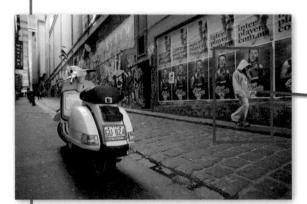 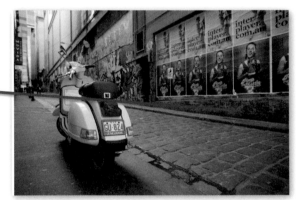

Figure 11.8 *The Photomerge Scene Cleaner option merges the content that you select from several images together to create a single photo. With this process you can do things like remove tourists from photos of monuments.*

Photomerge Scene Cleaner

The Photomerge Scene Cleaner is a new Photomerge option. The feature is a little like Group Shot in that it can be used to select parts from several images and merge them together, but differs slightly in that it is designed to montage the best bits of a series of photos of a single scene. This process will help build travel photos that are free of tourists that are frequently caught mid frame obscuring important details in the scene. See Figure 11.8.

The trick with using this feature is remembering that you have it in your Elements' kit bag when you are out and about photographing. If you are having trouble getting a clean shot then capturing a series of photographs of the same scene will give you the option of using the Photomerge Scene Cleaner to recreate the photo when you return to your desktop. See Figure 11.9.

Like other Photomerge options, Scene Cleaner has its own workspace that sits in the Elements' Editor. The screen contains two picture preview areas - Source, on the left, and Final. On the

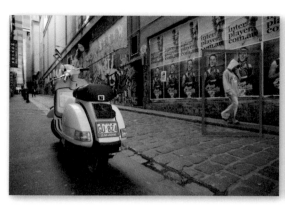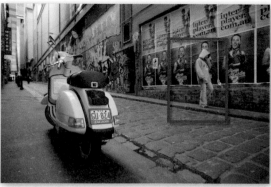

Figure 11.9 When shooting the photos to be used with the Scene Cleaner feature it is important to make sure that you photograph each important part of the scene, free of obstructions, over the series of pictures. If for instance, a tourist is sitting in the same place for all the photos, then it won't be possible for Elements to remove them from the picture.

right of these previews is a dedicated pane containing both instructions, as well as the tools (Pencil, Eraser and Alignment), settings (Show Strokes and Show Regions) and processing buttons (Done and Cancel) for the feature. Scene Cleaner works by the user drawing over parts of the source file that they want transferred to the Final photo. Elements automatically patches the new picture parts together.

The amount of the source photo used in the final image is controlled by the pencil strokes used. These can be modified with the Eraser tool. Removing marks reduces the size of the picture parts transferred. It can be helpful to select the Show Strokes and Show Regions, the areas being used for the montage, settings when fine-tuning your results.

It is possible to use the feature with only two files, using one as the source for changes and the other as the base for the final image, but the best results are obtained by selecting picture parts from several source images and in this way gradually building up the final photo. To do this the user can swap source files by simply clicking a new thumbnail in the Project Bin. Each source file is outlined with a different color and the same hue is used for the pencil marks used to select picture parts to transfer. By color coding pictures and pencil marks it is possible to locate which images are the source for specific picture parts.

Pro's Tip: When shooting Scene Cleaner source images try to ensure that the people that are obscuring the scene are in different positions in the photos with successive captures. This will ensure that Elements can build a people-free scene using picture parts from several photos.

FEATURE SUMMARY

1   Start by multi-selecting the source images in the Organizer workspace. Remember that you can drag a selection marquee around the thumbnails to choose more than one photo at a time.

2   With the source photos selected, choose the Photomerge Scene Cleaner option from the File > New menu. The pictures will be transferred to the Editor workspace and placed in the Project Bin.

3 The first image that you selected will be automatically placed in the Source position (left) in the workspace. The next step is to drag another one of the source photos and drop it into the Final position (right) in the workspace.

4 Now select the Pencil tool from the Photomerge Scene Cleaner pane on the right of the workspace and make a few marks over the areas on the Source image that you want to transfer to the Final image.

5 If too much of the source photo is being pasted to the Final image, select the Eraser tool from the pane and erase some of the Pencil strokes. Add more of the Source photo's contents by drawing more strokes on the image.

6 Click the Done button to process the files and create the montaged picture. Press the Cancel button to stop the feature, close the window and return to Elements.

What is the difference between Scene Cleaner and Group Shot?
With Scene Cleaner you paint on the Final photo to cover an unwanted feature, or person, that is not present in the Source photo. You can also paint on the Source (just like Group Shot) to bring over something from there. The ability to work back and forth lets you have exactly who or what you want in the final image.

Photomerge Panorama

Panoramic images have always been a very inspiring aspect of photography. Until now, making these types of pictures has been restricted to a small set of lucky individuals who are fortunate enough to own the specialized cameras needed to capture the wide images. With the onset of the latest image-editing packages, software manufacturers have now started to include features that allow users with standard cameras to create wonderful wide-angle vistas digitally.

These extra pieces of software are sometimes referred to as 'stitching programs', as their actual function is to combine a series of photographs into a single picture. The edge details of each successive image are matched and blended so that the join is not detectable. See Figure 11.10.

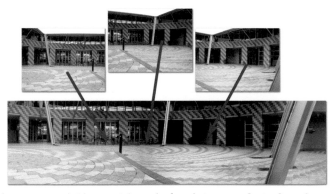

Figure 11.10 Digital panoramas are often created by stitching sequentially shot images together.

Once all the photographs have been combined, the result is a picture that shows a scene of any angle of anything up to a full 360°. See Figure 11.11.

Photomerge Panorama (Editor: File > New > Photomerge Panorama) started its life in Photoshop Elements (it now also exists in Photoshop) and is Adobe's version of the stitching technology. The feature has undergone a variety of enhancements over the last few releases so that now Photomerge Panorama includes enhanced support for larger file sizes, better fine-tuning controls, improved edge-matching capabilities and the option to produce the final composition as separate source picture layers.

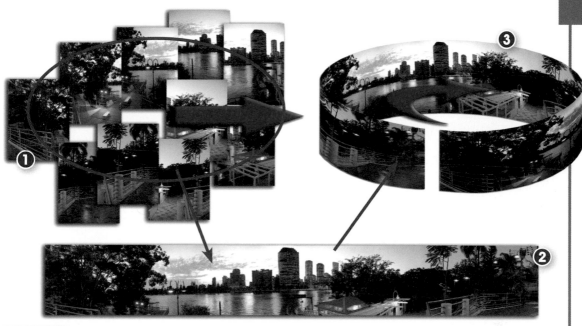

Figure 11.11 *The stitched result can be made up of many individual images and can encompass a view up to a full 360°. (1) Individual source photos. (2) Stitched panorama. (3) 360° spinning panorama.*

Taking images with Photomerge in mind

Although the Photomerge Panorama feature is designed to simplify and solve many of the problems associated with image stitching, a great deal of your own success will be based on how your source images are taken in the first place. A little care and planning at the shooting stage can ensure a more successful panorama with little or no 'touch-up' work later.

Though previous versions of Photomerge Panorama relied heavily on accuracy in the capture stage for the creation of successful panoramic results, the improvements and additional power of Photomerge Panorama as it appears in Photoshop Elements 6 and 7 means that great images are still possible with images shot in less than ideal conditions. That said, quality panoramas still result from careful planning and capture so use the following guidelines to help create the best source photos.

Image overlap

Photomerge Panorama works by identifying common edge elements in sequential images and using these as a basis for blending the two pictures together. When you are making your source photographs, ensure that they overlap by a minimum of 15% and a maximum of 30%. See Figure 11.12.

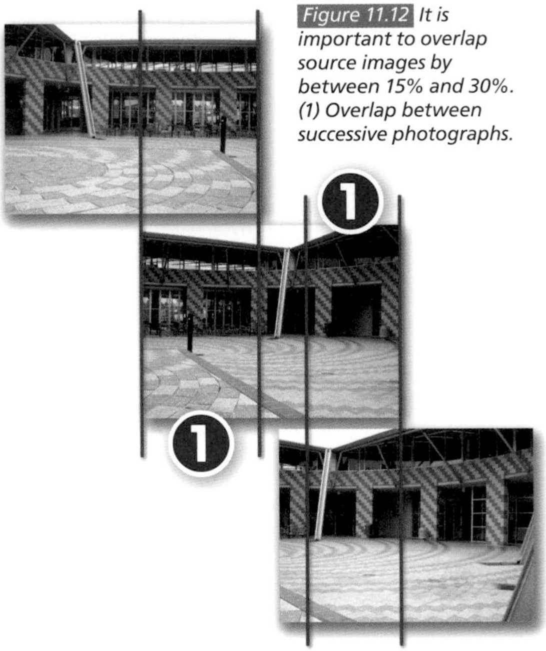

These settings give the program enough information to ensure accurate stitching. I find that if I locate a feature about one-third of the way in from the right-hand side of the viewfinder (or display screen) in one shot and then position the same detail one-third from the left in the next shot, I end up with sufficient overlap for Elements to process the picture. Overlapping images by more than 50% may seem like a good idea, but this can cause the image blending process to be less effective.

Figure 11.12 *It is important to overlap source images by between 15% and 30%. (1) Overlap between successive photographs.*

Keep the camera level

Although Photomerge Panorama is designed to adjust images that are slightly rotated, it is far better to ensure that all source images are level to start with. The easiest way to achieve this is by photographing your scene with your camera connected to a level tripod with a rotating head. If you are out shooting and don't have a tripod handy, try to locate a feature in the scene that remains horizontal in all shots and use this as a guide to keep your camera level when photographing your image sequence. See Figure 11.13.

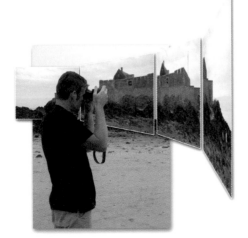

Figure 11.13 *Keep the camera level when shooting your scene.*

Maintain focal length

Sometimes it is tempting to zoom in to capture a closer view of important details when you are in the middle of shooting a panorama sequence. Doing so will change the focal length of the lens and will make it very difficult or impossible to stitch this picture with all the others from the scene. Check what is the optimum focal length for the vista before starting to photograph and once you start to shoot don't touch the Zoom control.

Pivot around the lens

Photomerge Panorama uses sophisticated perspective calculations to help reconstruct the scene you photographed. Changing your position, even by a few inches, will alter the perspective of all the images taken from that point on. Even the way that you hold and rotate the camera can alter the picture's vanishing point. To get the best results always try to pivot the camera around the axis (nodal point) of its lens; this will ensure that all the images in your sequence will have a similar perspective.

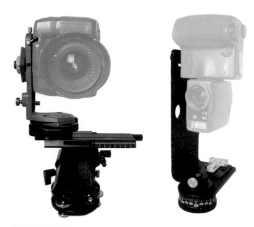

Figure 11.14 A panoramic head for tripods is available for users who regularly shoot wide vistas. (Source: Kaidan and Manfrotto panoramic tripod heads.)

Some compact digital cameras contain a special panorama capture mode design to help maintain overlap. A ghosted third of the previous capture is shown on the back of the camera screen to help align the next image to ensure accurate positioning and overlap. Often this special shooting feature also locks the white balance, focus and exposure settings and titles the source photos with a special number or letter sequence making their identification later easier.

Special panoramic heads designed to position the lens above the center of the tripod are available for this purpose. These virtual reality (VR) heads offset the camera so the nodal point of the lens is directly over the pivot point of the camera. Models are available for specific cameras or you can purchase a multi-purpose design that can be adjusted to suit a range of film and digital bodies. Shooting with these heads is by far the best way to ensure that your images stitch well. See Figure 11.14. If you are capturing your scene with a hand-held camera, then try to rotate your body around the camera, not the other way around. See Figure 11.15.

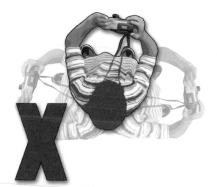

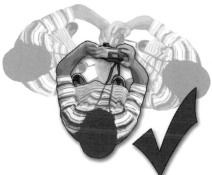

Figure 11.15 If no tripod is available, pivot the camera around its lens, not around your body.

Maintain exposure

Modern cameras contain specialized metering systems designed to obtain the best exposure for a range of lighting conditions. Each time the camera is aimed at a scene, a new calculation is made for the brightest and darkest areas of the view. This system, though very helpful for normal picture taking, can be problematic when shooting panoramas, as the exposure needs to be constant throughout the shooting sequence.

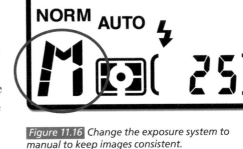

Figure 11.16 Change the exposure system to manual to keep images consistent.

Changing the exposure settings automatically for different image parts of the same scene will mean that key areas will appear as different tones in the stitched picture. If possible, you should change your camera's metering system to manual for the period whilst you are capturing panoramic source images to ensure consistent exposures. See Figure 11.16.

In shooting environments where there is a large range of brightness change from one part of the scene to the other, it is a good idea to shoot the source images for the scene twice using two different exposures – one set for the highlights and the other for the shadows. Before importing your images into Photomerge Panorama, you can combine the captured details from the two exposures and then stitch the evenly exposed result. See the 'Fixing panorama problems' section at end of this chapter for an example of this technique.

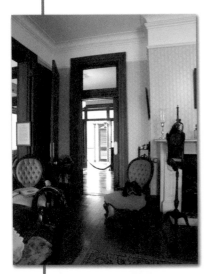
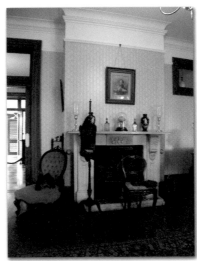
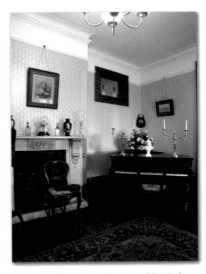

Figure 11.17 Be careful of changes in color cast from frame to frame resulting from inconsistent White Balance settings.

Keep white balance consistent

A similar problem can occur with the auto white balance system contained in many digital cameras. This feature assesses not the amount of light entering the camera but the color of the light, in order to automatically rid your images of color casts that result from mixed light sources in the scene. Leaving this feature set to Auto can mean drastic color changes from one frame to the next as the camera attempts to produce the most neutral result. Switching to manual can produce results that are more consistent, but you must assess the scene carefully to ensure that you base your White Balance settings on the most prominent light source in the scene. See Figure 11.17.

For instance, if you are photographing a wedding and two-thirds of the source shots are lit by sunlight, then this would probably be the best setting to use. For the experimenters amongst us, the one-third of the panorama not lit by sunlight could be shot a second time using a White Balance setting that suits and these images substituted before stitching.

Watch the edges

The edges of the image frame are the most critical part of the source picture. It is important to make sure that moving details such as cars, or pedestrians, are kept out of these areas. Objects that appear in the edge of one frame and not the next cause problems for the stitching program and may need to be removed or repaired later with other tools like the Clone Stamp. See Figure 11.18.

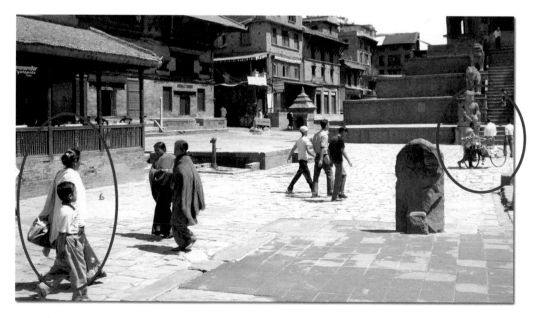

Figure 11.18 *Try to avoid placing moving objects at the edge of frames, as they will disappear or be ghosted when the images are stitched.*

Producing your panorama

Now that we have successfully captured our source pictures let's set about stitching them together to form a panorama. In version 6 of Photoshop Elements the panorama option of Photomerge was completely revamped to include several new auto modes as well as the manual method for stitching photos. Now when selecting the Photomerge Panorama option from inside the Editor workspace you are presented with an enhanced dialog that not only contains Browse/Open and Remove options, which prompt the user to nominate the picture files that will be used to make up the panorama, but also a list of stitching approaches (on the left of the dialog). See Figures 11.19, 10.20 and 10.21.

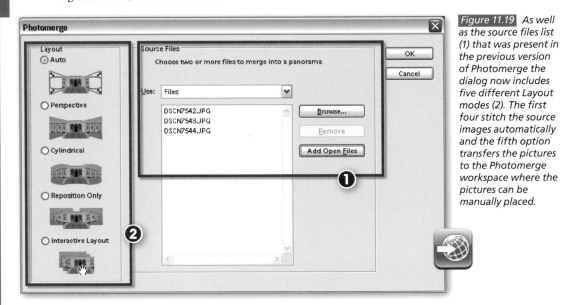

Figure 11.19 As well as the source files list (1) that was present in the previous version of Photomerge the dialog now includes five different Layout modes (2). The first four stitch the source images automatically and the fifth option transfers the pictures to the Photomerge workspace where the pictures can be manually placed.

New Photomerge Panorama stitching modes

The five different Photomerge Panorama Stitching and Blending or Layout options in Photoshop Elements are:

Auto – aligns and blends source files automatically.

Perspective – deforms source files according to the perspective of the scene. This is a good option for panoramas containing 2–3 source files.

Cylindrical – designed for panoramas that cover a wide angle of view. This option automatically maps the results back to a cylindrical format rather than the bow-tie shape that is typical of the Perspective option.

Reposition Only – aligns the source files without distorting the pictures.

Interactive Layout – transfers the files to the Photomerge workspace (which was the only option available in previous releases of Elements) where individual source pictures can be manually adjusted within the Photomerge composition. This is the only non-auto option.

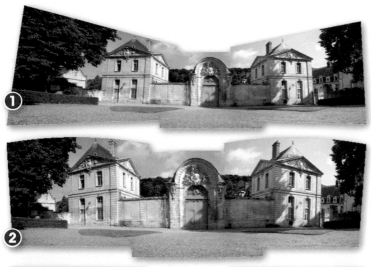

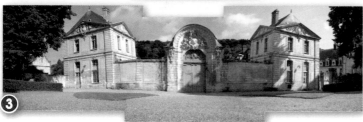

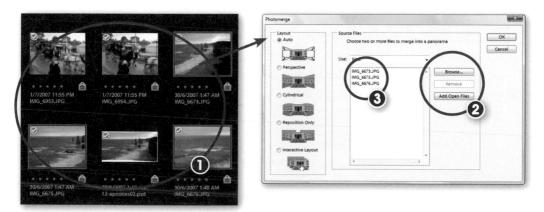

Figure 11.20 *The auto Layout options in the revised Photomerge dialog use different approaches when producing the final panoramic photo.*
(1) Auto and Perspective.
(2) Cylindrical.
(3) Reposition Only.

In most circumstances one of the auto options will easily position and stitch your pictures, but there will be occasions where one or more images will not stitch correctly. In these circumstances use the Interactive Layout option. This displays the Photomerge workspace (see Figure 11.22) where individual pieces of the panorama can be moved or rotated using the tools from the toolbar on the left-hand side of the dialog. Reposition Only and Perspective options are set using the controls on the right. Photoshop Elements constructs the panorama when the OK button is clicked.

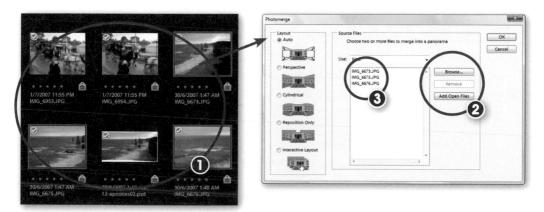

Figure 11.21 *Pick the files you want to use for the stitching process using the Browse dialog box. (1) Multi-selected source files in the Organizer space. (2) Add files window. (3) Browse and Remove buttons.*

You can also start the creation of a panorama from source images that you have multi-selected in the Organizer workspace. Simply Shift-click the thumbnails to include and then choose File > New > Photomerge Panorama and then click the Add Open Files option to insert these photos in the Photomerge Panorama Source Files dialog. The Browse option allows the user to locate suitable files which are then listed in the Source Files section of the box. Any of the files listed here can be removed if incorrectly added by highlighting the file name and clicking the Remove button. With the Layout mode selected, clicking OK exits the dialog and starts the initial opening and arranging steps in Photomerge Panorama.

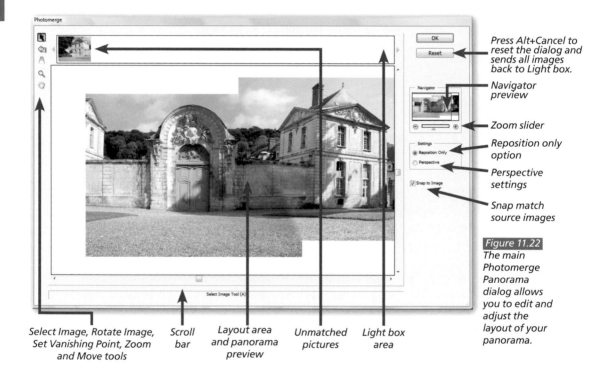

Press Alt+Cancel to reset the dialog and sends all images back to Light box.

Navigator preview

Zoom slider

Reposition only option

Perspective settings

Snap match source images

Figure 11.22
The main Photomerge Panorama dialog allows you to edit and adjust the layout of your panorama.

Select Image, Rotate Image, Set Vanishing Point, Zoom and Move tools

Scroll bar

Layout area and panorama preview

Unmatched pictures

Light box area

The auto workflow

If you have selected one of the auto Layout options then Photomerge will take care of the rest. The utility will open all images, combine them as separate layers into a single Photoshop Elements document and then align and blend the source photos. The final result will be the completed panorama.

The manual workflow

If you have selected the Interactive Layout option in the Photomerge dialog then the Photomerge dialog will display and you will see the utility load, match and stitch the source images together. If the pictures are stored in raw, or 16-bit form, they will be converted to 8-bit mode during this part of the process as well.

For the most part, Photomerge Panorama will be able to correctly identify overlapping sequential images and will place them side by side in the editing workspace. In some instances, a few of the source files might not be able to be automatically placed and Elements will display a pop-up dialog telling you this has occurred. Don't be concerned about this as a little fine-tuning is needed even with the best panoramic projects, and the pictures that haven't been placed can be manually moved into position in the main Photomerge Panorama workspace. See Figure 11.22.

Whilst in the Photomerge Panorama workspace you can use the Select Image tool to move any of the individual parts of the panorama around the composition or from the layout to the Light box area. Click and drag to move image parts. Holding down the Shift key will constrain movements to horizontal, vertical or 45° adjustments only. The Hand or Move View tool can be used in conjunction with the Navigator window to move your way around the picture. For finer control use the Rotate Image tool to make adjustments to the orientation of selected image parts. See Figure 11.23.

The Perspective settings option, together with the Set Vanishing Point tool, manipulates the perspective of your panorama and its various parts. Keep in mind when using the perspective tools that the first image that is positioned in the Composition area is the base image (light green border), which determines the perspective of all other image parts (red border). To change the base image, click on another image part with the Set Vanishing Point tool. It is not possible to use the perspective correction tools for images with an angle of view greater than 120°, so make sure that these options are turned off. After making the final adjustments, the panorama can be completed by clicking the OK button in the Photomerge Panorama dialog box. This action creates a layered stitched file.

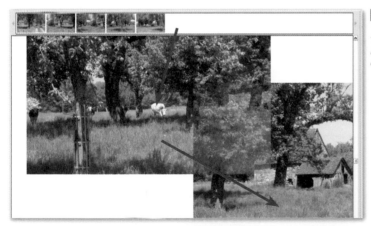

Figure 11.23
You can move source images to and from the Light box and Layout areas by clicking and dragging them.

Photomerge Interactive Layout pro's tips:

- Holding the Alt key lets you see borders around the images you mouse over, so it is easier to select a new Vanishing Point.
- Ctrl Z (Undo) is handy in this dialog because sometimes when you don't like a perspective correction and uncheck it, the result is not as it was before you applied the perspective.

Interactive Layout Step-by-Step

1 Select Photomerge Panorama from the File > New menu to start a new panorama.

2 Click the Browse button in the dialog box.

3 Search through the thumbnails of your files to locate the pictures for your panorama.

4 Click the Open button to add files to the Source Files section of the dialog.

5 Choose the Interactive Layout option at the base of the list.

6 Select OK to open the Photomerge Panorama main workspace. Edit the layout of your source images.

7 To change the view of the images use the Move View tool or change the scale and the position of the whole composition with the Navigator.

8 Images can be dragged to and from the Light box to the work area with the Select Image tool.

9 With the Snap to Image function turned on, Photomerge Panorama will match like details of different images when they are dragged over each other.

10 Ticking the Perspective box will instruct Elements to use the first image placed into the layout area as the base for the composition of the whole panorama. Images placed into the composition later will be adjusted to fit the perspective of the base picture.

11 To align the images without distorting the photos to fit select the Reposition Only option.

12 The final panorama file is produced by clicking the OK button.

FEATURE SUMMARY

When moving the cursor over the photos in the preview area, hold down the Alt key to see which image is active. This is useful when you are changing the vanishing point of your images.

Photomerge Panorama from the Photo Browser

Photo Browser: File > New > Photomerge Panorama

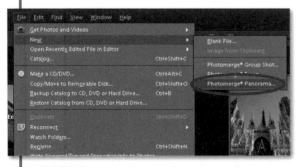

Figure 11.24 From version 3.0 onwards Photomerge Panorama can be accessed from the Photo Browser or Organizer workspace as well as from inside the Editor.

From version 3.0 of Elements for Windows, the Photomerge Panorama feature has also been able to be accessed from the Photo Browser or Organizer workspace as well as from within the Editor. This means that you can locate and multi-select a series of source files using the Photo Browser before selecting the File > New > Photomerge Panorama in the Editor menu option. This action will then open the Editor workspace. Next, select the Add Open Files option to add the selected pictures to the Photomerge Panorama Add Files dialog. At this point you can remove any of the files listed or add more pictures to the group. Once you click OK then Photomerge Panorama proceeds as normal. See Figure 11.24.

Photomerge Panorama in action

Vertical stitches

For most of the time you will probably use Photomerge Panorama to make horizontal panoramas of wide vistas, but occasionally you may come across a situation where you can make use of the stitching technology to create vertical panoramas rather than horizontal ones.

When capturing the vertical source images, be sure to follow the same guidelines used for standard panoramas – check exposure, focus, white balance, focal length and shooting position. See Figure 11.25.

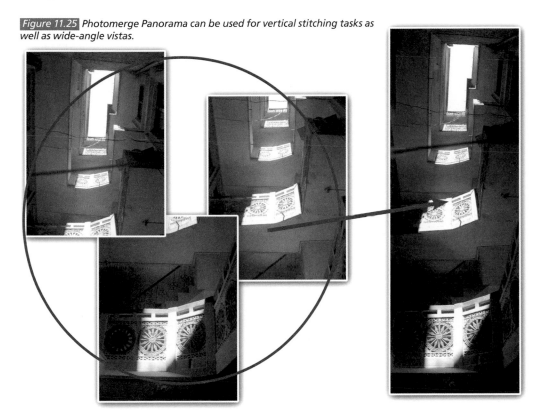

Figure 11.25 *Photomerge Panorama can be used for vertical stitching tasks as well as wide-angle vistas.*

Document stitches

Don't restrict yourself to using the Photomerge Panorama technology for creating architectural or landscape images; the tool can also come in handy when you are trying to scan a document that is larger than your scanner bed. Take the situation of recreating a digital version of an old wall map. The size of the document means that it will need to be captured in a series of overlapping section scans. The resultant files can then be stitched together to recreate a highly detailed digital version of the original document. Be sure to select the Reposition Only option in the Photomerge dialog when producing a document stitch as this will ensure that the source images are not distorted during the reassembly process. See Figure 11.26.

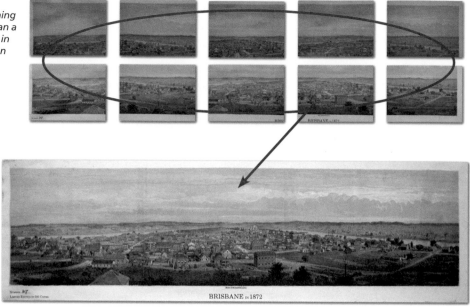

Figure 11.26
Document stitching allows you to scan a large document in sections and then 'glue' it all back together again.

Making panoramas that spin

When you produce a panorama that covers the full 360° of a scene, you not only have an image that can be used to make a wide vista print, but you also have the basic building block needed for creating an Apple QuickTime Virtual Reality (VR) movie. QuickTime allows the viewer to stand in the middle of the action and spin the image around themselves. It is like you are actually there.

Creating a QuickTime VR movie from your finished file is as simple as saving the stitched image as a Macintosh PICT file and then converting it to QuickTime format using Apple's free Make Panorama tool. The resulting file can be watched with any QuickTime player and has the added bonus of being able to be uploaded to the web and viewed online. See Figure 11.27.

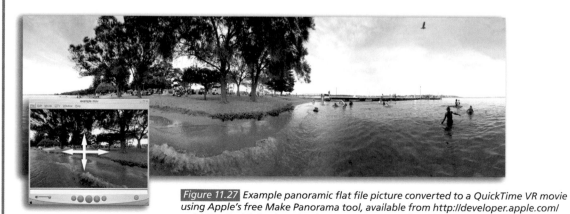

Figure 11.27 *Example panoramic flat file picture converted to a QuickTime VR movie using Apple's free Make Panorama tool, available from http://developer.apple.com/ quicktime/quicktimeintro/tools/. Image courtesy of Geoff Jagoe of Mastery Media. www.mastery.com.au.*

Windows users can make similar spinning panoramas using a small economical utility called Pano2exe. The program converts JPEG output from Photomerge Panorama to a self-contained EXE or program file, which is a single easily distributable file that contains the image itself as well as a built-in viewer. See Figure 11.28.

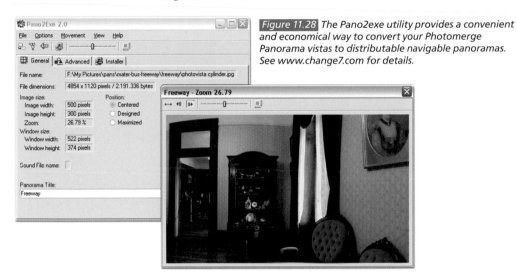

Figure 11.28 *The Pano2exe utility provides a convenient and economical way to convert your Photomerge Panorama vistas to distributable navigable panoramas. See www.change7.com for details.*

Fixing panorama problems

No matter how sophisticated the stitching technology Photomerge Panorama included, there are often some small problems in the final picture where the blending process has not produced perfect results. Some of these defects can be corrected by re-editing the panorama itself: arranging, rotating and manually moving the problem source images to create a better blend. But there are also occasions where the stitching process is not at fault.

The causes of these problems usually fall into one of two groups – subjects moving or changing at the edges of overlapping frames and differences in lighting and/or color between sequential images.

Solution 1 – Time your shooting sequence to accommodate moving objects in the frame. Wait until the objects are in the middle of the frame or are not in the frame at all before pushing the button.

Solution 2 – Shoot a single frame featuring the moving object so that, after stitching, the object can be cut and pasted into position over the top of the completed panorama.

Solution 3 – Shoot two complete sequences of source images: one with the camera's exposure system to suit the highlights of the scene and one with the settings adjusted for the shadows. Try adjusting your camera to 2 stops under the camera setting for the highlight picture and 2 stops over for the image in which the shadows are captured. Before stitching, combine the individual images into a single document. Arrange the layers so that the darkest picture is on

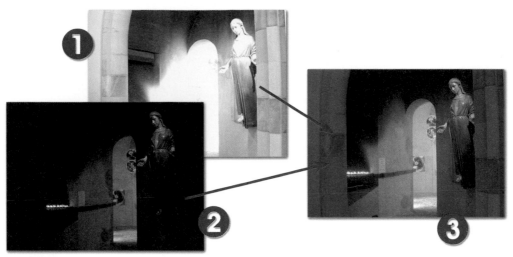

Figure 11.29 Tricky exposure situations can be solved by shooting twice – make one image so that the exposure is adjusted for shadows and one for highlights – and then combine the details of both shots to produce the frame that contains both shadows and highlights that will be used for stitching. (1) Shadow details captured. (2) Highlight details captured. (3) Combined photograph with both highlights and shadows.

top. Change the blend mode of the dark layer to Multiply and open the Levels feature. Drag the black point Output slider to the center of the dialog to add the highlight detail to the midtone and shadow areas of the layer beneath. Save the combined image and then use the correctly exposed and detailed picture as one of the source images used for creating the panorama. See Figures 11.29 and 11.30.

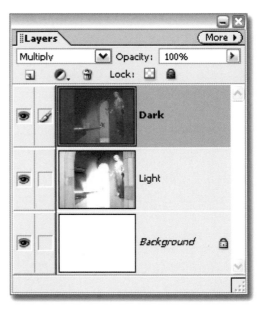

Figure 11.30 Combine the two images to form a composite with details in highlights and shadows.

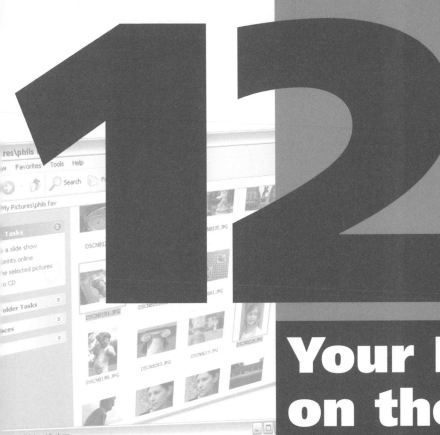

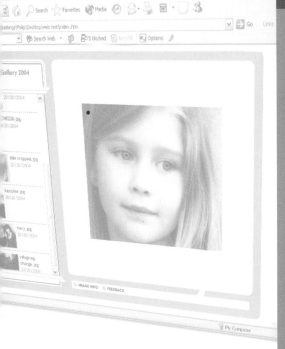

12

Your Images on the Web

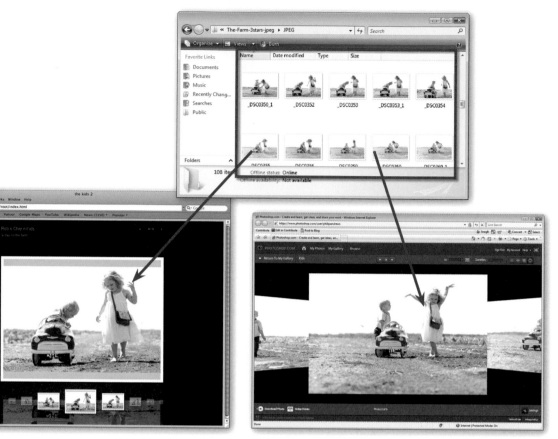

Figure 12.1 In the web age it is critical that users are able to output their images in a format that is suitable for Net use quickly and easily. Photoshop Elements has always been great at getting user's photos to the web quickly and easily, but in version 7.0, the level of interaction with the web is nothing short of revolutionary.

Since the first edition of this book, the World Wide Web has become an even greater part of our daily lives and, as I mentioned then, it is no longer sufficient to concentrate solely on the process of making great prints from digital files, as knowing how to output your pictures so that they are suitable for the web is not just a nice idea, it is now an essential part of the image-making process. In fact, there is a growing band of professional photographers whose work never becomes a print and only ever exists on our screens. See Figure 12.1.

Along with this change to display images online there is also a big move towards community sharing of ideas, techniques and photos. I'm not suggesting that this hasn't always been the case, just look at the level of commitment in your local camera club, but as we have all become more web literate many of the activities that used to occur at such clubs are now being conducted online. People from all over the world not only share their photos with each other, but they also provide feedback on the images and suggest different techniques that could be used to improve the pictures. All via the internet.

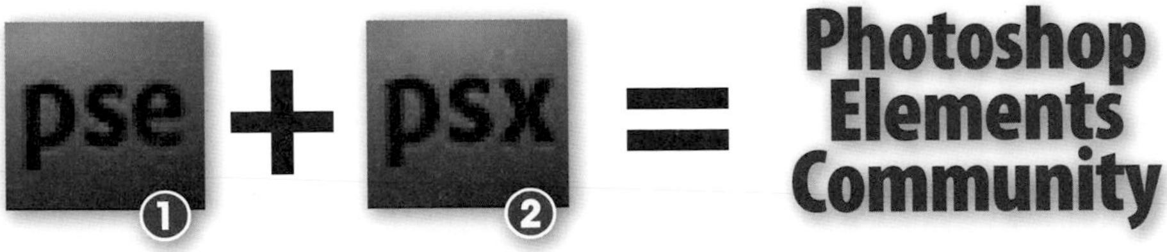

pse + psx = Photoshop Elements Community

① ②

Figure 12.2 The new web and community features in version 7.0 are a mix of the abilities of Photoshop Elements (1) and those found in Photoshop Express (2), Adobe's web based image management and enhancement offering.

In recognition of this situation, Adobe has been gradually introducing internet services and links to their software. Photoshop Elements 7.0 leads this change with the inclusion of a full community program with the new release. Elements users now have the opportunity to join a dedicated group of image makers and in doing so reap the benefits of the support that such involvement brings. All this is achieved by bringing together the abilities of Photoshop Elements and Photoshop Express, Adobe's free web based image management and editing program, which was released in Beta form early in 2008. See Figure 12.2.

This is a big change to how Photoshop Elements is used, but for many of you the degree of change may initially go unnoticed. Sure, the key features of the community are there, plain to see, at the Welcome Screen (community membership, photo backup, inspirational tutorials, web galleries and your own dedicated webspace) but once in Elements proper the differences are a little more subtle. See Figure 12.3.

Therefore, over the next few pages we will look at the skills you need to become a web-savvy image maker, and in the process we'll investigate some of the new web features that have been introduced in Photoshop Elements 7.0.

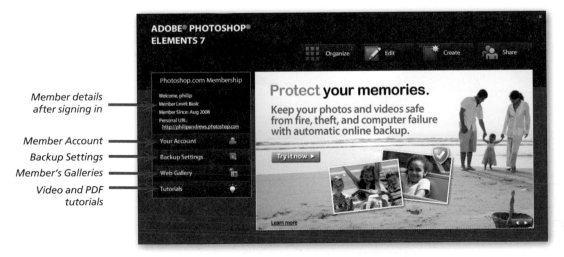

Figure 12.3 The key web based features in version 7.0 are displayed on the Welcome Screen, but you must become a member of Photoshop.com before seeing these and gaining access to them.

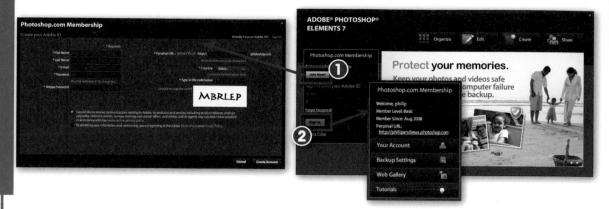

Figure 12.4 In version 7.0 it is possible to not only share your images on the web but also to share your ideas with fellow Element users. In this release Adobe provides a platform for the building of a energetic Photoshop Elements' community and it all happens via your Photoshop.com membership. If you don't have a membership, you can sign up for a free one at the Photoshop Elements Welcome Screen (1). Existing members can also sign in here (2).

The Photoshop Elements' community

The majority of the changes that we will cover over the next few pages are based around a membership system that is associated with both Elements and Photoshop.com. Joining one gives you access to the other and vice versa. There is two levels of membership – Free, which provides access to all the main features and 2Gb of storage space for your photos, and Plus, where for the price of a small annual membership fee, members receive extra storage space and regular deliveries of inspirational tutorials and creative content (templates, clip art, etc.) that they can use with their projects.

It is an easy process to get started. Just click the Join Now button located on the Welcome Screen of Photoshop Elements 7.0. A Photoshop.com membership screen will appear where you can fill in your details. Pressing the Create Account key will process you application allowing you to Sign In the next time you open Photoshop Elements or display the Welcome Screen. See Figure 12.4.

Note: Keep in mind that for your membership application to be processed or for you to be able to sign in and use the new web features, your computer must be connected to the internet.

What is Photoshop Express and Photoshop.com?

The last couple of years has seen some big changes in the world of imaging. Apart from the release of new cameras with more and more megapixels and the increasing power of the software used to manipulate our photos, there has also been a shift in the way that people work with these images.

Remember the days when photographers spent long hours by themselves in the darkroom carefully crafting prints? Well in the first years of digital such was the life of the digital photographer as well. Although with the new technology they weren't working in a darkroom, but rather they manipulated their photos in solitude at the desktop. Notice I said the first few years? That is because the lot of the image maker is changing. Now the process of working and presenting images is much more communal thanks to the connectivity of the internet. This change didn't go unnoticed by Adobe and early in 2008 they released of Photoshop Express (PSX) in a public beta form.

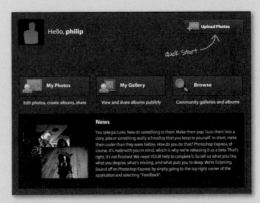

Photoshop Express was Adobe's initial answer to the growing need for an online image management, manipulation and storage solution.

Express was a free online image management, editing and presentation application. Employing a workflow that will be familiar to Elements users as well as photographers who have worked with other online photo applications such as Google's Picasso, shooters upload their images to Albums before making adjustments using simple, but effective, tools, and then presenting the photos to the world in the form of animated slideshows or web galleries. New users needed to sign up for an account before being able to upload images and access PSX features, but they did receive 2Gb of storage space and one of the slickest user interfaces

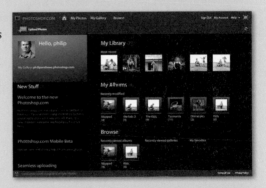

With the release of Elements 7.0, Photoshop Express has become Photoshop.com.

around for their trouble. With direct output to social networking sites such as FaceBook, the new application was loved by bloggers and those photographers who wanted a quick and easy way to get their images online.

With the release of Elements 7.0, Photoshop Express is now part of Photoshop.com. More features have been added to the site and stronger links have been created with the program itself. Now instead of a separate entity, Photoshop.com can be used as an online extension of Photoshop Elements. Cool!

Images and the Net

Even though fewer people are accessing the web through a modem and telephone line, the size of the images used for web work is still critical in the age of broadband. It is still true to say that the larger the picture file, the slower it will download to your machine. So preparing your files for Net use is about balancing picture quality and file size. See Figure 12.5. To help with this, several different file formats have been developed to include a compression system that shrinks file sizes to a point where they can be used on a website or attached to e-mails. The most popular of these is GIF and JPEG with the SWF, or Flash format, gaining more and more popularity in the last few years (especially with Photoshop Elements including several Flash output options for its Web Gallery, now called Online Album, feature). The problem with all these file formats is that small file size comes at a cost of image quality.

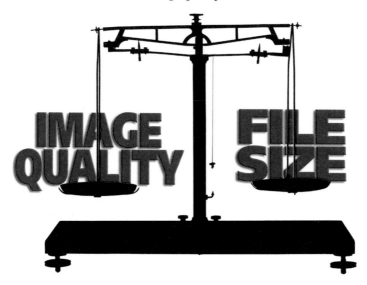

Figure 12.5 Preparing any content for web use is concerned with balancing quality and file size. This is especially true when placing your pictures on the Internet. Too much quality will mean that your photos will take a long time to display, too little and they will download quickly but be of poor quality.

GIF

With the GIF or Graphics Interchange Format, it is only possible to save a picture with a maximum of 256 colors. As most photographic pictures are captured and manipulated in 24-bit color (16.7 million colors), this limitation means that GIF images appear posterized and coarse compared with their full color originals. This isn't always the case, but because of the color restrictions this format is mainly used for logos and headings on web pages and not for photographic imagery. GIF is also used for simple animations, as it has the ability to flick through a series of images stored in the one file. See Figure 12.6.

JPEG

In contrast, the JPEG format was developed specifically for still images. It is capable of producing very small files in full 24-bit color. When saving in this format it is possible to select the level of quality, or the amount of compression, that will be used with a particular image. See Figure 12.7. In more recent years, two new formats – PNG (Portable Network Graphics) and JPEG 2000 – have been developed that build upon the file format technology of JPEG and GIF. At present, these file types are not used widely but as time passes they are gaining more popularity.

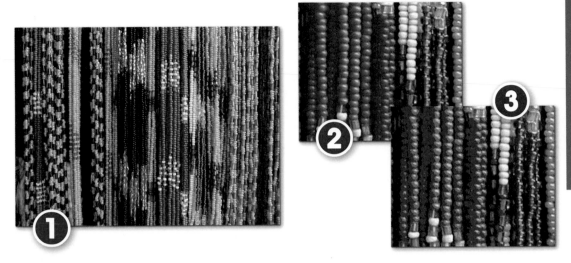

Figure 12.6 *The compression technology built into the GIF format makes files smaller by reducing the number of colors in your pictures to a maximum of 256 (8-bit color). This means that GIF images are small and fast to display but the lack of colors makes them unsuitable for use with photographs. (1) Original 3.53 Mb picture containing 16.7 million colors. (2) Detail of original. (3) Detail of the same file converted to GIF format so that it is 0.43 Mb in size and contains 32 colors only.*

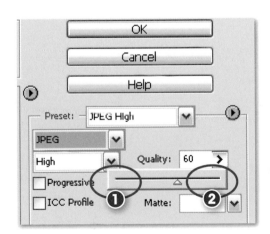

Figure 12.7 *The compression level in the JPEG format is selectable via the Quality slider in the JPEG dialog. Moving the slider to the left (1) creates a small, low quality file; moving it to the right (2) produces a better quality image but with a bigger file size.*

JPEG 2000

JPEG 2000 (JPX or JP2) uses wavelet compression technology to produce smaller and sharper files than traditional JPEG. The downside to the new technology is that to make use of the files created in the JPEG 2000 file format online users need to install a plug-in into their web viewers. Native (i.e. built-in) browser support for the new standard will undoubtedly happen, but until then Elements users can freely exchange JP2 files with each other as support for the format is built right into the software. From version 2.0 Elements has supported the saving of pictures to the newest version of the JPEG format – JPEG 2000. The controls for this format are accessed in the format's own preview dialog via the Save As option in the File menu.

PNG

PNG24 is a format that contains a lossless compression algorithm, the ability to save in 24-bit color mode and a feature that allows variable transparency (as opposed to GIF's on and off transparency choice). File sizes are typically reduced by 5–25% when saved in the PNG format. Greater space savings can be made by selecting the PNG8 version of the format, which allows the user to select the number of colors (up to 256) to include in the picture. Reducing the size of the color set results in smaller files and works in a similar way to the GIF. Most browsers and image-editing programs support the PNG format natively, so no extra viewer plug-in is necessary.

Flash

Elements 5.0 was the first version of the program released after Adobe's purchase of Macromedia. Since then Elements has embraced the Flash or SWF format that Macromedia developed for web sites. The galleries produced via the Elements' Online Album feature, as well as those displayed at the Photoshop.com website, all use the Flash file format rather than the more traditional HTML pages and JPEG or Png files. Like JPEG, the Flash format is designed to quickly display high quality photos on the Internet using small file sizes.

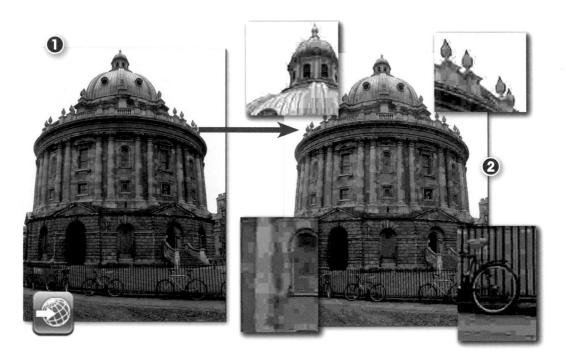

Figure 12.8 Too much JPEG compression introduces artifacts or visual errors into your pictures. (1) Original uncompressed picture. (2) Overcompressed version of the photo showing extensive artifacts.

Getting the balance right

Editor: File > Save for Web and Editor: File > Save As > JPEG 2000

Both JPEG formats, as well as GIF and PNG8, make small files by using 'lossy' compression algorithms. This means that image quality and information are lost as part of the compression process. In simple terms, you are degrading the picture to produce a smaller file. Too much JPEG compression, in particular, and the errors or 'artifacts' that result from the quality loss become obvious. See Figure 12.8.

So how much compression is too much? Well, Elements includes a special Save for Web feature that previews how the image will appear before and after the compression has been applied. See Figure 12.9. Start the feature by selecting the Save for Web option from the File menu of either the Standard or Quick Fix editor workspaces. You are presented with a dialog that shows 'before' and 'after' versions of your picture side by side. The settings used to compress the image can be changed in the top right-hand corner of the screen. Each time a value is altered, the image is recompressed using the new settings and the results redisplayed.

JPEG, GIF and PNG can all be selected and previewed in the Save for Web feature. To preview JPEG 2000 compressed images use the Save As option in the File menu and select JPEG 2000 as the file type. This step will open the preview dialog specifically designed for this format. See Figure 12.10.

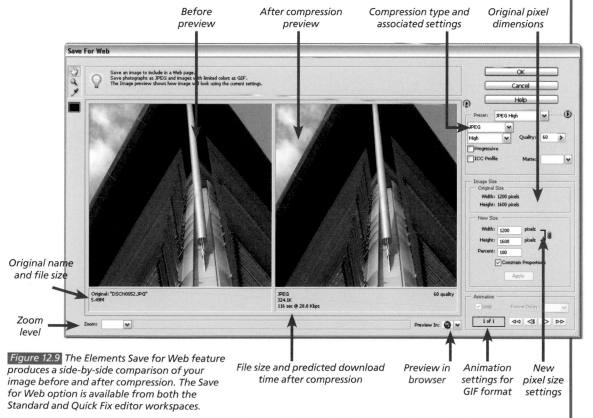

Before preview   *After compression preview*   *Compression type and associated settings*   *Original pixel dimensions*

Original name and file size

Zoom level

Figure 12.9 *The Elements Save for Web feature produces a side-by-side comparison of your image before and after compression. The Save for Web option is available from both the Standard and Quick Fix editor workspaces.*

File size and predicted download time after compression   *Preview in browser*   *Animation settings for GIF format*   *New pixel size settings*

By carefully checking the preview of the compressed image (at 100% magnification) and the file size readout at the bottom of the screen, it is possible to find a point where both the file size and image quality are acceptable.

By clicking OK it is then possible to save a copy of the compressed file to your hard drive ready for attachment to an e-mail or use in a web page.

FEATURE SUMMARY

1 With an image already open in Elements, pick the Save for Web (Editor: File > Save for Web) or Save As (Editor: File > Save As > JPEG 2000) option.

2 Adjust the magnification of the images in the preview windows to at least 100% by using the Zoom tool or the Zoom drop-down menu.

3 Select the file format from the Settings area of the dialog.

4 Alter the image quality for JPEG and JPEG 2000 or the number of colors for GIF and PNG8.

5 Assess the compressed preview for artifacts and check the file size and estimated download times at the bottom of the dialog.

6 If the results are not satisfactory, then change the settings and recheck file size and image quality.

7 Click OK to save the compressed, web-ready file.

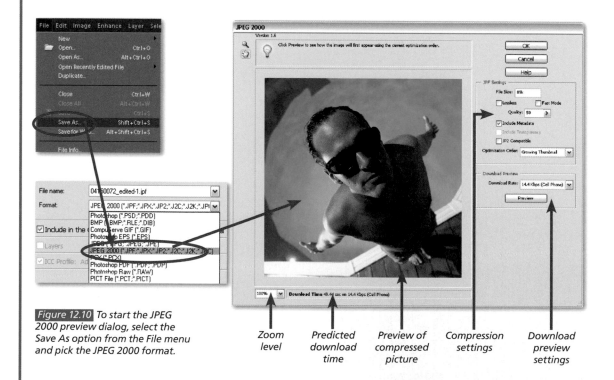

Figure 12.10 To start the JPEG 2000 preview dialog, select the Save As option from the File menu and pick the JPEG 2000 format.

Zoom level   Predicted download time   Preview of compressed picture   Compression settings   Download preview settings

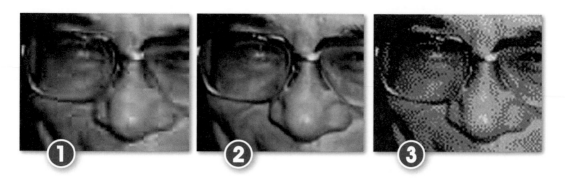

Figure 12.11 Details of compression comparisons. (1) JPEG maximum compression. (2) JPEG 2000 minimum compression. (3) PNG8, 16 colors.

Web compression formats side by side

To give an indication of the abilities of each particular format, I optimized the same image and saved it in five different web formats. The differences in image quality and file sizes, as well as the best uses and features of each format, can be viewed in Table 12.1 and Figures 12.11 and 12.12.

*Table 12.1 Comparison of file formats suitable for web use. * See detail of the compression type and setting applied to the same photograph in Figure 12.12.*

File format	Compression settings	Best uses or format features					File size	Detail*
		Photo	Logo	Heading	Anim-ation	Trans-parency		
JPEG	Minimum	✓					791 Kb	1
	Maximum	✓					60 Kb	2
JPEG 2000	Minimum	✓					880 Kb	3
	Maximum	✓					49 Kb	4
PNG8	256 colors		✓	✓		✓	502 Kb	5
	16 colors		✓	✓		✓	216 Kb	6
PNG24	—	✓				✓	1358 Kb	7
GIF	256 colors		✓	✓	✓	✓	398 Kb	8
	16 colors		✓	✓	✓	✓	201 Kb	9

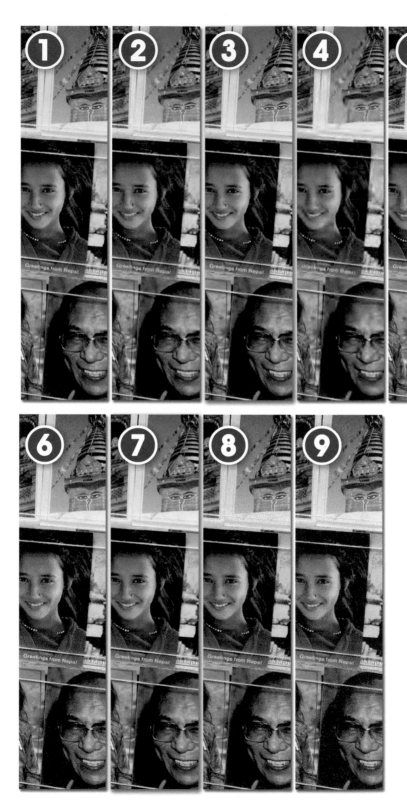

Figure 12.12 Side-by-side comparisons of the image quality of a variety of web optimized file formats at different compression settings.
(1) JPEG, minimum compression.
(2) JPEG, maximum compression.
(3) JPEG 2000, minimum compression.
(4) JPEG 2000, maximum compression.
(5) PNG8, 256 colors.
(6) PNG8, 16 colors.
(7) PNG24.
(8) GIF, 256 colors.
(9) GIF, 16 colors.

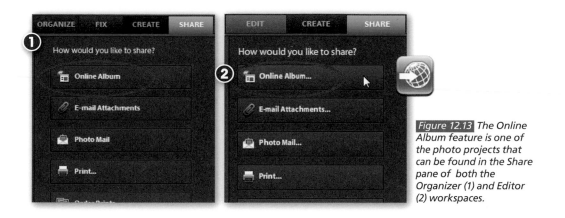

Figure 12.13 The Online Album feature is one of the photo projects that can be found in the Share pane of both the Organizer (1) and Editor (2) workspaces.

Making your own web gallery

Organizer: Share task pane > Online Album or Editor: Share task pane > Online Album

Never before in the history of the world has it been possible to exhibit your work so easily to so many people for such little cost. The web is providing artists, photographers and business people with a wonderful opportunity to be seen, but many consider making your own website a prospect too daunting to contemplate. For the last few versions of Elements, Adobe has included a feature that takes several images and transforms them into a fully functioning website in a matter of a few minutes. In version 7.0 this feature has been overhauled so that now it links directly with your Photoshop.com account and the photos which are stored there.

The Online Album feature (previously called the Online Galleries or Web Photo Galleries) can be found under the Share pane in both the Editor and Organizer workspaces. See Figure 12.13. Clicking the Online Album button displays the first window in a multi-step wizard. The steps allow you to choose your images, set the template and style of the website, input the heading and adjust the colors used on the pages, and choose where you want the project saved and more importantly how the website is to be shared. The feature even provides the option for free hosting via the Photoshop.com website. In the previous version, the sharing website was called Photoshop Showcase.

Online Gallery versus Online Album

In version 7.0 the Online Album option replaces the Online Gallery feature that was available in the previous release. Both features are designed to help you quickly and easily create a presentation that displays your photos on the internet, but Online Albums uses a workflow that duplicates the Albums found in the Organizer space of Photoshop Elements and places the copy online at Photoshop.com. This means that not only are your Online Albums a means of displaying your photos but they also become way to archive your photos. For more details about Album synchronization go to Chapter 4.

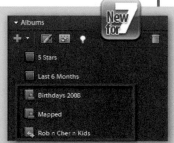

An Online Album provides both a way to view your images on the web and also an automatic backup of your photos.

YOUR IMAGES ON THE WEB

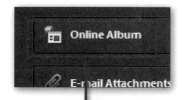

Figure 12.14 *The Online Album wizard is accessed by clicking the Online Album button in the Share task pane on the right of the workspace.*
(1) The first step is to title the new Album and use the Add and Remove buttons to alter the pictures included. (2) Click drag the photos to change their position in the album sequence. (3) The next pane contains displays a preview of the gallery, a Change Template button and three share options. (4) Clicking the change template option will display other designs for the gallery. Select one and click apply to change the design. (5) The next dialog provides a range of settings where the user can customize the album. (6) The same Share options found in step 3 are listed in the next pane. Select one of these to publish your album.

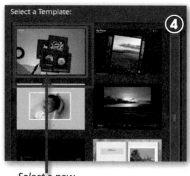

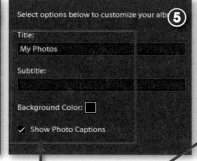

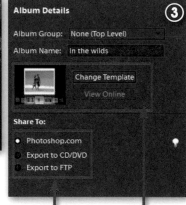

Images included in gallery   *Album title*   *Add or Remove photos to the list*

Click-drag to change image position in the sequence

Output options   *Change Template*

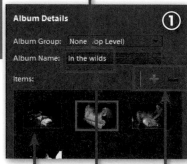

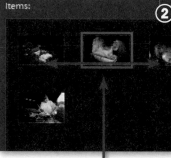

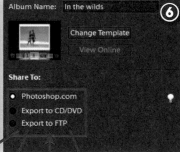

Select a new design for the gallery

Gallery details

Output options

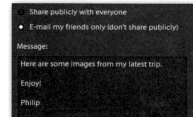

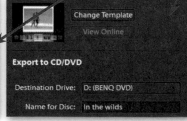

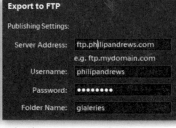

Photoshop.com web hosting service   *Write the gallery to a CD or DVD.*   *Upload to your own website*

Multi-select pictures to include

The photos that you use for the gallery can be multi-selected from the Photo Browser first, before entering the feature. This is different from earlier versions of Elements where you had to use all the pictures located in a single folder or directory. In the same vein, the revised Online Album wizard dialog contains a very useful Add/Remove pictures section (+ and − buttons on the top right) which displays a thumbnail list of those photos currently selected for inclusion in the website. In addition, the order that pictures appear in the web gallery can be changed by clicking and dragging thumbnails to new spots in the list. See Figure 12.14.

Gallery templates

For the first time version 5.0 included animated and interactive gallery types as well as the more traditional static thumbnail and display image templates. In version 6 the gallery choice was increased to now include a range of categories of design. In version 7.0 the template galleries have been arranged thematically and include the following groups: Classic, Family, Fun, Occasions, Seasons and Travel. See examples of some of the templates available on the next page in Figure 12.17. When creating an Online Album the gallery design is selected by default after clicking the Share button in the first pane. To select a different design the user needs to click on the Change Template button. They are then presented with the Template drop down menu and a list of representative thumbnails. See Figure 12.15.

The template menu also includes a Show All entry to display all available templates as well as a Photoshop.com option for listing the templates available from the website. In the top right of the pane is a double-sideways arrow button that allows you to set the content for the template pane. See Figure 12.16. The choices are:

*   Only Show Photoshop.com Content
*   Only Show Local Content
*   Show All Content

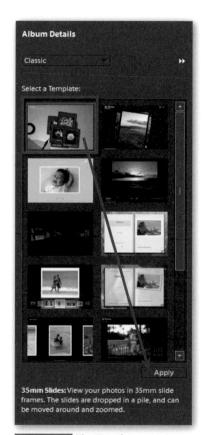

Figure 12.15 *The Template pane is accessed via the Change Template button and allows the user to select and apply a different design to their Online Album.*

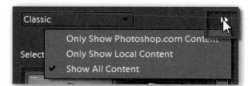

Figure 12.16 *The settings options for the pane adjust which templates are listed – local ones from Elements or those from Photoshop.com.*

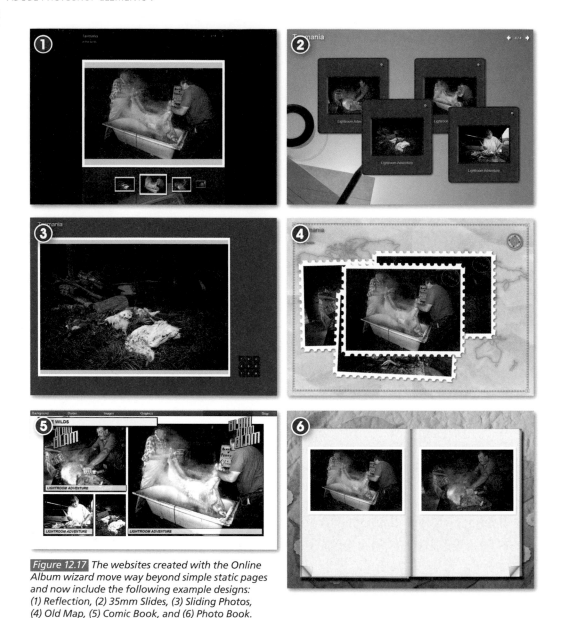

Figure 12.17 *The websites created with the Online Album wizard move way beyond simple static pages and now include the following example designs: (1) Reflection, (2) 35mm Slides, (3) Sliding Photos, (4) Old Map, (5) Comic Book, and (6) Photo Book.*

Going live

With the site design completed, the next step is to transfer all the files to some server space on the Net. Companies called ISPs, or Internet Service Providers, host the space. See Figure 12.18. The company that you are currently using for 'dial-up' or broadband connection to the Net will probably provide you space as part of your access contract. As an alternative, there is a range of hosting businesses worldwide that will store and display your gallery for free, as long as you allow them to place a small banner advertisement at the top of each of your pages. By far the best solution though is to make use of the space provided with your Photoshop.com membership.

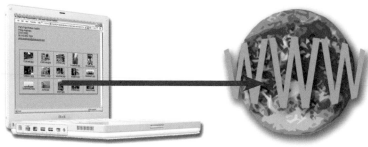

Figure 12.18 *The completed website has to be transferred from your computer to a space on the Net hosted by an Internet Service Provider. This space can be provided by the company that supplies your Internet or e-mail account or alternatively you can make use of the Photoshop.com hosting service which links directly to the Photoshop Elements Online Album wizard.*

This takes a lot of the hassle out of uploading your website as Adobe provides the ability to transfer your web pages to its own hosting service, Photoshop.com, from inside the Online Album's wizard.

Whichever route you take, you will need to transfer your site's files from your home machine to the ISP's machine. When using previous versions of Elements, this process was handled by an extra piece of software called an FTP or File Transfer Protocol program. Thankfully the Online Album feature contains an integrated FTP utility within the Share To section of the dialog. See Figure 12.19. You can choose between the following Share options:

Photoshop.com – Upload to a free online sharing area provided at Photoshop.com.

Export to FTP – Transfer to your own ISP or Net space provider.

Export to CD/DVD – An option for burning the gallery to a CD or DVD.

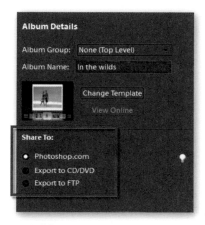

Figure 12.19 *The easiest way to get your completed album online is to make use of the the webspace that is provided with your Photoshop.com membership. That way when you choose the Share To > Photoshop.com option from the Online Album pane, the transfer process is handled automatically.*

Step-by-step Online Album creation

Use these steps to guide you through creating your first photo website.

1   Select the pictures you want to include in the site from those thumbnails displayed in the Organizer workspace. Hold down the Ctrl key to multi-select individual files and the Shift key to select all the files in a list. Alternatively, you can also drag a selection marquee around thumbnails in the Photo Browser.

2   Make sure the Task pane is displayed (Window > Show Task Pane). Click on the Create tab and then select the Online Album button.

3 Add in a title for the Album name. You can also select an Album group to include the new Album in. Remember that creating an online gallery is now a process of creating a Photoshop Elements' Album and then publishing the new Album online. So this part of the wizard is about setting up the Album structure (Album and the Album group it belongs to). See Figure 12.20

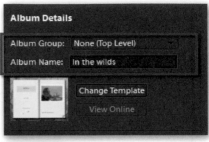

Figure 12.20

4 If you want to add the Album to a new Album Group then you will need to exit the wizard by clicking the Cancel button at the bottom of the pane and then create a new Album Group using the settings in the Albums pane of the Organize tab in the Organizer workspace. See Figure 12.21

5 Add or remove photos from the list of those to be included in the album (thumbnails listed in the panel) by clicking the '+' button to add more image or the '−' button to remove ones already listed.

6 Adjust the position of the images in the presentation sequence by click-dragging the thumbnail within the group. Click the Share button to move to the following step.

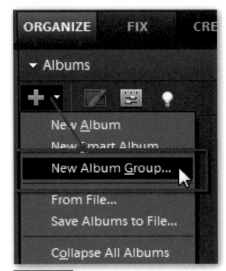

Figure 12.21

7 A preview of the images in the last template used is now displayed in the workspace. The pane contains a summary of the Album details as well as a Change Template button. If you are happy with the design, select a share option from the list in the Share To section of the pane. Click the Next button to proceed. See Figure 12.12.

8 If you want to alter the look of your online gallery then select the Change Template button. The pane's content changes to display a drop down menu of Template choices. Selecting one of these entries will display a list of thumbnails of the designs for each group. Clicking a thumbnail will display a description

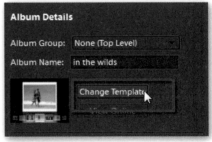

Figure 12.22

of the template features and its intended use. One entry on the Template list is titled Photoshop.com. Selecting this option will display templates from Photoshop.com rather than those stored with Elements on your computer. Click the Apply button to change the template to the new one selected from the list of press the Next button to proceed.

9   Automatically Photoshop Elements provides a preview of the web design complete with the images you selected in the main workspace to the left of the window. The content of the right side panel will be determined by the template selected in the previous step. Some web gallery designs have many settings and controls that can be used to adjust the look and feel of the gallery as well as the text included in it; others, particularly the highly automated ones, have few user-controlled settings to play with. You will need to click the Refresh button at the bottom of the panel to see the changes displayed in the preview section of the workspace. See Figure 12.23.

10   Many designs, however, do use photo details, like the caption entry, to provide titling for the individual photos. So if you want to, or need to, include these details in the design; exit the wizard by clicking the Cancel button. Add in caption details for your photos by adding text in the Properties palette (Window > Properties) and then restart the Online Album process. See Figure 12.24.

11   If available, adjust the color, opacity and text that will be used for the site and then choose whether you want to include any captions or file names under the display pictures.

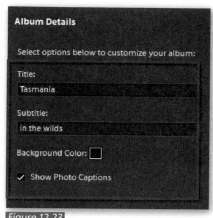

Figure 12.23

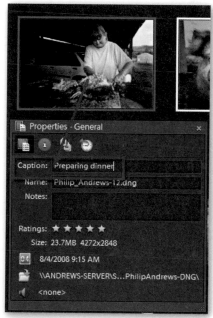

Figure 12.24

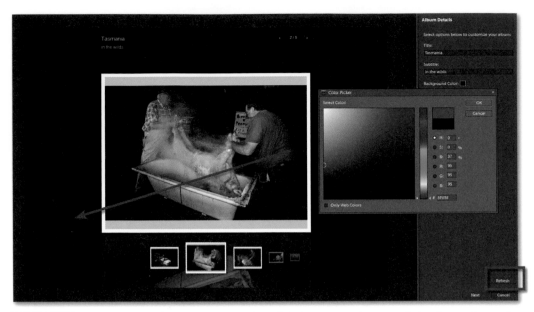

Figure 12.25 *There is no longer the need to preview the website in a separate browser window (as was the case in previous versions of the feature) as now the functioning website is previewed directly in the workspace. To be sure that the preview is updated with your latest settings click the Refresh button in the bottom right of the panel.*

12 With all the options set you can preview the way that the website looks and works in the workspace on the left of the panel. To update the preview to reflect your new settings click on the Refresh button at the bottom of the panel. Click Next to continue. See Figure 12.25.

13 There is no longer a formal Save step in the wizard as clicking the Share button in the final pane of the wizard automatically adds the new Album to list in the Organizer workspace as well as publishing it online.

14 Now select the way that you want to share your website from the three options listed in this panel. In this example the Export to FTP option was selected. Add in the details for your FTP site, which can be obtained from your service provider, and then click Upload to transfer the website to the web server. See Figure 12.26.

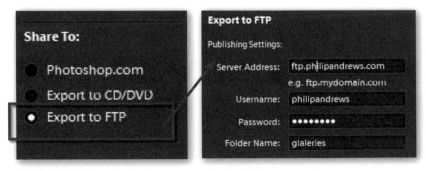

Figure 12.26 *After selecting Export to FTP, the FTP dialog will be displayed. Here you can input the settings provided by your ISP (Internet Service Provider). Next, click the Upload button to transfer your website files to the space on the web server.*

Sharing alternatives for your Online Album

As well as transferring your completed website to a space provided by your ISP, the Online Gallery feature provides two alternatives for sharing your pages – via CD/DVD or with the Photoshop.com. Both options are listed along with Export to FTP in the last panel of the Online Album wizard. See Figure 12.27.

CD/DVD distribution

1 After selecting the Export to CD/DVD option Elements will look for the CD/DVD drives installed in your computer and list these devices in a new Make a CD or DVD dialog.

2 Choose the drive to use for the writing and input a name for the disk in the area at the bottom of the dialog before clicking OK to start the writing process.

Uploading to Photoshop.com

1 Selecting the Photoshop.com option and clicking Next will re-display the details pane where you can adjust the settings for the Template. Click Next to continue.

2 Next, a new pane containing share settings is shown. Here you can choose to provide public access to the gallery via the Share publicly with everyone option, or share with friends via email invitations. If you select the second choice then you need to type in a message that will be sent with the invitation and select the contacts for the email.

3 Finally the choose the type of access that viewers will have from the entries at the bottom of the pane. The options are Download Photos and Order Photo Prints. Click Share to upload the files and send the invitations.

Share To:

- ● Photoshop.com
- ● Export to CD/DVD
- ● Export to FTP

Figure 12.27 *The Photoshop Showcase option allows you to upload and share websites and collections of photos with your friends over the Internet. The CD/DVD option provides the ability to save the completed website to disk for distribution separately.*

Album Details

Album Group: None (Top Level)
Album Name: In the wilds

Change Template
View Online

Export to CD/DVD

Destination Drive: D: (BENQ DVD)
Name for Disc: In the wilds

Album Details

Album Group: None (Top Level)
Album Name: In the wilds

Change Template
View Online

● Share publicly with everyone
● E-mail my friends only (don't share publicly)

Message:

Here are some images from my latest trip.

Enjoy!

Philip

Send E-mail To: Uncheck All

☐ Andrews, Philip

Another approach to publishing to the web

As we have already seen, the Online Albums feature is linked to the general Album options found in the Photoshop Elements' Organizer workspace. Given this link then it will come as no surprise that it is also possible for you to publish your pictures online via the settings in the Albums Pane. There are a couple of ways that you can create a gallery of images using this approach so let's look at each in turn.

Share a new Album

The first starts with the creation of a new Album. You might not have noticed that Share is one of the options that is available when creating a new Album. The Share button sits between the Done and Cancel buttons at the bottom of the Album Details pane that is used to create a new Album entry. See Figure 12.28. Selecting this option at the time of Album creation, transfers the album images straight to the Online Album wizard. With a couple more clicks of your mouse (to move through the wizard steps) the photos are published. In one easy sequence you have created an Album and published the contents online. Good job!

Now if you are an experienced Elements user then you probably have developed a workflow for publishing web galleries that involves:

1. creating an album,
2. adding selected images to the album,
3. adjusting the sequence of the pictures,
4. selecting the photos from the album that you want to use,
5. create the web gallery, and then
6. publish the gallery on line.

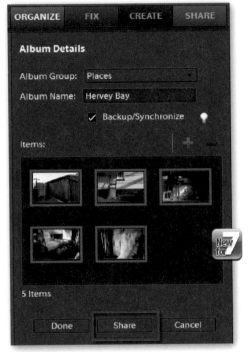

Figure 12.28 *Clicking the Share button in the New Album pane takes you directly to the Online Album wizard, fast tracking the web publishing process.*

As you can see, in Photoshop Elements 7.0 this process is much simplified. Now you can fast track your gallery production right from the Album pane. It may take a little time to get used to this way of working, but it is certainly faster than the old method. It also has the added bonus that if you select the Backup/Synchronize settings, located in the same pane, you will instruct Elements to automatically back up the contents of this album.

For more details about creating and using Albums go to Chapter 4.

Share an existing Album

Okay, so you say to me, 'This is great Phil. I can really speed up my organization and web publishing using this new way of working, but what of the Albums that I have already created?' Good question!. Thankfully these too can be easy uploaded to Photoshop.com in a template based web gallery of your own choosing. Here's how.

Display the Album pane first. Notice that there are different icons used for different Albums. These indicate the state of the Album. A double headed arrow shows the Album is marked for Backup/Synchronization and a small person indicates that the Album has been published online. See Figure 12.29.

To publish an existing Album, select its entry and then choose the Share icon (two people and a green arrow) on the left of the entry. This action will transfer the contents of the Album to the Online Album wizard. From here it is a simple matter of following the wizard steps to select the design of the gallery and published the photos to Photoshop.com. See Figure 12.30.

The photos in Synchronized Albums can be viewed online but only via the Photoshop.com file browser and only by you when you are signed in to the site. For your images to be seen publicly in a template based or themed Album then you must publish them from Photoshop Elements and select the 'Share publicly with everyone' setting in the Online Album wizard.

Alternatively, you can make a synchronized album visible to the public or viewable by a group of invited friends by clicking on the Lock icon to the right of the Album entry in the My Files or My Gallery sections of Photoshop.com. You don't get the choice of using a themed web gallery template when making images public in this way but it does provide another method of allowing others to see your photos. There are also options in the pop-up menu for allowing printing or downloading of the photos. See Figure 12.31.

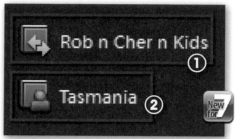

Figure 12.29 *The entries in the Albums pane are marked with different icons to signify their status. (1) A two way arrow is used for Backup/Synchronized albums. (2) A small person is used for Albums that have been Shared or published online.*

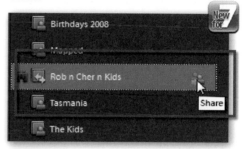

Figure 12.30 *To publish an existing Album just select the Album entry and then click on the Share icon (two people and a small green arrow). This will transfer the images in the current album directly to the Online Album wizard .*

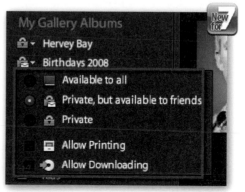

Figure 12.31 *Synchronized but not published Albums can be made viewable by friends or the public by clicking on the Lock icon and choosing the required action from the pop-up menu.*

Photoshop.com is your new partner

The partnership between Photoshop Elements and Photoshop. com goes way beyond merely providing a space on the web to view the pictures that you process in Elements. Because Photoshop.com grew out of Photoshop Express the site also contains simple editing features such as the ability to crop, resize, auto correct, alter white balance, adjust highlights, boost color, tint and distort photos. See Figure 12.32.

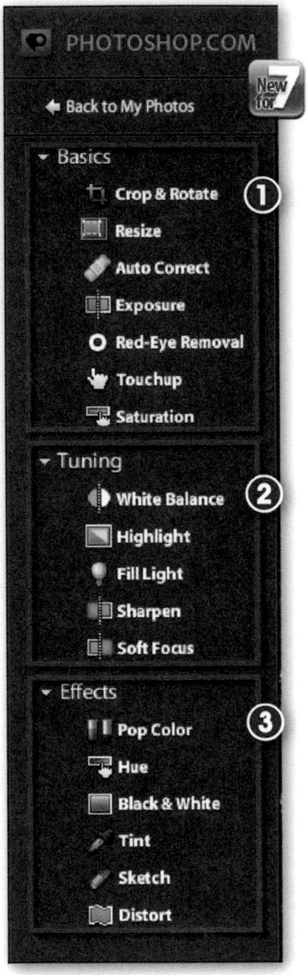

Enhancing online

To adjust an image online, click onto the My Photos heading first and then navigate to the photo. You can look for the photos visually by selecting an Album entry or Library heading on the left of the screen and then scrolling through the thumbnails in the main workspace. Alternatively, you can locate the photo by typing a search term into the Search box at the top right of the workspace and then hitting the Enter key. Photoshop.com tries to match the search term with album and file names, tags associated with the photos and picture captions.

Once you have located the photo, clicking on the picture's thumbnail switches the workspace to the edit mode and displays the photo as large as possible within the window. All the adjustments that can be applied to the photo, are grouped under three headings Basics, Tuning and Effects on the left. See Figure 12.33.

For most options, when an adjustment is selected from the list, a series of thumbnails displaying varying degrees of application for the adjustment are displayed above the image. Clicking a thumbnail will preview a change to the photo. With some adjustments a slider control is also provided below the thumbnails for finer control. One thumbnail of the group will be displayed with a curved yellow arrow. Click this entry to reset the photo to the way it was before selecting the current adjustment. Click the green tick (top right) to save the current adjustment changes and click the red cross to cancel the alterations.

Despite the preview being updated to reflect the changes that you have made, the adjustments are not actually applied to the image until they are saved upon exiting the Editing mode. This way of working allows you to revert the photo to its original state by clicking the Reset All button at the bottom of the window. Also contained at the bottom of the editing window is the View Original image which allows you to see how the photo looked before your adjustments.

Figure 12.32 Image enhancement options in Photoshop.com are broken into three broad groups. (1) Basics, (2) Tuning and (3) Effects. Each group contains a series of adjustment entries.

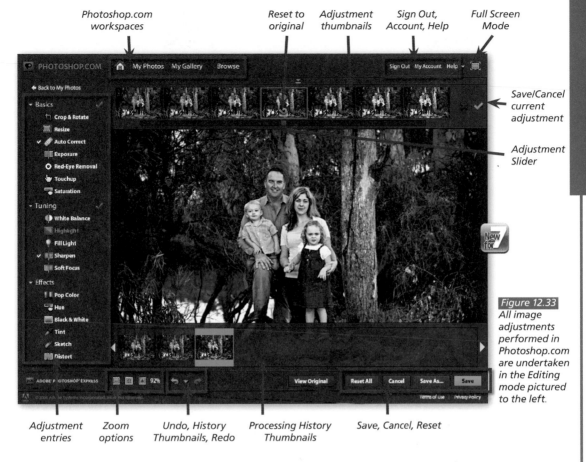

Photoshop.com workspaces

Reset to original

Adjustment thumbnails

Sign Out, Account, Help

Full Screen Mode

Save/Cancel current adjustment

Adjustment Slider

Figure 12.33
All image adjustments performed in Photoshop.com are undertaken in the Editing mode pictured to the left.

Adjustment entries

Zoom options

Undo, History Thumbnails, Redo

Processing History Thumbnails

Save, Cancel, Reset

Hold down the button to see the before image, let go of the button to return the picture to its current state.

Some enhancement options, such as Red-Eye Removal and Touchup, require the user to interact directly with the image. With these tools you will need to click on or paint over the parts of the photo that you want to change. The touchup tool in particular is very useful as it provides a way to remove small dust marks and spots from your photo. Once selected, you simply click and drag the a circle around the dust mark and then let the mouse button go. Automatically the dust spot is removed. If the result didn't work as you expected, just click the circular orange arrow icon at the top right of the window. This is the Reset button and pressing it will remove all your retouching changes, allowing you to start again.

Once you are satisfied with your changes, you can saved the altered photo by clicking the blue Save button at the bottom of the editing window. This action will update the photo in the Photoshop.com library and will also update the picture in your Photoshop Elements Catalog if the picture belongs to an Album that is set for Backup/Synchronisation. See Figure 12.34.

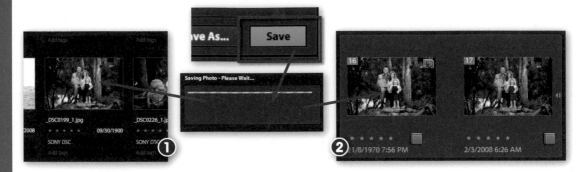

Figure 12.34 For photos that you have edited, and are part of a synchronized album, clicking the Save button updates the image at Photoshop.com (1) and in your Photoshop Elements catalog (2).

One great feature of the way that photos are saved is that it is always possible to return the photo back to its original state, that is, how it looked when you first imported it into Photoshop Elements or uploaded it to Photoshop.com. To do this when working at Photoshop. com, hover the mouse cursor over the thumbnail of the photo and a Photo Options menu heading will appear at the bottom of the thumbnail. Clicking on the downwards facing arrow, beside the heading, displays a pop up menu of choices. To remove the editing changes select the Revert entry. See Figure 12.35.

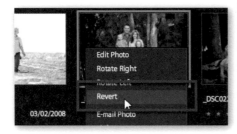

Figure 12.35 To remove the adjustments that you have made to a photo at Photoshop.com choose the Revert option from the Photo Options menu. Display this menu by hovering over the mouse cursor over the thumbnail and then clicking the menu heading when it appears.

The changed versions of the photo are saved in the Photoshop Elements catalog in a version set. The user can choose which version to display as the main thumbnail by using the selections found on the menu that is displayed when right-clicking the thumbnail.

Photoshop.com workspaces

As well as the editing mode we have been looking at here, Photoshop.com has four other key workspaces that can be used to manage and view your photos. To access any of these spaces select one of the options from the website's menu bar. See Figure 12.36.

The Home (house icon), My Photos and My Gallery areas are available only when you are signed in as a registered member of the site. These workspaces are private and viewable only by you. You can decided to invite specific friends and family to view the Online Albums stored here and marked as private, but apart from these selected viewers, no-one else can access the photos stored in this area. Even then, they only have access to the Albums that you choose. A special version of My Gallery complete with your details and any public albums is viewable when the

PHOTOSHOP.COM   ① 🏠   **My Photos**   ② **My Gallery**   ③   **Browse**   ④   New for 7

Figure 12.36 *When signed in as a registered member, Photoshop.com has four main work areas that you can navigate between by clicking the headings at the top left of the window. They are broken into two groups. The first group has three options that can be accessed by the member (1) Home, (2) My Photos and (3) My Gallery and are used to manage, manipulate and control the sharing of your photos. The second group contains (4) Browse plus a special version of My Gallery set up for public viewing. The Browse space is a dedicated public area of the website displaying the images that can be viewed by all.*

public navigates their way to your Photoshop.com webspace. The Browse area is the public part of the Photoshop.com website. Here you can not only view any of your Albums that you have chosen to mark as public, but also the public albums of all other Photoshop.com users. See Figure 12.37.

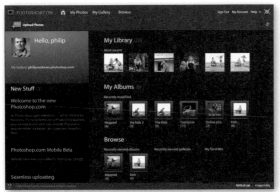

Home – *The Home area is access by clicking the small house icon on the left of the menu bar. It contains messages from Adobe on the left, a greeting to the user at the top left and clickable thumbnail previews of your library, albums and those places you have recently browsed. At the top left is a button for uploading files to Photoshop.com.*

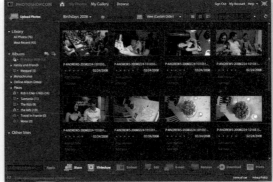

My Photos – *This area also contains an Upload Photos button. Just below this is a file manager view of your library and albums plus links to other photo sharing sites. The main workspace displays image thumbnails and their associated information. This is the starting point for most image actions including rating, editing, printing and emailing.*

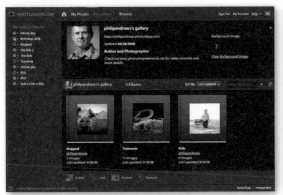

My Gallery – *This workspace displays any online albums that you have created in Photoshop.com or uploaded from Photoshop Elements. There is also space for displaying member details and buttons for linking your albums. Albums marked public can also bee seen here by anyone.*

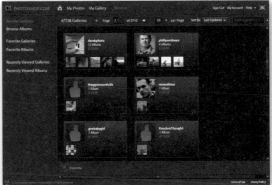

Browse – *Switch to the Browse space for viewing all the online albums created and shared by Elements users worldwide. Only albums that you mark as Available to All will appear here.*

Figure 12.37 Photoshop.com has four key work and viewing spaces. Home, My Photos and My Gallery areas are available to the signed-in user and the Browse area and a cut down version of My Gallery is what the public sees.

Book resources and video tutorials can be found at **www.photoshopelements.net**

My Gallery

The My Gallery area is unique among the workspaces in Photoshop.com as it can be viewed both by the public and also by the user. When signed in, you see a list of Albums, both public and locked, on the left of the screen, some details about the member that can be edited and thumbnails for the public albums in the main display area. Public Albums are marked with a brown album icon and those that are private are indicated with a small lock symbol. The state of any album can be changed by clicking onto the icon (lock or brown album) associated with the Album and selecting a new state from the menu that pops-up.

A different view of this My Gallery is displayed when a user navigates to your Photoshop. com website. The public will see a list of albums that you have marked as being able to viewed by everyone on the left of the screen and thumbnail versions of the same entries in the main workspace. The member details are displayed in the same spot but when viewed by the public this information is not editable. See Figure 12.37.

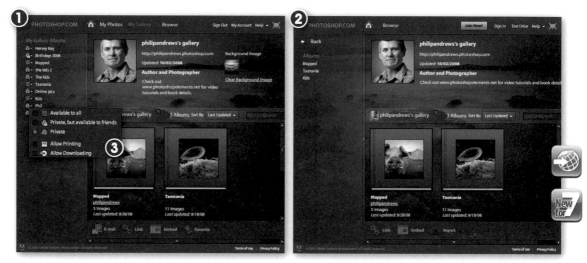

Figure 12.37 *The view of My Gallery that you see when you are signed in (1) and the view the public sees when displaying your Photoshop.com web page (2). Albums can be shared or made private by clicking on their icon in the list and selecting a different option from the list (3).*

Private and Public Albums

Using the idea of private and public albums provides the Elements user with security over the content that they produce, but the choice doesn't have to be one or the other. You also have the option to invite a set of individuals to view your otherwise private album. The invitations are sent out via email and each message contains a special link that the viewer can follow to see your photos.

Setting up and sending the viewing invitations can be be accomplished in several ways. The first is at the time of creating the Online Album in Photoshop Elements. As we saw earlier in this chapter, one of the options available to the user when working their way through the Online

Album wizard is to Email my friends only (don't share publicly). Here you can add a message and select the recipients before hitting the Share button to send out the email invitations.

As an alternative for Online Galleries that have already been published, you can select the Private, but available to friends, option from the Pop-up menu that is displayed when clicking the lock icon of an album entry. Albums that are marked private or public can be made semi-private, or is that semi-public, in this way. See Figure 12.38.

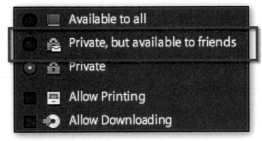

Figure 12.38 You can change the state of a published online album to Private, but available to friends by selection the option from the pop-up menu.

Order Prints

As you will see in the next chapter, Photoshop Elements has a very powerful print engine built into the program. It is just as easy to print individual photos, groups of images and order photos to be printed by a third-part printing laboratory, from the Organizer as it is the Editor workspaces. With the linking of Elements to Photoshop.com we now have a couple of extra printing options.

The same Order Print option found in Photoshop Elements is also available to use with images that are stored online. To use the feature, select one (or a few) of the images in the My Photos workspace and click the Prints button at the bottom of the window. This will transfer the file to Adobe's printing partner Shutterfly.com. By following the steps in the Shutterfly.com wizard you will then be able to choose the size and quantity of photos, pay for the order and have them printed and delivered.

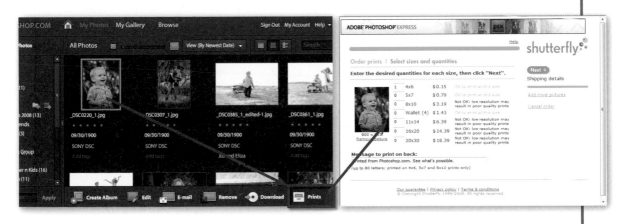

Figure 12.39 When clicking the Prints button in Photoshop.com, the selected images from the My Photo workspace are transferred to Shutterfly.com for printing.

If you prefer to print your own then is is also possible to right-click a photo and choose the Print option from the pop-up menu.

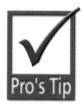

Pro's Tip: The right-click > Print approach certainly provides a quick and easy way to output your online photos but given the higher level of control that is possible with the Photoshop Elements print engine, it worth the extra to print the image from there. This may mean having to locate the photo in your Element's catalog, or if it is an online-only picture, downloading it first before printing.

Extra Photoshop.com features

If you look to the bottom of the My Photos window you will see a range of other Photoshop.com features that we have yet to cover. See Figure 12.40. These include an Edit Photo button that can be used instead of double-clicking the thumbnail to open the picture in the editing workspace and a Remove Photo option for clearing the images from the Photoshop.com image collection.

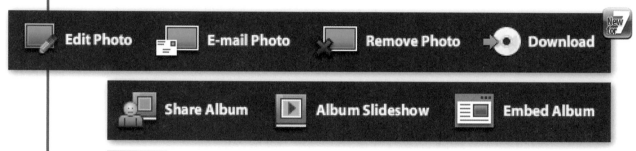

Figure 12.40 There are several different buttons for extra features at the bottom of the My Photos screen.

Download to desktop

Pressing the Download button will display the Download Photo dialog. See Figure 12.41. Here you can select the size of the file (the image dimensions) that you want to transfer, before pressing the Download to complete the process. This sizing option is very handy if you are wanting to add the photo to a website as the dialog presents you with options for downloading a thumbnail size as well as an image that is suitable for full screen viewing.

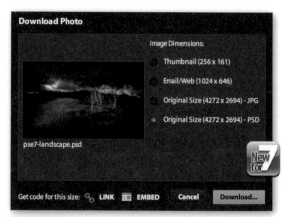

Figure 12.41 The Download Photo dialog is used to size the photo before downloading the image.

Link or Embed

Two extra buttons are also included at the bottom of the dialog – Link and Embed. Both features copy a piece of html code that describes the image, its size and where it is stored on the internet, to the clipboard. HTML or Hyper Text Markup Language is the coding used to build web pages. This piece of code can then be pasted (Ctrl V) into a webpage to either provide a link to the photo, or as a means of embedding the picture in the webpage.

A similar option, Embed Album, exists as an individual button in the bottom bar. Rather than embedding an individual image, this version of the feature embeds the whole album. Providing you with the ability to place Photoshop Elements Online Albums in websites other than Photoshop.com. Cool! See Figure 12.42.

These features may seem a little obscure to many of you, but they do provide a way of featuring your photos on other websites around the world quickly and easily. In the example above, the copied text was pasted into a new text document that was saved as the 'test-embed-album.html' file. The file was then opened into a web browser and the animated album appeared.

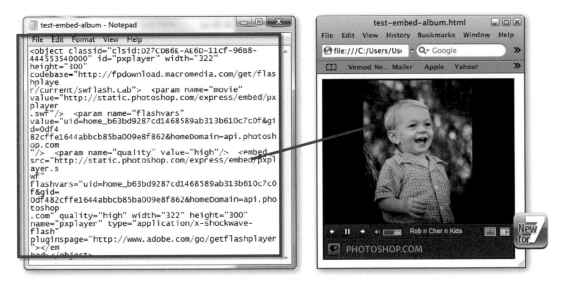

Figure 12.42 *By copying and pasting the code needed to display your album into new or existing web page, you can successfully display your photos in a range of websites other than Photoshop.com. .*

Slideshows at Photoshop.com

Alongside managing and editing your pictures Photoshop.com is also great at displaying images. As we saw earlier in the chapter, the Themed Online Albums, or slideshows as they are called in Photoshop.com, that you create in Elements can be uploaded to the website and viewed either by the general public or by a select group of fiends or family members. Using the Online Album feature in Elements to create these slideshows provides the user with the most control

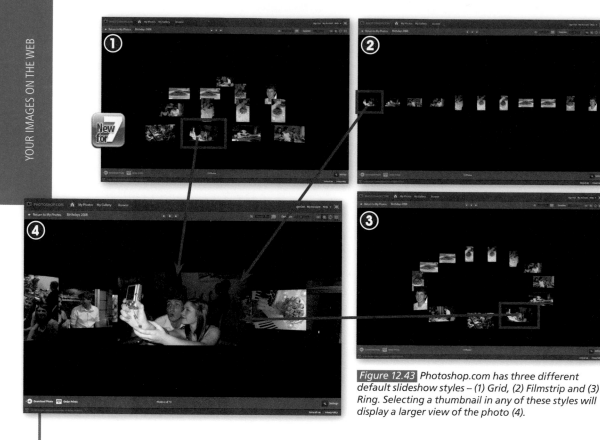

Figure 12.43 *Photoshop.com has three different default slideshow styles – (1) Grid, (2) Filmstrip and (3) Ring. Selecting a thumbnail in any of these styles will display a larger view of the photo (4).*

over the look of the final web gallery. Apart from being able to select from a range of designs or templates for the website, you also have the chance to adjust colors and titles for most designs.

However, this is not the only way to view your images on Photoshop.com. The website has several built-in slideshow styles that can be automatically applied to albums that are stored on the site. There are three main styles to choose from: Filmstrip, Grid and Ring. Each presents the Album's photos in a different animated style, allowing the user to select specific images which then snap into enlarged view. See Figure 12.43.

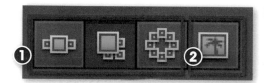

Figure 12.44 *Users can switch between slideshow styles by pressing the display buttons located in the top right of the slideshow screen. Buttons for the three default styles are always available (1) but the themed button (2) is only present for albums which have been created with the Elements' Online Album wizard.*

To view an Album as a slideshow, select its entry in the My Photos workspace and then click onto the Album Slideshow option at the bottom of the screen. To switch between slideshow styles click on one of the Display buttons at the top right of the slideshow window. If a Themed slideshow has been created for the Album then this will be the default slideshow view for the Album. You can still switch to the other styles using the display buttons, returning to the themed presentation if you wish, by clicking on the fourth, themed button. This extra display button is only available when a themed slideshow has been created for an online album. See Figure 12.44.

Photoshop.com has a variety of controls that can be used to adjust how your slideshows look and work. You can alter both the length of time that each slide is displayed, and the size of thumbnails and featured images using the Duration and Zoom In/Out sliders at the top of the slideshow screen. More specific controls for each slideshow style can be displayed by clicking the Settings button (wrench or spanner icon) at the bottom of the screen. See Figure 12.45. In the Settings panel you will find controls for Layout, Viewing Settings and Audio (Photoshop.com provides several different tracks that can accompany your presentation).

Emailing from Photoshop.com

In the next section of this chapter we'll look at different ways to email your photos to your friends and relatives from Photoshop Elements, but while we are discussing features found at Photoshop.com, we should examine the site's email potential as well.

Let's start with the simple task of how to email individual photos. After selecting the photo that you want to send from the My Photos workspace, click onto the E-mail Photo button at the bottom of the screen. This will display a small E-mail Photo window where you can add an address and a short message before clicking the Send button.

If you want to send the same image to multiple recipients then you can add several addresses as long as they are separated by a comma. See Figure 12.46.

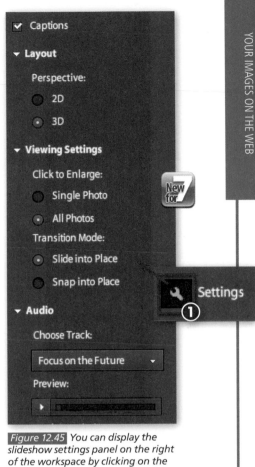

Figure 12.45 You can display the slideshow settings panel on the right of the workspace by clicking on the Wrench icon ('1') at the bottom of the screen.

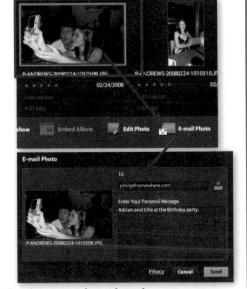

Figure 12.46 To send a photo via email just select the image in the My Photos area of Photoshop.com and then click onto the E-mail Photo button. Add an email address and a message in the window that is displayed and then hit the Send button.

Photoshop.com also lets you make use of the email contacts that you already have stored on your computer. Most users will already have a collection of addresses stored in their email program. Photoshop.com can import and use these contacts with its email features. To use existing contacts you first need to add them to your Photoshop Elements' Contact Book. Do this by displaying the book (Organizer: Edit > Contact Book) and then using the Import feature to add email addresses that you have stored in another program. Once this is completed, Elements will synchronize these new contacts with those used online at Photoshop.com as long as the Backup/Synchronization settings are active.

Now when emailing a photo from Photoshop.com you have the option of clicking onto the person icon in the top right of the E-mail Photo window and selecting the recipients for the message from the contacts listed. See Figure 12.47.

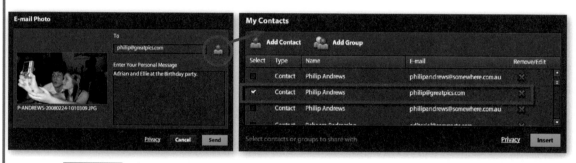

Figure 12.47 *After importing the addresses saved with your email program to Photoshop Elements you can use the entries with the mailing options at Photoshop.com.*

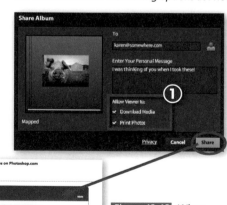

Figure 12.48 *When Sharing an Album from Photoshop.com you have the option to allow the viewer to download and/or print the photos (1). The feature sends an email message containing a link to the Online Album stored at your Photoshop.com website.*

Emailing an Album

Photoshop.com also has the ability to email an album of photos. At the moment this is the only way to email a group of images. So if you are wanting to send several pictures to your friends add them to an album first and then select the album entry from those listed on the left of the My Photos workspace. Next, select the Share Album button at the bottom of the screen. Insert the email addresses of the recipients and add a short message. Using the settings at the bottom of the Share Album window you can also decide if you want to let those you are sharing with to be able to download and/or print the Album photos. This option doesn't actually email all the photos in a message to your recipients. Instead, the feature sends a message containing a link that recipients can use to view the photos at your Photoshop.com webspace. See Figure 12.48.

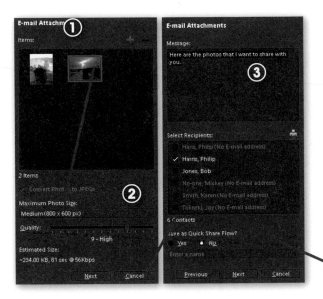

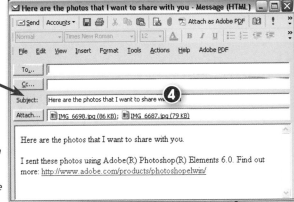

Figure 12.49 The E-mail Attachments wizard (1) provides the ability to adjust the size and compression (2) used with the photos you attach to your emails. Using the feature you can also add and remove contacts, via the Contacts Book, and type your message directly into the window (3). Pressing Next opens your email program (4), adds in your message and recipient details and attaches an optimized version of your picture to the new email document.

Sending images as email attachments

Organizer: Share task pane > Photo Mail or Editor: Share task pane > Photo Mail or E-mail Attachments

For many people, sharing images by sending them as email attachments has become a commonplace activity. Whether you are showing grandparents in another country just how cute their new granddaughter is, or providing a preview look at some holiday property, using email technology to send pictures is both fast and convenient.

Starting with Elements version 2.0 Adobe included a special Attach to E-mail function designed just for this purpose. Things have progressed with the new releases and now Elements users can email their images in two different ways – as Photo Mail or as E-mail Attachments. There is also a Contacts Book dialog in place of the old Add a Recipient option found in previous releases. Here you can add individual contacts, make groups from several e-mail addresses, and import and export to and from common e-mail contact formats such as vCards or Microsoft Outlook.

E-mail Attachments

The E-mail Attachment button starts the emailing process. Images are dragged from the content area in the Organizer workspace onto the Items section of the panel. The size and compression settings for the images are selected with the controls directly under the Items area. After clicking the Next button you can add a message and choose who to send the email to from the listed recipients. New recipients can be added with the Edit Contacts button (small person icon) in the top right of the panel. After all the participants have been selected, clicking the Next button will open your email program, create a new message and add in your pictures and recipients. See Figure 12.49 on the previous page.

FEATURE SUMMARY

1 You can select to use a photo that is currently open in the Editor workspace or multi-select images from inside the Organizer workspace.

2 Select the E-mail Attachments option in the Share task pane to start the feature.

3 Add or delete photos from the thumbnail list of those to include with the buttons at the top right of the dialog. Adjust size and compression of the photos and click Next.

4 Choose an existing recipient from the contacts list or add a new contact; add in a message and click Next to open your email program and create the new message.

Photo Mail

The second way to send your image by email is to use the Photo Mail option located in both the Share task pane of both the Organizer and Editor spaces. The first couple of screens are the same as the E-mail Attachment feature but, once you have selected the images and recipients to include in the message, clicking the Next button opens a new window where you can adjust the stationery, framing and layout of the images. See Figure 12.50.

FEATURE SUMMARY

1 After selecting the Photo Mail option from the Share task pane use the same steps as above (steps 1–3) to add images, choose recipients and include a message. Click Next.

2 In the new dialog that is displayed select the stationery (frames and background) style for the Photo Mail. Click the Next Step button.

3 Customize the look of the stationery by adjusting the background color, layout, photo size, font, borders and the inclusion of drop shadows.

4 Click Next to open your email program and create the new Photo Mail message.

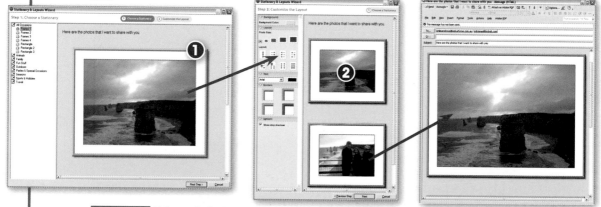

Figure 12.50 If, instead of using the E-mail Attachments option, you choose the Photo Mail format button then you will be prompted to choose the stationery (1) and decide on the layout (2) of the message in addition to the first couple of steps. The compression and size settings for this option are adjusted automatically.

Making simple web animations with Elements

In Chapter 7, we looked at how layers can be used to separate different image parts so that they are easier to enhance and manipulate. Here we will use layers to create simple animations for your website.

Traditional animation

Whether it is the production of a Disney classic or the construction of a small moving cursor for your web page, the basics of making animations remain the same. A series of images, or frames, is created with slight changes recorded from one picture to the next. The sequence is then compiled and each frame is shown in quick succession. As your eye sees a new image, your brain remembers the last, with the result that the still images appear to move.

Historically, the frame images were drawn and painted on a series of acetate cells. Large productions could use thousands of cells, each representing a small slice of movement, to produce just a few seconds of animation on screen. These days, many animation companies use digital versions of this old way of working but, despite all the technological changes, all animation is based on a sequence of still images.

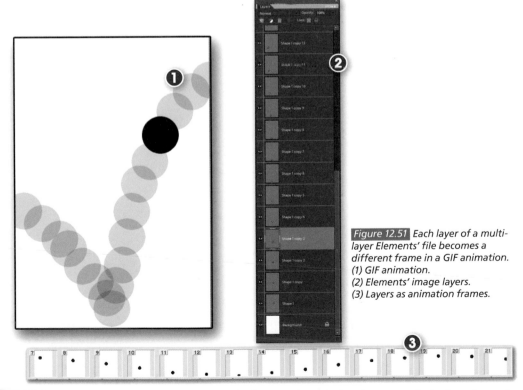

Figure 12.51 Each layer of a multi-layer Elements' file becomes a different frame in a GIF animation.
(1) GIF animation.
(2) Elements' image layers.
(3) Layers as animation frames.

Animation – the Elements' method

Adobe has merged traditional techniques with the multi-layer abilities of its PSD file structure to give Elements users the chance to produce their own animations. Essentially, the idea is to make an image file with several layers, the content of each being a little different from the one before. See Figure 12.51 on the previous page. The file is then saved in the GIF format. In the process, each layer is made into a separate frame in an animated sequence. As GIF is a format that is used for small animations on the Net, the moving masterpiece can be viewed with any web browser, or placed on the website to add some action to otherwise static pages.

The easiest way to save the GIF file is via the Save for Web feature. See Figure 12.52. The Save for Web dialog contains the original image and a GIF compressed version of the picture. By ticking the Animate check box you will be able to change the Frame Delay setting and indicate whether you want the animation to repeat (loop) or play a single time only. This dialog also provides you with the opportunity to preview your file in your default browser. The final step in the process is to click OK to save the file. See Figure 12.53.

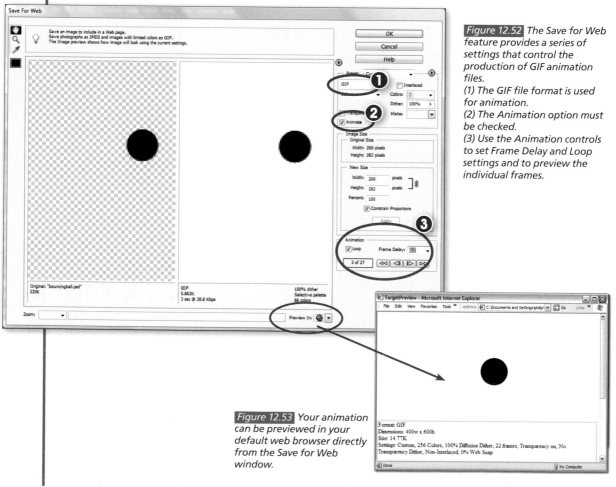

Figure 12.52 *The Save for Web feature provides a series of settings that control the production of GIF animation files.*
(1) The GIF file format is used for animation.
(2) The Animation option must be checked.
(3) Use the Animation controls to set Frame Delay and Loop settings and to preview the individual frames.

Figure 12.53 *Your animation can be previewed in your default web browser directly from the Save for Web window.*

Animation advice

Keep in mind when you are making your own animation files that GIF formatted images can only contain a maximum of 256 colors. This situation tends to suit graphic, bold and flat areas of color rather than the gradual changes of tone that are usually found in photographic images. So, rather than being disappointed with your results, start the creation process with a limited palette; this way you can be sure that the hues you choose will remain true in the final animation. It is also worth remembering that the Elements Animation feature is designed for short, non-complex compositions. If you are planning a major epic made up of large, high-resolution files that when compiled will play for an extended period of time, or even if you just want to add sound to your moving images, it would be best for you to use a dedicated animation package.

1 Create an Elements file with several layers of differing content.

2 Select File > Save for Web.

3 Ensure that the GIF setting is selected in the Settings section of the dialog.

4 Tick the Animate check box.

5 Adjust the Frame Delay option to control the length of time each individual image is displayed.

6 Tick the Loop check box if you want the animation to repeat.

7 Preview the animation by clicking the browser preview button. Close the browser to return to the Save for Web dialog.

8 Select OK to save the file.

Flipbooks – a new way to animate

Organizer: Share task pane > More Options > Flipbook

Flipbooks are a new way of creating small animations from a series of individual photographs. The results simulate the 'old school' animation technique where slightly different drawings were created on corners of successive pages of a small notebook. Flipping the pages between thumb and forefinger created a sense of motion.

The process for creating an Elements Flipbook is simple. Select the pictures to include from those displayed in the Organizer workspace and then choose the Flipbook entry in the More Options section of the Create task pane. See Figure 12.54. Set the Speed in frames per second, Order and Output options in the Flipbook dialog and then click Output to create. The resultant WMV (Windows Media Video) file can be played with any Windows machine with the latest version of Windows Media Player installed. See Figure 12.55.

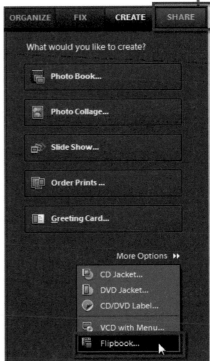

Figure 12.54 *After selecting the images to be included in the Flipbook choose the option from the More Options section of the Create task pane.*

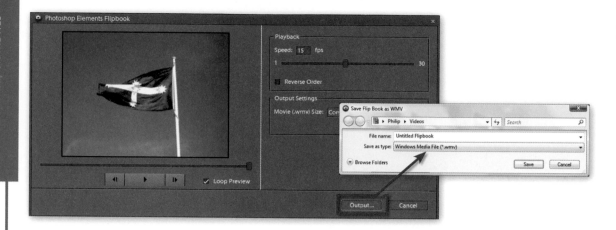

Figure 12.55 *Use the settings in the Flipbook dialog to adjust the frames per second that the photos are flipped, along with the size of the final video. Flipbooks are output in WMV format, which is compatible with most Windows machines.*

Creating your own slide shows

Organizer: Share task pane > Slideshow

Elements contains a Slide Show editor which can produce a variety of different types of presentations. The feature contains an easy-to-use interface and options that allow users to create true multimedia slide shows complete with music, narration, pan and zoom effects, transitions, extra graphics, and backgrounds and titles. The finished presentations can be output as a file, burnt to CD or DVD, e-mailed as a slide show, sent directly to your television (Windows XP Media Center Edition users only) or sent to Premiere Elements for further editing (for users who have this program installed). See Figure 12.56.

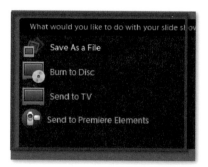

Figure 12.56 *The fully featured Slide Show editor in Elements provides more output options than ever before.*

Creating slide shows

Creating presentations in version 6 uses an approach that centers all production activities around a single editor interface and it is only at the time of outputting that you choose the type of slide show that you want to create. In this way you can create (and save) a single slide show project and then repurpose the presentation in many different forms (online, DVD, PDF slide show or direct to TV) by simply selecting different output options. See Figure 12.57.

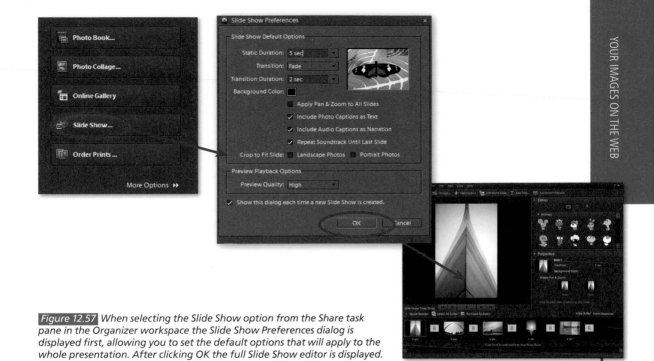

Slide shows in action

Though the Slide Show editor may at first seem a little complex, having all the controls in one place certainly means that you can create great multimedia presentations easily and efficiently. See Figure 12.58.

The following key features are included in the Editor:

- **Automatic editing:** Rotate, size, change to sepia, black and white or back to color and apply Smart Fix and Red Eye Fix to your photos without leaving the Slide Show editor. Click the Preview image to display the edit options in the Properties palette. See Figure 12.59.
- **Styled text:** Select from a range of text styles with click, drag and drop convenience ('1' in Figure 12.58).
- **Add graphics:** The Slide Show editor now includes a variety of clip art that can be added to your presentations. Double-click or click-drag to place a selected graphic onto the current slide ('2' in Figure 12.58).
- **Transitions:** Add individual transitions between slides by clicking the area in the middle of the slides in the storyboard and then selecting the transition type from those listed in the Properties pane ('3' in Figure 12.58).
- **Pan and Zoom:** Add movement to your still pictures by panning across or zooming into your photos. Simply select the slide in the storyboard and then check the Enable Pan & Zoom option in the Properties pane. Click on the left thumbnail (Start) and set the starting marquee's (green) size and position, then switch to the right thumbnail and adjust the ending marquee's (red) size and position ('4' in Figure 12.58).

Figure 12.58 *The Slide Show editor provides a single workspace for the creation and editing of your presentation creations.*

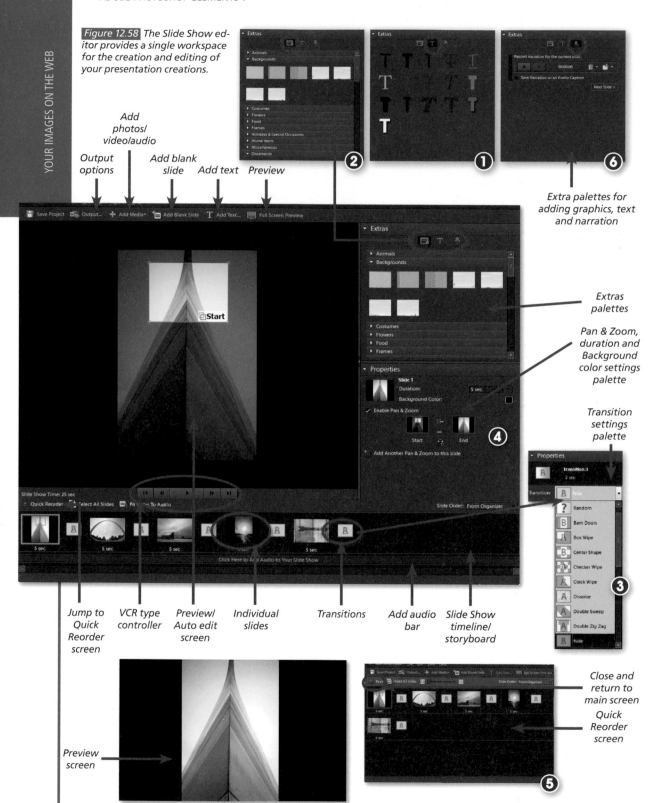

Add photos/video/audio

Output options

Add blank slide

Add text

Preview

②

①

⑥

Extra palettes for adding graphics, text and narration

Extras palettes

Pan & Zoom, duration and Background color settings palette

Transition settings palette

Jump to Quick Reorder screen

VCR type controller

Preview/Auto edit screen

Individual slides

Transitions

Add audio bar

Slide Show timeline/storyboard

③

Close and return to main screen

Quick Reorder screen

Preview screen

⑤

- **Quick Reorder:** This new sequencing screen enables you to quickly and easily adjust the position of any one photo in the presentation sequence using click and drag ('5' in Figure 12.58).
- **Music and narration:** Add music and extra audio to the show using the Add Media button and incorporate narration using the built-in slide show recorder ('6' in Figure 12.58).

Step-by-step Slideshow creation

1 Preselect the photos to include in the show from within the Photo Browser and then select Organizer: Create task pane > Slide Show.

2 Set the defaults for the presentation in the Slide Show Preferences dialog.

3 Adjust the slide sequence by click-dragging thumbnails within the storyboard or Quick Recorder workspaces.

4 Insert transitions by clicking the space in between slides and selecting a type from the menu in the Properties pane.

5 Add graphics and text by click-dragging from the Extras pane.

6 Record voice-over by selecting a slide and then using the Narration option in the Extras pane.

7 Add existing audio by clicking the soundtrack bar at the bottom of the storyboard.

8 Produce the slide show by selecting File > Output Slide Show and picking the type of presentation to produce from the Slide Show output dialog.

FEATURE SUMMARY

Editing the slide photos

The Properties palette displays several simple editing controls when you click a photo in the preview area of the Slide Show editor. Although the best approach is to ensure that all editing and enhancement changes are applied to the photos before their inclusion in a presentation project, these controls can be used for making quick simple changes to the images used in individual slides. The options include:

Rotate – Pivots the photo 90° left or right.

Scale – Makes the photo bigger or smaller.

Crop to Fit – Enlarges the photo to fill the whole slide frame even if this action crops the edges of the picture.

Crop to Slide –Fits the photo within the boundaries of the slide without cropping any image details.

Auto Smart Fix – Applies automatic adjustment of colour, contrast, brightness and sharpness to the picture.

Convert to Black and White – One-click conversion to black and white.

Convert to Sepia – One-click conversion to sepia toned monochrome.

Auto Red Eye Fix – Removes red eye from portraits taken with a flash.

More Editing – Opens the slide in Elements' Editor workspace where the edited file is saved as a Version Set and added to a catalog once complete. See Figure 12.59.

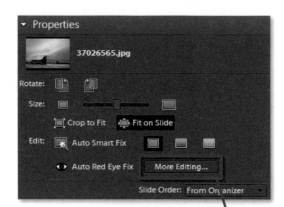

Figure 12.59 Clicking the photo in the preview area of the Editor switches the contents of the Properties palette to contain simple editing tools. These include Rotate left and right, Scale and Crop options, Auto Smart Fix, Convert to black and white or sepia buttons and Auto Red Eye Fix. For more advanced editing tasks click the More Editing button to transfer the photo to the Full Edit workspace.

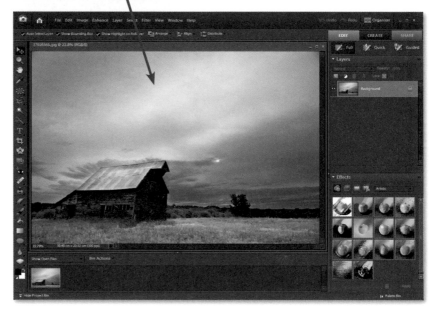

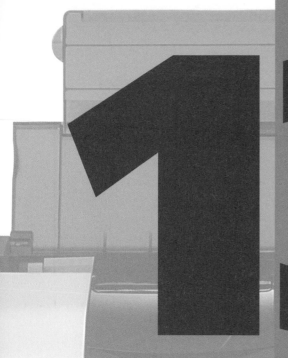

13

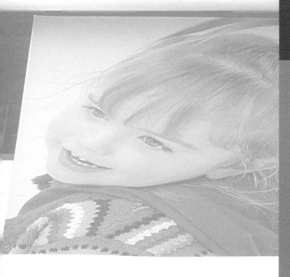

Preparing Images for Printing

Printing the Elements way

The link between paper type and quality prints

Making your first print

Making multiple prints

Web-based printing

Despite the great rush of picture makers to 'all things web', most treasured digital images still end up being printed at some stage during their existence. Contributing to this scenario is the current crop of affordable high quality inkjet printers whose output quality is nothing short of amazing. As little as 11 years ago it was almost impossible to get photographic quality output from a desktop machine for under £5000, now the weekend papers are full of enticing specials providing stunning pictures for as little as £100. See Figure 13.1.

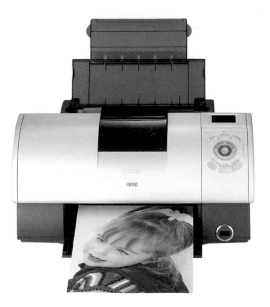

Printer manufacturers have simplified the procedure of connecting and setting up their machines so much that most users will have their printer purring away satisfactorily within the first minutes

Figure 13.1 *Current inkjet printers are capable of providing photographic quality images at a fraction of the cost of comparative technology just a few years ago.*

of unpacking the box. Software producers too have been working hard to simplify the printing process so that now it is generally possible to obtain good output from your very first page.

Elements is a good example of these developments, providing an interactive printing system that previews the image on the paper background 'virtually' before using any ink or paper to output a print. As we have already seen in Chapter 3, the package also includes the ability to print a section of an open image, make a contact sheet of images contained within a folder and produce a print package of different sized pictures optimized to fit on a specific paper stock. See Figure 13.2.

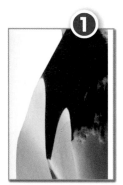 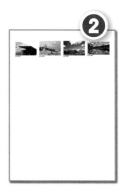 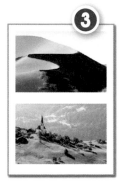 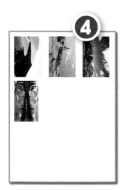

Figure 13.2 *Elements contains an interactive print system that can not only produce single image prints, but also contact sheets, picture labels and multi-print packages. (1) Individual print. (2) Contact print. (3) Picture package. (4) Picture labels.*

Book resources and video tutorials can be found at **www.photoshopelements.net**

Printing the Elements way

Editor: File > Print, Editor: File > Page Setup, Editor: File > Print Multiple Photos

All of the print settings in Elements are contained in four separate but related dialog boxes (see Figure 13.3): Print – Editor: File > Print (1); Page Setup – Editor: File > Page Setup (2); Print Photos – Editor: File > Print Multiple Photos (3); and Order Prints Online – Editor: File > Order Prints (4). Similar output dialogs were included in previous versions of Elements but the upgraded features in the new release of the program have made the printing process much easier and more flexible. The Print, Order Photos and Print Multiple Prints options are also available in the Organizer workspace.

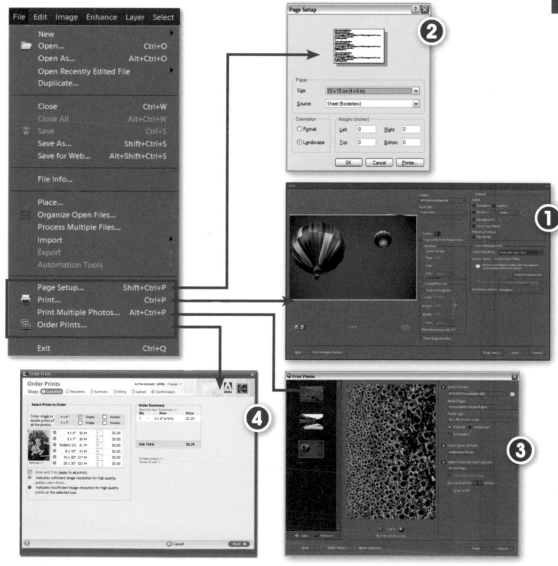

Figure 13.3 *Four separate dialogs control the majority of settings and options in the in Elements' printing system. (1) Print dialog. (2) Page Setup dialog. (3) Print Photos dialog. (4) Order Prints dialog.*

The **Print** dialog (previously called Print Preview) is the first stop for most users wanting to make a hard copy of their digital pictures. Here you can interactively scale your image to fit the page size currently selected for your printer. By deselecting the Center Image option and ticking the Show Bounding Box feature, it is possible to click and drag the image to a new position on the page surface. These advanced preview features alone will make a lot of digital photographers very happy. See Figure 13.4.

In Photoshop Elements 6 the dialog was revamped and now displays extra settings previously accessed by clicking the Show More Options button at the bottom of the window on the right side of the dialog. Here you find Output option settings such as printing the file name or caption alongside the photo, or adding a colored border, crop marks or even a background color. Just underneath the output options is the Color Management settings where you can choose to let Elements, or the printer, manage the transition of colors from your photo to print.

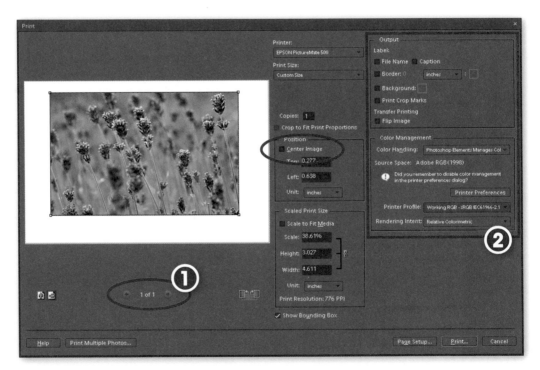

Figure 13.4 *You can change the size and position of your image on its paper background via the Print (Editor: File > Print) dialog. (1) When printing a multi-page Photo Creations document or multiple pictures the next/ previous page Navigation buttons appear at the base of the preview area. New for version 6 was the inclusion of Output and Color Management settings in the main dialog (2). Previously these controls have been accessed via a Show More Options button at the bottom of the window.*

Once you are satisfied with the picture size and position, you can proceed to the **Page Setup** dialog using the button provided. It is here that you are able to change the settings for the printer, such as media type, size and orientation, printing resolution and color control, or enhancement. The extent to which you will be able to manually adjust these features will depend on the type of printer driver supplied by the manufacturer of your machine. When complete, click OK to return to the Print dialog. To complete the output process, click the Print button. This step produces a general Print dialog where the user has another opportunity to check the printer settings via the Properties button, before sending the image on its way with a click of the OK button. See Figure 13.5.

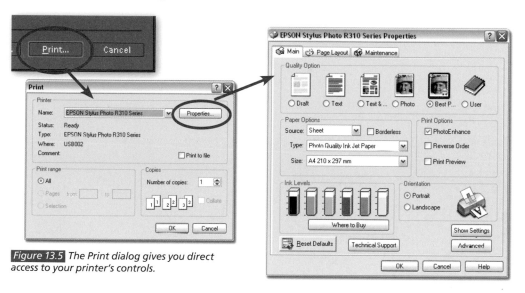

Figure 13.5 *The Print dialog gives you direct access to your printer's controls.*

Printing from the Organizer workspace

Photo Browser: File > Print, File > Page Setup

As we have already seen in our brief introduction to printing in Chapter 3, you can output your pictures directly from the Photo Browser. In fact, the Print options available from the Organizer workspace are very similar to those available via the Editor. For quick printing tasks the Photo Browser: File > Print option takes you directly to the same multi-print dialog that is available in the Editor (File > Print Multiple Photos) and there is no practical difference between outputting your files from either space. See Figure 13.6.

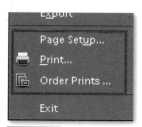

Figure 13.6 *The Organizer offers similar printing options to those found in the Editor workspaces.*

The link between paper type and quality prints

When you first start to output your own images, the wide range of printer settings and controls can be confusing. To start with it is best to stick to a standard setup and allow the built-in features of the driver to adjust the printer for you. For most printing tasks, selecting the media type in the Print Properties dialog will be sufficient to ensure good results. The manufacturers have determined the optimum ink and resolution settings for each paper type and, for 90% of all printing tasks, using the default settings is a good way to ensure consistently high quality results. So if you are using gloss photographic paper, for example, make sure that you select this as your paper type in the Printer Settings dialog. See Figure 13.7.

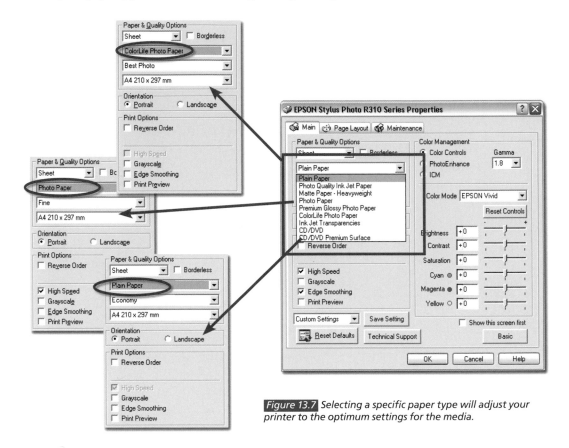

Figure 13.7 *Selecting a specific paper type will adjust your printer to the optimum settings for the media.*

Making your first print

Editor: File > Print

With an image open in the Editor workspace, display the Print dialog (File > Print). Check the thumbnail to ensure that the whole of the picture is located within the paper boundaries. To change the paper's size or orientation, select the Page Setup and Printer Properties options. Whilst here, adjust the printer output settings to suit the type of paper being used. Work your way back to the Print dialog by clicking the OK buttons. See Figure 13.8.

To alter the position or size of the picture on the page, deselect the Center Image option and then select the Show Bounding Box feature. Change the image size by clicking and dragging the handles at the edge and corners of the image. If you can't see the handles try inputting a number smaller than 100% in the Scale box until the edge of the picture is visible. Move the picture to a different position on the page by clicking on the picture surface and dragging the whole image to a different area. See Figure 13.9. To print, select the Print button and then the OK button.

PREPARING IMAGES FOR PRINTING

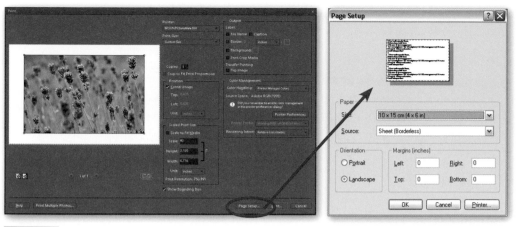

Figure 13.8 Change paper size, orientation and type via the Page Setup and Printer Properties dialogs.

1 Select Print (File > Print) after ensuring that the file has sufficient resolution for printing. Use a minimum of 220 dpi for photo-quality printing.

2 Click the Page Setup button.

3 Pick the Printer option to set the paper type, page size and orientation, and print quality options.

4 Click OK to exit these dialogs and return to the Print dialog.

5 At this stage you can choose to allow Elements to center the image automatically on the page (tick the Center Image box) and enlarge, or reduce, the picture so that it fits the page size selected (choose the Fit on Page option from the Print Size menu).

6 Alternatively, you can adjust the position of the picture and its size manually by deselecting these options and ticking the Show Bounding Box feature. To move the image, click inside the picture and drag to a new position. To change its size, click and drag one of the handles located at the corners of the bounding box.

7 With all the settings complete, click Print to output your image.

FEATURE SUMMARY

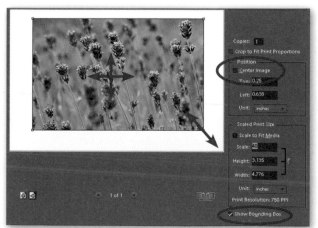

Figure 13.9 Change the size and position of the image on the page with the controls in the Print dialog.

Color Management in the Print Dialog

There are several settings in the Color Management Section of the Print dialog that are useful for ensuring that you get the best color match between screen and print. These settings are also the ones that many users have difficulties in understanding how and when to use them. See Figure 13.10. Let's look at each in turn

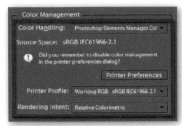

Figure 13.10 The settings in the Color Management area control the way that photo colours are match with printer capabilities.

Color Handling

One of the key tasks that needs to be handled when printing is the massaging of the colors in the photo so that they fit the range of colors that can be output by the printer. The choices in the Color Handling menu of the Print dialog determine how this massaging will be handled. See Figure 13.11. There are three options:

Printer Manages Color – The picture is sent to the printer and the printer massages the colors to fit. This option provides good results and is simplest to use.

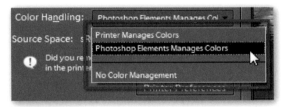

Figure 13.11 Three Color Handling options are available to Elements users.

Photoshop Elements Manages Color – Photoshop Elements controls the adjustment of the images tones to suit the printer's capabilities. This provides the best results but does require the user to set both the Printer Profile and Rendering intent carefully as well as making sure that the printer is not using its own color management system. This needs to be switched off.

No Color Management – This option is not recommended as using it will mean that the photo, printer and Photoshop Elements will not share a common understanding about the colors in the photo.

Printer Profile

The Printer Profile is a small settings file that describes to Photoshop Elements the range of colors that are capable of being printed by the device. Most often these files are downloaded to your computer when you install the drivers for a new printer. Some printers have a single printer profile, others have several different versions depending on the paper surface that you are printing on. If you have selected the Photoshop Elements Manages Colors option then you need to also correctly choose the printer profile from the drop down list in the Color Management section of the Print Dialog.

Rendering Intent

At various points in the digital photography process it is necessary to change or alter the spread of colors in a picture so that they fit the characteristics of an output device, such as a screen or printer, more fully. The Photoshop Elements user has four choices of approach that the program can use in this conversion process. Each approach produces different results and is based on a specific conversion or 'rendering intent'. Specific conversion approaches can be selected from the Rendering Intent drop-down menu in the Color Management section of the print dialog. The options are:

The **Relative Colorimetric** setting squashes or stretches the range of colors in the original photo so that they fit the range of possible colors that the new device can display or print.

The **Saturation** option tries to maintain the strength of colors during the conversion process (even if color accuracy is the cost).

The **Perceptual** setting puts conversion emphasis on ensuring that the adjusted picture, when viewed on the new output device, appears to the human eye to be very similar to the original photo.

The **Absolute Colorimetric** option translates colors exactly from the original photo to the range of colors for the new device. Those colors that can't be displayed are clipped.

Sound a little confusing? Well don't worry. The default setting, Relatvie Colormetric, is usually a fine choice for most subjects.

Printing directly from Photoshop.com

Once your photos have been uploaded to Photoshop.com it is possible to print directly from the site to your desktop printer. Just choose the Print option from the menu that appears when you right-click a thumbnail. The is also an Order Prints button at the bottom of the window. Use this feature to place an order for prints to be made by Shutterfly.com. These options are great for the Photoshop Elements users, but even better news for their friends and relatives as they too can print to a desktop machine or Order Prints that you have shared with them online. It is even possible to allow the general public to print any photos displayed in the Browse workspace of Photoshop.com.

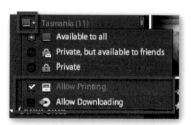

Figure 13.12 Control whether your images can be printed, or downloaded, from your online albums via the settings in the Album pop-up menu. Click onto the Album icon (on the left) to display it.

Of course being so generous as to allow every Tom, Dick and Harry, the ability to print your pictures might not be something that you want to do, so Photoshop.com provides a setting to control the printability of the photos you place on line. To allow users to print photos locate the Online Album in the My Photos workspace. Click onto the Album icon (on the left of the entry) and select the Allow Printing option. To restrict access to just viewing, that is, no printing (or downloading) allowed, make sure that the setting is not selected in this menu. See Figure 13.12.

Making multiple prints

In the last few years the digital camera market has exploded. Now digital camera sales easily outstrip their film-based counterparts over the same selling period. And with the onslaught of these new silicon shooters has come a change in the way that people take pictures.

Users are starting to alter the way they shoot to accommodate the strengths of the new technology. One of these strengths is the fact that the act of taking a picture has no inherent cost. In comparison, film-based shooting always involves a development cost associated with the production of negatives and prints, as well as the initial purchase of the film, whereas digital picture taking is essentially costless. Yes, there is the outlay for the camera and the expense associated with the storage, manipulation and output of these images, but the cost of shooting is zero. Hence, it seems that the typical digital camera user is shooting more pictures, more often, than they were when capturing to film. See Figure 13.13.

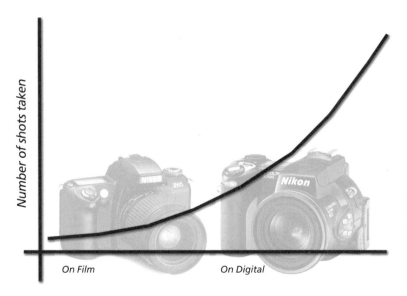

Number of shots taken

On Film   *On Digital*

Figure 12.13 *As there is no cost associated with shooting, digital camera users now take more pictures than when they were using film-based cameras.*

Contact sheets

Editor: File > Print Multiple Photos > Contact Sheet

Digital photographers are not afraid to shoot as much as they like because they know that they will only have to pay for the production of the very best of the images they take. Consequently, hard drives all over the country are filling up with thousands of pictures. Navigating this array of images can be quite difficult and many shooters still prefer to edit their photographs as prints rather than on screen. The people at Adobe must have understood this situation when they developed the Contact Print feature for Photoshop and Elements. Elements 6 and 7 contains a version of the feature that is part of the Print Multiple Photos dialog.

From within one feature, the imaging program creates a series of small thumbnail versions of all the images in a catalog or those that were multi-selected before opening the tool. These small pictures are arranged on pages and can be labeled with file name, captions and dates. From there it is an easy task to print a series of these contact sheets that can be kept as a permanent record of a folder's images. The job of selecting the best pictures to manipulate and print can then be made with hard copies of your images without having to spend the time and money to output every image to be considered. See Figure 13.14.

The options contained within the Contact Sheet dialog allow the user to select the number of columns of image thumbnails and the content of the text labels that are added. The page size and orientation can be chosen via the Page Setup button.

1 If working in the Editor workspace, open the images to be printed; otherwise multi-select the pictures from inside the Photo Browser.

2 Select File > Print Multiple Photos and choose Contact Sheet from the Select Type of Print menu. From the Photo Browser select File > Print and then choose Contact Print.

3 Use the Add and Remove Photos buttons to adjust the list of pictures to be included in the contact sheet.

4 Select the printer from the drop-down list in section 1 of the dialog. If need be, click the Printer Preferences button next to the printer selection to adjust the hardware settings to suit your output. See Figure 13.14.

5 In section 2 of the dialog select Contact Sheet from the drop-down list of print types. See Figure 13.14.

6 In the final section 3 choose the number of columns to use (and therefore the total number of thumbnails to place on a single sheet) and select the content of the label text to be included. See Figure 13.15.

7 Click Print to output the contact sheet.

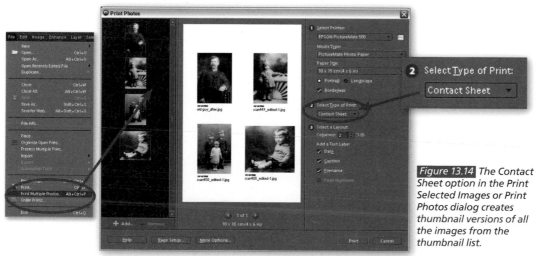

Figure 13.14 The Contact Sheet option in the Print Selected Images or Print Photos dialog creates thumbnail versions of all the images from the thumbnail list.

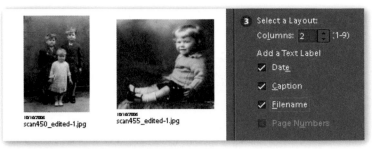

Figure 13.15 *The options in the Contact Sheet dialog allow the user to select the number of thumbnails per page by adjusting the columns value as well as what text will be included as labels.*

Picture packages

Editor: File > Print Multiple Photos > Picture Package or Organizer: File > Print > Picture Package

At some stage in your digital imaging career you will receive a request for multiple prints of a single image. The picture might be the only shot available of the winning goal from the local football match, or a very, very cute picture of your daughter blowing out the candles on her birthday cake, but whatever the story, multiple requests mean time spent printing the same image. Adobe included the Picture Package feature in its Elements and Photoshop packages to save you from such scenarios. Previously located in the Print Layouts section of the File menu where the Contact Sheet command was placed, the revamped Picture Package has now been integrated into the Print Multiple Photos dialog. The feature allows you to select one of a series of predesigned multi-print layouts that have been carefully created to fit many images neatly onto a single sheet of standard paper.

There are designs that place multiples of the same size pictures together and those that surround one or two larger images with many smaller versions. The feature provides a preview of the pictures in the layout. You can also choose to repeat the same image throughout the design by

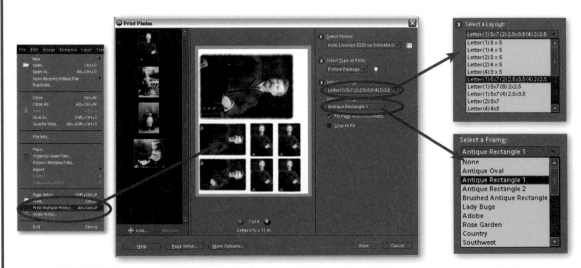

Figure 13.16 *The Picture Package option lays out multiple versions of the same image or several different pictures on a single sheet of paper and includes an option for surrounding the photos with a fancy frame.*

selecting the One Picture per Page option. There is also the option to select a frame from one of the many listed to surround the photos you print.

Whichever layout and frame design you pick, this feature should help you to keep both family members and football associates supplied with enough visual memories to make sure they are happy. See Figure 13.16.

1 If working in the Editor workspace, open the images to be printed; otherwise multi-select the pictures from inside the Photo Browser.

2 Select File > Print Multiple Photos and choose Picture Package from the Select Type of Print menu. From the Photo Browser select File > Print and then choose Picture Package.

3 Use the Add and Remove Photos buttons to adjust the list of pictures to be included in the contact sheet.

4 Drag the photos on the preview page to reorder their sequence or alter their position in the layout. You can also add more pictures from the film strip by dragging them from the left of the dialog into the preview area.

5 Select the printer from the drop-down list in section 1 of the dialog. If need be, click the Printer Preferences button next to the printer selection to adjust the hardware settings to suit your output. See Figure 13.16.

6 In section 2 of the dialog select Picture Package from the drop-down list of print types. See Figure 13.16.

7 In the final section 3 choose the Layout and Frame design to be included. See Figure 13.17.

8 To repeat a single image on a page click the One Photo per Page option. To add many different pictures to the same page leave this item unchecked.

9 Click Print to output the Picture Package pages.

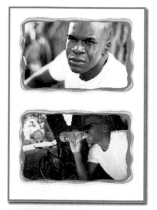 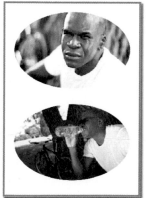 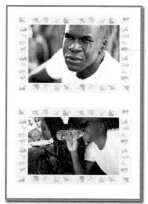 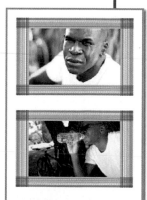

Figure 13.17 There are many different Layout and Frame designs included in the revised Picture Package feature.

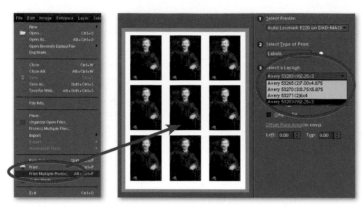

Figure 13.18 *The Labels option lays out multiple versions of the same image or several different pictures in a format to suit commercially made sheets of adhesive labels.*

Picture labels

Editor: File > Print Multiple Photos > Labels or Organizer: File > Print > Labels

First introduced in Elements 3.0 for Windows, this additional Multi-photo Printing option lays out and sizes the images to suit the design of commercially available sheets of adhesive labels. The Layout box contains a variety of label sheet designs and just as with the Picture Package feature you can add frames to your label photos. To help with precise aligning of the print to the label sheet Adobe has also included an offset print settings box. Here you can make slight adjustments of where the pictures print on the paper surface. If the print is misaligned to the left then add a positive number to the settings; if the error is to the right then you will need to add a negative number to the dialog. See Figures 13.18 and 13.19.

1   If working in the Editor workspace, open the images to be printed; otherwise multi-select the pictures from inside the Photo Browser.

2   Select File > Print Multiple Photos and choose Labels from the Select Type of Print menu. From the Photo Browser select File > Print and then choose Labels.

3   Use the Add and Remove Photos buttons to adjust the list of pictures to be included in the labels sheet.

4   Select the printer from the drop-down list in section 1 of the dialog. See Figure 13.18. If need be, click the Printer Preferences button next to the printer selection to adjust the hardware settings to suit your output.

5   In section 2 (see Figure 13.18) of the dialog select Labels from the drop-down list of print types.

6   In the final section 3 (see Figure 13.18) choose the Layout and Frame design to be included.

7   To repeat a single image on a page click the One Photo per Page option. To add many different pictures to the same page leave this item unchecked.

8   Click Print to output the label pages.

9   If the label print doesn't quite match the perforations on the sheet then adjust the print position using the Offset Print Area settings.

FEATURE SUMMARY

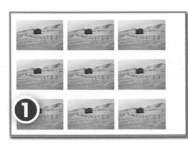

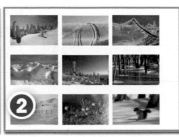

Figure 13.19 As with the other Print Multiple Photos options, the Picture Labels feature allows you to print a page of labels with different images (1) or, by selecting the One Photo per Page setting, produce a whole sheet with multiple copies of the one picture (2).

Individual Prints

Editor: File > Print Multiple Photos > Individual Prints or Organizer: File > Print > Individual Prints

Also included in Elements 7 is the ability to set up and print several individual photographs at one time. Until this version of the program the traditional Print dialog (Editor: File > Print) was the only way you could print one photo on a page. This approach is fine if all you want to do is print a single photo, but what if you have 10 pictures that you want to print quickly and easily? Well, this is where the Individual Print option in the Print Multiple Photos feature comes into play. This option allows the user to 'batch' a variety of one-image-to-one page photos at the same time. Though you don't have as many options when outputting your picture with this feature you can still choose the size of the photo on the page and whether it will be cropped in order to fill the paper size fully. And for those times when you need a couple of prints of a group of pictures simply change the number of times the pictures will be used in the print batch. See Figure 13.20 on the next page.

1 If working in the Editor workspace, open the images to be printed; otherwise multi-select the pictures from inside the Photo Browser.

2 Select File > Print Multiple Photos and choose Individual Prints from the Select Type of Print menu. From the Photo Browser select File > Print and then choose Individual Prints.

3 Use the Add and Remove Photos buttons to adjust the list of pictures to be included in the labels sheet.

4 Select the printer from the drop-down list in section 1 of the dialog. See Figure 13.20. If need be, click the Printer Preferences button next to the printer selection to adjust the hardware settings to suit your output.

5 In section 2 of the dialog (see Figure 13.20) select Individual Prints from the drop-down list of print types.

6 In the final section 3 (see Figure 13.20) select the Print Size you desire. If you are using the Fit on Page option then you can also select the Crop to Fit feature designed to ensure the picture fills the print paper fully.

7 To obtain more than one print of each picture adjust the value in the Use each Photo option.

8 Click Print to output the individual prints.

FEATURE SUMMARY

Book resources and video tutorials can be found at **www.photoshopelements.net**

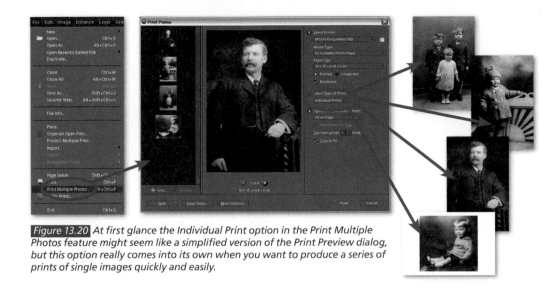

Figure 13.20 At first glance the Individual Print option in the Print Multiple Photos feature might seem like a simplified version of the Print Preview dialog, but this option really comes into its own when you want to produce a series of prints of single images quickly and easily.

Balancing image size and picture quality

The printing techniques detailed above can be used for producing good prints for the majority of images, papers, inks and printers. To gain the ultimate in control over your printed output, however, you need to delve a little deeper. Let's start by revisiting the factors that underpin good image quality.

Great prints are made from good images, and we know from previous chapters that digital image quality is based on high image resolution and high bit depth. Given this scenario, it would follow that if I want to make the best prints possible, then I should at first create pictures with massive pixel dimensions and huge numbers of colors. The problem is that such files take up loads of disk space and, due to their size, are very, very slow to work with, to the point of being practically impossible to edit on most desktop machines.

The solution is to find a balance between image quality and file size that still produces 'good prints'. See Figure 13.21. For the purposes of this book, 'good prints' are defined as those

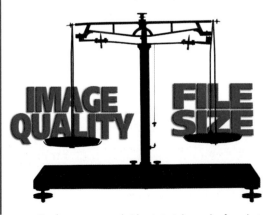

that appear photographic in quality and can be considered visually 'pixel-less'. The quality of all output is governed by a combination of the printer mechanism, the ink set used and the paper, or media, the image is printed on. To find the balance that works best with your setup, you will need to perform a couple of simple tests with your printer.

Figure 13.21 Just as is the case with photos optimized for web usage, good prints are made from files that balance file size and image quality .

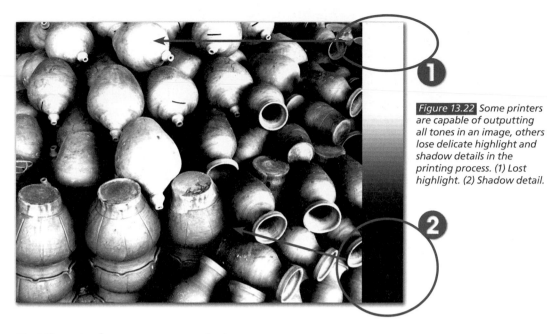

Figure 13.22 Some printers are capable of outputting all tones in an image, others lose delicate highlight and shadow details in the printing process. (1) Lost highlight. (2) Shadow detail.

Getting to know your printer

Testing tones

There are 256 levels of tones in each channel (Red, Green and Blue) of a 24-bit digital image. A value of 0 is pure black and one of 255 is pure white. Desktop inkjet machines do an admirable job of printing most of these tones, but they do have trouble printing delicate highlight (230–255) and shadow (0–40) details. Some machines will be able to print all 256 levels of tones, others will only be able to output a smaller subset. See Figure 13.22.

To test your own printer/ink/paper setup, make a stepped grayscale that contains separate tonal strips from 0 to 255 in approximately five tone intervals. Alternatively, download the example grayscale from this book's website. Print the grayscale using the best quality settings for the paper you are using. Examine the results. In particular, check to see at what point it becomes impossible to distinguish dark gray tones from pure black and light gray values from white. Note these values down for use later, as they represent the range of tones printable by your printer/paper/ink combination. See Figure 13.23.

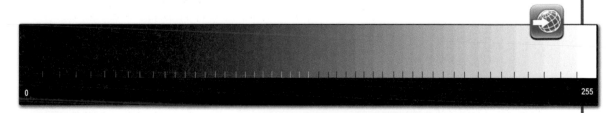

Figure 13.23 Print the example grayscale, noting down the tones that your machine fails to print.

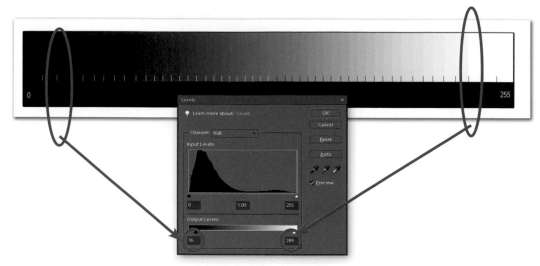

Figure 13.24 *Drag the black and white Output sliders until they match the values of those found in the grayscale or tone test.*

When you are next adjusting the levels of an image to be printed, move the output sliders at the bottom of the dialog until black and white points are set to those you found in your test. The spread of tones in your image will now meet those that can be printed by your printer/paper/ink combination. See Figure 13.24.

Testing resolution

Modern printers are capable of incredible resolution. Some are able to output discrete dots at a rate of over 5000 per inch. Many users believe that to get the utmost detail in their prints they must match this printer resolution with the same image resolution. Although this seems logical, good results can be achieved where one pixel is printed with several printer dots. Thank goodness this is the case, because the result is lower resolution images and therefore more manageable, and smaller, file sizes. But the question still remains – exactly what image resolution should be used?

Again, a simple test can help provide a practical answer. Create a high-resolution file with good sharp detail throughout. Using Image > Resize > Image Size makes a series of 10 pictures from 1000 to 100 ppi, reducing in resolution by 100 ppi each time (i.e. 1000, 900, 800, etc.). Alternatively, download the resolution examples from this book's website (www.photoshopelements.net). Now print each of these pictures at the optimum setting for your machine, with ink and paper you normally use. Next, examine each image carefully. Find the lowest resolution image where the picture still appears photographic. This is the minimum image resolution that you should use if you want your output to remain photographic quality.

For my setup, this setting varies between 200 and 300 ppi. I know if I use these values I can be guaranteed good results without using massive file sizes.

Managing color in practice

As computer operating systems have developed, so too has the way that they have handled the management of color, from capture through the manipulation phase to output. A central part of this process is a group of settings, called a color profile, that governs the conversion of an image's color from one device to another. A well-calibrated system will contain a profile for scanner/camera, screen, printer and a working profile that is used when editing the file in Elements. These profiles are used so that the image is passed from one managed space to another.

When printing with Adobe Elements it is possible to select the type of color management you want to apply to the output. If your printer came supplied with a profile, you can select it in the Print Space area of the Print dialog. Some printers are supplied with several profiles matched to different paper types. In previous versions of Elements you will need to select Show More Options to make the Color Management section of the dialog visible. If no profile is supplied, then you can either elect to use the same space the image was captured in or select the Printer Manages Color option in the Color Handling section of the Print dialog. Alternatively you may be able to download and install profiles for your printer from the companies website. See Figure 13.25.

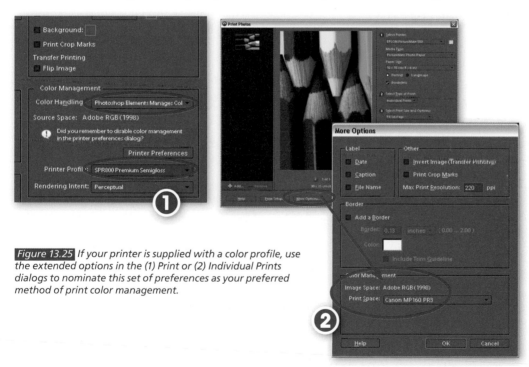

Figure 13.25 If your printer is supplied with a color profile, use the extended options in the (1) Print or (2) Individual Prints dialogs to nominate this set of preferences as your preferred method of print color management.

For the majority of output scenarios these options will provide good results. If you do happen to strike problems where images that appear neutral on screen continually print with a dominant cast, then most printer drivers (the special printer software that manages the activity of printing) include a feature that can be used to change individual colors to eliminate casts. See Figure 13.26.

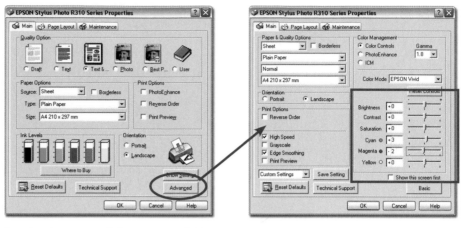

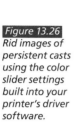

Figure 13.26
Rid images of persistent casts using the color slider settings built into your printer's driver software.

Typical printing problems and their solutions

Surface puddling (pooling)

Prints with this problem show puddles of wet ink on the surface of the paper resulting from too much ink being applied. To help this situation, reduce the Cyan, Yellow and Magenta sliders in the printer's dialog box. Make sure that you make the same change to all three sliders, otherwise you will introduce a color cast into the print. Also increase the Saturation slider; this will decrease the volume of ink going to the black nozzle. See Figure 13.27.

Banding

This problem usually results from one or more of the print heads being clogged. Consult your printer's manual to find out how to activate the cleaning sequence. Once completed, print a 'nozzle test' page to check that all the print needs are working correctly. If banding still occurs after several cleaning attempts it may be necessary to install a new cartridge. See Figure 13.28.

Figure 13.27 Surface puddling results from too much ink hitting the paper surface.

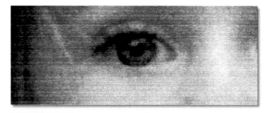

Figure 13.28 Cleaning the print heads usually solves banding problems.

Edge bleeding

Edges of the print appear fuzzy and shadow areas are clogged and too dark. This usually occurs when using an uncoated paper. Use the corrective steps detailed in 'puddling' above, as well as choosing a media or paper type such as 'Plain Paper' or 'Backlit Film'. These measures will change the amount of ink being applied, and the spacing of the ink droplets, to account for the absorbency of the paper. See Figure 13.29.

Book resources and video tutorials can be found at **www.photoshopelements.net**

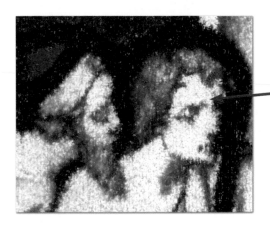
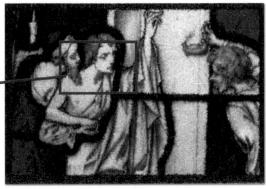

Figure 13.29 Edge bleeding can result from using an uncoated porous paper.

Web-Based Printing

Editor: File > Order Prints, Organizer: File > Order Prints

In designing Elements, Adobe realized that the web plays, and will continue to play, a large role in the life of most digital image makers. The inclusion of a Web-Based Printing option in the package shows just how far online technology has developed.

Although many images you make, or enhance, with Elements will be printed right at your desktop, occasionally you might want the option to output some prints on traditional photographic paper. The Order Prints option, located in the File menu, provides just this utility. See Figure 13.30.

Using the resources of kodakgallery.com in the USA, Elements users can upload copies of their favorite images to the company's site and have them photographically printed in a range of sizes. The finished prints will then be mailed back to you. This service provides the convenience of printing from your desktop with the image and archival qualities of having your digital pictures output using a photographic rather than inkjet process.

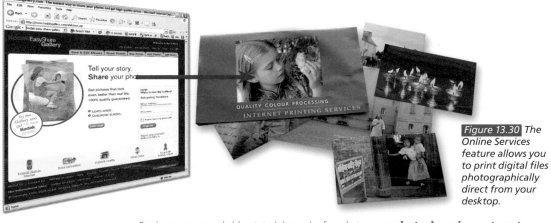

Figure 13.30 The Online Services feature allows you to print digital files photographically direct from your desktop.

Book resources and video tutorials can be found at **www.photoshopelements.net**

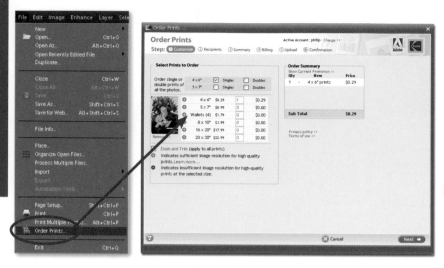

Figure 13.31 Images that are already opened in Elements can be uploaded directly to the kodakgallery.com website.

Making your first online prints

In previous versions of Elements you needed to access the Online Services feature before uploading your pictures to print, but Elements 7 streamlines the process by allowing you to upload directly from the Editor or Organizer workspace. The first time you use the feature you will need to register for the service but from that time onwards the feature works seamlessly from inside the Elements package. See Figure 13.31.

Although kodakgallery.com does provide a set of simple online editing and enhancement tools at its main site, I prefer to alter my images in Elements first before uploading. In addition to printing your favorite pictures, kodakgallery.com also provides album creation and image-sharing services, allowing you and your friends to upload your favorite photos, review them and then print those that you like the most. See Figure 13.32.

If you like the look of true photographic quality prints, then this online option provides a quick, easy and reliable service to output your digital images from your desktop.

To print online

1 Select or multi-select pictures from Photo Browser.

2 Choose File > Order prints.

3 Choose print numbers and size from the Customize section of kodakgallery.com. Click Next.

4 Select the recipient of the prints from the list or add new contact details and then click Next.

5 Review print and shipping charges at the next screen and then click Next.

6 At the Billing section insert your credit card information and add the billing address. Click Place Order, which will upload your pictures and then display an order confirmation.

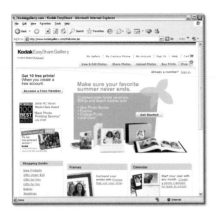

Figure 13.32 The uploaded pictures can be stored in a series of photo albums on the kodakgallery.com website ready for sharing and printing. The online service can also be used for creating and printing cards, calendars and photo books.

To upload files for sharing

1 Select or multi-select pictures from the Organizer workspace.

2 Choose the Share Online option from the Share button in the shortcuts bar.

3 Choose the person you want to share the pictures with from the list or add new contact details for a new recipient. Click Next.

4 The files will now be uploaded and an invitation to share the pictures will be sent to the recipients selected in the previous step.

Options for web printing

Since version 5.0 Elements has contained a streamlined method of ordering online prints. Individual or multi-selected thumbnails are dragged and dropped onto contact names in the Quick Share pane (previously Order Prints). The photos to print are associated with the contact name and once the order is confirmed they are uploaded, printed and sent to the contact using the delivery details first entered when creating the contact. See Figure 13.33.

Using the Order Prints pane

1 Open the Quick Share pane by selecting Organizer: Window >Quick Share.

2 Select or multi-select images from the Photo Browser (Organizer) workspace to print.

3 Drag the selected prints to the Contact name (Target) in the pane. When the target changes color let go of the mouse button to drop the pictures.

4 Press the Confirm Order button to process the order with the online print company.

To add a new Order Print contact

1 Open the Quick Share pane and press the Add New Contact button by selecting Organizer: Window > Quick Share. Insert the details in the dialog displayed. '1' in Figure 13.33.

To review and confirm an order for a specific contact

1 Open the Quick Share (Order Prints) pane, select a contact name from those listed and then press the View Photos in Order button. Review the photos shown in the dialog and then press the Confirm Order button to place the online print order. '2' in Figure 13.30.

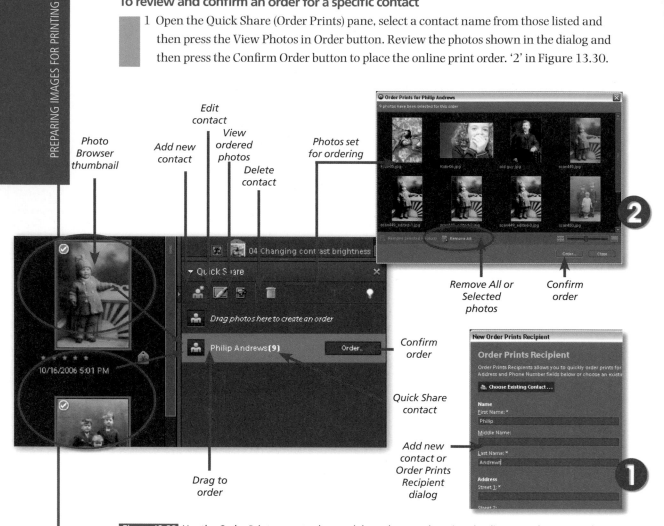

Figure 13.33 Use the Order Prints pane to drag and drop photos to be printed online onto the contact that they are to be sent to.

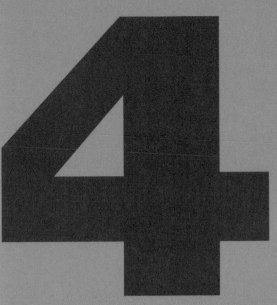

14

Photo Projects

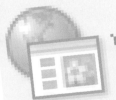

ADOBE PHOTOSHOP ELEMENTS 7

As we have already seen in previous chapters, Photoshop Elements includes a variety of ways to use the photos that you enhance with the program. The various output options can be broken into two broad groups that are reflected in the headings in the Task pane – Create and Share. The Create options are sophisticated imaging projects that enable users to quickly and easily include their pictures in a range of project forms. The Share entries on the other hand provide a variety ways that you can distribute your photos. These divisions are broad categories and not exclusive, so you will find that some photo projects, such as Order Prints, fall under both headings.

A few years ago it would have been sufficient for a good image-editing package to include a print command and maybe a way to export pictures in a variety of different file formats, but these days photos are compiled, shared, distributed and displayed in a much broader range of ways. With the inclusion of the Create and Share photo projects in Elements you too can start to use your pictures in forms that you may never have thought possible.

Photo projects

Organizer/Editor: Share task pane or Create task pane

Photo projects can be accessed from the Organizer and the Editing spaces by selecting an option from the Share or Create task panes on the right of the workspace. If these options are not visible choose Window > Show Task Pane or select them from the Project Bin menu. A list of key project types are grouped in each pane with other options available via the More Options button. See Figure 14.1. Some of the projects will already be familiar to Elements users as they have appeared in various forms in previous versions of the program, but others such as the Photo Collage and revamped Photo Book entries are new and exciting ways to share your pictures with others. See Figure 14.2.

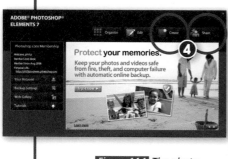

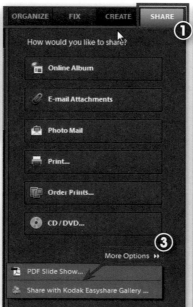

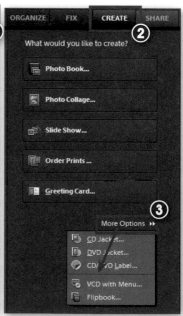

Figure 14.1 *The photo projects are accessed from either the Organizer or Editor workspaces via the Share (1) or Create (2) task panes. Key projects are listed in the pane with extra projects accessed via the More Options buttons (3). Users can also access these options directly from the Photoshop Elements Welcome window (4).*

Book resources and video tutorials can be found at **www.photoshopelements.net**

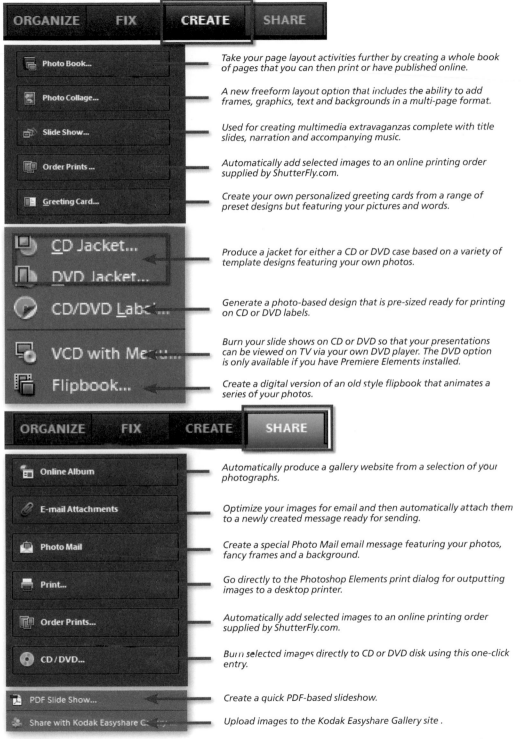

Take your page layout activities further by creating a whole book of pages that you can then print or have published online.

A new freeform layout option that includes the ability to add frames, graphics, text and backgrounds in a multi-page format.

Used for creating multimedia extravaganzas complete with title slides, narration and accompanying music.

Automatically add selected images to an online printing order supplied by ShutterFly.com.

Create your own personalized greeting cards from a range of preset designs but featuring your pictures and words.

Produce a jacket for either a CD or DVD case based on a variety of template designs featuring your own photos.

Generate a photo-based design that is pre-sized ready for printing on CD or DVD labels.

Burn your slide shows on CD or DVD so that your presentations can be viewed on TV via your own DVD player. The DVD option is only available if you have Premiere Elements installed.

Create a digital version of an old style flipbook that animates a series of your photos.

Automatically produce a gallery website from a selection of your photographs.

Optimize your images for email and then automatically attach them to a newly created message ready for sending.

Create a special Photo Mail email message featuring your photos, fancy frames and a background.

Go directly to the Photoshop Elements print dialog for outputting images to a desktop printer.

Automatically add selected images to an online printing order supplied by ShutterFly.com.

Burn selected images directly to CD or DVD disk using this one-click entry.

Create a quick PDF-based slideshow.

Upload images to the Kodak Easyshare Gallery site .

Figure 14.2 *Photo projects are listed in both the Create and Share task panes. Some options are present in both lists as they constitute both a creation project and a way to share your photos. The options available in the panes are listed above.*

Each project requires you to have some basic resources prepared before starting out. For the most part this means that you should have selected, enhanced and edited any pictures you wish to include before commencing the creation process.

In the case of the VCD or DVD with Menu options you will need to create the slide shows that you want to feature before selecting these options. For this reason it is a good idea to follow the workflow detailed below when making your Photo Creations. See Figure 14.3.

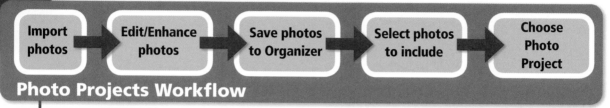

Photo Projects Workflow

Import photos → Edit/Enhance photos → Save photos to Organizer → Select photos to include → Choose Photo Project

Figure 14.3 As you need to have all your pictures edited and enhanced before adding them to your Photo Creation projects, start by enhancing your pictures then save the finished file back to the browser. Now select the pictures to include and then select the Photo Creations project. The selected images will now appear in the Project dialog.

Photo Book and Photo Collage

The Photo Book and Photo Collage options use a similar interface to projects that make use of the special frames, backgrounds, themes (matched backgrounds and frame sets), graphics and text to create multi-page documents from a group of selected photos. The big difference between the two options is that with Photo Books, the creation is optimized for production with an online book publisher (Kodak Easy Share Gallery), whereas the Photo Collage option creates a series of layouts which can be printed using your desktop machine. The Theme and Layout options allow the user to automatically design their pages and insert pictures using one of a range of templates and styles, and then edit or add to the layouts after creation. For more details on creating Photo Books and Collages see Chapter 10.

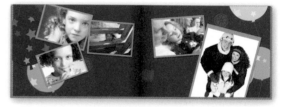

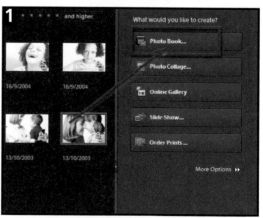

Start by selecting the photos that you wish to include from the thumbnails displayed in the Organizer workspace. To select a group of pictures click on the first thumbnail and then hold down the Shift key whilst selecting the last photo. To pick individual images Ctrl-click on the thumbnails. Next choose the Photo Book option in the Create task pane.

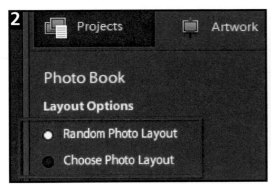

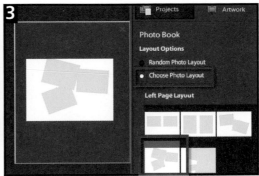

The Photo Book panel is then displayed on the right of the workspace. The first step is to choose between Random Photo Layout or Choose Photo Layout. The former allows you to select the themes to be used with the pages but Elements selects the arrangement of the images on each page. The second option allows the user to choose both. Here I selected 'Choose'.

Choose a Layout design for both the left and right pages by clicking the example thumbnail. A larger version of the design is displayed in a pop-up window to the left of the Task pane. As we are creating a Photo Book there is no need to pick a page size as only one is available for online book production, but when working with Photo Collages you also select the page size here. Click Next.

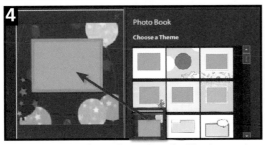

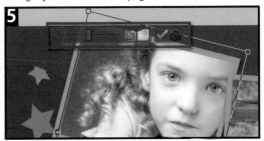

In the next step select a theme (matched background and frame set) to use for the Photo Book. Also choose if you want Elements to 'Auto-fill' the frames with the images you selected and if you want to include captions with the images. Drag images to a new location in the Project Bin to change their position in the book. The first photo will be seen through a die-cut opening in the front of the book. Click Done to produce the book.

Adjust the size and positioning of frames by clicking onto each in turn and dragging the corner handles. Alter the size and position of the photos inside the frames by double-clicking on the photo and either using the corner handles, the tools in the edit bar at the top of the frame or the options in the right-click pop-up menu. With the adjustments complete, save the project.

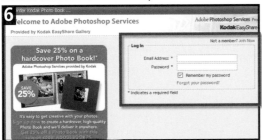

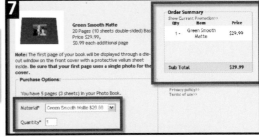

To print the book to a desktop printer open the saved project in the Edit space and then choose File > Print. To have the multi-page document professionally printed and bound using the Kodak Easy Share Gallery service, press the Order button in the floating Photo Book options bar at the bottom of the book preview. A new web dialog is displayed requesting the new user to register for the service and returning users to log in.

After logging in, select the style of book to be produced and then complete the rest of the order conditions before clicking OK to submit the book order.

Note that you can also create documents without images and add photos later from the Project Bin at the bottom of the Editor.

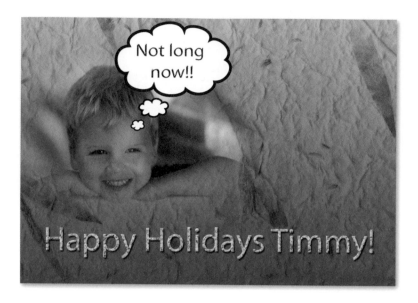

Greeting Cards

Creating greeting or birthday cards customized with your own pictures and heartfelt message is a good way to make the card-giving experience a little more personal. The Greeting Card project in Elements contains many different templates and styles ranging from formal, season's greetings, valentine and baby cards. Most have decorative borders, appropriate color schemes and places for you to add your message. Like other photo projects, greeting cards are created by selecting edited images from the Organizer before having them automatically placed in one or a range of templates. From here you can add graphics and text and even more images before outputting the final design to your desktop printer.

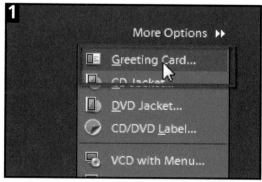

Start by multi-selecting photos from the Organizer workspace before choosing Greeting Card from the More Options section in the Create task pane. Unlike in previous versions of the feature, from version 6 the size is predetermined as standard postcard dimensions. The Greeting Card panel will be displayed on the right of the Editor workspace.

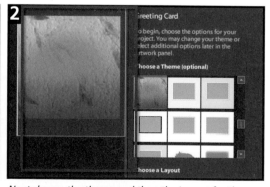

Next choose the theme and then the Layout for the card. You can pick between a range of basic designs based on the number of images to be included. Don't panic if the position of the photos is not exactly what you want as this can be changed later. Click Done to create the card.

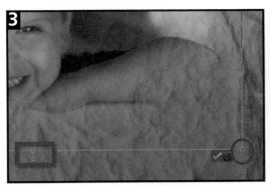

Adjust the position, size, shape and orientation of the photos placed on the greeting card using the corner and side handles. See Chapter 9 for more details. When finished click the Commit button (green tick) at the bottom of the frame to apply the changes.

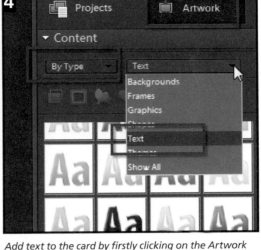

Add text to the card by firstly clicking on the Artwork heading in the Create task pane and then choosing the By Type heading on the left and Text entry on the right drop-down menus. To add some type double-click on the text style thumbnail that you want from those listed in the Text pane. Replace the text that is automatically placed on the card with your own and alter color and font style in the normal manner. See Chapter 7 for more details on making changes to text.

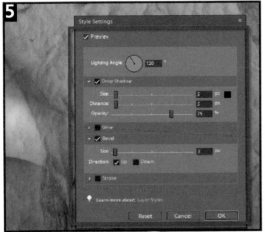

Add graphics, shapes, special effects and extra photos to the card by selecting the desired option from the Content panel and then clicking the Apply button. Alter the look of characteristics of shadows, strokes and bevels using the controls in the Style Settings dialog accessed by selecting the Edit Layer Style option from the right-click menu.

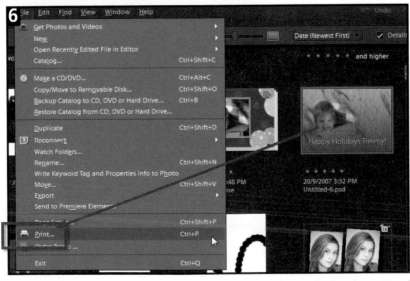

Once the card design is completed you can print the card with a desktop machine connected to your computer. Do this by selecting the saved Greeting Card project in the Organizer space and selecting the File > Print option.

Book resources and video tutorials can be found at **www.photoshopelements.net**

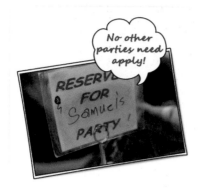

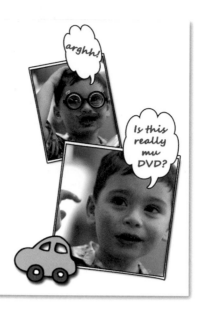

CD and DVD Jackets

CD and DVD jackets are the sheets of paper or thin card that wrap around the inside of the CD/DVD case. The inclusion of a photo project option for the creation of these jackets first appeared in Elements 5.0. There is no real difference between the two choices except for the size of the finished document. For this reason I have presented only one step-by-step technique here. After creating a jacket with a combination of your images and one of the themes provided in the Creation dialog, the final design is printed, the edges trimmed and the paper inserted into the cover space of the case.

CD/DVD cases normally open like a book so remember to position the front cover details on the right-hand side of the design.

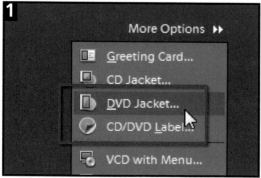

Start by multi-selecting photos from the Organizer workspace before choosing CD or DVD Jacket from the More Options section in the Create task pane.

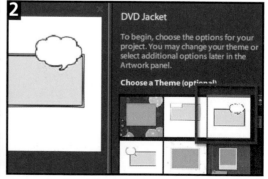

Choose the theme for the jacket from the thumbnails listed in the menu of the panel. Next, select the number of photos to include in the Layout section before pressing Done to instruct Elements to automatically create the document and insert the pictures into the frames.

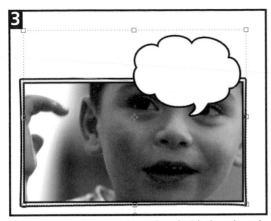

A new project document is produced with the selected images inserted into the frames and placed onto the background. If more images were selected than the places available in the document then Elements uses only those images it needs to fill the frames in the layout.

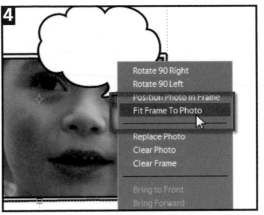

Right-click on each image in turn and choose Fit Frame To Photo. Next adjust the size and orientation of the photo and the frame using the side and corner handles. For more details on how to manipulate frames and the pictures they contain go to Chapter 9.

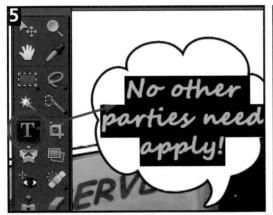

With the images in place we can now turn our attention to adding other details to the design. Here extra text is inserted in the Speech Bubble section of the theme's background. The user can match the color and style of the text with the comic style already in the design.

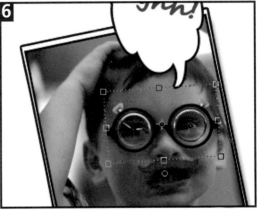

For a finishing touch extra graphics and/or shapes can be added to the composition by selecting them from the Content panel and then clicking Apply to add the item to the jacket design. The size, shape, rotation and position of these images are adjusted in the same way as the frame photos.

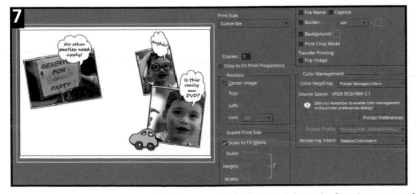

After saving the completed composition the CD/DVD jacket is then printed using the Actual Size setting to ensure that the jacket fits the case.

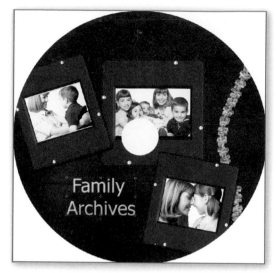

CD/DVD Labels

Another inclusion for image makers saving their files to disk is the CD/DVD Label project. This photo project produces a circular design that is suitable for printing onto the surface of printable CDs or on perforated label paper. Like the other revised creation projects in Elements 6, an image or images are selected from the Organizer workspace or Project Bin, before selecting the CD/DVD Label option from the More Options menu in the Create task pane. Once selected the panel options will not provide a choice for the document's size as all the templates are designed with dimensions to suit a standard DVD or CD disk. The choice of layouts is largely based on the number of images to include on the CD label, but the selection you make here doesn't restrict you from adding (or taking away) images later in the design process. Some of the same themes that are available in the CD/DVD Jacket creation are also contained here and so it is possible to create matching label and jacket sets for your projects.

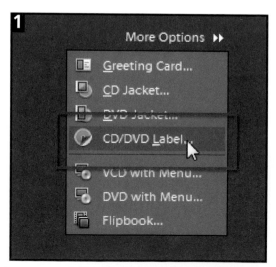

Start by multi-selecting photos from the Organizer workspace before choosing CD or DVD Label from the More Options menu in the Create task pane. There is no need to select the size as it is predetermined to suit the dimensions of a standard CD/DVD disk. Choose the theme and layout based on the number of photos to include and the design you like. Click Done to create the label and insert the images.

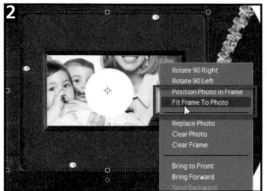

Right-click on the photo and choose Fit Frame To Photo. Next adjust the size and orientation of the photo and the frame using the side and corner handles. Keep in mind that the edges will be cut to suit the disk shape. For more details on how to manipulate frames and the pictures they contain go to Chapter 9.
Note: Some frames are designed for specific photo orientations, i.e. landscape or portrait, selecting the Fit Frame to Photo option when the frame and photo are not the same orientation will still result in cropping the photo.

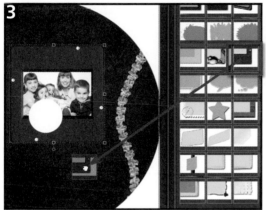

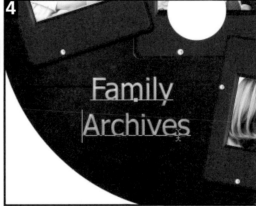

If you want to add more images to the design then locate a frame to include from the Artwork panel and then click and drag the thumbnail onto the document. A new frame will appear. To add a photo either drag one from the Photo Bin to the frame or click in the center and browse for a picture file in the file dialog that opens. To find out more about adding, removing and replacing photos in a Photo Projects document go to Chapter 9.

After positioning the pictures we can now add some text to the composition. As we are matching the design used in the CD/DVD Jacket creation the text is inserted in an appropriate section in the theme's background. The color and style of the text are matched with the design.

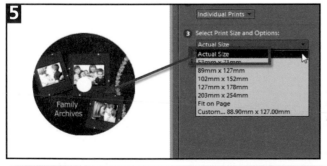

Once the design is completed save the creation project and then insert the CD/DVD or label sheet into the printer ready for printing. Select File > Print and ensure that the print size is set to Actual size (scale = 100%). This will guarantee that the final label is an exact match to the CD/DVD disk.

Note that for some label types some repositioning of the design might be required. I would recommend doing a test print on plain paper and making sure that the design lines up with the label paper.

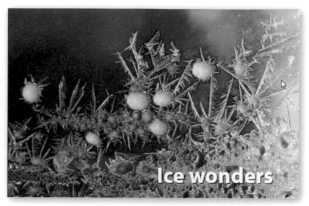

Ice wonders

Slide shows on your computer or TV

As we have already seen in Chapter 10, the Slide Show option in Elements is very sophisticated. Gone is the simple menu-based wizard that Elements featured in earlier versions of the product. Now, using a single Slide Show editor, you create and arrange slide shows, add music, text, graphics and narration then finally produce the show in one of a range of formats. For more specific detail about how to use the Slide Show feature see Chapter 10.

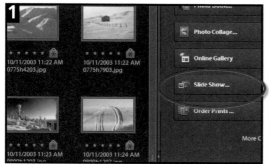

Start creating your slide show by selecting the photos that you wish to include from the thumbnails displayed in the Organizer workspace.

To select a group of pictures click on the first thumbnail and then hold down the Shift key whilst selecting the last photo. To pick individual images Ctrl-click on the thumbnails.

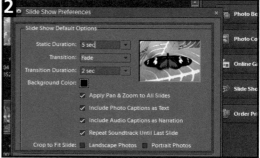

With the pictures selected, choose the Slide Show option from the Create task pane. This action will display the Slide Show Preferences dialog. Using the controls here set the general slide duration, transition, transition duration, background color, cropping and caption options that will be used for the whole show. There are also options to adjust how the soundtrack will be added to the presentation and the overall quality of how the show previews in the Editor space.

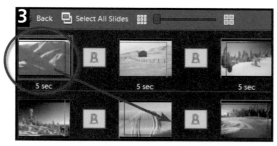

The Slide Show editor is displayed after clicking OK at the Preferences dialog. Adjust the sequence of the photos in the presentation by switching to the Quick Reorder screen (View > Quick Reorder). Click and drag photos to a new position to change their place in the show's sequence. When finished choose View > Quick Reorder to change back to the Slide Show editor view.

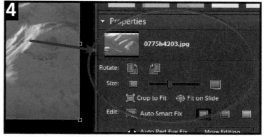

To make basic (automatic) editing changes to the slides in the presentation click on the preview picture (large) and then adjust the settings in the Properties pane. Here you can rotate, adjust picture size, alter cropping and apply Auto Smart Fix and Auto Red Eye Fixes. There are also three quick Photo Effect buttons that convert the slide to black and white, sepia and back to color.

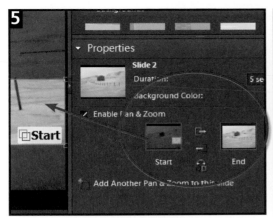

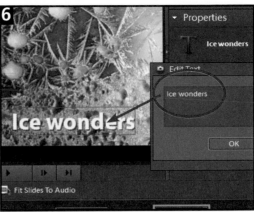

Along with the basic transition effects there is also the ability to animate the pictures in the presentation. This effect is created with the Pan and Zoom controls, which are displayed in the Properties pane when the slide thumbnail is selected in the timeline. Click the check box to enable the feature and then set the Start (Green) and End (Red) marquees on the slide preview.

In addition the Editor allows you to add graphics, text and narration to your show. Simply select the heading in the Extras pane and then drag and drop the text or graphics onto the slide and adjust size and color or effects using the options in the Properties pane. Select the Narration option to record any comments to be added to the slide.

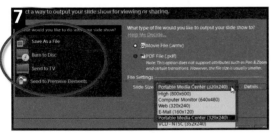

To add a music track to the show click the music bar below the timeline and browse for the file to include. The transitions added to all slides can be changed or customized by clicking on the 'A-B box' between slides in the timeline and altering the settings in the Properties pane.

Once you are happy with the presentation design save the show (File > Save Slide Show Project) before outputting (File > Output Slide Show) the presentation in one of the formats listed in the Output dialog.

Slide shows in PDF format

Elements can also produce simple presentations of your images in the PDF (Adobe Acrobat) format that is suitable for emailing. There are two ways to produce PDF slide shows: one from within the Slide Show editor and one via the options in the Share task pane.

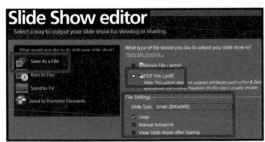

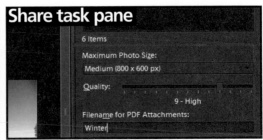

After creating your presentation in the Slide Show editor, save the production and then select File > Output Slide Show. Choose the Save as a File option and then the PDF File entry to set the dialog for Adobe Acrobat output. Next select the slide size from the drop-down menu and choose Loop, Manual Advance and View Slide Show after Saving options as appropriate.

Alternatively, multi-select your images in the Organizer and then choose the PDF Slide Show entry from the More Options entry in the Share task pane. Adjust the sequence of pictures, the photo size and quality and input the name for the presentation then click the Next button. Add in Recipient details and a message before clicking Next to build the show and create a new email message.

VCD/DVD with Menu

I'm sure that it wouldn't take too much prompting for readers to recall the dreaded family slide shows that seem to occur regularly on lazy Sunday evenings in many households around the country. Everyone's favorite uncle would present a selection of the family archives and we would all sit around amazed at how much we had changed and try not to make rude comments about clothing styles and receding hairlines.

Well, the days when most photographers recorded the family history on slide film have long gone but the slide show events that accompanied these images are starting to make a comeback, thanks in part to the ease with which we can now organize and present our treasured digital photos on new media like CD and DVD. Gone too are the dusty projectors, being replaced instead by DVD players hooked to widescreen 'tellies'. This project converts your Elements slide shows to VCD format ready for viewing on most DVD players or computers with a DVD drive but, to be sure that your machine is compatible, check the equipment manual first.

In Elements 6.0 and 7.0 slide shows can be written directly to VCD or DVD with the output options found in the revised Slide Show editor; however, DVD burning does require Premier Elements to be installed alongside Photoshop Elements.

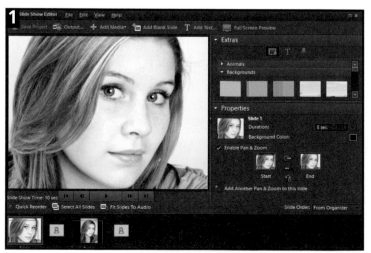

Before you can create a DVD or VCD with a menu you must have at least one slide show saved into the Photo Browser. If you don't have a candidate slide show then start the process by selecting the Slide Show option and creating a multimedia presentation complete with sound. Save the project to the Organizer.

Book resources and video tutorials can be found at **www.photoshopelements.net**

PHOTO PROJECTS

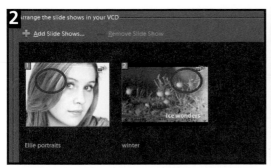

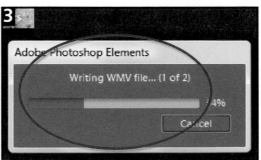

Select the slide shows that you want to include in the VCD from the Photo Browser and then pick VCD with Menu from the More Options menu in the Create task pane. Add or Remove slide shows from the thumbnail list if you are unhappy with your selection. Click and drag slide shows to new positions in the list to adjust where they will be placed in the menu of the VCD. The small number in the top left of each thumbnail indicates the sequence. Click Burn when you are happy with the arrangement.

The burn step is a two-part process. First, any slide show not in the Windows Media Video file will be converted to that format. The conversion can be quite lengthy if you are burning slide shows containing many high-resolution files. If you want to speed up this section of the process, convert your shows to WMV beforehand from inside the Slide Show project dialog.

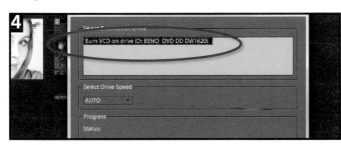

The second part of the burn process is writing the CD/DVD itself. After converting the slide shows to WMV files a Burn dialog will appear. Make sure that a new blank CD/DVD is inserted into the writer and click the OK button to create the VCD.

Archiving files direct to CD/DVD

As well as the ability to write slide shows to disk with an associated menu, Elements also can be used to save a copy of your photos to CD/DVD. After selecting the photos to include from the Organizer workspace, select the CD/DVD option from the Share task pane, choose the destination drive in the pop-up dialog and click OK to burn the disk.

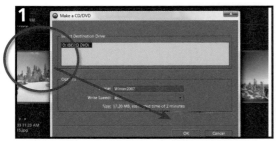

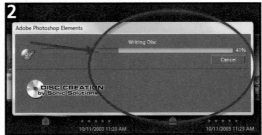

With the exception of photo projects such as Photo Books and Slideshows, Elements users can archive, or save a copy of their files directly to CD or DVD disk. Simply multi-select the photos in the Organizer space and then choose the CD/DVD entry from the Share task pane. Next select the Destination Disc Drive from those listed, add in a Name for the disk and click OK.

Elements then displays a writing dialog showing the progress of the archiving process. If the number and size of the photos that you have selected exceeds the capacity of the selected disk then Elements prompts you for further disks to include in the writing process. At the conclusion of writing, Elements prompts you to name the disks accurately so that the files can be easily located later.

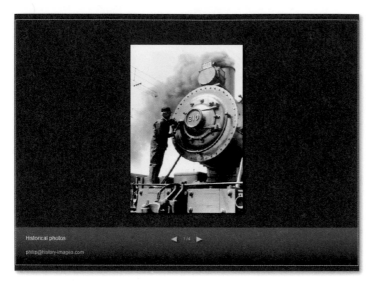

Online Album

Photoshop Elements 7.0 sees the continued development of the web gallery production prowess of the program with a revamped featured called Online Album (previously called the Online Gallery, HTML Photo Gallery or Web Photo Gallery). Now located in the Share task pane, the revamped wizard now simplifies the creation process which is now centred around the main workspace with the gallery settings grouped in a side panel on the right. The first step in the process is selecting and sequencing the images to include in the gallery. The next pane displays a menu and list of thumbnails for selecting the type (category) and style (template) of gallery that you create. Then you set about customizing the design and adding site details such as the photographer's contact information and where and how you want to display the resultant website.

For more details on using the Online Gallery feature and preparing images for web display see Chapter 12.

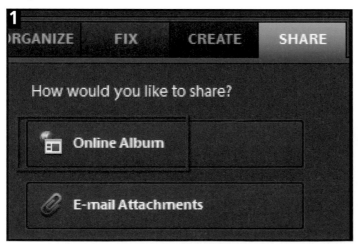

As is the case with most Photo Creation projects, you should adjust, edit or enhance the photos that are to be included in your gallery before selecting them from the Organizer workspace. Here I made use of the Rotate and Auto Smart Fix options located in the menu that is displayed when you right-click a thumbnail for some quick general adjustments. With the adjustments complete the photos are multi-selected before choosing the Online Album option from the Share task pane.

Book resources and video tutorials can be found at **www.photoshopelements.net**

2

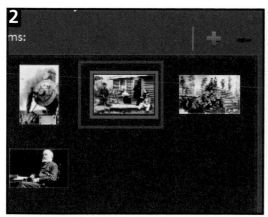

When the Online Album pane is displayed you will notice that the images you selected are listed as thumbnails. The + 'add' and − 'remove' buttons at the top of the group of thumbnails allow you the chance to alter the photos that are to be used in producing the gallery. In addition you can click-drag the images to new positions in the sequence they will be shown in the gallery pages.

3

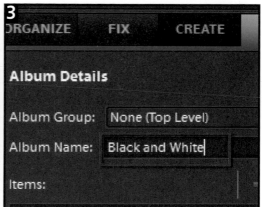

The next step is to input a name for the new Album. As the process of creating a web gallery in Elements 7.0 is based on the new synchronized album structure, you must create an album. You can choose to to have the album sit within an existing album group by selecting the group entry from the drop down menu. If you want to use a new Album Group then you need to quit the wizard, create the album group and then start again.

4

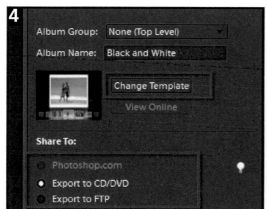

Clicking the Share button at the bottom of the screen builds a preview of the Online Album and displays it on the right in the main workspace. Here you can choose to Share the album to Photoshop.com, Export to a DVD/ CD or Export to FTP. If you don't like the look of the current template you can choose to change it by selecting the Change Template button.

5

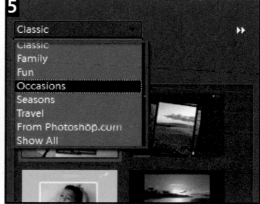

If you choose to change template then you will be presented with a new pane containing a drop down menu of template groups. Selecting one of these headings will display a list of thumbnails representing the design of each template. Picking the Show All option will display all templates and selecting From Photoshop.com will show only those templates available from the website. Click Next.

6

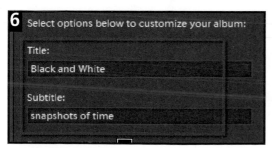

Now you will be presented with a pane that allows you to customise the look of the template and also add in details such as the title and sub-title text. Clicking the Next button will take you back to the pane seen in step 4 where you can select how you want to share the Album. Depending on your choice you will be presented with a further pane full of settings.

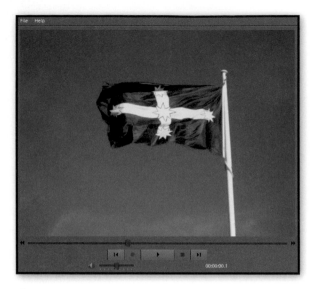

Flipbook

Until version 5.0 the only way to create a short animation in Elements from a series of still images was to save the file as a GIF image (see Chapter 12), but now you can produce a short production with the Flipbook feature. The feature derives its name from the old technique of drawing a slightly different picture on the successive pages of a small notebook. You would then animate the sequence by grasping the edge of the pages, arching the book and flipping the pages in quick sequence.

Unlike the animations produced in GIF format where each layer of the Elements document becomes a frame in the movie, the Flipbook feature uses a series of different images that have been selected in the Organizer space as the basis for the animation. This approach makes the feature particularly good for creating snippets of action from sequences of photos captured on the Burst or Continuous Shooting mode with your digital camera.

For more details on using the Flipbook feature see Chapter 12.

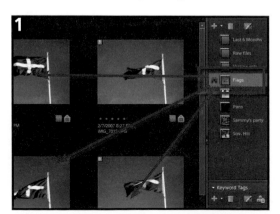

It is not just the images that you select which are important to the creation of a successful Flipbook – the position each image takes within the sequence also impacts upon the overall effect of the animation. For these reason it is a good idea to add the source photos to an Elements Album (previously Collection) as the first step in the creation process. Of course, this should happen after each image has been enhanced and corrected.

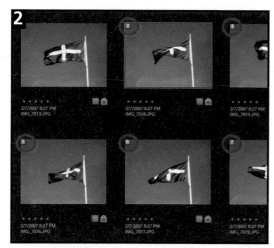

Elements Albums (Collections) are a unique grouping of images in that the sequence of the photos is recorded as well as their membership in the group. When an Album of photos is displayed in the Photo Browser workspace the user can alter the position of any photos within the sequence by simply click-dragging the thumbnail to another spot. In the example here I added the photos to an Album called Flags. To display the collection of images you just click the heading in the Album palette.

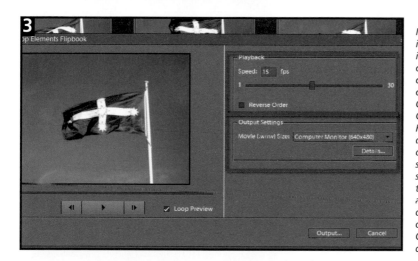

Next, select the images to be included in the book from the open Album and choose the Flipbook option from the More Options menu in the Create task pane. The Flipbook dialog is then displayed. Here you can set the playback speed in frames per second (FPS), the order the sequence is played and the pixel dimensions of the output. Click the Output button to create the movie.

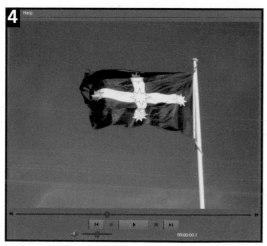

The newly created Flipbook movie is stored in the WMV or Windows Media Video file format at the top of the Organizer. The animation can be played by most Windows machines. Double-clicking the file in the Photo Browser displays the video with the Elements video player utility.

Sharing photos as E-mail Attachments

Photoshop Elements contains two ways to share your photos with your friends and relatives via email. The first, and probably the most traditional approach, allows the user to adjust the size and compression settings for the photos and then optimizes the images using these settings before adding them to a newly created email message as attachments. Also see Chapter 12 for more details on sending your files by email.

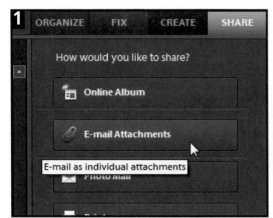

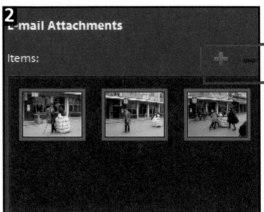

After multi-selecting the files to send from those available in the Organizer workspace choose the E-mail Attachments entry from those listed in the Share task pane. As with most photo projects there isn't an opportunity to edit or enhance the photos when stepping through the process so make sure that the images you include have been adjusted before starting.

The first screen in the E-mail Attachments panel lists the photos you have selected for inclusion. Use the '+' and '−' buttons to add or remove extra images from the list or simply drag photos from the Organizer to the List area. Using the controls below the List area adjust the photo size and quality (compression) checking the total Estimated Size of the optimized photos to be sure that they don't exceed the email message limit before clicking Next.

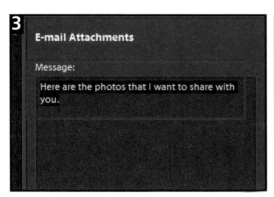

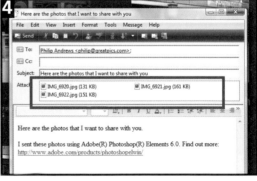

Type in a message to be included in the email and select the Recipients from those listed. If this area of the panel is empty then add new recipients by clicking the Edit Recipient button in the top right of the panel (person icon). This displays the Adobe Contacts Book where the user can add, edit or remove recipients and their details. Note that you can import existing contact lists and details from vCard and email programs using the Import feature.

Clicking Next will optimize copies of your photos, create a new email message in your default message program and attach the files. It is then a simple matter of hitting the Send button to email your photos to all the listed recipients.

Sending images as a Photo Mail

The second way to distribute your masterpieces via email is to incorporate them into the special Photo Mail format that is unique to Photoshop Elements. The feature essentially frames and presents your photos against a colored, or textured, background in a range of different layout combinations. The final composition is then sent to your friends and relatives as an email message. See Chapter 12 for extra information on using Photo Mail.

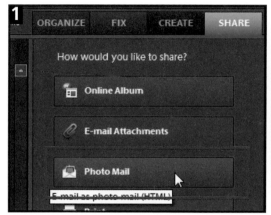

To start the Photo Mail creation process, multi-select enhanced images from those listed in the Organizer space and then choose the Photo Mail option from the Share task pane. If the panes are not displayed then select the Window > Show Task pane menu entry.

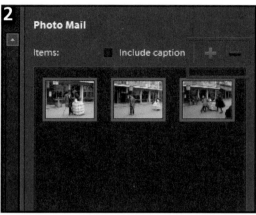

Unlike the E-mail Attachment feature, Photo Mail doesn't provide an option to adjust the size and quality settings used for the email optimization process. This is handled automatically in Photo Mail. This means that in the first panel, users only have the chance to add or remove images using the '+' or '–' buttons and alter the position of the photos in the sequence (drag to a new location). There is also an option for including photo captions in the Photo Mail design.

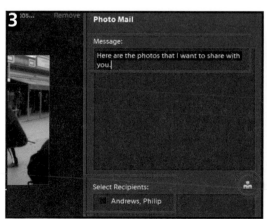

Clicking Next displays a new panel where users have the opportunity to add a message for the email and select recipients. If no contacts are listed in the Select Recipient section of the panel, new contacts can be added by clicking on the Edit Recipient button (small person icon) on the right of the panel.

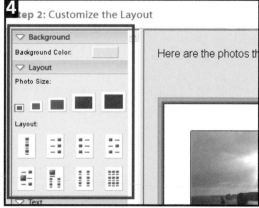

Use the options in the next two dialogs to customize the look of your Photo Mail message. There are settings for frame design, background color, layout design, photo size and the inclusion of drop shadows. Once completed click the Next button to create a new email message and add the Photo Mail design and recipient list. Click send to email.

Sharing online

The online sharing facilities that are available inside Elements are an interesting alternative to creating Online Albums, Synchronized Albums or Photo Mail projects. Multi-selected pictures or even whole catalogs can be uploaded and shared online. The pictures are stored on the web in an album format that has options to run as a slide show via space provided by third parties such as the Kodak Easy Share Gallery service. Selected friends and relatives are automatically emailed and invited to view (and, of course, buy prints) as part of the sharing process. This approach is a lot easier than creating your own web pages and then having to upload them to an ISP server space that you have to organize. The downside to e-sharing your photos this way is that you have few choices over the way that the pictures are displayed.

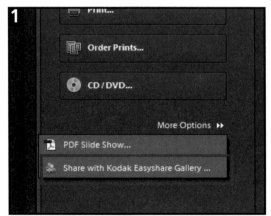

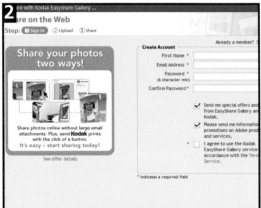

Multi-select the files to include from the Organizer workspace then choose Share with Kodak EasyShare Gallery from the More Options menu of the Share task pane. Register for the sharing service using the next few screens or if you are already a member simply log in. Select the recipients that you want to invite to share your online album from those in your contacts book. Add extra names and contact details if need be.

Add a subject heading and message to be included in the notification email and choose whether the viewers need to sign in to see the album. The photos will then be uploaded and the invitation emails sent out to the people in your contact list that you selected. At the same time a confirmation email is sent to your own email address letting you know that the album has been shared.

Don't forget that Photoshop Elements 7.0 users can also take advantage of the sharing abilities offered by the Photoshop.com website. As well as being an online space that can be used to store and display the Online Albums you create in Elements, the site can store and share images and videos in much the same way as the Kodak EasyShare Gallery does.

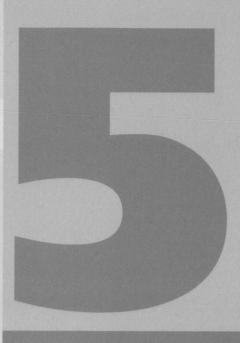

15

Theory into Practice

The Project – 'A Family History'

Now that you have an understanding of the program and many of its great features let's look at how you can use these features with a real life project. You can download all the resources you need to complete the tasks from the book's website (www. photoshopelements.net) and then you can follow along with the included video tutorials in which I perform all the steps detailed in the text. Once you are feeling confident with your new skills and abilities with Photoshop Elements 7.0 you can move on to the next step and start to substitute your own pictures for the ones I supplied.

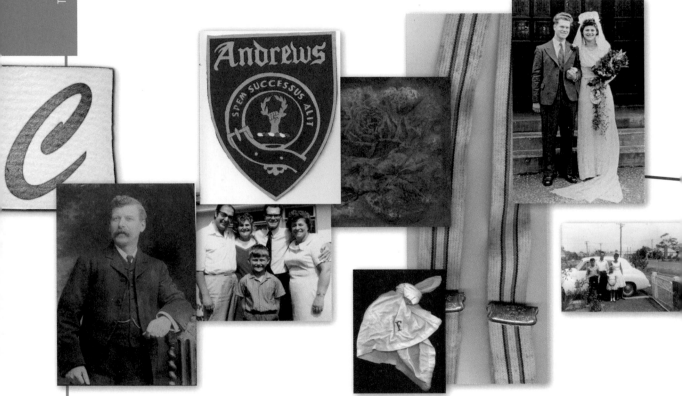

The Project – 'A Family History'

In previous versions of this book I detailed several different projects in this 'Theory into Practice' chapter. In a break from this tradition, I thought that to give a fuller view of the way that users can get the most out of Photoshop Elements, it would be useful to take a more in depth look at a single, multi-faceted project. So here I will be outlining the various steps involved in creating a multi-page Photo Book.

The content of this project will, no doubt, be very familiar to most readers, as it usually doesn't take too long before some well-meaning relative discovers that your newly acquired digital imaging skills can be put to good use restoring the pictures from your family's past. After all, most people have a collection of historical documents stored away in their lofts, or in a set of rarely-used drawers. Usually contained in boxes, or old suitcases, these collections are a

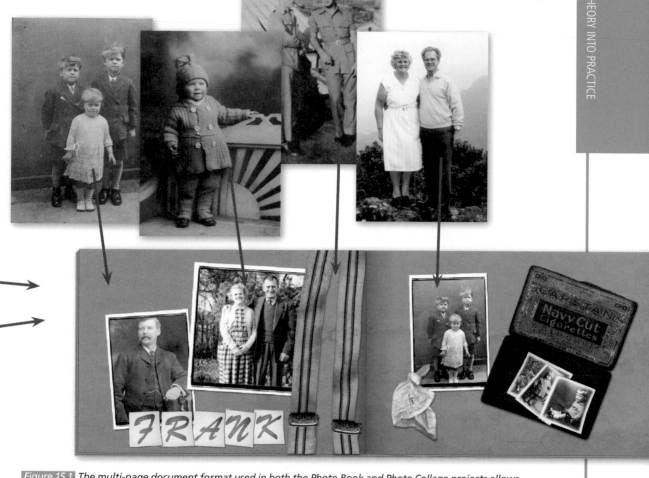

Figure 15.1 The multi-page document format used in both the Photo Book and Photo Collage projects allows the user to showcase their digital imaging skills and take advantage of design and layout options provided by these features. In this extended tutorial we take a bunch of photos and scanned mementos and produce a photo book. Along the way we take a closer look at the workflow that is best used for such projects.

mixture of photographs, special items, and letters. Undoubtedly, before long the family member with a new interest in digital imaging will inherit the task of restoring such heirlooms back to their former glory. Suffering from a mixture of scratches, stains and fading, the images can be improved and repaired with a combination of easy-to-use Elements techniques. The keepsakes too, can be converted to digital by being photographed, or even scanned, and together with the restored photos, the complete collection carefully laid out in an Elements' multi-page document.

Ready-made themes combining feature frames and textured backgrounds added as part of the creation process can be adjusted or even replaced. Extra objects can be manually added and the whole composition fine-tuned before outputting the pages to print, screen or web. So, without any more introduction, let's get started.

1. Capturing the source files

The content for this type of project is wide and varied; from old photos, slides and negatives to letters and documents and small items and mementos. A scanner is invaluable for converting a variety of object types to a digital format. As well as being able to be used with prints, some models are capable of scanning negatives and slides as well. This ability is usually provided with an auxiliary attachment to flatbed units or via a special transmission lid. Small three-dimensional objects can also be converted to digital with a scanner. Simply place the item on the cleaned glass platen before scanning as usual. Larger items can be lit and photographed separately.

As is the case whenever photographing, it is important that the scanner (or camera) settings ensure that both delicate highlight and subtle shadow details are captured. Too much contrast and these areas will be saved as pure white and pure black. If in doubt, make a test scan and check the results in Elements. If there is a problem adjust the contrast setting and scan again.

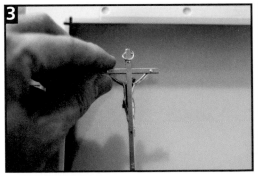

It might seem a little pedantic but it is worth spending some time cleaning the glass surface before commencing scanning operations. Remember, removing dust and marks at this stage means less work later. When capturing items that may damage the platen, cover the surface first with plastic wrap.

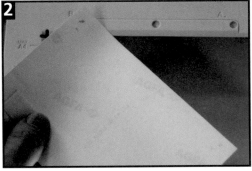

Next, clean the item to be scanned. If this is a photograph, use an anti-static cloth to help ensure no dust sticks to the surface. Place the photo on the platen making sure that the photo is orientated correctly. Close the lid and ensure that the photo is held flat against the glass.

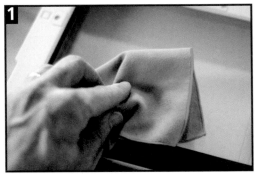

When scanning objects or mementos carefully place them on the platen, ensuring that they are sitting in contact with the glass surface as much as possible. If possible, close the scanner lid. This creates a clean background that can be easily removed later.

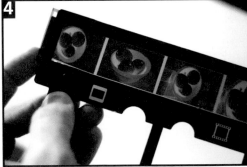

If the original is a negative (color negative shown here) then after cleaning, insert the negative into the holder making sure that the strip is oriented correctly. When setting the scanner controls select the color negative option in the scanning software.

2. Importing, tagging and creating Albums

With the source files created, import, tag and group the pictures into an Elements Album. The images used in this project are included on the book's website. After downloading the ZIP file you must de-compress or Expand the files before you can use them. Then select File > Get Photos and Videos > From Files and Folders and navigate to the now decompressed Project-Images directory on your computer.

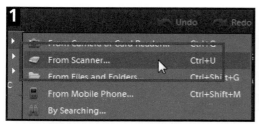

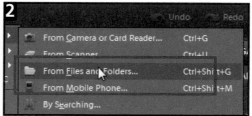

The next step is to get your photos into Photoshop Elements. If you are using the Get Photos and Video > From Scanner option then the pictures will already be imported into the Organizer workspace.

If, instead, you want to transfer your photos from your hard drive, select the From Files or Folders option. To download from a camera card choose the From Camera or Card Reader entry.

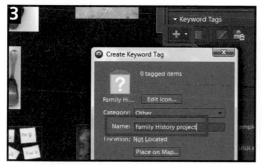

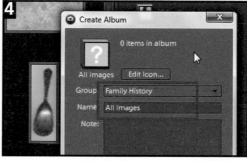

Once the photos have been transferred to Elements they will be displayed in the Organizer workspace. Add a Keyword Tag to the group by creating the tag and then selecting all of the imported images (Select > All) and dragging the tag to the pictures.

If the sequencing of the images is important for the type of project you are creating then as well as adding a keyword tag it is also a good idea to include the project images in an Album. In this example I created a new Album Group first (Family History) and then add the All Images Album heading to the group.

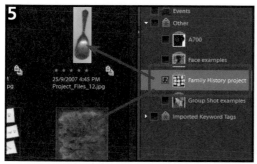

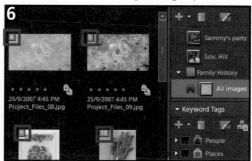

Now when you want to display the Keyword Tagged photos it is a simple matter of clicking onto the entry in the Keywords Tags section of the Organize pane. To restore the view of all images in the Catalog press the Show All button at the top of the thumbnail display.

Similarly, to show the contents of an Album click onto the entry heading. Once the Album images are displayed you can change the position of an image by dragging it to a new spot in the sequence. The number in the top left corner indicates the position of the image in the sequence.

3. Crop, Straighten, Trim

As we have seen in previous chapters, it is best to edit and enhance your photos before including them in one of the Create or Share projects, as performing these changes after the event is often more difficult or, in some cases, not even possible. So the first task is to crop, straighten or trim the photos. To perform these edits the photos must be opened from the Organizer into the Full edit workspace. To do this, select the photo and then choose the Full Edit option from the right-click menu.

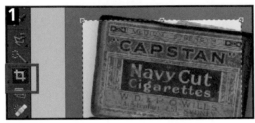

To start a new crop select the Crop tool and click-drag a marquee over the parts of the picture you want to keep. You don't have to be exact with this first rectangle as you can adjust the size and shape of the marquee by click-dragging the corner and side handles.

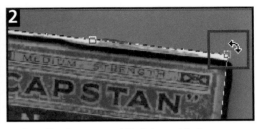

By dragging the cursor whilst it is outside the marquee it can be rotated to crop and straighten at the same time. This enables you to straighten a crooked scan or realign a horizon line that is less than horizontal. The crop is executed by clicking the 'tick' at the bottom right of the crop marquee.

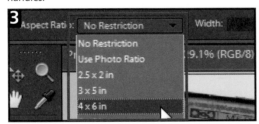

You can make a crop of a specific format, size and resolution by adding these values to the options bar before drawing the cropping marquee. Using this feature you can crop and resize in one step. To reset the Crop tool to normal choose the No Restriction option from the Aspect Ratio drop-down menu.

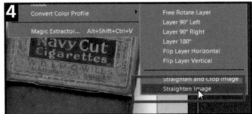

Sometimes scanned pictures can end up being slightly crooked because the original was not placed squarely on the scanning platen. The automatic Image > Rotate > Straighten Image function is designed for this scenario. When selecting this option Elements automatically rotates the main content in the photo to straighten it.

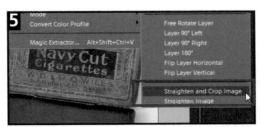

Extending the automatic squaring-off action of the Straighten feature, the Image > Rotate > Straighten and Crop Image option adds an automatic removal of the white space surrounding the corrected picture to the process. The feature works by identifying the color that surrounds the straightened image and uses this as a basis of the ensuing crop.

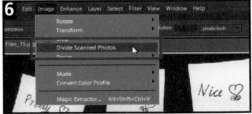

If you want to assemble and scan several images in one go then the Image > Divide Scanned Photos feature will prove a godsend. With this feature Elements will separate each of the individual pictures and place them in a new document. To ensure accurate division of photos place a colored backing sheet on top of the prints to be scanned. This helps the program distinguish where one picture starts and the other ends.

4. Brightness, Contrast, Color

The next step in the process is to make some basic enhancement changes to the brightness, contrast and color in the photo. In Photoshop Elements you can perform such changes in a variety of ways. The simplest method is to select one or more of the auto options from the Fix pane in the Organizer space and apply it to selected thumbnails. For a little more control the images can be transferred to the Full or Guided workspaces where features such as Brightness/Contrast, Levels, Color Variations or Remove Color Cast can be used.

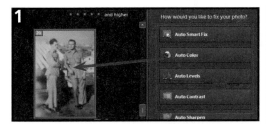

For the quickest and easiest changes to brightness, contrast and color, select the images to be enhanced and then choose one of the auto options from the list in the new Fix Pane. Select Edit > Undo if the correction is not satisfactory.

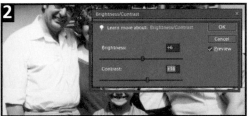

The Enhance > Adjust Lighting > Brightness/Contrast feature provides a quick and easy adjustment of the overall brightness of the image. Pushing the slider to the right lightens the midtones. Contrast is increased by moving the slider to the right and decreased by dragging it to the left.

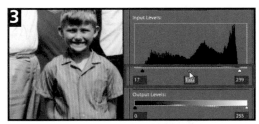

The Levels feature provides a higher level of control over both brightness and contrast. To increase contrast in a photograph move the Highlight and Shadow Input sliders in the Levels dialog towards the center of the histogram. Moving the Midtone Input slider to the left increases the brightness of the photo.

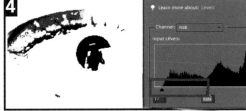

To help ensure quality adjustments holding the Alt key whilst moving the Input sliders will preview the pixels that are being converted to pure black or white (clipped). Move the sliders in until you see the first few pixels and then adjust the sliders slightly to ensure no pixels are being clipped.

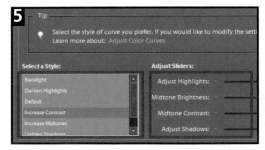

The simplest way to increase contrast with the Adjust Color Curves feature is to click on the Increase Contrast entry in the Select Style menu. To decrease contrast in a photo click on the Backlight or Darken Highlights entries. You can fine-tune the results by moving the Adjust sliders.

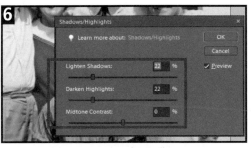

The Shadows/Highlight feature provides some brightness control using the Lighten Shadows slider. Moving this control to the right brightens the darkest portions of the image.

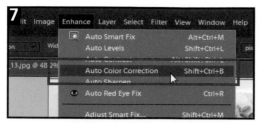

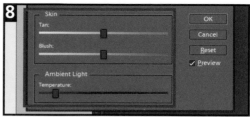

The Auto Color Correction feature provides a handy one-click correction of many color cast problems. The Auto Levels option can also provide good results and you should try these options first before moving on to more manual approaches if necessary.

When the Adjust Color for Skin Tone dialog first opens click on a section of skin tone to adjust the dialog's default settings then use the Tan, Blush and Ambient Light sliders until the skin color (and the rest of the photo) is more natural.

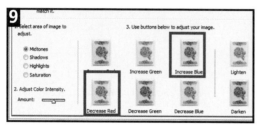

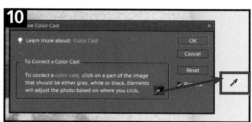

Using the Color Variations requires you to recognize the nature of the cast in your photos and then to click on a thumbnail sample that will help reduce the problem. In this example Decrease Red and Increase Green were both used to help correct the picture. The Amount slider is used to alter the degree of change applied when each thumbnail sample is pressed.

The Remove Color Cast feature works well if there is a part of the problem picture that is meant to be a neutral gray or white. After selecting the feature you then use the eyedropper cursor to click on the neutral picture part. Elements will change the color at this point to even amounts of red, green and blue and then apply the same changes to the rest of the photo.

 # 5. Removing backgrounds

With the photos straightened, cropped and enhanced, let's now turn our attention to object images. These mementos are often included in compositions without their backgrounds and with the addition of a simple drop shadow to make them appear as though they are sitting on the surface of the layout. So removing backgrounds is a task that you may encounter in your

project creation adventures and thankfully Photoshop Elements has several ways to ease the pain of this sometimes frustrating activity – from the simple Magic Eraser tool, to the more interactive Magic Extractor option and then, for the really tricky situations, a two-step process of selecting the background (using the new Quick Selection tool) and then deleting the background. In all techniques the background layer needs to be changed to a standard image layer first by double-clicking on the Layer entry and then okaying the New Layer dialog.

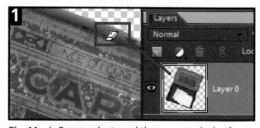

The Magic Eraser selects and then erases pixels of similar tone and color. The Tolerance setting determines how alike the pixels need to be before they are erased. High settings will include more pixels of varying shades and colors. Select the Contiguous option to force the tool to select pixels that are adjacent to each other and choose Use All Layers if you want to sample the color to be erased from a mixture of all visible layers.

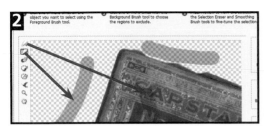

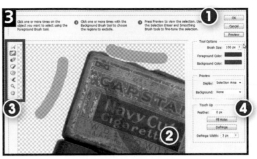

The Magic Extractor feature quickly removes the background of a picture whilst retaining the subject in the foreground. The feature works by marking, with a scribbled line or a series of dots, the foreground (to be kept) and the background (to be removed) parts of the picture. Elements then automatically finds all the background parts in the picture and removes them from the document, filling the space with your choice of black, gray, white or transparency.

The Magic Extractor works within its own window (1), which includes a zoomable preview area (2), a set of tools for marking the fore- and background parts of a photo (3), touch-up options to refine extraction results (4) as well as settings to select what will fill the background area once it is removed.

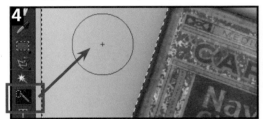

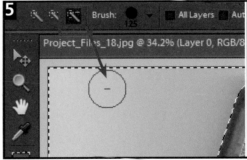

The new Quick Selection tool combines the outlining ability of a Marquee tool with the color selection characteristics of the Magic Wand. The selection is created by painting over the parts of the picture that you want to select. In this case it is the background of the photo that we want to include in the selection. The selection outline will grow as you continue to paint. When you release the mouse button the tool will automatically refine the selection further.

Like other selection tools, the Quick Selection tool also provides the option to add to or take away from an existing selection using either the Shift (add) or Alt/Option (take away) keys, or by clicking one of the selection mode buttons in the tool's options bar.

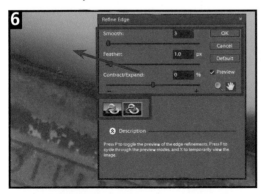

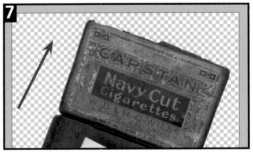

To coincide with the release of this new Selection tool, Adobe has also created a new way to customize the selections you make. The Refine Edge feature is accessed via Select > Refine Edge. The feature brings together four different controls for adjusting the edges of the selection with two selection edge preview options. Use the settings here to preview and then fine-tune the quality of the selection edge used to outline the background of the photo.

With the background now carefully selected, this part of the photo can be deleted by hitting the Delete key. This will cause the selected area to be replaced with a checker board pattern indicating the area is now transparent. One way to ensure that the items placed in your composition look like they are meant to be there is to pay attention to the quality of the edge between the item and the transparent background. A harsh, sharp edge looks artificial whereas a softer edge seems more realistic. Be sure to add a slight Feather of 1 pixel to the selection before deleting the background.

THEORY INTO PRACTICE

 ## 6. Restore and retouch

Now onto restoring some of those older images. The most basic of tools used for repairing spots, marks and in some cases tears across the photo, is the Clone Stamp tool. The tool is a good place to start when first restoring your photos. Using the tool is a two-step process – select the area to be sampled and then paint over the mark. The same process is used when working with the more sophisticated Healing Brush tool. So skills built here can be easily transferred to Healing Brush work later.

In contrast the Spot Healing Brush provides a simpler, one-step solution, where the texture and color of the area surrounding the brush tip are used to paint over the mark or scratch. In most cases this tool works extremely well, but if you do find unwanted detail creeping into your retouched areas switch to the Clone Stamp (or Healing Brush tool) and select your own sample points.

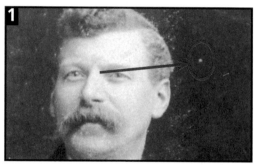

The Clone Stamp tool works by sampling a selected area and pasting the characteristics of this area over the blemish, so the first step in the process is to identify the areas in your picture that need repair. Make sure that the image layer you want to sample is selected.

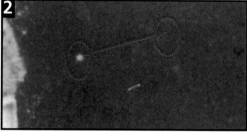

Next, locate areas in the photograph that are similar in tone, texture and color to the areas needing to be fixed. Use these areas to paint over the dust and scratches marks. Select the area to be sampled by holding down the Alt key and clicking the mouse button when the cursor (now changed to cross hairs) is over a part of the image that suits the area to be repaired.

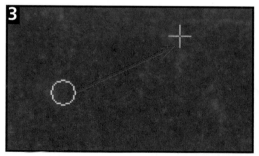

With the sample point selected you can now move the cursor to the area to be fixed. Click on the blemish and a copy of the sample point area is pasted over the mark. Depending on how well you chose the sample area, the blemish will now be blended into the background seamlessly. Continue to click, repairing more blemishes as you go.

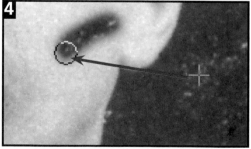

You may need to reselect your sample point if you find that the color, texture or tone doesn't match the surrounds of the blemish. It may also be necessary to change brush size to suit different repair tasks. Changing the brush size will alter the size of both the Sample and Stamp areas.

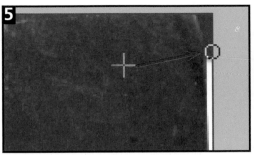

For difficult repair jobs where you need to recreate picture elements select a similar part from the photograph as your sample point. Here, the background is sampled to help repair the missing section of the scan in the upper right-hand corner.

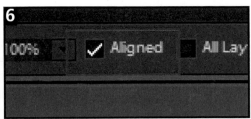

Switching between aligned and non-aligned can really help you with rebuilding picture parts. **Aligned** sets the sample point so that it remains the same distance from the stamped area no matter where on the picture you start to click, and **Non-aligned** repositions the sample point back to the original sample spot each time the mouse is moved and then clicked.

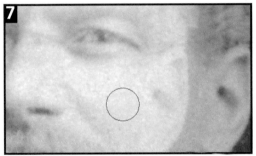

The Clone Overlay option was new for Photoshop Elements 6 and provides a ghosted view of the sampled area over the main image when painting with the Clone Stamp tool. This can be very helpful when trying to align specific sample parts with the background image. Activate the feature by selecting the Show Overlay setting in the Clone Overlay options dialog accessed via the feature's button in the Clone Stamp tool bar.

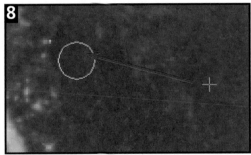

The Healing Brush is designed to work in a similar way to the Clone tool; the user selects the area (Alt-click) to be sampled before painting and then proceeds to drag the brush tip over the area to be repaired. The tool achieves such great results by merging background and source area details as you paint. Just as with the Clone Stamp tool, the size and edge hardness of the current brush determines the characteristics of the Healing Brush tool tip

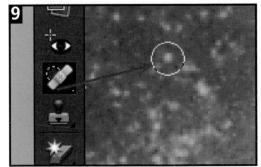

The Spot version of the Healing Brush removes the sampling step from the process. To use the brush you simply select the feature, adjust the brush tip size and harness and then click onto the blemish. Almost magically the Brush will analyse the surrounding texture, color and tones and use this as a basis for painting over the problem area.

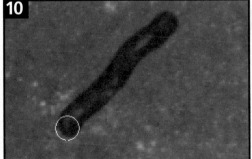

The Spot Healing Brush can also be used for removing marks, hairs, streaks or cracks by click-dragging the tool across the offending blemish.
Pro's tip: If unwanted detail is used to cover the repaired area, undo the changes and then draw around the area to be healed with the Lasso tool and apply the brush again. This restricts the area around the blemish that the tool uses to heal.

7. Convert to gray and tint

With the bulk of the enhancement tasks out of the way, it is now time to consider some more aesthetic options. When thinking of historical photos most people can recall the sepia toned images of their relatives found in family photo albums. You can recreate the look and feel of these old style pictures by converting color photos to gray and then tinting them the familiar sepia brown hue. There are several options for changing color photos to monochrome including the Convert to Black and White feature first introduced in 5.0 as well as saturation and mode changes. In terms of tinting, Elements contains features for applying a single color change across the whole of the image or for separately tinting the highlights and shadows.

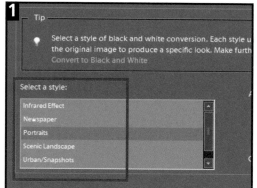

The Convert to Black and White feature (Enhance > Convert to Black and White) provides custom mapping of color to gray. Use the Style presets in the Convert to Black and White dialog to establish the basic look of the conversion. Preview the results in the After image in the top right of the dialog.

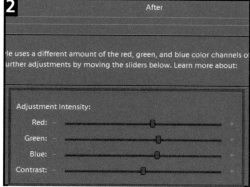

Next, fine-tune how colors map to specific grays using the Adjustment Intensity sliders. Drag to the right to emphasize these colors in the conversion and drag the controls for the opposite colors to the left to add more contrast to the conversion.

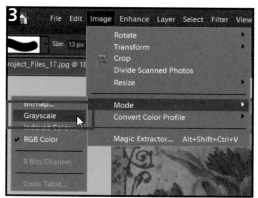

The simplest way to convert a color photo to monochrome is to select the Image > Mode > Grayscale option and then click on the OK button in the Discard Color warning box. However, you may need to adjust the image's contrast after performing this change. Also, the mode of the photo will need to be changed back to RGB Color when it comes time to tint the picture.

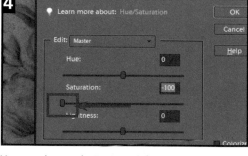

You can also use the Remove Color option (Enhance > Adjust Color > Remove Color). This feature has the advantage of keeping the photo in RGB mode after the conversion, allowing hand coloring of the photo. The one-step Remove Color feature produces the same results as manually desaturating the photo using the controls in the Hue/Saturation feature (Enhance > Adjust Color > Adjust Hue/Saturation). With the Hue/Saturation dialog open, drag the Saturation slider all the way to the left (a setting of -100) to produce a grayscale result.

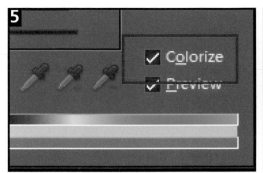

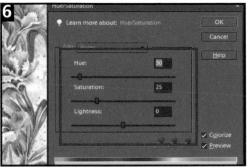

The simplest way to add a tint to your color photos and convert them to monochrome in one step is to make use of the Colorize option in the Adjust Hue Saturation feature in the Enhance > Adjust Color menu. After the Hue/Saturation dialog is opened proceed to the bottom right-hand corner of the dialog and select the Colorize option. Immediately the image will be changed to a tinted monochrome.

With the dialog still open use the Hue slider to alter the color of the tint. Traditional looking sepia tone is approximately a value of 30 and a blue tone equivalent can be found at a value of 215. The strength of the color is controlled by the Saturation slider.

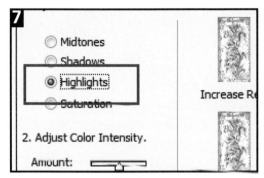

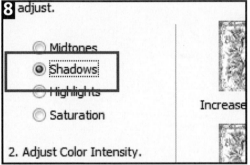

To create a split tone effect (highlights one color and shadows a different hue) select the Color Variations option from the Enhance > Adjust Color menu. Check the Highlights option and then click on the thumbnail for the color to apply to these tones. Here I decreased Blue.

Without closing the Color Variations dialog now check the Shadows option and add a different color to these image tones. In the example the shadows were colored blue by clicking the Increase Blue thumbnail repeatedly. Click OK to apply the split toning changes.

 ## 8. Creating a Photo Book

Following the suggested Elements workflow we now have successfully enhanced, edited and adjusted the candidate photos so that they are now ready for inclusion in a new photo project. In this case the family history pictures and mementos will be used as the basis for a new multi-page Photo Book project. Keep in mind when creating such books that the minimum number of pages accepted by the online publisher (Kodak EasyShare Gallery) is 20, and so unless you particularly want a few pages free of photos, ensure that you have enough content to fill all 20 book pages. Also remember that the first image in the Project Bin (or Album used for the project) is featured on the title page, which can be seen through a die-cut hole in the front cover. For this reason, it is a good idea to create a specific Elements document that can be used for the title page.

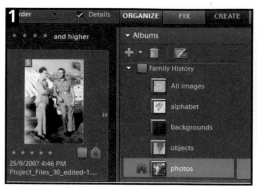

When working with a range of different types of project content it is helpful to break the content into different categories. Here I have separated the documents into several Albums arranged under one Album Group heading.

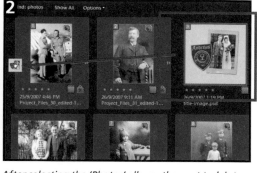

After selecting the 'Photos' album, the next task is to drag the individual images around the workspace to adjust the sequencing of the group. For example the specially created title photo is dragged to the first position in the album so that it will be used on the title page of the Photo Book.

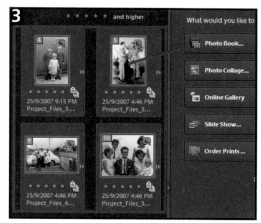

The thumbnails of the photos to include are then selected in the Organizer workspace before clicking on the Photo Book entry in the Create task pane.

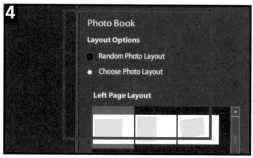

The Edit workspace opens and the selected images are automatically placed into the Project Bin at the bottom of the screen. The Task pane on the right of the workspace displays the first group of Photo Book creation settings. Choose the Layout option to use for the book. Here I use the Choose Photo Layout entry to allow more design options for left and right pages. Click Next to display a second group of settings.

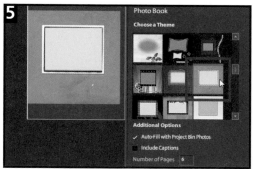

Select a theme (matched background and frames set) from the list of thumbnails. A larger preview of the design will be displayed next to the pane to help with selection. In this example I chose the Auto Fill but not the Add Captions option in the section beneath the Themes area. Click the Done button to create the multi-page document.

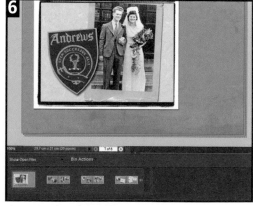

The pages are created and the photos are inserted with associated frames onto ready-made backgrounds. The book is displayed in a new preview mode with the pages listed separately in the Project Bin.

9. Add extra elements and fine-tune

As you can see from the results the Photo Book creation process automatically places images in frames and positions them on the pages. The next step in the process is to fine-tune the layout and how the images are framed. After that, extra content can be added to the pages. This can include text and graphics plus those all important mementos that you have so carefully extracted from their backgrounds. To make these changes use the steps below.

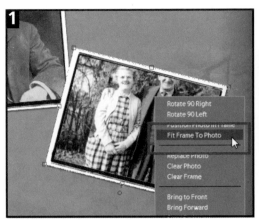

The frame and its contents (together) can be edited using either the handles on the edge or options in the right-click menu. Keep in mind that the frame and the picture that it holds can be edited separately. Single-clicking the frame selects the frame and the picture together so that any changes made in this mode will affect both components. The quickest way to enlarge a frame to suit an image that has been cropped is to select the Fit Frame to Photo option.

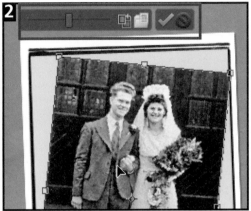

The picture inside the frame can be scaled and rotated independent of the frame by firstly double-clicking the photo (to select the picture without the frame) and then click-dragging the side, corner or rotate handles. Alternatively you can scale, rotate 90° left, replace the current picture with a new one and apply or cancel the changes with the buttons in the pop-up control that appears at the top of the picture border.

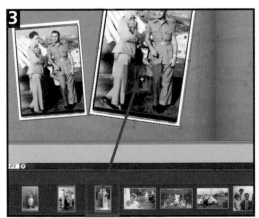

To replace existing photos with different images whilst still retaining the frame, select the frame first and then click-drag a picture from the Project Bin to the frame. This action swaps the two pictures. Alternatively you can select the Replace Photo entry from the right-click menu and choose a new picture via the file dialog that is displayed.

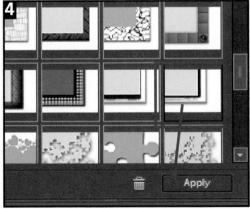

To add new photos to an existing layout you need to start by adding a new blank frame to the composition. Do this by clicking on the selected frame in the Artwork section of the Artwork panel in the Create pane and pressing the Apply button. A new frame will be created in the middle of the current page of the document.

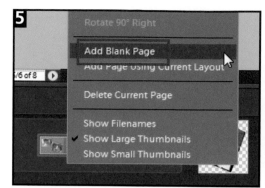

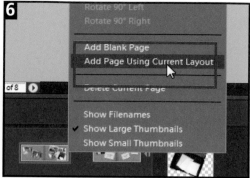

In Elements you have two options for creating new pages that are displayed in the right-click menu when the cursor is over the pages in the Project Bin. The Add Blank Page option is used to add a white page with no frames, backgrounds or themes present. Once the page is created then text, graphics, shapes, frames, backgrounds and special effects can be added from the Artwork panel.

The second option is the Add Page Using Current Layout. This feature duplicates the layout settings of the selected page when creating the new one. Use this option to add new pages to a group of pages that already contain a background and frames as it will help to keep the look of the whole document consistent. The new page is then added to the document and a new thumbnail is displayed in the Project Bin to the right of the selected page.

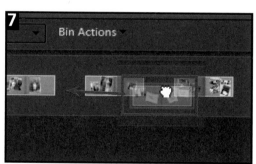

Multi-page Photo Creation (.PSE) documents are displayed in the Photo Bin with a shaded background. The document can be expanded or collapsed via the sideways arrow button on the right of the last thumbnail. Changing the position of the page's thumbnail in the Project Bin alters the page's actual position in the document. Moving pages is a simple task, just click on the page to move and drag it to a new location in the document, release the mouse button and the page is relocated.

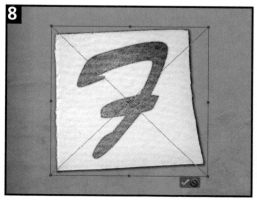

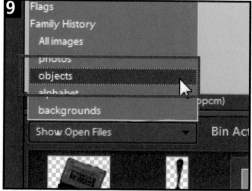

To add in the mementos (minus their backgrounds) that you created earlier you will need to use the File > Place option in the Edit space. Other images (without transparent backgrounds) can be opened and then dragged from the Project Bin onto the Photo Book.

Alternatively, you can display the contents of any Elements Album inside the Project Bin. Simply click on the Show menu positioned in the top left of the Project Bin. Choose the Album entry from the list provided and the bin will then show the album images.

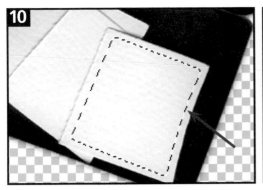

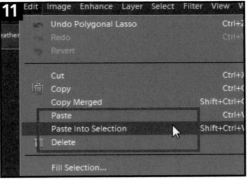

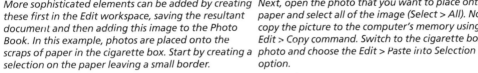

More sophisticated elements can be added by creating these first in the Edit workspace, saving the resultant document and then adding this image to the Photo Book. In this example, photos are placed onto the scraps of paper in the cigarette box. Start by creating a selection on the paper leaving a small border.

Next, open the photo that you want to place onto the paper and select all of the image (Select > All). Now copy the picture to the computer's memory using the Edit > Copy command. Switch to the cigarette box photo and choose the Edit > Paste into Selection option.

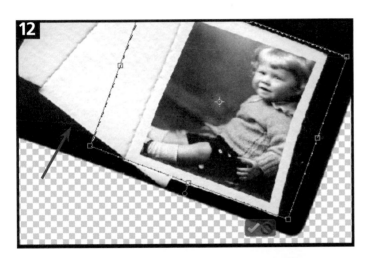

Before doing anything else choose the Free Transform feature (Ctrl T) and use the corner handles to make the image smaller and the rotate handle to pivot the photo. When you have finished click on the Commit button to apply the transformation.

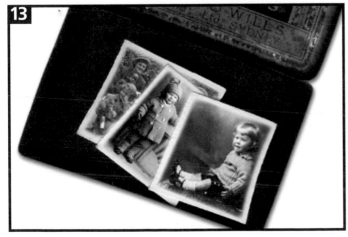

Repeat these steps until all three papers have been filled with project images. Save the document and then use File > Place to add the image to the Photo Book composition. Use Free Transform again to adjust its size to suit the other elements on the page.

10. Output to print

With the book pages now completed, you can output the multi-page document. You have two options – to upload the Photo Book to a print company for professional printing or binding, or output the document to a desktop machine for printing at home.

The Photo Book project is designed specifically to make the process of ordering online much simpler than in previous editions. Kodak EasyShare Gallery still handles the printing and binding but both Kodak and Adobe have streamlined the process and steps between completing the book document and completing the order. Printing at home is also a viable alternative as many paper companies can supply double-sided paper allowing you to print your book document 'back to back' just like the professionals. The binding component can be handled by your corner office supplies store for a small charge.

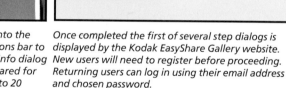

With the multi-page document open click onto the Print button in the floating Photo Book options bar to start the process. Elements then displays an Info dialog indicating that the book files are being prepared for uploading and that this process can take up to 20 minutes.

Once completed the first of several step dialogs is displayed by the Kodak EasyShare Gallery website. New users will need to register before proceeding. Returning users can log in using their email address and chosen password.

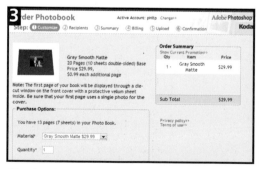

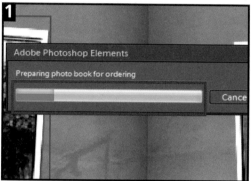

After logging in Kodak takes you through a six-step process that involves selecting the finish of the completed book, choosing recipients, billing details, uploading the files and confirming the order. With this process complete the book is printed and bound and shipped back to you via post or courier.

For outputting to a desktop printer select the File > Print option with the document open in the Edit workspace. Elements will then display the standard Print dialog with the exception that just beneath the preview area there are Forward and Back buttons enabling you to flip through the pages of the document.

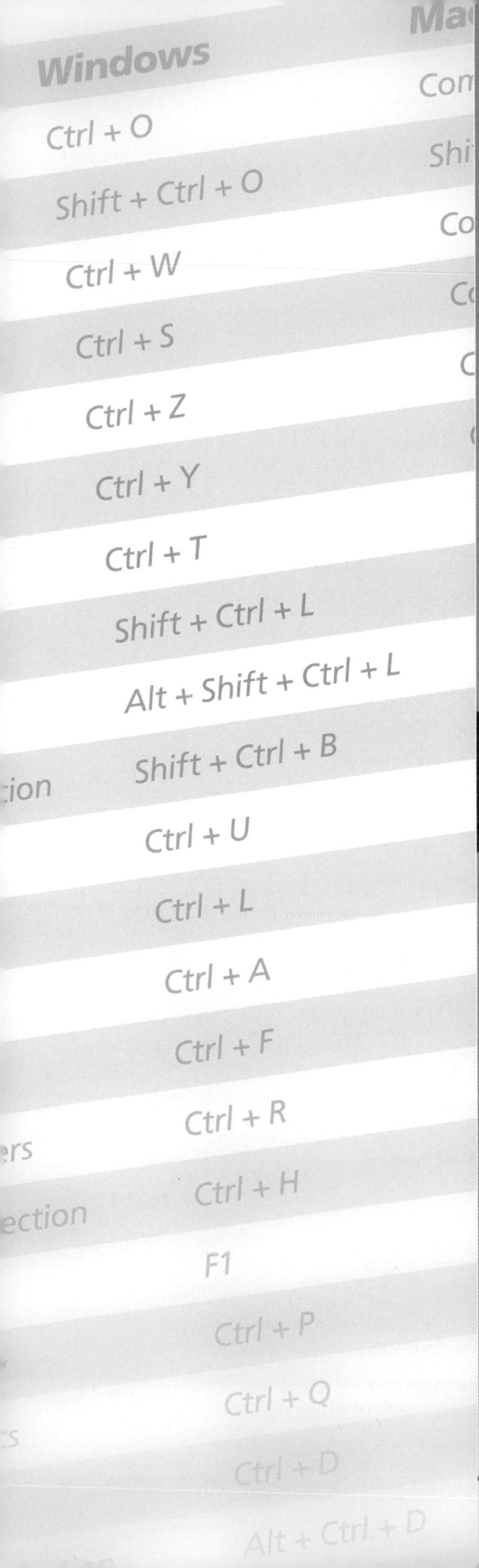

Windows

Ctrl + O

Shift + Ctrl + O

Ctrl + W

Ctrl + S

Ctrl + Z

Ctrl + Y

Ctrl + T

Shift + Ctrl + L

Alt + Shift + Ctrl + L

Shift + Ctrl + B

Ctrl + U

Ctrl + L

Ctrl + A

Ctrl + F

Ctrl + R

Ctrl + H

F1

Ctrl + P

Ctrl + Q

Ctrl + D

Alt + Ctrl + D

Appendices

Jargon buster

Keyboard shortcuts

Elements/Photoshop feature
equivalents

Jargon buster

A >>

Aliasing The jaggy edges that appear in bitmap images with curves or lines at any angle other than multiples of 90°. The Anti-aliasing function in Elements softens around the edges of images to help make the problem less noticeable. See Figure A.1.

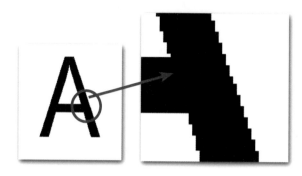

Figure A.1 Aliasing is most noticeable on the edges of text and objects with diagonal or curving edges.

Aspect ratio This is usually found in dialog boxes concerned with changes of image size and refers to the relationship between the width and height of a picture. The maintaining of an image's aspect ratio means that this relationship will remain the same even when the image is enlarged or reduced. See Figure A.2.

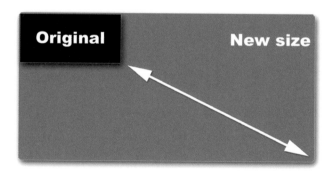

Figure A.2 Maintaining the aspect ratio of your photograph when you enlarge or reduce sizes will help guarantee that all your picture elements remain in proportion.

B >>

Background printing A printing method that allows the user to continue working whilst an image or document is being printed.

Batch processing or **Process Multiple Files** as it is known in Elements 6 and 7. Refers to a function or a series of commands being applied to several files at one time. This function is useful for making the same changes to a folder full of images. In Elements this function is found under the File menu and is useful for converting groups of image files from one format to another.

Bit Stands for 'binary digit' and refers to the smallest part of information that makes up a digital file. It has a value of only 0 or 1. Eight of these bits make up one byte of data.

Bitmap or **'raster'** The form in which digital photographs are stored which is made up of a matrix of pixels. Many people confuse this term with Bitmap mode, which refers to a pure black and white picture that contains no colors or gray tones.

Blend mode The way in which a color or a layer interacts with others below it. The most important after Normal are probably Multiply, which darkens everything, Screen, which adds to the colors to make everything lighter, Lighten, which lightens only colors darker than itself, and Darken, which darkens only colors lighter than itself. Both the latter therefore flatten contrast. Color maintains the shading of a color but alters the color to itself. Glows therefore are achieved using Screen mode, and Shadows using Multiply.

Brightness range The range of brightnesses between shadow and highlight areas of an image.

Burn tool Used to darken an image; can be targeted to affect just the shadows, midtones or highlights. Opposite to Dodge. Part of the toning trio, that also includes the Sponge.

Byte This is the standard unit of digital storage. One byte is made up of 8 bits and can have any value between 0 and 255. 1024 bytes are equal to 1 kilobyte. 1024 kilobytes are equal to 1 megabyte. 1024 megabytes are equal to 1 gigabyte.

C ≫

CCD or **Charge Coupled Device** Many of these devices placed in a grid format comprise the sensor of most modern digital cameras. See Figure A.3.

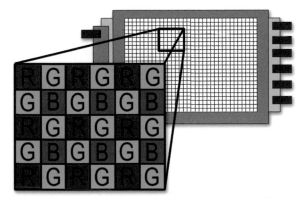

Figure A.3 The CCD sensor is the digital equivalent of film and is used to record the photograph.

Clone Stamp or **Rubber Stamp tool** Allows a user to copy a part of an image to somewhere else. It is therefore ideal for repair work, e.g. unwanted spots or blemishes. Equivalent to Copy and Paste in a brush.

Color mode The way that an image represents the colors that it contains. Different color modes include Bitmap, RGB and Grayscale.

Compression A process where digital files are made smaller to save on storage space or transmission time. Compression is available in two types – lossy, where parts of the original image are lost at the compression stage, and lossless, where the integrity of the file is maintained during the compression process. JPEG and GIF use lossy compression whereas TIFF is a lossless format.

D >>

Digitize This is the process by which analog images or signals are sampled and changed into digital form.

Dodge tool Used for lightening areas in an image. See also Burn tool.

DPI or ***Dots per inch*** A term used to indicate the resolution of a printed photo. PPI or Pixels Per Inch refers to the resolution of a digital picture. Generally, the higher the DPI or PPI the better quality the photo. See Figure A.4.

Dynamic range The measure of the range of brightness levels that can be recorded by a sensor.

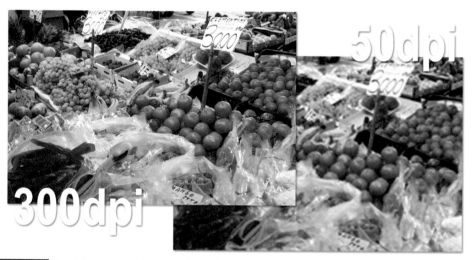

Figure A.4 *The dpi or dots per inch term is used as a measurement of the resolution of a printed picture. The higher the dpi value the higher the image's resolution will be.*

E >>

Enhancement A term that refers to changes in brightness, color and contrast which are designed to improve the overall look of an image.

F >>

File format The way that a digital image is stored. Different formats have different characteristics. Some are cross-platform, others have inbuilt compression capabilities.

Filter In digital terms a filter is a way of applying a set of image characteristics to the whole or part of an image. Most image-editing programs contain a range of filters that can be used for creating special effects.

Front page Sometimes called the home or index page, refers to the initial screen that the viewer sees when logging on to a website. Often the name and spelling of this page file are critical if it is to work on the web server. Consult your ISP staff for the precise name to be used with your site.

G >>

Gamma The contrast of the midtone areas of a digital image.

Gamut The range of colors or hues that can be printed or displayed by particular devices.

Gaussian Blur When applied to an image or a selection this filter softens or blurs the image.

GIF or ***Graphic Interchange Format*** An indexed color mode that contains a maximum of 256 colors that can be mapped to any palette of actual colors. It is extensively used for web graphics, buttons and logos, and small animated images.

Grayscale A monochrome image containing just monochrome tones ranging from white through a range of grays to black.

H >>

Histogram A graph that represents the tonal distribution of pixels within a digital image. From version 3.0 of Elements the histogram is located under the Windows menu. See Figure A.5.

History Adobe's form of Multiple Undo.

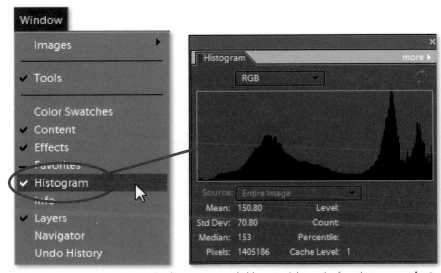

Figure A.5 The histogram is a visual representation of the pixels that make up your digital photograph.

Hot linked A piece of text, graphic or picture that has been designed to act as a button on a web page. When the viewer clicks the hot linked item they are usually transported to another page or part of a website.

HTML The Hyper Text Mark Up Language is the code used to create web pages. The characteristics of pages are stored in this language and when a page file is downloaded to your computer the machine lays out and displays the text, image and graphics according to what is stated in the HTML file.

Hue Refers to the color of the light and is separate from how light or dark it is.

I >>

Image layers Images in Elements can be made up of many layers. Each layer will contain part of the picture. When viewed together all layers appear to make up a single continuous image. Special effects and filters can be applied to layers individually. See Figure A.6.

Interpolation This is the process used by image-editing programs to increase the resolution of a digital image. Using fuzzy logic the program makes up the extra pixels that are placed between the original ones that were generated at the time of scanning.

ISP The Internet Service Provider is the company that hosts or stores web pages. If you access the web via a dial-up account then you will usually have a portion of free space allocated for use for your own site; others can obtain free (with a small banner advert attached) space from companies like www.tripod.com.

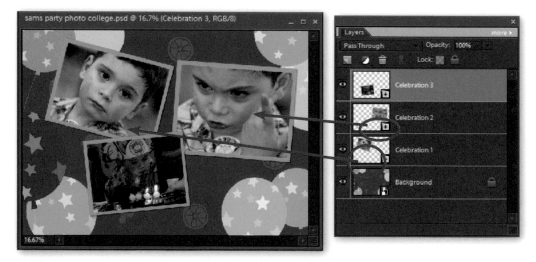

Figure A.6 *Layers help keep different parts of a complex image separate. This makes editing and enhancement steps easier.*

Book resources and video tutorials can be found at **www.photoshopelements.net**

J >>

JPEG A file format designed by the Joint Photographic Experts Group that has inbuilt lossy compression that enables a massive reduction in file sizes for digital images. Used extensively on the web and by press professionals for transmitting images back to newsdesks worldwide. See Figure A.7.

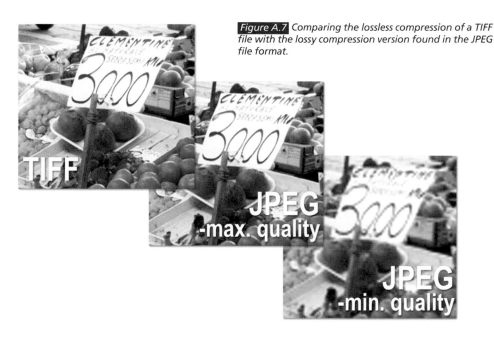

Figure A.7 *Comparing the lossless compression of a TIFF file with the lossy compression version found in the JPEG file format.*

L >>

Layer opacity The opacity or transparency of each layer can be changed independently. Depending on the level of opacity the parts of the layer beneath will become visible. You can change the opacity of each layer by moving the Opacity slider in the Layers palette.

LCD or **Liquid Crystal Display** A display screen type used in preview screens on the back of digital cameras, in laptop computers and more and more as replacement desktop screens.

Liquify A tool that uses brushes to perform distortions upon selections or the whole of an image.

M >>

Marquee A rectangular selection made by clicking and dragging to an opposite corner.

Megapixel One million pixels. Used to describe the resolution of digital camera sensors.

N >>

Navigator In Elements, a small scalable palette showing the entire image with the possibility of displaying a box representing the current image window frame. The frame's color can be altered; a new frame can be drawn (scaling the image window with it) by holding the Command/Ctrl keys and making a new marquee. The frame can be dragged around the entire image with the Hand tool. The Zoom tools (mountain icons) can be clicked, the slider can be dragged, or a figure can be entered as a percentage.

O >>

Optical resolution The resolution that a scanner uses to sample the original image. This is often different from the highest resolution quoted for the scanner as this is scaled up by interpolating the optically scanned file.

Options bar Long bar beneath the menu bar, which immediately displays the various settings for whichever tool is currently selected.

P >>

Palette A window that is used for the alteration of image characteristics: Properties palette, Layers palette, Styles palette, Hints palette, file browser, History, etc. These can be docked together vertically around the main image window or if used less frequently can be docked in the Palette Bin to the right of the main workspace or in the Palette Well (for earlier versions of Elements) at the top right of the screen (dark gray area).

Pixel Short for 'picture element', refers to the smallest image part of a digital photograph.

Process Multiple Files see **Batch processing**.

R >>

RGB All colors in the image are made up of a mixture of Red, Green and Blue colors. This is the typical mode used for desktop scanners, painting programs and digital cameras.

S >>

Sponge tool Used for saturating or desaturating part of an image that is exaggerating or lessening the color component as opposed to the lightness or darkness.

Status bar Attached to the base of the window (Mac) or beneath the window (PC). Can be altered to display a series of items from Scratch Disk usage and file size to the time it took to carry out the last action or the name of the current tool.

Stock A printing term referring to the type of paper or card that the image or text is to be printed on.

Swatches In Elements, refers to a palette that can display and store specific individual colors for immediate or repeated use.

T >>

Thumbnail A low-resolution preview version of larger image files used to check before opening the full version.

TIFF or ***Tagged Image File Format*** A file format that is widely used by imaging professionals. The format can be used across both Macintosh and PC platforms and has a lossless compression system built in.

W >>

Warp Text feature A means of creating differing distortions to pieces of text such as arcs and flag ripples.

Keyboard shortcuts

General >>

Action	Windows (ver. 7.0)	Macintosh (ver. 6.0)
Open a file	Ctrl + O	Command + O
Open file browser	–	Shift + Command + O
Close a file	Ctrl + W	Command + W
Save a file	Ctrl + S	Command + S
Step backward	Ctrl + Z	Command + Z
Step forward	Ctrl + Y	Command + Y
Free Transform	Ctrl + T	Command + T
Auto levels	Shift + Ctrl + L	Shift + Command + L
Auto contrast	Alt + Shift + Ctrl + L	Option + Shift + Command + L
Auto Color Correction	Shift + Ctrl + B	Shift + Command + B
Convert to Black and White	Alt + Ctrl + B	Option + Command B
Hue/Saturation	Ctrl + U	Command + U
Levels	Ctrl + L	Command + L
Select All	Ctrl + A	Command + A
Apply last filter	Ctrl + F	Command + F
Show/Hide rulers	Shft + Ctrl + R	Command + R
Show/Hide selection	Ctrl + H	Command + H
Help	F1	Command + ?
Print Preview	Ctrl + P	Command + P
Exit Elements	Ctrl + Q	Command + Q
Deselect	Ctrl + D	Command + D
Feather a selection	Alt + Ctrl + D	Option + Command + D

Viewing >>

Action	Windows	Macintosh
Fit image on screen	Ctrl + 0	Command + 0
100% magnification	Alt + Ctrl + 0	Option + Command + 0
Zoom in	Ctrl + +	Command + +
Zoom out	Ctrl + -	Command + -
Scroll image with Hand tool	Spacebar + drag mouse pointer	Spacebar + drag mouse pointer
Scroll up or down 1 screen	Page Up or Page Down	Page Up or Page Down

Selection/Drawing tools >>

Action	Windows	Macintosh
Add to an existing selection	Shift + Selection tool	Shift + Selection tool
Subtract from an existing selection	Alt + Selection tool	Command + Selection tool
Constrain Marquee to square or circle	Shift + drag Selection tool	Shift + drag Selection tool
Draw Marquee from center	Alt + drag Selection tool	Option + drag Selection tool
Constrain Shape tool to square or circle	Shift + drag Shape tool	Shift + drag Shape tool
Draw Shape tool from center	Alt + drag Shape tool	Option + drag Shape tool
Exit Cropping tool	Esc	Esc
Enter Cropping tool selection	Enter	Return
Switch Magnetic Lasso to Lasso	Alt + drag tool	Option + drag tool
Switch Magnetic Lasso to Polygonal Lasso	Alt + drag tool	Option + drag tool
Switch from Selection to Move tool	Ctrl (except if Hand tool is selected)	Command

Painting >>

Action	Windows	Macintosh
Change to Eyedropper	Alt + painting or Shape tool	Option + painting or Shape tool
Cycle through blending modes	Shift + + or -	Shift + + or -
Set exposure or opacity for painting	Painting tool + Number key (%= number key × 10)	Painting tool + Number key (%= number key × 10)
Display Fill dialog box	Shift + Backspace	Shift + Delete
Perform Fill with background color	Ctrl + Backspace	Command + Delete
Change Brush tip size	[to decrease size] to increase size	[to decrease size] to increase size
Change Brush tip hardness	Shift + [to decrease hardness Shift +] to increase hardness	Shift + [to decrease hardness Shift +] to increase hardness

Type editing >>

Action	Windows	Macintosh
Select word	Double-click	Double-click
Select line	Triple-click	Triple-click
Decrease font size by 2 points/pixels	Selected text + Shift + <	Selected text + Shift + <
Increase font size by 2 points/pixels	Selected text + Shift + >	Selected text + Shift + >

Elements/Photoshop feature equivalents

Activity	Elements	Photoshop
Lighten shadow areas in an image	Fill Flash feature (ver. 1.0/2.0), Shadows/Highlights (ver. 3.0-7.0) Adjust Color Curves (ver. 5.0-7.0)	Curves and Shadow/ Highlight feature
Darken highlight areas in an image	Backlighting feature (ver. 1.0/2.0), Shadows/Highlights (ver. 3.0-7.0) Adjust Color Curves (ver. 5.0-7.0)	Curves and Shadow/ Highlight feature
Transformation	Image > Transform	Edit > Transform
Rotate layer	Image > Rotate > Layer 90° left	Edit > Transform > Rotate 90° CCW
Rotate canvas	Image > Rotate > 90° left	Image > Rotate Canvas > 90° CW
Resize image	Image > Resize > Image Size	Image > Image Size
Resize canvas	Image > Resize > Canvas Size	Image > Canvas Size
Batch dialog	File > Batch Processing or File > Process Multiple Files	File > Automate > Batch
Web Photo Gallery	File > Create Web Photo Gallery or Create>HTML Photo Gallery	File > Automate > Web Photo Gallery
Contact Sheet	File > Print Layouts > Contact Sheet or File > Process Multiple Files	File > Automate > Contact Sheet II
Picture Package	File > Print Layouts > Picture Package or File > Process multiple Files	File > Automate > Picture Package
Auto Levels	Enhance > Auto Levels	Image > Adjustments > Auto Levels
Auto Contrast	Enhance > Auto Contrast	Image > Adjustments > Auto Contrast
Auto Color Correction	Enhance > Auto Color Correction	Image > Adjustments > Auto Color
Hue/Saturation	Enhance > Adjust Color > Hue/ Saturation	Image > Adjustments > Hue/Saturation
Color Variations	Enhance > Adjust Color > Color Variations	Image > Adjustments > Variations
Brightness/Contrast	Enhance > Adjust Brightness/Contrast > Brightness/Contrast	Image > Adjustment > Brightness/Contrast
Levels	Enhance > Adjust Brightness/Contrast > Levels	Image > Adjustments > Levels

Book resources and video tutorials can be found at **www.photoshopelements.net**

Index

INDEX

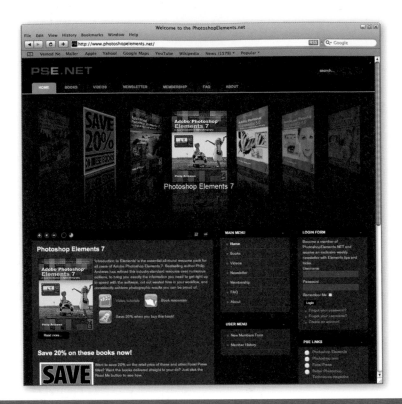

On the Website.....

To coincide with the release of Photoshop Elements 7.0, and a new edition of this, my best selling book, I have put together an extensive series of video tutorials for book owners on the supporting website (www.photoshopelements.net) that will help you make the most out of the new features in the program. This time around, Adobe has not only changed the interface and added new features but they have also added new ways to use and share your images in creative projects. Use these videos alongside the details and step-by-step instructions in the book to help get you quickly up to speed on Photoshop Elements 7.0.

There are also a bunch of free resources that are featured in the book. Use these images to work along with me when building your Elements' skills.

To view the video tutorials included on the website you will need to have the latest version of Adobe's Flash player installed on your computer. To get the free player go to

www.adobe.com

www.PhotoshopElements.net